1
UNCOMMON
GUIDE
TO
EUROPE

MW00978433

THE UNCOMMON GUIDE TO EUROPE

JOHN WHITMAN

ST. MARTIN'S PRESS   NEW YORK

All rights reserved. For information write:
St. Martin's Press, Inc., 175 Fifth Ave., New York, N.Y. 10010
Manufactured in the United States of America
Library of Congress Catalog Card Number: 77-10376

Library of Congress Cataloging in Publication Data

Whitman, John.
    The uncommon guide to Europe.

    1. Europe—Description and travel—1971-
—Guide-books.   I. Title.
D909.W538   914.04'55   77-10376

ISBN 0-312-82862-4
ISBN 0-312-82863-2 pbk.

ABOUT THE AUTHOR

For the past 16 years John Whitman has been crisscrossing the Continent of Europe in search of the offbeat and unusual. His bent for the unordinary took him to places thoroughly European and noncommercial. Now he shares this information with you in *The Uncommon Guide to Europe*, his sixth travel guide.

WHITMAN'S OFF SEASON TRAVEL
GUIDE TO EUROPE, St. Martin's Press,
1976

STARTING FROM SCRATCH, *A Guide to Indoor Gardening*, Quadrangle, the New York Times Book Company, 1976. (A main selection of the Organic Gardening Book Club and an alternate selection of the Book-of-the-Month Club).

WHITMAN'S RESTAURANT GUIDE TO
MINNESOTA, Nodin Press, 1976.

WHITMAN'S TRAVEL GUIDE TO MINNESOTA,
Nodin Press, 1977.

EUROPE

NORWAY
Oslo

SCOTLAND
Edinburgh

NORTHERN
IRELAND
Belfast

NORTH
SEA

DENMARK
Copenhagen

Dublin

IRELAND

ENGLAND

WALES
Cardiff
London

English *Channel*

EAST

Amsterdam
The Hague
NETHERLANDS
Brussels
BELGIUM
Bonn

ATLANTIC

OCEAN

LUXEMBOURG

Paris

WEST
GERMANY

LIECHTENSTEIN
Bern
SWITZERLAND

FRANCE

ITALY

MONACO

SAN
MARINO

SPAIN

ANDORRA

CORSICA
Ajaccio

PORTUGAL

Madrid

BALEARIC ISLANDS
Palma
MINORCA
MAJORCA

SARDINIA

Cagliari

Lisbon

IBIZA

MEDITERRANEAN

SEA

GIBRALTAR

CUCL

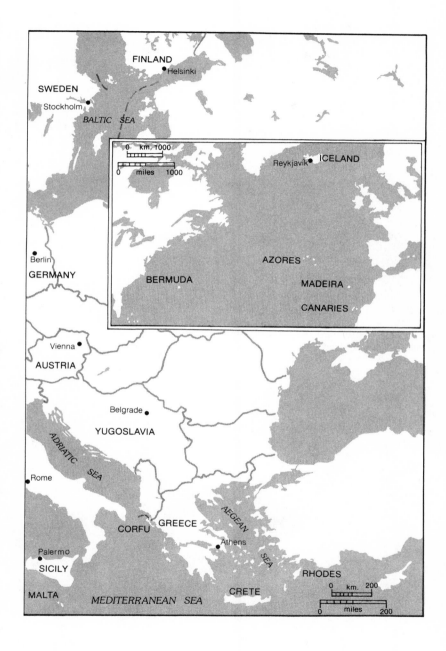

To Tom Dunne for his confidence
and encouragement when it counted.

CONTENTS

ICELAND

IRELAND

ITALY

LIECHTENSTEIN

LUXEMBOURG

MALTA

NETHERLANDS

NORWAY

PORTUGAL

SPAIN

SWEDEN

SWITZERLAND

YUGOSLAVIA

INTRODUCTION

There's a growing suspicion that Europe has become common and commercialized. Certainly, in the larger cities the skyscrapers and Golden Arches suggest this. Nevertheless, a world of European charm waits to be uncovered. This book is an invitation to that world, one that is truly typical of the countries you plan to visit.

HOW TO USE THE GUIDE

The format of this guide is really quite simple. You'll find a map at the beginning of each chapter with many cities numbered on it. These cities serve as reference points for the hotels and restaurants listed alphabetically at the end of the chapter. This will help you locate them as quickly as possible. You'll also find information on what to see (briefly), the weather, and local peculiarities that could cause minor problems abroad.

WHAT YOU'LL FIND INSIDE THE GUIDE

SMALL, TYPICAL HOTELS IN EUROPE'S MAJOR CITIES

Tucked into the hidden corners of all major cities are charming, authentic hotels that offer comfortable rooms, personal service, and fine regional cooking. You'll sleep in four-poster beds, under beamed ceilings, or next to an ancient clock that chimes the hours. Antiques, fresh flowers, fruit in a crystal bowl—these are the touches that reward the selective traveller shying away from more commercial hotels. The price tag in these small hotels often is considerably lower than you would expect to pay. That's why we've included so many in this guide. They offer great value and an uncommon touch of class.

A SELECT NUMBER OF COUNTRY INNS AND
REGIONAL RESTAURANTS

Europe offers a unique opportunity if you're willing to get off-the-beaten-path. You'll uncover exceptional hotels and restaurants in rural areas barely touched by most Americans. We've included nearly 3,000 of these in this guide so that you can unfold the map of Europe, toss a dart at it, and be within an easy drive of the kind of place you'd cross the Atlantic to stay or eat in. These places are usually typical of the country you're visiting. You may end up snuggling under a down cover or trying local specialties from fresh octopus in a Greek taverna to a pint of bitter in an English pub. The uncommon traveller will find that these are the kinds of places that make a trip memorable.

EUROPE'S 100 BEST RESTAURANTS[1]

No one should pass up the chance to eat in Europe's finest restaurants, at least in some or one of them. We've included a hundred that we think are great. These places combine superb cuisine with elegance and attentive service. With their wonderful European charm they make an ideal splurge. You'll have to make reservations far in advance for many of these fine restaurants. Expect the meal to last at least two or three hours, especially in the evening. Dress tends to be quite formal. Most gourmets suggest that you avoid hard liquor before one of these meals which are usually accompanied by fine wines. Americans should note that some restaurants *refuse* to serve water with a meal insisting that this would be in bad taste. Never hesitate to ask the waiter for advice (and prices) when in doubt.

[1]These are marked by three stars *** in the sections reviewing hotels and restaurants.

HELPFUL SUGGESTIONS ON. . . .

TRANSATLANTIC PLANE TRAVEL

Regulations and fares are so complex and change so frequently that information in most publications is dated within a few months. However, you can get up-to-date information from competent travel agents. It costs no more to buy a ticket from them (their commission is included in the price). Generally, the sooner you buy a ticket, the better the price. But ask to have all cancellation penalties explained in detail. If you're interested in a bargain, be sure to ask the agent about flights on Laker or Icelandic.

PACKING

Take the *minimum* amount of clothing and travel gear possible. If you can get by with one small bag that you can carry onto the plane, then you're travelling the right way.

HOTEL RESERVATIONS

Travel agents can make reservations for you, but they charge a 10 percent service fee on all individual travel arrangements. If you buy your plane tickets through AAA (Worldwide Travel), you can sometimes have reservations made for free. You'll have to check on this with your local branch. All airlines make free reservations for their customers at stopover and final destination points. For instance, if you're flying to Vienna and stopping off in London, the airlines will make reservations in those two cities. You can make reservations yourself by writing individual hotels. In your letter you must include international reply coupons to cover the cost of return postage. These coupons can be purchased in most post offices. Be sure to make hotel reservations in the peak season from mid-May to late September.

INTER-EUROPEAN TRAVEL

If you're planning to fly to major cities within Europe, make your reservations ahead of time in the United States. Get your route worked out as far ahead of time as possible. If you wait until you're abroad, you may find the flights filled. If you plan extensive rail travel abroad, check into the Eurailpass, which you can buy only in the United States. All travel agents sell the pass (the price you pay already includes their commission). Remember that rail travel is quite inexpensive abroad, so that you'll have to be travelling long distances to make the pass pay for itself. Car travel, a favorite of many travellers, calls for some advance planning in the peak summer season. Rental cars can be difficult to find unless you've reserved one far in advance. Major car rental companies will make reservations from the United States as will travel agents and airlines. I suggest that you use the airlines for this service since they'll always have a booth that you can go to if some problem arises abroad.

MAPS

The maps in this guide will be extremely helpful in giving you the general location of a city or small town. This kind of help is invaluable, but it's not enough. You can get free maps from the tourist offices (p. xix), from travel organizations such as AAA (if you buy tickets from them), from oil company clubs (Amoco), and so on. But, if you plan extensive travel in rural areas, then I think you should buy maps that are as detailed as possible in a bookstore abroad where the selection will be best. You'll find that many of the hotels and restaurants listed in this guide are in tiny towns, typical of the country but often hard to locate on general maps.

COMMUNICATION

If you've made reservations abroad, have your mail sent directly to the hotels where you'll be staying. If you're travelling on a loose schedule, ask friends to send letters to the American Express offices in cities you'll be visiting (you must have their credit card or some of their traveller's checks to benefit from this free service). Ask friends to type your name and address on the envelope. This makes it easier to spot in a stack of several hundred letters. If you phone home from Europe, be sure to check on the service charge before calling from a hotel. In some hotels you'll be socked with a 40–60 percent rate increase. There's no surcharge on phone calls from central post offices. You'll find long distance operators in these offices in all major cities.

REACHING THE AUTHOR

We'd be delighted with any suggestions or information that you would like to send to John Whitman. Your letters should be addressed to him c/o St. Martin's Press, 175 Fifth Avenue, New York, N.Y. 10010.

TRAVEL INFORMATION AND GUIDES

Free travel information on every aspect of a country is available from national tourist offices listed below. Written requests for information are generally answered within three weeks. The offices suggest that you be as specific as possible about the information you need. Many of these offices have booklets and guides that might interest you. You can ask for a list in your letter. There is usually a reasonable charge for these to cover the cost of publication although most information from tourist offices is free.

New York

Austrian Tourist Office
545 Fifth Avenue
New York, N.Y. 10017
tel: 697-0651

British Tourist Authority
680 Fifth Avenue
New York, N.Y. 10019
tel: 581-4700

Belgian Tourist Office
720 Fifth Avenue
New York, N.Y. 10019
tel: 582-1750

French Tourist Office
610 Fifth Avenue
New York, N.Y. 10020
tel: 757-1125

German Tourist Office
630 Fifth Avenue
New York, N.Y. 10020
tel: 757-8570

Greek Tourist Office
601 Fifth Avenue
New York, N.Y. 10017
tel: 421-5777

Irish Tourist Board
590 Fifth Avenue
New York, N.Y. 10036
tel: 246-7400

Italian Tourist Office
630 Fifth Avenue
New York, N.Y. 10020
tel: 245-4822

Luxembourg Tourist Office
1 Dag Hammerskjold Plaza
New York, N.Y. 10017
tel: 751-9650

Netherlands Tourist Office
576 Fifth Avenue
New York, N.Y. 10036
tel: 245-5320

Portuguese Tourist Bureau
570 Fifth Avenue
New York, N.Y. 10036
tel: 581-2450

Scandinavian National Tourist
   Office
75 Rockefeller Plaza
New York, N.Y. 10019
tel: 582-2802

Spanish National Tourist Office
665 Fifth Avenue
New York, N.Y. 10022
tel: 697-3385

Swiss National Tourist Office
608 Fifth Avenue
New York, N.Y. 10020
tel: 757-5944

Yugoslav Tourist Office
630 Fifth Avenue
New York, N.Y. 10020
tel: 757-2801

Chicago

Austrian National Tourist Office
332 S. Michigan Avenue,
   Suite 1401
Chicago, Illinois 60604
tel: 427-9629

British Tourist Authority
Suite 2450, John Hancock Center
875 N. Michigan Avenue
Chicago, Illinois 60611
tel: 787-0490

German Tourist Office
11 South LaSalle Street
Chicago, Illinois 60603
tel: 263-2958

Irish Tourist Board
224 N. Michigan Avenue
Chicago, Illinois 60601
tel: 726-9356

Italian Tourist Office
500 N. Michigan Avenue
Chicago, Illinois 60611
tel: 644-0990

Spanish Tourist Office
180 N. Michigan Avenue
Chicago, Illinois 60601
tel: 641-1842

Los Angeles

Austrian Tourist Office
Suite 901, 3440 Wilshire Blvd.
Los Angeles, Cal. 90010
tel: 380-7990

British Tourist Authority
612 South Flower Street
Los Angeles, Cal. 90017
tel: 623-8196

Greek National Tourist Office
627 West Sixth Street
Los Angeles, Cal. 90017
tel: 626-6696

Montreal

German Tourist Office
P.O. Box 417, 47 Fundy
Place Bonaventure
Montreal, Canada
tel: 878-9885

Italian Travel Office
3 Place Ville Marie
Montreal, Canada
tel: 866-7667

Portland

Austrian National Tourist Office
1007 N.W. 24th Avenue
Portland, Oregon 97210
tel: 244-6000

San Francisco

German Tourist Office
323 Geary Street
San Francisco, Cal. 94102
tel: 986-0796

Irish Tourist Board
681 Market Street
San Francisco, Cal. 94105
tel: 781-5688

Italian Tourist Office
St. Francis Hotel, Post Street
San Francisco, Cal. 94119
tel: 392-6202

Netherlands Tourist Office
681 Market Street
San Francisco, Cal. 94105
tel: 781-3387

Spanish Tourist Office
209 Post Street
San Francisco, Cal. 94102
tel: 986-2125

Swiss Tourist Office
661 Market Street
San Francisco, Cal. 94105
tel: 362-2260

Toronto

British Tourist Authority
151 Bloor Street West
Toronto, Ontario
tel: 925-6326

Irish Tourist Board
7 King Street East
Toronto, Ontario
tel: 364-1301

Netherlands Tourist Office
Royal Trust Tower, Suite 3310
Toronto Dominion Center
Toronto, Ontario
tel: 364-5339

Swiss Tourist Office
Commerce Court Postal Station
Toronto, Ontario
tel: 868-0584

TRAVEL REPORTS

The following four reports have newsletters that are a good source of unusual information and helpful cost-cutting hints. You may want to subscribe to one or more if you plan extensive travel abroad.

Association of Informed
   Travelers
228 Overlook Road
New Rochelle, N.Y. 10804

Joyer Travel Report
8401 Connecticut Avenue
Washington, D.C. 20015

Passport
20 North Wacker Drive
Chicago, Illinois 60606

Travel Smart
Communications House
40 Beechdale Road (Dobbs Ferry)
New York, N.Y. 10522

INTERNATIONAL AIRLINES

All airlines offer special tours to European countries at attractive rates. You can get this information directly from the airlines or from travel agents. Airlines will also make hotel and car rental reservations free of charge at any of your stopover points or final destination in Europe. Many airlines have free pamphlets and books on countries abroad. You can write them for this information or ask at one of their branch offices.

Aer Lingus-Irish
564 Fifth Avenue
New York, N.Y. 10035
tel: 757-9200

Aeroflot Soviet Airlines
545 Fifth Avenue
New York, N.Y. 10017
tel: 661-4050

Air Canada
488 Madison Avenue
New York, N.Y. 10022
tel: 421-8000

Air France
683 Fifth Avenue
New York, N.Y. 10022
tel: 758-6300

Air India
345 Park Avenue
New York, N.Y. 10022
tel: 935-7500

Alitalia
666 Fifth Avenue
New York, N.Y. 10019
tel: 582-8900

British Caledonian
415 Madison Avenue
New York, N.Y. 10017
tel: 935-9550

British Airways
245 Park Avenue
New York, N.Y. 10017
tel: 687-1600

El Al Israel Airlines
850 Third Avenue
New York, N.Y. 10022
tel: 751-6824

Finnair
10 East 40th Street
New York, N.Y. 10016
tel: 689-9300

Iberia Air Lines of Spain
565 Fifth Avenue
New York, N.Y. 10017
tel: 793-5000

Icelandic Loftleidir Airlines
630 Fifth Avenue
New York, N.Y. 10020
tel: 757-8585

KLM Royal Dutch Airlines
609 Fifth Avenue
New York, N.Y. 10017
tel: 759-3600

LOT Polish Airlines
500 Fifth Avenue
New York, N.Y. 10036
tel: 564-8116

Lufthansa German Airlines
1640 Hempstead Turnpike
East Meadow, L.I., N.Y. 11554
tel: 357-8400

National Airlines
P.O. Box 2055
Miami, Florida 33159
tel: 874-5000

Olympic Airways
647-649 Fifth Avenue
New York, N.Y. 10019
tel: 956-8462

Pakistan International Airlines
608 Fifth Avenue
New York, N.Y. 10020
tel: 581-0600

Pan American Airways
200 Park Avenue
New York, N.Y. 10017
tel: 973-4000

Sabena Belgian World Airlines
720 Fifth Avenue
New York, N.Y. 10019
tel: 961-6200

SAS Scandinavian Airlines
638 Fifth Avenue
New York, N.Y. 10020
tel: 657-7700

Swissair
608 Fifth Avenue
New York, N.Y. 10020
tel: 995-8400

TAP Portuguese Airways
601 Fifth Avenue
New York, N.Y. 10017
tel: 421-8500

THE UNCOMMON GUIDE TO EUROPE

ANDORRA

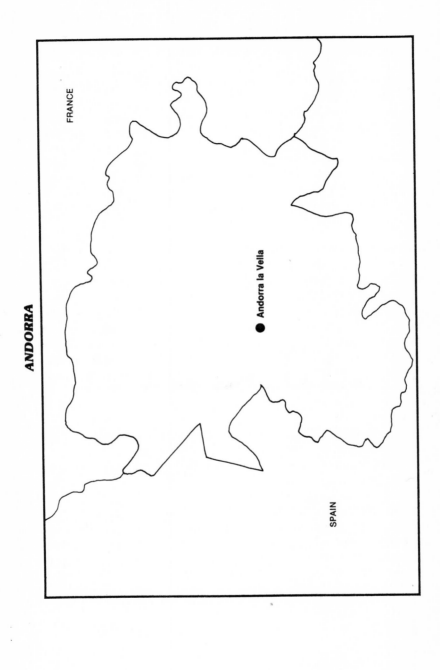

ANDORRA

FRANCE

● Andorra la Vella

SPAIN

WHAT TO SEE

Andorra is a tiny principality isolated in the Pyrénées mountains between Spain and France. Famed as a shopper's paradise, it's also an unusual destination for someone seeking the calm and beauty of a mountain retreat. Both the French and Spanish swarm into the miniscule country at all times of year to take advantage of the low prices; but the crowds are at their worst in July and August. This is an uncommon destination for Americans and will appeal especially to hikers, photographers, shoppers, and people trying to come down from a nervous high.

WHAT'S THE WEATHER REALLY LIKE?

Not so great much of the year. During the winter, roads can be blocked with drifts of snow on the French side although the roads leading into Spain generally stay open. Spring comes fairly late breaking into sunny weather in mid-June. The weather is best in July and August, unfortunately the peak vacation months for most Europeans. It can be quite pleasant here in the fall although you should come prepared for cool and damp weather. You should expect snow by November.

SOME SUGGESTIONS FOR A MORE ENJOYABLE TRIP

Be sure to make reservations if you plan a trip to Andorra in late June, July, and August. Or you can beat the crowds by staying here in early June or early September (still reserve a room). If you're planning a trip to Andorra in the winter, be sure to check ahead with one of the mountain hotels to see whether all roads are open. Americans generally have few problems going through Spanish or French customs, but you might want to keep packages of liquor and cigarettes well hidden.

WHERE TO STAY

Andorra La Vella

Park Hotel   Plana Guillemo   tel: 20 979
Large, pleasant mountain hotel with traditional atmosphere and reasonably comfortable rooms. Lovely view. Garden, pool. Moderate.

Hotel Andorra Palace   Prat de la Creu   tel: 21 072
Large, modest hotel with reasonably comfortable rooms and a restaurant with a nice view. Pool. Moderate.

Pyrénées   20 Avenue Princep Benlloch   tel: 20 508
Large, modest hotel with functional rooms. Lovely view. Inexpensive.

AUSTRIA

AUSTRIA

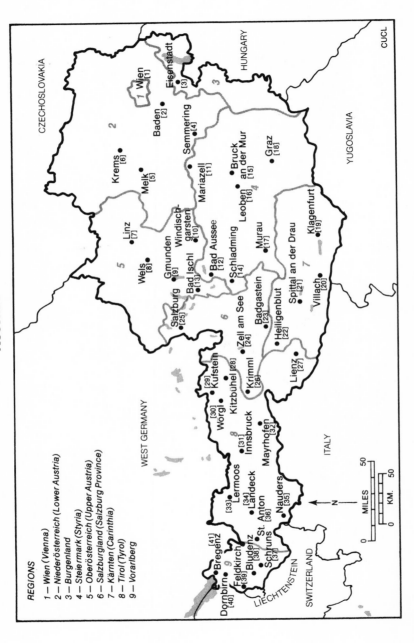

REGIONS

1 — Wien (Vienna)
2 — Niederösterreich (Lower Austria)
3 — Burgenland
4 — Steiermark (Styria)
5 — Oberösterreich (Upper Austria)
6 — Salzburgland (Salzburg Province)
7 — Kärnten (Carinthia)
8 — Tirol (Tyrol)
9 — Vorarlberg

CZECHOSLOVAKIA

HUNGARY

YUGOSLAVIA

WEST GERMANY

ITALY

SWITZERLAND

LIECHTENSTEIN

1 Wien [1]
Eisenstadt [3]
Baden [2]
Semmering [4]
Krems [6]
Melk [5]
Mariazell [11]
Bruck an der Mur [15]
Graz [18]
Linz [7]
Windisch-garsten [10]
Leoben [16]
Wels [8]
Gmunden [9]
Bad Aussee [12]
Murau [17]
Bad Ischl [13]
Schladming [14]
Klagenfurt [19]
Salzburg [25]
Spittal an der Drau [21]
Zell am See [24]
Badgastein [23]
Villach [20]
Heiligenblut [22]
Krimml [26]
Lienz [27]
Kufstein [29]
Wörgl [30]
Kitzbühel [28]
Innsbruck [31]
Mayrhofen [32]
Lermoos [33]
Landeck [34]
Nauders [35]
St. Anton [36]
Bludenz [38]
Schruns [37]
Feldkirch [39]
Dornbirn [40]
Bregenz [41]

N

MILES 0   50
KM. 0   50

WHAT TO SEE

Austria really has two main tourist seasons. During the winter people flock to the fabulous ski resorts which are packed during Christmas and Easter vacations. During the summer from late June to early September, you'll find the major cities of Innsbruck, Salzburg, and Vienna jammed. A good suggestion for the uncommon traveller is to try to see the major cities in late spring or fall, although the winter is extremely interesting if you're into music or art. If you do plan a trip in the summer, try to combine stays in the major cities with excursions into the countryside. It's the rural areas of Austria that relatively few Americans have toured, and they have a charm that can be just as memorable as the Boys' Choir or the Spanish Riding School. Listed in this chapter are delightful places to stay throughout the country which offer regional cooking, comfortable beds covered with eiderdown quilts, and a chance to relax in a romantic setting.

For sightseeing, most people won't miss _Vienna_ (Wien) [1] because it's one of Europe's most active and exciting destinations offering a fascinating cultural life, the Vienna Boys' Choir, Spanish Riding School, and numerous sights to fill several days of active sightseeing. Please note that the summer is not really the best time to visit this city. It's much livelier in the off-season. Other popular cities are _Salzburg_ [25] with the Residenz Palace, Schloss Mirabell, and Hellbrunn Castle, and _Innsbruck_ [31] noted for the Hofburg, Golden Roof, and Schloss Ambras. Both are delightful in the summer and active in the off-season as well. In all three of these major cities you'll get tons of free travel information in local tourist offices and hotels with ample directions on how best to visit popular tourist sights.

The uncommon traveller will want to make some lesser-known but still wonderful excursions: to medieval _Dürnstein,_ the abbey of _Klosterneuburg_ near Vienna [1], the Schloss Eggenberg in _Graz_ [18], romantic _Sankt Wolfgang,_ ancient _Freistadt_ [7], the sixteenth-century Hochosterwitz fort east of _St. Veit an der Glan_ [19], the St. Florian Abbey south of _Linz_ [7] (also the starting point of a river trip to Vienna), _Krems_ [6] set in wine country (great in the fall), and the abbey of _Melk_ [5]. For resort living try _Baden_ [2], _Bad Aussee_ [12] or _Badgastein_ [23]. Of the 200 lakes in the Salzkammergut the _Faakersee_ is the most beautiful, the _Wörthersee_ is the best known, and the *Weissensee* is the warmest. Try to get to at least one. One of the most stunning drives is along the *Grossglockner Highway*, a series of hairpin turns along steep mountain terrain from *Lienz* [27] to *Zell am See* [24]. Allow a full day for this fabulous drive, inquire ahead of time about the weather conditions (skip it if it's not sunny), and be prepared for a stiff charge (have plenty of Austrian currency). You might also want to bring along a picnic lunch and be sure to have enough film with you. Fill up *before* you make the trip since gas stations disappear as soon as the needle reaches empty. In another part of the country you'll find a truly uncommon destination, the lake of *Neusiedlersee* [3], a favorite of artists, poets, bird lovers, and hunters. It's rarely seen by foreign tourists and is lovely from late April to late October. You'll find one of the loveliest falls in Austria at *Krimml* [26]. The Eisriesenwelt Caves near *Werfen*, the Dachstein Ice Caves east of *Hallstatt*, and the Hallein Mines near *Salzburg* [25] are fascinating to tour. Skiers flock to the great slopes of *Kitzbühel* [28], *Seefeld* [31], *Saint Christophe* [36], *Lech* [42], *Zürs* [42], and a host of other fine resorts during the December to late-March season.

WHAT'S THE WEATHER REALLY LIKE?

Quite good in the valleys from mid-May to mid-September although you should be prepared for rainy days even during the peak summer season. Winter in the major cities tends to be drab with frequent showers, light snows, and cold weather. The ski resorts often bask in brilliant sunshine when the valleys are shrouded in gray mists.

SOME SUGGESTIONS FOR A MORE ENJOYABLE TRIP

The major cities of Salzburg, Vienna, and Innsbruck are all packed during the summer season, thanks in part to the superb music festivals held at this time. Tickets to all music festivals must be purchased months in advance, and hotel reservations should be made three months ahead of time. Should you arrive in Vienna without a room reservation, head immediately to the local tourist office in the train station where a special booth is set aside for both information on sight-seeing and help in finding an available room. You may have to settle for a bed in a dormitory or student hotel, and you should expect a wait of an hour or more. It's somewhat easier finding rooms in the country where over 2,500 farms offer beds to foreign tourists (look for little signs such as *zimmer frei*). If you can avoid the peak periods of June, July, and August, try to. Not only will you miss the crowds, but you'll be rewarded with a chance to take in the off-season attractions of the Spanish Riding School, Vienna Boys' Choir, and superb performances in the State Opera House (note that tickets for these should be purchased as soon as you know your estimated date of arrival in Vienna. Try to buy them three months in advance if possible). Skiers will want to avoid the peak periods of Christmas and spring holidays. They should note too that Zürich is often a better gateway to Austrian resorts than Vienna. Offbeat travellers take in Austria in either spring or fall when relatively few tourists are around. However, some mountain resorts do close at these times. Motorists should be warned that there is a steep charge for some of the superhighways and an equally steep charge ($12) to take the Grossglockner Highway. They should also be warned that the roads in Austria tend to be poor, that the traffic is often bad, and that conditions in winter often demand the use of chains. Allow yourself plenty of time for travel by car.

WHERE TO STAY

Anif [25] (Salzburg)

Hotel Schlosswirt   A-5081 Anif   tel: (06 246) 21 75
Main building dates back to 1607 while farm across road has been skillfully converted to inn as well. Overly popular in summer, but a good choice in the off-season. Ask for nonroadside rooms; no. 55 is particularly fine. Only four miles from Salzburg center (off superhighway at Salzburg-Süd exit). Moderate.

Aschach [7]

Faust-Schlossl Hotel   Landshaag   tel: 02
Small, dignified castle-hotel on lovely grounds. Period furnish-

ings. Golf, tennis, fishing. Expensive. Twelve miles northwest of Linz.

Baden Bei Wien [2]

Clubhotel Schloss Weikersdorf   Baden   tel: 40 71
Castle converted into luxury hotel similar to an elegant country club. Original antiques in most rooms. Pools. Wide variety of sports. Very expensive.

Krainerhütte   Baden   tel: 45 11
Small country inn three miles west of Baden. Forest setting. Some superb rooms. Good cooking. Fishing, tennis, and riding. Moderate.

Badgastein [23]

Parkhotel Bellevue   Waggerlstrasse   tel: 25 71
Huge old-world hotel, the town's most famous, in lovely park setting. Elegant throughout. Comfortable, recently renovated rooms. Fine cooking. Lively social life including fashion shows. Pool, tennis, and golf. Very expensive. Closed from October to mid-December.

Hotel Elisabethpark   Hauptstrasse   tel: 25 51
Large traditional hotel with elegant rooms. Nice setting near the casino. Good restaurant. Friendly service. Lively in the winter. Pool. Very expensive.

Grüner Baum   Badgastein   tel: 25 16
Small and charming Alpine hotel with lots of local flavor. Good food. Pool. Moderately expensive.

Der Kaiserhof   Badgastein   tel: 25 44
Traditional old world hotel on lovely grounds. Comfortable rooms recently revamped. Fine dining. Excellent spa hotel. Very expensive. Closed late fall and early spring.

Straubinger   Badgastein   tel: 20 12
A fine "family" hotel for centuries. Lovely atmosphere. Quite comfortable. Delightful historic restaurant. Expensive. Closed late fall.

Bad Hall [7]

Schloss Feyregg   Feyregg 1   tel: 591
Tiny luxury castle-hotel south of Linz. Small and elegant. Beautiful furnishings for romantic and antique flavor. Splendid dining. Moderately expensive. A peaceful haven open all year.

Bad Tatzmannsdorf [3]

Schlosshotel Jormannsdorf   Jormannsdorf   tel: 223
Small castle converted into hotel just outside of town. Lovely setting. Modest rooms. Inexpensive.

Bernstein [3]

Schloss Bernstein   Bernstein   tel: 220
Modest rooms in a medieval castle high on the hill. Limited kitchen. Southwest of Eisenstadt.

Bregenz [41]

Weisses Kreuz   Römerstrasse 5   tel: 22 488
Small traditional hotel with simple but comfortable rooms. One of the better hotels in the region. Good restaurant. Moderate.

Bruck an der Mur [15]

Hotel Bauer-Zum Schwarzen Adler   Bruck an der Mur   tel: 51 331
Large ancient hotel—totally up-to-date comfort. Authentic atmosphere. Excellent cuisine emphasizing local specialties. Expensive.

Drassburg [3]

Hotel Schloss Drassburg   Drassburg   tel: 220
Small castle-hotel in the country. Simple yet elegant rooms. Lovely setting in park near forest. Very quiet. Hunting arranged for guests. Expensive. Open April to December. Ten miles south of Eisenstadt.

Durnstein [17]

Hotel Richard Löwenherz   Dürnstein   tel: 222
Large rambling hotel which was once a convent. Nice garden atmosphere overlooking the Danube. Some fine rooms—ask to see yours first. Delightful dining. Expensive. Closed mid-November until Christmas. Near Friesach southeast of Murau.

Hotel Schloss Dürnstein   Dürnstein   tel: 240
Large castle hotel overlooking the Danube. Varied rooms—some with fine furnishings and antiques. Good restaurant. Pool and fishing. Very popular. Excellent in early fall when vineyards are changing color. Moderate. Open mid-March until late November.

Eisenstadt [3]

Park Hotel   Eisenstadt   tel: 43 61
Small modern hotel. Not fancy, but pleasant. Moderately expensive.

Feldkirch [39]

Alpenrose   Rosengasse 6   tel: 21 75
Small old hotel with simple authentic rooms. Good food. Moderate.

Central Hotel Löwen   Neustadt 15-19   tel: 20 70
Large traditional hotel with authentic flavor. Compact and cheery rooms. Fine restaurant for the region. Moderate.

Flattnitz [17]

Winterthalerhof Hotel   Flattnitz   tel: 27 112
A fine resort with modern and comfortable rooms. Set up for deer and chamois hunting. The hotel has its own grounds. Hunting is inexpensive. Pool. Moderate. South of Murau; to west of Friesach.

Frohnleiten [15]

Schloss Rabenstein   Frohnleiten   tel: 203
Small castle hotel with antique rooms. Charming. Lovely views.

Popular. Moderately expensive. Open April to mid-October. South of Bruck an der Mur.

Fuschl am See [25]

Schloss Fuschl   Fuschl am See   tel: 253
Large luxury castle-hotel—one of the finest in Austria. Perched on a cliff overlooking a lake. Totally isolated and serene. Antiques throughout, with fine hunting museum. Very comfortable and sports-oriented. Riding, fishing, hunting, pool, tennis, and golf. Exceptional cuisine with game in the off-season. Ultraexpensive. Open late April to November. Only twelve miles southeast of Salzburg.

Gosau [13]

Schlosshotel Gosau   Gosau   tel: 203
Sixteenth-century castle-hotel in secluded area. Modest rooms. Pleasant surroundings. Moderate. Ten miles south of Bad Ischl.

Gosing [11]

Alpen Hotel   Gösing   tel: 217
Fine hunting hotel with own grounds for chamois and deer. Moderate to expensive. Open June to December. North of Mariazell.

Grünau im Almtal [9]

Almtalhof   A-4645 Grünau   tel: (07 616) 204
Idyllic, rustic retreat well into the mountains and away from it all. Comfortable rooms and lots of atmosphere. Filled to the brim with antiques and charm. Good regional cooking. Moderate. Southeast of Gmunden.

Hirschegg [40]

Ifenhotel   Hirschegg   tel: 321
Large traditional hotel with spacious and modern rooms. Elegant throughout. Excellent cuisine in candlelit dining room. Superb game and trout in the off-season. Ideal retreat for the sportsman:

sailing, golf, tennis, and skiing. Expensive. Although east of Dornbirn, the village is in the Kleines Walsertad, a mountainous region accessible from Germany. Closed November to mid-December.

Igls [31]

Agidihof   Bilgeristrasse   tel: 71 08
Small, typical hotel. Charming and comfortable. Expensive. Closed late October to mid-December.

Schlosshotel Igls   Igls   tel: 72 17
Luxury castle-hotel on large private grounds. Sumptuous mansion with a few choice rooms and elegant suites. Excellent cuisine. Pool, riding, and walking. Very expensive. Southern edge of Innsbruck.

Innsbruck [31]

Goldene Rose   Herzog-Friedrich Strasse 39   tel: 22 041
Authentic simple hotel dating back five centuries. Quite comfortable. Good restaurant. Moderate.

Goldener Adler   Herzog-Friedrich Strasse 6   tel: 26 334
Lovely historic hotel. Small and classy. Charming atmosphere. Comfortable if compact rooms. Seductive in its authentic simplicity. Very fine cuisine. Moderately expensive.

Roter Adler   Seilergasse 4-6   tel: 21 069
Small, quiet hotel, recently revamped. Simple, enjoyable. Lots of atmosphere. Popular restaurant and bar. Moderate.

Hotel Schwarzer Adler   Kaiserjäger Strasse 2   tel: 27 109
Near the Imperial Palace and a short walk from the Old Town. Simple, yet comfortable rooms—not for the stuffy. Best ones in back (more quiet). Small wine cellar and a charming, wood-panelled dining room for a romantic meal. Moderate.

Irdning [12]

Schloss Pichlarn   Irdning   tel: 28 41
Lavish medieval castle converted into lovely hotel. On huge estate in the Enns Valley. Elegant throughout with wonderful an-

tiques and atmosphere. Spacious and very quiet rooms. Exquisite dining. Pool, golf, tennis, riding, fishing, and hunting on its
own reserve. Very expensive. Closed November to mid-December. Only sixty miles from Salzburg. East of Bad Aussee.

Kitzbuhel [28]

Grand Hotel   Kitzbühel   tel: 43 95
Large "château" hotel with spacious and very comfortable
rooms. Just east of town on lovely grounds. Winter season very
lively. Good cooking. Tennis. Closed late September to mid-December. Expensive.

Guido Reisch   Kitzbühel   tel: 44 44
Revamped older hotel. Quite comfortable. The tea dance at five
is the most popular in town. Moderate to expensive.

Goldner Greif   Hinterstadt 24   tel: 43 11
Famous thirteenth-century Tyrolean inn with modern facilities.
Comfortable and quiet. Authentic atmosphere. Lots of antiques.
Fine dining. Swinging social life. Casino. Pool. Expensive.
Closed late autumn and early spring.

Hotel Hirzingerhof   Schwarzseestrasse 8   tel: 32 11
Small luxury inn just outside of town in quiet location. Ancient
building with romantic and charming flavor. Antiques throughout. Spacious rooms. Fine cuisine. Expensive. Closed late fall
and early spring.

Die Postkutsche   Ehrenbachgasse 30   tel: 30 18
Tiny chalet made from ancient mansion. Luxurious and quite
exclusive. Superbly furnished rooms. Ultrafine dining and service. Popular and posh. Very expensive. Closed late fall and
spring.

Schloss Lebenberg   Lebenbergstrasse 17   tel: 43 01
Luxury castle-hotel. Spacious and elegant rooms—mostly suites.
Fine dining. Pool, tennis, golf, and winter sports. Very expen-
sive. Closed November.

Schlosshotel Münichau   Kitzbühel   tel: 29 62
Old hunting lodge (castle) just west of town in quiet lovely setting. Chic old-world flavor. Comfortable and charming rooms.

Fine dining. Moderately expensive. Closed late fall and early spring.

Tennerhof   A-6370 Kitzbühel   tel: 31 81
On a hill overlooking town. Lovely in any season. Ask for delightful rooms with patio or for the south side if interested in the view. Inside and outside pools. Quite good cooking with one room reserved for residents. Expensive.

Klagenfurt [19]

Musil   10 Oktober Strasse 14   tel: 70 544
Quite lovely little hotel with striking Italian influence—atrium and marble stairs. Comfortable rooms. Number 6, nice double; number 8, four-poster; and number 10 with typical old farmer's beds. Relaxing coffee house next to the hotel's own bakery with delicious strudel (blackberry, apricot, or apple). Two distinctive dining areas for those interested in sampling regional specialties. Moderate.

Sandwirt   Pernhartgasse 9   tel: 82 430
Small, comfortable old world hotel with spacious rooms. Charming atmosphere. One of the better restaurants in town. Moderate.

Schloss Freyenthurn   Klagenfurt-See   tel: 21 174
Small castle-hotel on the Wörthersee. Elegant old-world ambience. Quiet and comfortable. Fishing and hunting. Expensive. Open April through October.

Klosterneuburg [1]

Schlosshotel Martinschloss   Martinstrasse 34-36   tel: 74 26
Large medieval castle on spacious grounds. Charming with fine atmosphere. Pool, tennis. Good dining. Expensive, worth it. Convenient to Vienna.

Kuhtai [31]

Jagdschloss Kühtai   Kühtai   tel: 201/225
Deluxe sixteenth-century hunting lodge high in the mountains. Lovely rooms. Very fine cuisine with delicious fresh trout. Moderately expensive. Open mid-December until the end of April to

match the skiing season. Only twenty miles west of Innsbruck.

Lech/Arlberg [42]

Hotel Arlberg   Lech   tel: 321
Large lively Alpine hotel with quiet and comfortable rooms. Many sports—fishing, tennis, riding, pool, and skiing. Very expensive. Closed late fall and late spring.

Gasthof Post Hotel   Lech   tel: 206
Small, delightful inn geared to families. Authentic atmosphere. Superb apartments. Good food. Pool. Very expensive.

Lienz [27]

Hotel Traube   Hauptplatz 14   tel: 25 51
A gem. In the center of town. Comfortable rooms, many with nice view. Rooms 412 and 315 highly recommended. But all nice. Pool. Fresh and flowery dining room with nice terrace for informal snacks. Outstanding regional cuisine (try the *schlipfkrapfen*, even if you have to special order them). Wines come from the family vineyard. Not far from the ski slopes, ideal for offbeat skiing. Nursery available. Expensive, worth it.

Micheldorf [7]

Hofgut St. Michael   In der Schön   tel: 26 61
Small old world hunting lodge converted into fine hotel with tasteful décor. On lovely grounds. Comfortable. Lots of antiques. Fine restaurant. Pool, skiing, fishing, tennis, and riding. Quite expensive. Thirty miles south of Linz.

Neumarkt am Wallersee [25]

Schloss Sighartstein   Neumarkt   tel: 251
Tiny deluxe palace hotel. Ancient mansion filled with exquisite antiques in ideal setting by lake. Very comfortable with elegant dining. The kind of place where you pour your own drinks. Trout fishing for guests. Ultraexpensive. Written reservations necessary. Open April to November. Fifteen miles northeast of Salzburg.

Oberalm [25]

Schloss Haunsperg   Oberalm   tel: 26 62
Tiny medieval castle converted into fine traditional hotel with
lovely antiques. Spacious grounds and nice atmosphere. Quite
comfortable. Tennis, riding, and fishing. Moderately expensive.
South of Salzburg.

Oberlech [42]

Hotel Montana   Oberlech   tel: 460
Small, popular resort hotel with comfortable rooms and very
good cooking. Expensive. Closed late fall and late spring.

Sporthotel Sonnenburg   Oberlech   tel: 208
Fine hotel—both sporty and sophisticated. Good casual dining.
Expensive. Closed late fall and late spring.

Patsch [31]

Grüwalderhof   Patsch   tel: 73 04
Small hunting lodge converted into comfortable hotel with traditional atmosphere. Ideal for skiers. Moderate. Closed late fall
and early spring. Just south of Innsbruck.

Portschach am Worthersee [19]

Schloss Leonstein   Hauptstrasse 226   tel: 28 16
Fifteenth-century castle-hotel of distinction. Near the lake with
lovely garden. Charming atmosphere with lots of antiques.
Beautiful rooms. Exceptional dining. Special concerts given in
honor of Brahms. Beach, tennis, fishing. Moderately expensive.
Open May to November. Only nine miles west of Klagenfurt.

Parkhotel   Elisabethstrasse 22   tel: 26 21
Very large lakeside hotel with airy rooms. Lovely suites. Fine di-
ning. Fishing and tennis. Quite expensive. Open May through
October.

Schloss Seefels   Töschling 1   tel: 23 77
Small castle-hotel set on the lake in lovely setting west of town.
Lots of atmosphere. Large rooms. Good dining. Active social

life. Fishing, tennis, and golf. Very expensive. Open May
through September.

Salzburg [25]

Dr. Wührers Haus Gastein   *Ignaz-Rieder-Kai 25*   *tel: 22 565*
Small delightful inn with quiet and comfortable rooms. Moderate
to expensive. Open all year.

Gastschloss Mönchstein   *Mönchsberg 26*   *tel: 41 363*
Tiny charming castle-hotel perched above town with a spectacu-
lar view. Elegant, if compact, suites. Very quiet and luxurious.
Fine cuisine. Tennis. Closed in the winter. Expensive.

Goldener Hirsch   *Getreidegasse 37*   *tel: 87 019*
"The Golden Stag," with its superb location near the shopping
street, is one of Austria's great historic inns. Truly authentic and
romantic throughout. Charming, quiet, and quite comfortable
rooms. Exceptional restaurant with award-winning cuisine and
fine wines. Delicious game in the off season. Very expensive.

Hotel Kobenzl   *Gaisberg*   *tel: 21 776*
Small chalet overlooking the city from the suburb of Gaisberg.
Spectacular view and lovely grounds. Charming and warm.
Quite comfortable. Fine dining. Pool, riding, and fishing. Expen-
sive. Closed in the winter.

Osterreichischer Hof   *Schwarzstrasse 5-7*   *tel: 72 541*
Large traditional hotel with a quiet riverside location. Spacious
and nicely furnished rooms—most with fine view. Good cooking. Quite expensive.

Schlosshotel Fondachhof   *Gaisbergstrasse 46*   *tel: 20 906*
An artists' favorite—a tiny intimate hotel on spacious grounds
just two miles from the center of town. The two-hundred-year-
old castle offers quiet and comfortable rooms (avoid those in the
annex). Antiques throughout. Fine dining. Pool. Very expensive.
Open from April through October.

Schlosshotel Klesheim   *Salzburg*   *tel: 31 178*
Small ancient home converted into fine hotel in secluded setting.
Comfortable. Very expensive. Open only from June to Sep-
tember.

Schlosshotel St. Rupert   *Morzgerstrasse 31*   *tel: 41 231*
Tiny charming castle-hotel in serene park with lovely view. Just
outside of town. Wonderful décor including fine antiques. Excellent cuisine. Only open from April to October.

Seefeld [31]

Astoria   Geigenbühel 185   tel: 22 72
Large attractive hotel in lovely grounds above the city. Spacious
rooms. Pool and fishing. Very expensive. Closed mid-September
to mid-December.

Karwendelhof   Bahnhofstrasse 124   tel: 26 55
Quite large rustic inn with authentic and comfortable rooms.
Friendly. Pool. Quite expensive.

Hotel Klosterbräu   Seefeld   tel: 26 21
Large monastery converted into modern hotel. Lots of antiques.
Comfortable, if compact, rooms. Exquisite dining. Pool and
fishing. Golf nearby. Expensive. Closed late fall and early
spring.

Schlosshotel Seefeld   Seefeld   tel: 26 58
Tiny castle-hotel in scenic setting. Original antiques. Simple and
quite comfortable. Good dining. Very expensive. Closed April,
October, and November.

Semmering [4]

Silvana   Semmering   tel: 309
Intimate hotel with elegant décor. Delicious food. Moderate.
Open all year.

Südbahnhotel Astoria   Semmering   tel: 455
Large traditional mountain hotel with fine views. Spacious
grounds. Comfortable. Good dining. Pool, tennis, hunting, and
fishing. Moderate. Closed mid-September to mid-December.

St. Anton am Arlberg [36]

Alte Post   St. Anton   tel: 25 53
Ancient building with modern rooms and some atmosphere.
Popular. Good dining. Expensive. Closed in May.

Post Hotel   *St. Anton*   *tel: 22 13*
Large Tyrolean inn—very popular. Comfortable. Fine dining. Expensive. Closed late fall.

Schwarzer Adler   *St. Anton*   *tel: 22 44*
Large authentic mountain resort with attractive décor and lots of atmosphere. Very comfortable and friendly. Lively in the winter. A favorite of serious skiers. Very expensive.

St. Wolfgang

Hotel Auhof   *St. Wolfgang*   *tel: 262*
Fine hotel one mile east of town on the lake. Large rooms with superb views. Good fishing. Closed in November.

Hotel Weisses Rössl   *Marktstrasse 74*   *tel: 306*
The White Horse Inn of operetta and White Christmas fame— beautiful lakeside setting. Comfortable rooms—number 4 is superb. Excellent cuisine. Pool, tennis, and fishing. Expensive. Closed November to March.

Vienna [1] (see Klosterneuburg)

Clima Villen Hotel   *Nussberggasse 2C*   *tel: 37 15 16*
Pleasant resort surrounded by vineyard with nice view. Comfortable rooms with bath. Pool. Oriented to motorists. Expensive.

Kahlenberg Hotel   *Josephs Dorf 26*   *tel: 32 12 51*
Small (only 33 rooms), modern, quite comfortable. Most rooms with bath. Pleasant hillside location with quite nice view. Geared to motorists in its out-of-the-way location. Moderate.

Ring Hotel Vienna   *Maria am Gestade 1*   *tel: 63 77 01*
Small tasteful inn with lots of atmosphere. Quiet and comfortable. Good food. Warm Service. Moderate to expensive.

Römischer Kaiser   *Annagasse 16*   *tel: 52 77 51*
Baroque building converted into comfortable hotel in the heart of the city. Now part of the Romantic hotel chain. Moderate to expensive.

Velden am Worthersee [20]

Schlosshotel Velden   Am Korso 24   tel: 26 55
Beautiful lakeside castle dating from the seventeenth century. Splendid décor. Restful and relaxing atmosphere. Comfortable if cozy rooms. Good restaurant. Casino. Tennis and trout fishing. Expensive. Open April to November.

Seehotel Europa   Wrannpark 1   tel: 27 70
Small modern lakeside hotel in fine park. Nice and comfortable. Fine dining. Good fishing. Moderate. Open May to October.

Villach [20]

Hotel Post   Hauptplatz   tel: 61 01
Seventeenth-century patrician house converted into large hotel, a bit rough around the edges and a little too busy with tours. But dining on local specialties can be outstanding. The restaurant just off the cozy bar is the nicest and most in demand. Rooms are modest. Moderate.

Wals-Siezenheim [25]

Schlosshotel Klessheim-Kavalierhaus   Wals   tel: 78
Fine castle-hotel in secluded setting. Quiet·and comfortable. Delightful atmosphere. Expensive. West of Salzburg.

Wolfnitz Bei Klagenfurt [19]

Schloss Seltheim   Wölfnitz   tel: 75 218
Small traditional inn on fine estate. Quite comfortable. Hunting and fishing. Moderate. Open May to September. On the lake west of Klagenfurt.

Wörgl [30]

Schloss Itter   Wörgl   tel: 25 61
Superb location for medieval castle converted into modern hotel. Traditional flavor. Fishing and hunting. Up-and-down reputation—it may be closed. Worth a side trip for the view.

Ybbs an der Donau [5]

Royal Hotel Weisses Rössel   Ybbs   tel: 292
Small, comfortable hotel—ideal for wine tours and tasting. Fishing and hunting available. Moderate. Open April to October. Fifteen miles west of Melk.

Zurs/Arlberg [42]

Hotel Alpenrose-Post   Zürs   tel: 271
Large, somewhat commercial hotel with some local flavor. Comfortable rooms. Fine restaurant. Sporty and casual. Pool. Expensive. Open December through April.

Albona   Zürs   tel: 341
Large, fine hotel. Good small restaurant. Lots of life, especially at night. Open winters only. Quite expensive.

Central-Sporthotel Edelweiss   Zürs   tel: 246
Modern and lively mountain hotel with comfortable rooms and fine dining. Great for families. Open winters only. Quite expensive.

Lorünser   Zürs   tel: 254
Large, recently revamped hotel with comfortable rooms. Good cooking. Great for families and serious skiers. Open winters only. Quite expensive.

Hotel Zürser Hof   Zürs   tel: 513
Large luxury hotel—one of the finest resort hotels in Europe. Sumptuous and elegant throughout. Spacious rooms with antiques. Declining restaurant. Nice clientèle. Very expensive. Open from December through April. Northeast of Schruns via Stuben.

WHERE TO EAT

Graz [18]

Herzl-Weinstube   Prokopigasse 12   tel: 83 365
Ancient inn with rustic atmosphere and Austrian specialties. Moderate.

Innsbruck [31]

Das Alte Haus Delevo   *Maria Theresien Strasse 9*   *tel: 28 088*
Fine regional cooking in this old-style restaurant. Moderate.

Ottoburg   *Herzog-Friedrich Strasse 1*   *tel: 26 371*
Wine tavern with fine Austrian cuisine. Moderate.

Lans [31]

Wilder Mann   *Lans*   *tel: 73 87*
Fabulous continental cuisine with Austrian touches. Quite expensive. Worth a detour. Southeastern edge of Innsburck.

Vienna [1] (Wien)

Alter Hofkeller   *Schauflergasse 1*   *tel: 52 31 77*
Lively wine tavern with typical Austrian fare. Zither music. Moderate.

Csardasfürstin   *Schwarzenbergstrasse 2*   *tel: 52 92 46*
Only a short walk from the Opera. Small restaurant with Hungarian and Balkan specialties (quite spicy). Gypsy music. Lively. Moderate.

Demel   *Kohlmarkt 14*   *tel: 63 55 16*
An institution. Vienna's most famous pastry shop once serving the Emperor. Fabulous sweets. Excellent coffee and light lunches. Very elegant. Expensive.

***Drei Husaren   *Weiburggasse 4*   *tel: 52 11 91*
Soft and sensual. One of the most elegant French restaurants with an excellent wine list. Wonderful atmosphere. Expensive. Reserve well in advance.

Fischerhaus   *Höhenstrasse*   *tel: 44 13 20*
Lovely setting on a hill in the Vienna Woods overlooking the city. Viennese cooking. Moderate.

Franziskaner   *Franziskanerplatz 6*   *tel: 52 11 72*
Rather small and elegant restaurant with original paintings and antiques enhancing the atmosphere. Fine French and continental cooking. Superb service. Lively social center. Expensive.

Rotisserie Coq d'Or   *Führichgasse 1*   *tel: 52 12 75*
Quite large with modern and attractive décor. Fine grills. Good for lunch. Moderate to expensive.

****Sacher*   *Philharmonikerstrasse 4*   *tel: 52 55 75*
Very elegant and popular meeting place in the Sacher Hotel. World-famous for its chocolate cake.

Schwarzenberg   *Kärtner Ring 17*   *tel: 52 73 93*
Typical coffeehouse serving delicious coffee. A place where people sit for hours to relax and meet people.

Urbanikeller   *Am Hof 12*   *tel: 63 91 02*
Lively wine cellar with fine local cooking. However, the emphasis is on the wine. Viennese music. Moderate.

Wegenstein   *Nussdorfer Strasse 59*   *tel: 34 16 50*
Viennese specialties including game in the off-season. Good home cooking. Casual. Inexpensive to moderate.

Wiener Stadkrug   *Weiburggasse 3*   *tel: 52 79 55*
Typical Viennese setting. Wonderful regional cooking. Expensive.

****Winter*   *Simmeringer Lände 262*   *tel: 77 65 17*
A rustic charmer with a liberal use of wood. Nice atmosphere. Quite intimate. Excellent regional cooking and fine wines. Very expensive.

Zur Spanischen Hofreitschule   *Josefsplatz 6*   *tel: 52 56 81*
Fine intimate restaurant with motifs of the Spanish Riding School. Good continental cuisine. Quite expensive.

BELGIUM

BELGIUM

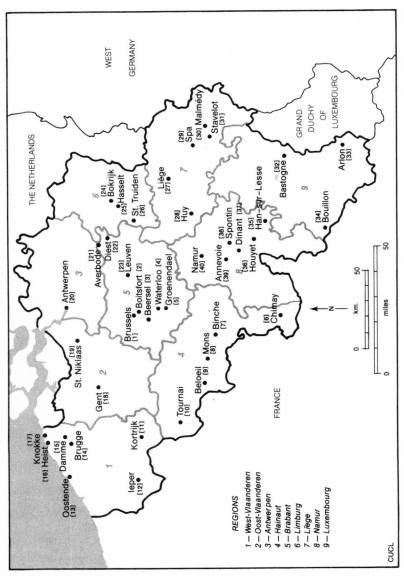

THE NETHERLANDS

WEST GERMANY

GRAND DUCHY OF LUXEMBOURG

FRANCE

Knokke [17]
Heist [15]
Oostende [13]
Damme [14]
Brugge [16]
St. Niklaas [19]
Kortrijk [11]
Ieper [12]
Gent [18]
Antwerpen [20]
Averbode [21]
Diest [22]
Bokrijk [24]
Hasselt [25]
St. Truiden [26]
Leuven [23]
Boitsfort [2]
Brussels [1]
Beersel [3]
Waterloo [4]
Groenendael [5]
Tournai [10]
Beloeil [9]
Mons [8]
Binche [7]
Chimay [6]
Liège [27]
Huy [28]
Spa [29]
Malmédy [30]
Stavelot [31]
Namur [40]
Annevoie [39]
Spontin [38]
Dinant [37]
Houyet [36]
Han-sur-Lesse [35]
Bouillon [34]
Bastogne [32]
Arlon [33]

1
2
3
4
5
6
7
8
9

N

km.   0   50
miles 0   50

REGIONS

1 — *West-Vlaanderen*
2 — *Oost-Vlaanderen*
3 — *Antwerpen*
4 — *Hainaut*
5 — *Brabant*
6 — *Limburg*
7 — *Liège*
8 — *Namur*
9 — *Luxembourg*

CUCL

WHAT TO SEE

Belgium has much to offer the uncommon traveller: romantic castles, superb restaurants (some of my favorites), historic country inns, inspiring *béguinages* (nunneries), and art museums filled with masterpieces from the mystical Middle Ages to the whimsical baroque period. And, you'll find scenic variety as well: rolling hills in the rugged Ardennes with its scented forests to a coastline with forty miles of fine beaches euphemistically called the "Sahara." Since Belgium is no larger than Maryland, you'll find that it's easy to uncover in a relatively short stay.

Don't miss *Brussels* [1]. It's a rather unimpressive city overall, but its Grand'Place fringed with historical buildings makes up for it, as do the dozens of superb restaurants. From September to May you'll want to take in a performance of opera or ballet at the outstanding *Théâtre Royal de la Monnaie*. Recommended excursions from the capital include the *béguinage* of *Leuven* [23], the castles at *Beersel* [3] and *Gaasbeck*, and perhaps, the battlefield at *Waterloo* [4] (frankly, disappointing to many).

South of Brussels, you won't want to miss two of the country's outstanding castles: *Beloeil* [9] and *Chimay* [6]. The latter hosts a music festival in June and July (reserve seats months in advance). Try too to get to *Tournai* [10] to see its Romanesque cathedral. A unique off-season event (early March) is the Carnaval de *Binche* [7] (takes place on Shrove Tuesday). It's one of the most interesting folkloric events in Europe.

Toward the coast you'll find one of Europe's great *small* cities: *Brugge* [14]. It's a marvel at any time of year although the surrounding region is most beautiful from late May to early October. During the summer Belgians invade the region's fashionable beaches, staying in resorts such as *Knokke* [17] or *Oostende* [13]. If you drive through this region, take the scenic route from *Gent* [18] to *Brugge* [14] to see the colorful blankets of blooming begonias, most brilliant in August. You won't want to miss excursions to the charming typical towns of *Lissewege* and *Damme* [15] (eat in nearby Oostkerke).

In *Gent* [18] take your time to see the historic mansions, museums, ancient guild, and patrician houses, and the fine cathedral protecting Jan Van Eyck's world-famous *Adoration of the Mystic Lamb*. The Thursday market in nearby *Sint-Niklaas* [19] makes for a photogenic and fun outing. Try some fricaseed chicken *waterzooi* in the artists' haven of *Deurle*.

Rubens fans devote some of their travel time to three of his works in the Gothic Cathedral of *Antwerp* **[20]**. Note that these are generally covered until noon. You'll find other works of Rubens in the Royal Gallery of Fine Arts, in the artist's seventeenth-century home, and in the Plantin-Moretus Museum. Try to avoid arriving in Antwerp on a Monday, since most sights close on this day. Two fine sights in the surrounding region are the *béguinage* at *Lier* and the St. Rombaut Cathedral in *Mechelen*.

Heading southeast you'll visit the medieval (recreated) village in *Bokrijk* **[24]**, shop for Val St. Lambert crystal in *Liège* **[27]**, gamble in *Spa* **[29]**, or just relax in any of dozens of authentic country inns described in the sections on where to stay and eat in Belgium. This area is a gourmet's delight.

Annevoie-Rouillon **[39]** must be ranked as one of the finest châteaux in Belgium. It's open from Easter until the end of June, then again in the first two weeks of September. Annevoie is a forty-nine-mile drive from Brussels and worth a special detour. Also of interest to some travellers will be the animal park at *Han-sur-Lesse* **[35]** as well as the shops touting brass and copper items in *Dinant* **[37]**. Near the French border you'll find a medieval castle at *Bouillon* **[34]**.

WHAT'S THE WEATHER REALLY LIKE?

Weather tends to be reasonably good from May through September, although everyone should come armed with a solid umbrella. October is an unpredictable month. The weather is generally poor from November through March (the worst month) with frequent rains and occasional snowfalls. Sometimes in the middle of November you'll find crisp and clear weather known as *St. Martin's Summer*. Days can be surprisingly bright and sunny at this time. April, like October, represents a change in season and is unpredictable.

SOME SUGGESTIONS FOR A MORE ENJOYABLE TRIP

Belgium is a small country best visited by car. Allow at least a week (two days in Brussels and five in other areas, which should include a rural inn). In the major cities I'd suggest that you park your car to sightsee on foot. You may want to use taxis for side trips to popular restaurants in suburban areas. Fares on meters now include a 15 percent tip. Although tips are included on the bills in most restaurants, you should add another tip for the waiter if the service and food were outstanding. Hotels in major Belgian cities often offer 20 percent discounts for weekend stays, but you must ask about these before checking in. Belgium is famous for its local celebrations, and you might want to get a calendar of events either from the Belgian National Tourist Office (p. xix) or from the Belgian Airlines (Sabena). Note that Belgian francs are good in Luxembourg (but not vice versa).

WHERE TO STAY

Antwerpen [20] (Antwerp)

Plaza   Charlottalei 43-49   tel: (031) 39 59 70
Fairly small deluxe hotel in a quiet area. Very comfortable with excellent service. Expensive.

As [25]

Hotel Mardaga   Stationstraat 89   tel: (011) 65 70 34
Tiny, delightful hotel with comfortable rooms and fine food. Moderate. Northeast of Hasselt.

Bastogne [32]

Lebrun   8 Rue de Marche   tel: (062) 21 11 93
Tiny inn with excellent restaurant specializing in ham, trout, and game. Moderate.

Beersel [3]

Auberge des Chevaliers   Château de Beersel   tel: 376 26 47
Small hunting lodge near the moated castle. Great atmosphere and fine cuisine. Quite expensive.

Bouillon [34]

Tyrol   Rue audessus de la Ville 21   tel: (061) 46 62 93
Charming tiny inn with comfortable rooms. Peaceful. Moderate.

Poste   1 Place St. Arnould   tel: (061) 46 65 06
Quite small hotel with pleasant rooms. Moderate.

Brugge [14] (Bruges)

Portinari   Garenmarkt   tel: (050) 33 61 12
Quite small mansion turned into a near-luxury hotel with extremely comfortable and spacious rooms. Tasteful. Quiet. Good restaurant. Expensive.

Duc de Bourgogne   Huidenvettersplein 12   tel: (050) 33 20 38
A tiny, pleasant antique hotel with a canalside location bringing out the mood for which Brugge is justly famous. Original oils throughout. The restaurant is one of the finest in the region. A winner. Expensive.

Brussels [1] (Bruxelles)

L'Hôtel Amigo   1-3 Rue de L'Amigo   tel: 511 59 10
Large and very charming hotel with a superb location only a few steps from the Grand'Place. Calm, comfortable, and tastefully furnished rooms. Quiet and deluxe. Pleasant service. Very expensive, but worth it.

Park Hotel   Avenue de l'Yser 21   tel: 734-7871
Small residential hotel with comfortable, quiet rooms and pleasant garden atmosphere. Most rooms with bath. Quite good restaurant. Moderate to expensive.

Deurle [18]

Rally Saint Christophe   Pontstraat 63   tel: (091) 52 31 06
A riverside inn southwest of Gent. Full of atmosphere. Comfortable. Delightful restaurant. Moderate to expensive.

Auberge du Pècheur   Pontstraat 42   tel: (091) 82 31 44
Another delightful rural inn with fine atmosphere and food. Moderate to expensive.

Deurne [20]

Rivierenhof   Turnhoutsebaan 244   tel: (031) 35 25 64
In the eastern suburb of Antwerpen is a château hotel in a park setting. Only a few rooms. Tennis. Expensive.

Durbuy-Sur-Ourthe [27]

Hostellerie Le Sanglier des Ardennes   Durbuy-sur-Ourthe tel: (086) 21 10 88
In the northern part of the province. Charming inn, secluded and calm. Lots of atmosphere. Superb food with trout as the specialty. Fishing. Expensive. Closed January. Southwest of Liège.

Essene [1]

Hostellerie Bellemolen   Stationstraat 4   tel: 66 238
About eleven miles northwest of Brussels. A fine rustic inn dating back to the medieval period. Several comfortable rooms, and a superb kitchen. Quite expensive.

Gent [18]

Parkhotel   Wilsonplein 1   tel: (091) 25 17 81
Small hotel—one of the better choices in town, with a fine restaurant. Nice wines. Moderate.

Groenendael [1]

***Romeyer   109 Chaussée de Groenendael   tel: 657 05 81
Only eight miles from Brussels. Pleasant rural inn noted for topflight cooking. Quite expensive. Be sure to call ahead. A must if you're nearby!

Château de Groenendael   Avenue A. Dubois 1   tel: 657 08 01
Charming inn with gourmet dining. Expensive. Closed in February.

Châlet de la Forêt   Drève de Lorraine 43   tel: 374-3993
Tiny deluxe hotel with a superb restaurant. Expensive.

Keerbergen [1]

Hostellerie Berkenhof   Valkeniersdreef   tel: (015) 51 18 03
Fifteen miles northeast of Brussels. Fine country inn with excellent cooking. Quite expensive.

Havelange [38]

Hostellerie de la Poste   5 Route de Dinant   tel: 63 090
Northeast of Spontin. Fine tiny inn with an excellent restaurant. Expensive. Closed February.

Herbeumont-sur-Semois [34]

Prieuré des Conques   Herbeumont-sur-Semois   tel: (061) 41 14 17
A short drive southeast of Bouillon. Formerly an abbey, now a modern hotel with exquisite antiques. Lovely park setting close to the Semois River. Comfortable rooms. Excellent cooking. Expensive. Closed January to mid-March.

Heyd [27]

Le Lignely   Heyd   tel: (086) 49 90 26
Small, delightful inn with very comfortable rooms. Nice restaurant specializing in fish dishes. Moderate to expensive. Closed mid-January to mid-February. Halfway between Liège and Bastogne.

Honnay-Pondrome [37]

L'Ermitage Canadien   Beauraing   tel: 71 211
South of Houyet via Beauraing. Wooden exterior in charming setting. Simple rooms. Excellent food with accent on fresh trout. Some fishing. Lots of fun. Expensive.

Huy [28]

L'Aigle Noir   8 Quai Dautrebande   tel: (085) 21 10 64
Small country hotel with several comfortable rooms and an excellent restaurant. Moderate. Closed July and August.

Ieper [12] (Ypres)

Hostellerie St. Nicholas   G. de Stuersstraat 6   tel: (057) 20 06 22
Small hotel with a long and rich history. Elegant but simple. Quite comfortable. Nice restaurant. Moderate. Closed July and August.

Kemmel [12]

Hostellerie Mont Kemmel   Bergstraat 339C   tel: (057) 44 41 45
South of Ieper. Small country inn with a delightful atmosphere and serene setting. Nice view from comfortable rooms. Excellent cuisine. Tennis. Expensive.

Knokke-Heist [17]

La Réserve   132 Elisabethlaan   tel: (050) 60 27 12
Small luxury resort in a superb setting. Comfortable and tasteful rooms. Just a short walk to the sea. Excellent restaurant with special gastronomic weekends. Very lively on gala weekends at Christmas and January, for which reservations are necessary. Casino. Tennis. Fishing. Expensive.

Lugano   Villapad 8   tel: (050) 60 44 71
Small resort hotel with a refreshing outdoor feeling. Comfortable rooms at moderate rates. A good in-between hotel.

La Roche-en-Ardennes [32]

Hôtel de l'Air Pur   11 Route de Houffalize   tel: (084) 41 12 23
Serene setting with view to the Ourthe River. Simple rooms, but famed for its superb cuisine. Expensive. Only a mile and a half from La Roche, northwest of Bastogne. Closed January until Easter.

La Chalet et Beau Séjour   Route de Marche   tel: (084) 41 12 23
Tiny inn with chalet atmosphere. Good restaurant with game as specialty. Moderate to expensive. Closed in winter.

Liège [27]

Hôtel de la Couronne   11 Place des Guillemins
tel: (041) 52 21 68
Fine hotel with central location. Large and elegant. Very comfortable. Good restaurant. Expensive.

Lokeren [19]

Parkhotel   Antwerpse Steenweg 1   tel: (091) 48 20 46
Only a few miles southwest of Sint Niklaas. Delightful and quiet hotel filled with antiques. Superb restaurant specializing in seasonal dishes with an emphasis on fresh game. Excellent wines. Moderate. Closed in July. Worth a detour.

Mont-Malmédy [30]

Hostellerie Trois Marets   Mont-Malmédy   tel: (080) 77 79 17
Lovely scenic location for this fine inn with simple but comfortable rooms. Excellent restaurant specializing in fish dishes. Moderate. Closed mid-November until mid-December.

Noirefontaine [34]

Auberge du Moulin Hideux   Rue de Dohan 1   tel: (061) 46 62 15
Lovely old mill with only ten comfortable rooms. Great atmosphere—one of Europe's finest country inns. Intimate. Superb cooking. Northwest of Bouillon. Closed January and February.

Nukerke [10]

Hostellerie Shamrock   Ommegangstraat 136   tel: (055) 21 55 29
Attractive and calm retreat. Only six rooms, comfortable and elegant. Very fine restaurant specializing in game. Northeast of Tournai.

Oostkamp [14]

Château des Brides   Breidelstraat 1   tel: (050) 82 20 01
Tiny, charming estate five miles from Brugge. Very quiet and comfortable with lots of atmosphere. Moderate.

Rochehaut-sur-Semois [34]

Chalet Ardennais   Route de Alle 120   tel: 46 530
A short drive northwest of Bouillon. Overpowering view from
this tiny, delightful inn noted for its superb cuisine. Expensive.
Reserve well in advance.

Solre Saint-Gery [8]

Le Prieuré Saint-Géry   9 Rue Lambot   tel: (071) 79 85 71
Southeast of Beaumont. Eighteenth-century atmosphere. Only a
few rooms available. Restaurant specializes in fresh fish. Closed
mid-January to mid-February. Expensive. Southeast of Mons.

Spa [29]

***Grand Cerf   111 Rue Sauvenière   tel: (087) 77 26 80
Small traditional hotel with one of the best restaurants in town.
Known for its superb paté and fresh trout. Expensive.

Château Sous Bois   22 Chemin de la Platte   tel: (087) 77 23 00
Small traditional hotel in lovely park setting. Very quiet and
comfortable. Good restaurant. Expensive. Closed October to Easter.

Stambruges-Grandglise [10]

Le Vert Gazon   Route de Mons 1   tel: (069) 57 59 84
Several rooms in this small inn with a lovely scenic location. Excellent restaurant with great fish dishes (lobster in season). Expensive. Closed February. East of Tournai.

Val de Poix [32] (Hatrival)

Val de Poix   Val de Poix   tel: (061) 61 13 08
Hunting lodge in forest. Converted into superb restaurant with
duck as the specialty. Moderate. Closed mid-January to mid-
March. Two and one-half miles southwest of St. Hubert; west of
Bastogne.

Villers-le-Temple [27]

La Commanderie   *28 Rue Joseph Pierce*   tel: *(085) 51 17 01*
Fifteen miles southwest of Liège. Medieval atmosphere in a charming and calm country inn. Excellent cooking. Superb choice for short rural vacation. Closed January. Expensive. ˙

Waimes [30]

Hôtel des Bains   *Lac de Robertville*   tel: *(080) 67 95 71*
Just east of Malmédy. Small and intimate hotel and restaurant. Comfortable. Quite expensive. Closed February.

Yvoir [40]

Hostellerie Vachter   *22 Chaussée de Dinant*   tel: *(082) 61 13 14*
Twelve miles south of Namur to the west of Spontin. Superb cooking in this tiny inn with an exquisite garden atmosphere. Expensive. Reserve well in advance. Closed February.

WHERE TO EAT

Aartselaar [20]

Château Linderboos   *Chaussée de Boom 139*   tel *(031) 78 09 65*
Southeast of Antwerpen. Old home with superb atmosphere. Regarded as one of the finest restaurants in the region—an experience. Very expensive. Closed August.

Angleur [27]

Le Sart Tilman   *Route du Condroz 531*   tel: *(041) 65 42 24*
Excellent rural restaurant serving superb local specialties. Just south of Liège. Moderate.

Antwerpen [20] (Antwerp)

La Cigogne d'Alsace   *Wiegstraat 7-9*   tel: *33 97 16*
Small, delightful, and fun restaurant with very good regional cooking. Moderately expensive.

Le Criterium   *25 Avenue de Keyserlei 25*   *tel: (031) 33 01 58*
Turn-of-the-century atmosphere in a restaurant ranked among the top in the city by gourmets. Expensive.

La Pérouse   *Ponten Steen*   *tel: (031) 32 35 28*
A special off-season restaurant open from October to May. On a ship offshore. Superb food and music in the background. Reservations a must. Expensive.

La Rade   *Ernest Van Dijckkaai 8*   *tel: (031) 33 49 63*
A classic restaurant with superb cuisine. Open all year. Expensive. Again, reservations a must.

Sint Jacob in Gallicië   *Braderijstraat 14*   *tel: (031) 33 74 65*
Fine restaurant in sixteenth-century atmosphere with a delightful wine-cellar ambience. Expensive. Best reserve.

Sir Anthony Van Dijck   *16 Oude Koorn Markt*   *tel: 31 61 70*
Quiet and relaxed spot, noted for superb fish dishes. Expensive.

Binche [7]

Phillippe II   *18 Avenue Albert 1er*   *tel: (064) 33 13 05*
Large and friendly restaurant with a wide choice of continental dishes. Very nice. Expensive.

Brugge [14]

Duc de Bourgogne   *Huidenvettersplein 12*   *tel: (050) 33 20 38*
Mentioned in the hotel section. A superb restaurant with both Belgian and French cuisine. Lovely setting and flavor. Expensive.

Brussels [1] (Bruxelles)

***Les Arcades*   *Chaussée de Waterloo 1441*   *tel: 374-3516*
Very small, somewhat plain-looking restaurant serving delicious dishes prepared from the freshest and finest ingredients available. Not at all showy, but discreet and reserved. Set up for knowing gourmets who are willing to spend time and money to get what they want. Limited number of dishes. Fine, moderately priced wines. Closed Sunday, Monday, and August.

L'Auberge de Boondael   *Square du Vieux Tilleul 12*
tel: 672 70 55
Rustic farmhouse atmosphere with wooden beams and open grill. Specialities are steak and chicken. Smoky, busy, and very popular. Quite expensive. Taxi needed from center of town.

Auberge du Souverain   *1 Avenue de la Fauconnerie*
tel: 672 16 01
You'll need a cab to get to this elegant restaurant with a lakeside setting. Superb cuisine. Expensive.

Auberge Pittorsque   *30 Drève Pittoresque*   *tel: 358-0149*
You'll have to take a taxi to find this out-ot-the-way spot that's a favorite with residents. Charming atmosphere and open fireplace. Good regional dishes. Expensive.

Au Bon Vieux Temps   *12 Marché Aux Herbes*   *tel: 218 15 46*
Trying to find this charming seventh-century house in its narrow passageway is half the fun of this small restaurant. Lots of atmosphere in a crowded way. Trout and Coquille St. Jacques are its specialties. Best at lunch. Expensive.

Au Roi d'Espagne   *9 Petit Sablon*   *tel: 512 65 70*
Tiny restaurant with a Spanish décor. Both Spanish and international dishes. Very popular. Moderate. Reserve.

Chalet de la Fôret   *43 Drève de Lorraine*   *tel: 374 39 93*
You'll need a taxi to get to this serene and superb restaurant in a forest setting. Best in warm weather, when dining is al fresco. Very expensive. A few rooms available.

Chez Bernard   *93 Rue de Namur*   *tel: 512 88 21*
Small and expensive. One of the best restaurants in town for fresh seafood.

***Chez Marcel*   *84 rue Wayez*   *tel: 521-9957*
Excellent formal restaurant. Superb fish dishes and fine wines. Very expensive.

Chez Marius "En Provence"   *1 Place du Petit Sablon*
tel: 512 27 89
Fine southern French cooking in a pleasant atmosphere. Hearty portions. Superb sauces. Expensive.

***Comme Chez Soi (Just Like Home)*   *Place Rouppe 23*
tel: 512 29 21
An insider's favorite where it helps to be known. Turn-of-the-century atmosphere. Specialties according to the season, including salmon and game birds. Expensive.

La Couronne   28 Grand'Place   tel: 511 14 09
Ideal location on the main square. Seventeenth-century décor for this elegant restaurant appealing mainly to English-speaking tourists. The upstairs is highly recommended. A bit snooty and very expensive.

***Dupont   Avenue Vital-Riethuisen 46   tel: 427-5450*
A gastronomic temple, drawing in an élite group of gourmets. Not at all snobbish, but very knowing. Varied menu, with outstanding selection of wines. Each meal is made up of a number of courses, of which you can eat as much as you like. Expensive. Closed Monday evening, and mid-July to late August.

L'Ecailler du Palais Royal   18 Rue Bodenbroek (near the Place Sablon)   tel: 512 87 51
Housed in an old romantic building across from the church. The atmosphere is matched by the seafood specialties, including fresh oysters in season. Lots of fun. Expensive.

L'Epaule de Mouton   16 Rue des Harengs   tel: 511 05 94
Geared to gourmets. A tiny restaurant with a vast menu (sixty-two house recipes). You get what you pay for—that's a lot.

Le Filet de Boeuf   8 Rue des Harengs   tel: 511 95 59
Excellent atmosphere and superb stews and beef. Expensive.

Le Londres   21-23 Rue de l'Ecuyer   tel: 218 06 43
Classic continental cuisine with a flair. Fancy. Expensive.

La Maison du Cygne   2 Rue Charles Buls   tel: 511 82 44
Superb atmosphere and cuisine near the Grand'Place. Very expensive. Large menu with emphasis on superb fowl. Fanciful and fun.

***Parc Savoy   Place Marie-Savoy 9   tel: 649 98 65*
A calm and pleasant restaurant in a garden setting with an open and airy feeling. Fine varied menu. Formal and expensive. Taxi needed from the center of town.

Le Pré au Bois   15 *Chaussée de Waterloo*   tel: *358 12 06*
An outstanding new restaurant with very fine cuisine. Expensive and very popular. About thirteen miles from the city center.

Les Provençaux   22 *Rue Grétry*   tel: *218 06 23*
Refined atmosphere for a fine restaurant specializing in French cuisine. Expensive.

Ravenstein   *Rue Ravenstein 1*   tel: *512 77 68*
Marvelous old building with terrace—ideal in warm weather. Luxury restaurant with oysters and langoustines as its specialties.

Rôtisserie Vincent   8-10 *Rue des Dominicains*   tel: *511 23 03*
Down-to-earth and enjoyable. Open kitchen in a noisy, hurried atmosphere. Varied and reasonable menu.

***Villa Lorraine*   *Chaussée de la Hulpe 28*   tel: *374-2587*
An elegant restaurant in a park setting. Exceptional menu, considered by many to be the best in Belgium. Excellent choice of wines. Very expensive. Taxi needed from the center of town.

Chaudfontaine [27]

La Cense Blanche   *Chaussée de Liège 33*   tel: *(041) 65 68 61*
Five miles southeast of Liège. Lovely rustic restaurant with excellent cuisine. Moderate.

Damme [14]

Drie Zilveren Kannen   *Grote Plaats 9*   tel: *(050) 33 56 77*
Fine restaurant with a Flemish flair. Steep prices for hearty fare. Northeast of Brugge.

Le Siphon   *Damme*   tel: *(050) 35 02 50*
About one mile from Damme. An "in" place for thick steaks. Expensive.

Gent [18]

Cordial   *Kalandenbert 9*   tel: *(091) 25 77 10*
A fine restaurant popular late at night for its superb steaks and fowl. Expensive.

Dauphin   Vlaanderenstraat 7   tel: (091) 25 89 36
One of the finest restaurants in Belgium specializing in classic French cuisine with a large choice of delicious dishes. The seafood is superb and matched by flawless service. Expensive.

Jésus-Eik [1]

Restaurant Barbizon   95 Welriekendedreef   tel: (02) 657-0462
Isolated in woods to the southeast of Brussels. Delightful restaurant specializing in fish (lobster in season). Expensive. Closed Tuesday and Wednesday. Closed February.

Keerbergen [1]

Hostellerie Berkenhof   Valkeniersdreef 5   tel: (015) 51 18 03
Delightful farm restaurant in peaceful setting. Excellent fish dishes. Closed Sunday evening and Monday. Closed last three weeks in July. Expensive. Northeast of Brussels to east of Mechelen.

Kermt [25]

Salon's van Dijk   Kiezel op Lummen 17-19   tel: (011) 22 20 02
Fine country restaurant with pleasant atmosphere. Excellent regional dishes. Moderate. Northwest of Hasselt.

Liège [27]

Chez Septime   12 rue Saint Paul   tel: 23 22 55
Outstanding regional restaurant with delicious asparagus in season. Wonderful poultry and game. Good wines. Nice atmosphere. Expensive.

Vieux Liège   41 Quai Goffé   tel: (041) 23 77 48
Superb restaurant with fine cellar housed in a sixteenth-century building. Lots of atmosphere. A must. Expensive.

Clou Doré   33 Rue Mont-Saint-Martin   tel: (041) 23 79 30
Exclusive inn with great traditional atmosphere. A few rooms available—filled with antiques. A restaurant with some of the region's finest cooking. Expensive. Reserve well in advance.

Limbourg [27]

Le Dragon   31 Place St. Georges   tel: (087) 76 23 10
East of Liège and a short drive west of Eupen. Pleasant restaurant. Moderate. Closed end of July to mid-August.

Lorce [27]

Vallée   Lorce   tel: (080) 78 58 26
South of Liège via Aywaille. Take road east from Houssonloge. Restaurant with stunning view of the Amblève valley. Superb cooking. Moderate. Closed January and February.

Meise [20]

De Molen   Meise   tel: 269-1452
A long-time favorite of gourmets in a secluded location just off the Bruxelles-Antwerpen highway (signs show the way). Expensive.

Auberge Napoléan   Drève du Château Royal   tel: 269-3078
Large dining room with vast menu specializing in French dishes. Hearty and delicious cooking. Moderate.

Morlanwelz [8]

Chez Mairesse   77 Chaussée de Mariemont   tel: (064) 44 21 96
A short drive northeast of Mons and only twelve miles from Charleroi. Superb restaurant near the museum. Expensive. Reservations a must.

Namur [40]

Le Champeau   14 Avenue Golenvaux   tel: 22 92 92
This is one of the finest restaurants in the region, with excellent service and cuisine, making it an ideal stopover for lunch or supper. Expensive.

Neuville-en-Condroz [27] (Liège)

Le Chêne-Madame   Avenue de la Chevauchée   tel: 71 41 27
Worth the special detour you'll make to get here. Excellent

offering of fine dishes and wines. Nice ambience. Very expensive. Southwest of Liège.

Nivelles [4]

Gueulardière   102 Faubourg de Mons   tel: (067) 22 45 47
Fine cuisine in a lovely park setting. Expensive. Southwest of Waterloo.

Pascall   Grand'Place   tel: (067) 22 17 16
Excellent regional restaurant specializing in fresh game during the off season. Expensive.

Aigle Noir   Place Shiffelers   tel: (067) 22 20 48
A delightful restaurant with a superb reputation. Accent on both meat and fowl with delicate sauces. Expensive.

De la Collègiale   Avenue Jeuniaux 2   tel: (067) 22 28 43
Small and cozy with delicious food. Expensive.

Oostende [13] (Mariakerke)

***Au Vigneron   Aartshertogstraat 80   tel: 74 816
Very fine formal restaurant with lots of atmosphere. Superb seafood and regional specialties complemented by outstanding wines. Very expensive, worth it.

Sint Idesbald-Koksijde [13]

***L'Aquilon   Koninklijkebaan 318   tel: (058) 51 22 67
Southwest of Oostende on the coast near the border is a delightful authentic cottage turned into a fine restaurant. Expensive. Closed January and October.

Sint Michiels Brugge [14]

Weinebrugge   Koning Albertlaan 342   tel: (050) 31 44 40
Just on the outskirts of Brugge to the southwest. An elegant and relaxing restaurant specializing in fish—superb oysters and lobsters. Closed September. Closed Sunday evening and Monday. Expensive.

Temse [20]

Watermolen   Grote Kaai 17   tel: (031) 71 07 50
Elegant restaurant with nice atmosphere. Superb regional dishes. Expensive. Southwest of Antwerpen.

Tournai [10]

Trois Pommes d'Orange   Pied de Beffroi   tel: (068) 22 52 78
Simple and very pleasant restaurant serving nice steaks. Reasonable.

Trou Normand   35 Grand'Place   tel: (068) 22 17 22
Another simple restaurant specializing in game dishes in season—grouse is excellent. Moderate.

Vieuxville [27]

Au Vieux Logis   Route de Logne 20   tel: (086) 21 14 60
South of Liège. An excellent restaurant with trout and crawfish as specialties. Moderate. Closed January.

Waregem [11]

't oud Konijntje   Bosstraat 53   tel: (956) 60 19 37
Ten miles northeast of Kortrijk is a delightful inn with a superb restaurant—not to be missed. Expensive. Closed late July to mid-August.

DENMARK

DENMARK

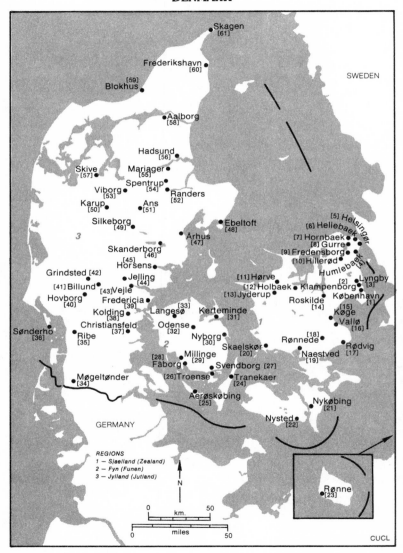

Skagen [61]

Frederikshavn [60]

SWEDEN

[59] Blokhus

Aalborg [58]

Hadsund [56]

Skive [57]   Mariager [55]

Viborg [53]   Spentrup [54]

Karup [50]   Ans [51]   Randers [52]

Silkeborg [49]

Skanderborg [46] [45]

Ebeltoft [48]

Århus [47]

[5] Helsingør

[6] Hellebaek

[7] Hornbaek [8] Gurre

[9] Fredensborg

[10] Hillerød

Humlebaek

Grindsted [42]

[41] Billund   [43] Vejle [44]

Horsens

[11] Hørve

[12] Holbaek ● Klampenborg

[2] Lyngby [3]

Hovborg [40]

Fredericia [39]

Kolding [38]

Langesø [33]

[13] Jyderup

Roskilde [14]

København [1]

Kerteminde [31]

[15] Køge

Sønderho [36]

Christiansfeld [37]

Odense [32]

Ribe [35]

Nyborg [30]

Skaelskør [20]

Rønnede [18]

Vallø [16]

Rødvig

[28] Millinge [29]

Faborg

Naestved [19] [17]

Møgeltønder [34]

[26] Troense

Svendborg [27]

Tranekaer [24]

Aerøskøbing [25]

Nykøbing [21]

GERMANY

Nysted [22]

REGIONS
1 — Sjaelland (Zealand)
2 — Fyn (Funen)
3 — Jylland (Jutland)

N

Rønne [23]

0 ____ 50
km.

0 ____ miles ____ 50

CUCL

WHAT TO SEE

Denmark is a fanciful land of delightful country inns (*kroer*), green copper spires, and crooked cobblestone streets winding between weathered cottages. *Copenhagen* [1] (København), one of the livelier European capitals, attracts virtually all first-time visitors with its Amalienborg Palace (see the changing of the guard at noon), Ny Carlsberg Glyptotek (superb collection of impressionist paintings), crown jewels in the Rosenborg Castle, fun-filled Tivoli, and shops in the streets making up the Strøget. Short excursions to the Frederiksborg Castle in *Hillerød* [10], the delightful eighteenth-century suburb of *Dragør* [1], Hamlet's Kronborg Castle in *Helsingør* [5], the Louisiana Art Museum in *Humlebaek* [4], and the Gavnø Manor near *Naestved* [19] are all recommended. Longer trips would take in the *Egeskov* Manor, *Odense* [33] (birthplace of Hans Christian Andersen), Den Gamle By (collection of ancient houses) in *Aarhus* [47], and the charming village of *Ebeltoft* [48]. The sunny resorts on the island of *Bornholm* appeal to naturalists and sun lovers during the warmer summer months (June, July, and August).

WHAT'S THE WEATHER REALLY LIKE?

Not bad at all from mid-May to mid-September, and occasionally quite nice in April, late September, and early October. Winters are cold and dark. Note that an umbrella may be necessary at any time.

SUGGESTIONS FOR A MORE ENJOYABLE TRIP

Copenhagen tends to be packed from mid-May to early September. Since the weather's generally quite good in early May and late September, why not beat the crowds by travelling at that time? Although the weather's drab in the winter, you can take advantage of the Royal Danish Ballet, special sales, and low off-season rates at that time. During the packed summer months you can arrive in Copenhagen without a reservation and still get a room in a private home. Head immediately to Kiosk P in the railway station. There you'll pay a small fee to reserve a room (best deal imaginable). Taxis are expensive, and you'll probably prefer to use public transportation to cut costs. If you do take a taxi, note that tips are not expected. Transportation from the airport into town is provided at low cost on local bus number 32. Liquor tends to be expensive in all Scandinavian countries. Surprisingly, some wines are quite reasonable. You'd be very smart to bring in one bottle of your favorite brand of booze. Distances are short, but expect slow driving if you travel by car. And remember to make ferry reservations far in advance if you plan to travel to either Sweden or Germany by boat.

WHERE TO STAY

Ans [49]

Kongensbro Kro   *Ans*   *tel: 87 01 77*
West of Arhus and north of Silkeborg on the Gudenaa River is a small and charming inn noted for its fishing and bird watching. Comfortable and quiet rooms in secluded setting. Fine Danish cooking. Moderate.

Arhus [47]

Marselis Hotel   *Strandvejen 25*   *tel: 14 44 11*
Small modern hotel close to the beach. Secluded and quiet location. Very comfortable. Attractive. Good food. Moderately expensive.

Bedsted [57]

Morup Mølle Kro   *Bedsted*   *tel: 94 80 31*
Comfortable, modernized inn only 6 miles from the North Sea and its fascinating beaches. Quite good restaurant. Pool. Moderate. Northwest of Skive.

Copenhagen [1] (København)

Ascot Hotel   *Studiestraede 57*   *tel: 12 60 00*
Small, ancient building converted into comfortable hotel with pleasant, compact rooms. Nice overall atmosphere. Expensive.

Codan Hotel   *Sankt Annae Plads 21*   *tel: 13 34 00*
Large, lovely hotel in a noncentral location, but with a charming and quite elegant air. Comfortable, modern rooms with bath. Very expensive.

Hotel Corona   *Cort Adelersgade 8-10*   *tel: 12 44 90*
Small, livable hotel with comfortable, clean rooms. Nothing fancy, but pleasant. Moderate. Open late March to end of September.

Missionshotellet   *Løngangsstraede 27*   *tel: 12 65 70*
Very large, comfortable, and Christian. Clean and convenient. No booze. Moderate.

Hotel Neptun   *Sankt Annae Plads 18*   *tel: 13 89 00*
Quite small, older hotel on charming street near the Royal Palace. Clean, but compact rooms, most with shower or bath. Friendly. Expensive.

71 Nyhavn Hotel   *71 Nyhavn*   *tel: 11 85 85*
Small nineteenth-century warehouse converted into a modern hotel with simple and rustic flavor. Wooden beams throughout. Pleasant and charming. Near the harbor. Good restaurant. Expensive.

Hotel Opera   *Tordenskjoldsgade 15*   *tel: 12 15 19*
Small, intimate hotel with comfortable rooms. Private atmosphere. Great in off-season. Excellent restaurant. Expensive.

Hotel Residenz   *160 Gothersgade*   *tel: 15 15 36*
Small, comfortable hotel in a noncentral location (take tram 5, 6 or 16). Pleasant. Only two rooms with private bath. Moderate.

Copenhagen Admiral   *Toldbodgade 24*   *tel: 11 82 82*
Large, eighteenth-century warehouse converted into charming and very comfortable hotel. Earthy and somewhat rustic in atmosphere. Expensive.

Skovriderkroen   *Strandvejen 235*   *tel: (0143) Helrup 6340*
Hunting lodge in the suburbs converted to pleasant country hotel, about thirty minutes by bus from central Copenhagen. Pleasant courtyard, good location near bathing, and excellent regional restaurant. Expensive.

Skovshoved Hotel   267 Strandvejen   tel: (01 66) Ordrup 28
Delightful country inn dating back to 1675 with pleasant rooms, half with bath. Simple, yet traditional flavor. Nice park and close to the sea. Out of the way. Moderate to expensive.

Christiansfeld [38]

Strickers Hotel   Lindegade 25   tel: 56 11 16
South on A10 from Kolding is an ancient hotel (1773) with lots of atmosphere and antiques. Comfortable.

Ebeltoft [48]

Hvide Hus   Ebeltoft   tel: 34 14 66
Large luxury hotel with lovely view. Comfortable rooms. Fine restaurant. Golf, riding, fishing, pool. Expensive.

Faborg [28]

Rasmussen's Hotel   Torvet 12   tel: 61 16 16
Near the Egeskov manor is a small hotel catering to a Danish clientèle. Comfortable. Moderate.

Feldballe [48]

Hubertus Kroen   Møllerup Estate   tel: 37 10 03
Tiny inn only seven miles from Ebeltoft. Quite comfortable. Faces riding grounds. Inexpensive.

Fredensborg [9]

Store Kro   6 Fredensborg Slotsgade   tel: 28 00 47
Ten miles southwest of Helsingør is a superb country inn—one of Denmark's best. Most rooms are spacious with bath. Elegant throughout. Fine restaurant—an excellent spot for lunch before or after the castle tour. Moderately expensive.

Grindsted [42]

Filskov Kro   Grindsted   tel: 34 81 11
Grindsted is northeast of Esbjerg on Highway A1. In the midst of Jutland's heather country is a fine inn with good cooking and comfortable rooms. Pool. Moderate.

Hadsund [52] (Gjerlev)

Øster Tørslev Kro   Gjerlev J.   tel: 47 62 50
A fine inn located between Hadsund and Randers. Modest rooms, but excellent Danish food, served here since 1720. Inexpensive.

Hammel [51]

Pøt Mølle Kro   Hammel   tel: 96 11 75
A few modest rooms and attractive romantic restaurant in an old watermill, only a few miles northeast of Hammel. Inexpensive to moderate. Southeast of Ans.

Hanstholm [57]

Hanstholm Hotel   Byvej 2   tel: 96 10 44
Quite large, new hotel surrounding court. Attractive rooms, most with bath. Expensive. Northwest of Skive on the northern coast.

Hellebaek [6]

Hellebaek Kyst Hotel   Strandvejen 123   tel: 10 96 00
Northwest of Helsingør you'll find a large beach resort in a secluded area. Comfortable; geared to sportsmen; riding, fishing, golf, and so on. Moderate.

Helsingør [5]

Hotel Marienlyst   30 Nordre Strandvej   tel: 21 18 01
Twenty-eight miles north of København, where the ferry crosses
to Sweden. A large and elegant hotel just north of town with a
view to the sea. Spacious rooms. Fine restaurant. Great turn-of-
the-century ambience. Pool. Denmark's only casino. Very fine
and very expensive.

Holbaek [12]

Strandparken Hotel   58 Kalundborgvej   tel: 43 06 16
Just west of town is a small attractive hotel in a secluded setting.
Spacious and comfortable rooms. Good food. Moderate.

Hornbaek [7]

Hotel Trouville   20 Kystvej   tel: 20 22 00
Smart modern resort hotel in a secluded area by the sea. Superb
beach. Fishing. Expensive. North of Helsingør.

Horsens [45]

Snaptun Faergegaard   Horsens   tel: 68 30 03
Delightful inn directly on the Horsens Fjord. Gorgeous scenery.
Excellent restaurant. Fishing, golf, and sailing.

Bygholm Parkhotel   Schuttersvej   tel: 62 23 33
Small manor once part of a castle with garden atmosphere.
Old-world charm. Excellent restaurant. Comfortable and calm.
Moderate.

Jørgensens Hotel   Sondergade 7   tel: 62 16 00
Lovely home converted into comfortable hotel. Expensive.

Hørve [11]

Dragsholm Slot   Hørve   tel: 45 33 66
Not a kro but a castle—the only one in Denmark with accommodations. Exquisite, richly appointed rooms. This eight-hundred-

year-old palace has all modern facilities. Each room is unique and luxurious. Large park for quiet and calm stay. Excellent restaurant. Expensive and worth it.

Hovborg [40]

Hovborg Kro   Hovborg   tel: 39 60 33
North of Holsted between Esbjerg and Kolding on Highway A1. Authentic inn with thatched roof in a scenic area. Comfortable rooms in a building dating back to 1790. Very quiet. Fine Danish cooking. Fishing on the Holme River. Moderate.

Karup [50]

Karup Hotel   Karup   tel: 10 10 19
Tiny inn geared to fishermen, who can try to catch perch and pike in both the spring and fall. Inexpensive.

Køge [15]

Vallø Slotskro   Køge   tel: 66 74 16
Tiny centuries-old inn with attractive and comfortable rooms. Lots of atmosphere. Very calm. Fishing. Moderate.

Langeland [29]

Tranekaer Gjaestgivergard   Tranekaer   tel: 59 12 04
Small, 160-year-old inn near the castle and large park. Beautifully furnished. Comfortable. Restaurant in stables. Moderate. North of Rudkøbing.

Mariager [56]

Apotekergaarden   Fuglsangsgade 12   tel: 54 11 88
Romantic inn, built as a pharmacy in 1700, in a town famous for its roses. Southwest of Hadsund.

Hotel Postgaarden   Torvet 6   tel: 54 10 12
Small, inexpensive hotel on the main square. Pleasant.

Millinge [29]

Steensgard Herregardspension   Assensvej   tel: 61 12 90
A six-hundred-year-old manor house on a twenty-one-acre estate with pond, gardens, and woods has been converted into
Denmark's most exclusive hotel. Dignified and as beautiful inside as out. Elegant public rooms. Spacious private rooms decorated in rich period furnishings. One of the best is number 1,
with its own private entrance. Fine French cuisine. Riding, tennis, and fishing. Expensive, but worth it. Reserve well in advance. Four miles northwest of Faborg.

Falsled Kro   Millinge   tel: 68 11 11
Fine inn with rooms in varied styles. The restaurant is excellent
with an emphasis on smoked salmon and superb pastries. Sailing. Six miles north of Faborg. Closed February. Expensive.

Møgeltønder [34]

Schackenborg Kro   Møgeltønder   tel: 14 83 83
Go south of Ribe to Tonder. Close to the border and just across
from Schackenborg Castle, you'll find a tiny inn built in 1687.
On a charming old village street, it's one of the best-known
kroer in Denmark with its authentic atmosphere and excellent
food. Worth a detour.

Naestved [19]

Mogenstrup Kro   Naestved   tel: 76 11 30
Northeast of Naestved is an ancient inn known for its fine
cooking. Modest rooms available. Worth a side trip. Expensive
dining. (Modern rooms recently added).

Nyborg [30]

Hesselet Hotel   Kristianslundsvej   tel: 31 30 29
Near the Nyborg Castle is a superb small hotel on the water in a
garden setting. Modern and spacious rooms—all very comfortable. Fine restaurant and bar. Golf, pool, tennis, and riding. Expensive, but worth a detour.

Odense [32]

Grand Hotel   Jernbanegade 18   tel: 11 71 71
Large old-style hotel with compact and comfortable rooms. Excellent restaurant. Moderately expensive.

Oure [30]

Majorgarden   Oure   tel: 28 10 50
Tiny country inn with delightful atmosphere between Svendborg and Nyborg. Moderate.

Randers [52]

Hotel Kongens Ege   Skovbakken   tel: 43 03 00
Large modern hotel in a peaceful park setting. Spacious and luxurious rooms. Fine food. Golf. Expensive.

Ribe [35]

Weis' Stue   Torvet   tel: 42 07 00
The inn is on the main square of Ribe, opposite the cathedral. Its interior dates back to 1720. Small but comfortable rooms. Fine food.

Dagmar Hotel   Ribe   tel: 42 00 33
Large but charming hotel with comfortable rooms and fine antiques. Moderate.

Rødvig [17]

Rødvig Kro   Rødvig   tel: 70 60 98
Southeast of Køge is an excellent inn with comfortable rooms. Inexpensive.

Silkeborg [49]

Kongensbro Kro   Ans   tel: 87 01 77
Fifteen miles north of Silkeborg and only three miles from Ans is an attractive old Danish inn with fine river fishing in the spring. Moderate.

Skanderborg [46]

Munkekroen · Adelgade 49   tel: 52 08 88
In the heart of Skanderborg near the Lake District is this medieval inn noted for its excellent menu.

Skanderborghus   Skanderborg   tel: 52 09 55
Small inn with comfortable rooms in a beautiful location. Very peaceful. Fishing. Ideal for visits to the Lake District. Expensive.

Spentrup [54]

Hvidsten Kro   Spentrup   tel: 47 70 22
North of Randers is a historic inn dating back to 1634, noted as a drop for arms from England during World War II. The center for the Danish Resistance is now a fine inn with excellent food. Modest rooms. Inexpensive.

Vallø [16]

Vallø Slotskro   Vallø   tel: 66 74 16
Ancient inn with pleasant rooms and good regional cooking. Moderate.

Vejle [43]

Munkebjerg Hotel   Vejle   tel: 82 75 00
Attractive modern hotel in pleasant setting at Vejle Fjord. Casual atmosphere with golf nearby. Expensive.

Vestbjerg [59]

Hotel Luneborg Kro   Vestbjerg   tel: 26 51 00
Tiny delightful inn in the far north. Charming, historic atmosphere. Moderate. East of Blokhus.

WHERE TO EAT

Aerøskøbing [25] (Aerø Island)

Købinghus   Sondergade 36   tel: 52 11 00
Interesting café dating back to the seventeenth century. Danish dishes. Moderate.

Arhus [47]

Moesgaard Skovmølle   Arhus   tel: 27 12 14
A rustic restaurant near the old water mill six miles south of Arhus in forest setting at Moesgaard open-air museum.

Blokhus [59]

Strandingskroen   Blokhus   tel: 24 90 07
Near the beach is a delightful restaurant in an old skippers' house.

Copenhagen [1] (København)

Royal Hotel   1 Hammerichsgade   tel: 14 14 12
Superb candlelight dinner each Wednesday evening from October 31 until the end of March. Excellent Continental cuisine. Exquisite setting and atmosphere. Dancing. Formal. Expensive.

Hotel Imperial   Vester Farimagsgade 9   tel: 12 80 00
The "Atrium." Fine French cuisine. Quiet and tasteful. Expensive and worth it—one of the best in town.

Plaza Hotel   4 Bernstorffsgade   tel: 14 92 62
The "Baron of Beef." French cuisine. Extensive wine list. Cocktails in elegant library room. Expensive.

7 Sma Hjem   Jernbanegade 4   tel: 11 02 95
Seven small homes as dining rooms. Charming atmosphere. International cuisine. Nice cellar bar. Moderate.

Krogs Fiskerestaurant   Gammelstrand 38   tel: 15 89 15
Excellent fish dishes of all varieties. Very popular. Moderate to expensive. Don't miss it!

Den Gyldne Fortun   Ved Stranden 18   tel: 12 20 11
Basement restaurant. Delicious Danish cold table. Best for lunch.
Expensive.

Bof and Ost   Grabrødre Torv 13   tel: 11 99 11
Intimate cellar setting. French style. Very fine international
cuisine with Danish delicacies. Expensive.

Ebeltoft [48]

Den Skaeve Kro   Villadsgyde   tel: 34 18 38
On the main street of Ebeltoft. One of the oldest houses in
town.

Mellem Jyder   Juulsbakke 3   tel: 34 11 23
Delightful restaurant behind the Town Hall. Small garden.
Restored in 1660. Moderate.

Fanø [36]

Sønderho Kro   Sønderho   tel: 16 40 14
In the heart of a town famous for its old skippers' cottages. Tiny
entrance into this delightful inn built in 1722. Near the beach.

Grena [48]

Mejlgaard Slotskro   Grena   tel: 31 71 74
Thirteen miles from Grena on the peninsula. The stables of a
manor converted into a rustic restaurant. Moderate. Northeast of
Ebeltoft.

Hillerød [10]

Slots Kroen   Hillerød   tel: 61 87 62
An attractive café serving regional dishes within the castle area.
Moderate.

Holte [1]

Søllerød Kro   Søllerødvej 35   tel: 80 25 05
Twelve miles northwest of København on A5, near a forest, is one
of the great restaurants in Denmark. In a thatched seventeenth

century building, it offers superb international and Danish dishes in warm weather—mostly summer. Worth a detour. Expensive.

Jyderup [13]

Bromølle Kro   Jyderup   tel: 55 00 90
Directly west of Roskilde is the oldest (1199) kro in Denmark. Fine restaurant with lovely view of park from the terrace in late spring and early fall. Moderate.

Klampenborg [2]

Strandmøllekroen   Strandvejen 808   tel: 63 03 22
Near the Deer Park on the coast road ten miles north of København. Fine cooking in a restful location. Expensive.

Kolding [38]

Krybily Kro   Kolding Landevej 160   tel: 56 25 55
Six miles north of Kolding on Highway 1. An inn dating back to 1737 still serving fine food.

Odense [33]

Den Gamle Kro   Overgaden 23   tel: 12 14 33
Built in 1683, this charming inn has a wonderful historic flavor and superb food.

Sortebro Kro   Funen Village   tel: 13 28 26
Part of the open-air museum in the Funen Village. Quite good Danish dishes.

Under Lindetraet   Ramsherred 2   tel: 11 43 08
Opposite the Hans Christian Andersen House. Charming small cafe serving delicious Danish dishes. Moderate.

Rønnede [19]

Rønnede Kro   Rønnede   tel: 71 10 86
An historic inn built in 1645 near Køge by the Gisselfeld and

Bregentved manor houses. Nice restaurant. Moderate. On main road number 2.

Roskilde [14]

Svogerslev Kro   Roskilde   tel: 38 30 05
West of København is a delightful inn with a thatched roof. The building dates from 1727. Charming restaurant serving both continental and Danish cuisine. Moderate.

Svanninge [28]

Staevnegarden   Svanninge   tel: 12 48
Delightful, seventeenth-century inn specializing in fresh fish. Moderate.

Svendborg [27]

Vester Skerninge Kro   Svendborg   tel: 24 10 04
Six miles from Svendborg on the road to Faborg is a fine inn serving Danish specialties in a lovely setting.

Tasinge [26]

Breininge Kro   Troense (Taasinge)   tel: 22 54 75
Just outside the town of Troense. Fine Danish food in an antique setting. No rooms.

Breininge Mölle   Taasinge   tel: 22 52 55
Colorful restaurant in an old mill. Moderate.

Admiralen Valdemar Slot   Troense   tel: 21 09 80
Cafe in the cellar of the Valdemar Slot castle, now a naval museum. Inexpensive.

FINLAND

FINLAND

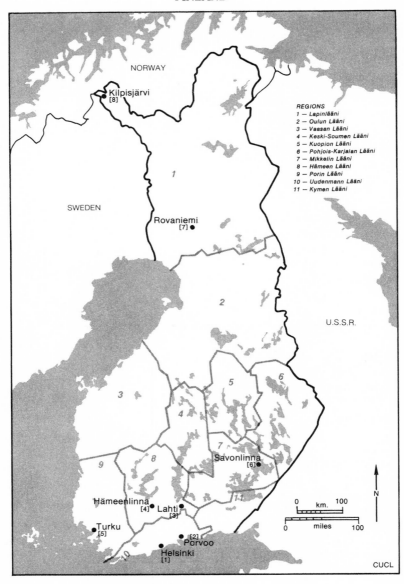

NORWAY

Kilpisjärvi
[8]

REGIONS
1 — Lapinlääni
2 — Oulun Lääni
3 — Vaasan Lääni
4 — Keski-Soumen Lääni
5 — Kuopion Lääni
6 — Pohjois-Karjaian Lääni
7 — Mikkelin Lääni
8 — Hämeen Lääni
9 — Porin Lääni
10 — Uudenmann Lääni
11 — Kymen Lääni

SWEDEN

Rovaniemi
[7]

U.S.S.R.

5

6

3

4

7

Savonlinna
[6]

9

8

Hämeenlinna
[4] Lahti
[3]

Turku
[5]

[2]
Porvoo

Helsinki
[1]

0   km.   100

0   miles   100

N

CUCL

WHAT TO SEE

The natural gateway to this northern land of sixty thousand lakes and a half million saunas is *Helsinki* [1], appreciated by some for its Suomenlinna Fortress, Botanical Gardens, Helsinki Design Center, and open air market with wriggling (almost) fish and fresh flowers. However, the real appeal of Finland lies in its fresh air, scented forests, and isolated wilderness. You may want to relax in such a resort complex as *Hämeenlinna* [4] or at the inn in *Porvoo* [2]. Try to make an excursion to see the medieval fortress at *Savonlinna* [6] and the Sibelius Museum in *Turku* [5]. Trout fishermen may wish to make the long trek to *Kilpisjärvi* [8] to try their favorite sport.

WHAT'S THE WEATHER REALLY LIKE?

Almost all tourists travel to Finland from mid-May to late September during the warmer summer months, which offer long hours of daylight.

SOME SUGGESTIONS FOR A MORE ENJOYABLE TRIP

In Helsinki, you can take an excursion around the city on the tourist tram for a token amount. Note that rooms are at a premium and that you should reserve one far in advance. Swingers may want to take the *night* boat from Stockholm to Helsinki (often quite wild).

WHERE TO STAY

Hameenlinna [4]

Hotel Aulanko   Hämeenlinna   tel: 21 271
Very large, lovely resort in beautiful park setting. Comfortable. Geared to the sportsman, with tennis, golf, and riding. Moderate.

Helsinki [1]

Hotel Helsinki   Hallituskatu 12   tel: 63 07 01
Comfortable commercial hotel with contemporary rooms. Attractive. Good restaurant. Moderate to expensive.

Hotel Palace   Eteläranta 10   tel: 11 114
Small, attractive hoel with contemporary rooms. Great view. Very comfortable. Excellent choice and very Finnish. Expensive.

Hotel Seurahuone   Kaivokatu 12   tel: 10 441
Small, traditional hotel with elegant rooms and flavor. Expensive.

Imatra [6]

Valtionhotelli   Imatra   tel: 63 244
Small castle converted into attractive and very comfortable hotel with nice atmosphere. Moderate. South of Savonlinna.

Inari [6]

Tourist Hotel   Inari   tel: 29
Small, very simple inn in idyllic setting. Inexpensive. Far northeast of Savonlinna.

Jyvaskyla [3]

Jyväshovi   35 Kauppakatu   tel: 21 33 22
Large, comfortable, traditional hotel. Simple and functional throughout. Moderate. Straight north of Lahti.

Lahti [3]

Seurahuone   14 Aleksanterinkatu   tel: 25 161
Attractive hotel with comfortable rooms. Superb regional cooking. Moderate.

Porvoo [2] (Borga)

Haikko Manor Hotel   Porvoo   tel: 13 033
Small, traditional hotel on 25 acres of lovely grounds near the

sea. Very comfortable with period furnishings. Fine restaurant. Fishing. Expensive. Thirty miles east of Helsinki. Large health spa recently added.

WHERE TO EAT

Helsinki [1]

Kalastajatorppa   4 Kalastajatorpantje   tel: 48 17 87
Modern restaurant in lovely setting. Very attractive with excellent seafood. Expensive. Reserve.

Adlon   14 Fabianinkatu   tel: 66 46 11
Both international and Finnish specialties served in this fine restaurant with dancing. Expensive. Reserve.

Karl König   4 Mikonkatu   tel: 13 911
Sophisticated and very attractive international restaurant with some regional dishes. Expensive. Reserve.

FRANCE

FRANCE

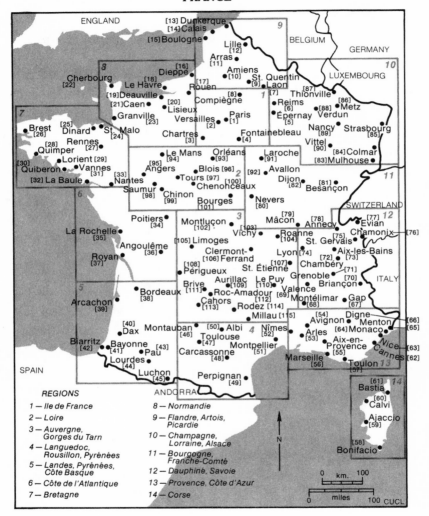

ENGLAND

[13] Dunkerque
[14] Calais
[15] Boulogne
Lille **[12]**
Arras **[11]**
Amiens **[10]**
St. Quentin **[9]**
Laon
[16] Dieppe
Cherbourg **[22]**
[18] Le Havre **[17]**
[19] Deauville Rouen **[8]**
[21] Caen **[20]** Compiègne **[1]** **[7]**
Granville Lisieux Versailles **[2]** **[1]**
[23] Chartres **[3]**
Fontainebleau **[4]**
BELGIUM
GERMANY
LUXEMBOURG
[87] Thionville
Reims **[6]**
Épernay **[5]** **[88]** Verdun Metz **[86]**
Nancy **[89]**
Vittel **[90]** **[84]** Colmar
[83] Mulhouse
Strasbourg **[85]**

[7]
Brest **[26]** **[25]** Dinard St. Malo **[24]**
Rennes **[27]**
[28] Quimper Lorient **[29]**
[30] Quiberon Vannes **[31]**
[32] La Baule Nantes **[33]**
Saumur **[98]** Chinon **[99]**
Le Mans **[94]** Orléans **[93]**
Angers **[95]** Blois **[96]**
Tours **[97]** **[100]** Chenonceaux
Bourges **[101]**
Laroche **[89]**
[92] Avallon
Dijon **[82]** **[81]** Besançon
Nevers **[80]**

[6]
La Rochelle **[35]**
Angoulême **[36]**
Royan **[37]**
Poitiers **[34]**
Montluçon **[102]**
Vichy **[103]**
Limoges **[105]**
Clermont-Ferrand **[106]**
Périgueux **[108]**
Mâcon **[79]**
Roanne **[104]**
Lyon **[74]**
St. Étienne **[107]**
Le Puy **[110]**
Annecy **[78]**
St. Gervais **[75]**
Aix-les-Bains **[73]**
Chambéry **[72]**
Grenoble **[71]**
SWITZERLAND **[12]**
Evian **[77]**
Chamonix **[76]**

[5]
Arcachon **[39]**
Bordeaux **[38]**
Brive **[111]**
Aurillac **[109]**
Roc-Amadour **[112]**
Cahors **[113]**
Rodez **[114]**
Montélimar **[69]** **[68]**
Briançon **[70]**
Gap **[67]**
ITALY

[40] Dax
Biarritz **[42]**
Bayonne **[41]**
Lourdes **[44]**
Pau **[43]**
Luchon **[45]**
Montauban **[46]**
Toulouse **[47]**
Carcassonne **[48]**
Perpignan **[49]**
Albi **[50]**
Nîmes **[52]**
Montpellier **[51]**
[4]
Millau **[115]**
Arles **[53]**
Avignon **[54]**
Aix-en-Provence **[55]**
Marseille **[56]**
Digne **[54]**
Menton **[65]**
Monaco **[64]** **[66]**
Nice **[63]**
Cannes **[62]**
Toulon **[57]** **[13]**

SPAIN
ANDORRA

[14]
Bastia **[61]**
Calvi **[60]**
Ajaccio **[59]**
Bonifacio **[58]**

REGIONS

1 — Ile de France
2 — Loire
3 — Auvergne, Gorges du Tarn
4 — Languedoc, Rousillon, Pyrénées
5 — Landes, Pyrénées, Côte Basque
6 — Côte de l'Atlantique
7 — Bretagne

8 — Normandie
9 — Flandre, Artois, Picardie
10 — Champagne, Lorraine, Alsace
11 — Bourgogne, Franche-Comté
12 — Dauphiné, Savoie
13 — Provence, Côte d'Azur
14 — Corse

N

0 km. 100

0 miles 100 CUCL

WHAT TO SEE

Half of the Americans travelling to France never get out of Paris. The city is one of the world's greatest, but it's only one aspect of a varied and challenging country. I spent three years researching this chapter, and I hope that you'll have a chance to explore some of the places listed here. The inns and regional restaurants in France are outstanding and among the best values in Europe.

No one is going to go to France without visiting *Paris* [1]. You'd have to spend a week there just to become familiar with the most famous sights. Free guides to the city are distributed in most hotels, as are small maps of the *métro* (subway). This is a convenient, fast, and inexpensive way to get around. If you find the *métro* complicated, ask your concierge for a quick explanation. Combined with walking, the subway is unbeatable. Following is a list of the most popular sights with subway stops listed for your convenience:

Arc de Triomphe (Etoile métro)
Notre Dame (Cité metro) (Go at 10:00 a.m. for Mass)
Sainte Chapelle (Cité metro)
Louvre (Palais Royal métro)
Musée de Jeu de Paume (Concorde métro)
Invalides and Tomb of Napoleon (Invalides métro)
Eiffel Tower (Trocadero métro)
Sacré Coeur (Abbesses métro)
Versailles (Pont de Sèvres métro, then bus 171)
Pantheon (St. Michel métro)

If your time is limited, you can still take some quick excursions from Paris. Try to see the thirteenth-century cathedral of *Chartres* [3]. Its stained glass windows are magnificent and at their radiant best at sunset. The palace at *Fontainebleau* appeals to many as does the Château de Vaux-le-Vicomte at *Maincy*. Try to visit the gardens and royal residence of *Versailles* [2] in the middle of the week to avoid the depressing weekend mob. With the exception of the cathedral in *Amiens* [10] there's little to draw you into the north. But to the east there's *Champillon* and *Epernay* [5] (famed for its cellars of champagne). They're snuggled into the hills of a wine region that shouldn't be missed during the wine harvest of September and October.

Following are brief suggestions for fabulous and very uncommon trips through France.

Normandy (Normandie): scenic shoreline and fabulous country inns. Don't miss the tapestry in *Bayeux* and *Mont St. Michel*. *Rouen* [17] is a bit flat but popular for its Great Clock. *Deauville* [19] is one of the most popular resorts and packed in the summer. Try to visit Normandy in spring or fall.

Brittany (Bretagne): an artist's favorite and a region noted for delicious shellfish. The port fortress of *St. Malo* [24] and the authentic town of *Vannes* [31] are pleasant, but nature is really what Brittany has to offer along with its picturesque harbor scenes at *Concarneau* and *Perros-Guirec.*

Farther south you'll travel through a region famous for its five hundred Romanesque churches. Try to take in *Poitiers* [34] and sample brandy in *Cognac*, which produces 170 million bottles a year of the "heart of wine."

The southwestern corner of France is one of the loveliest with its scented forests, sandy beaches, plush resorts, and great food complemented by outstanding wine. Famous resorts include *Arcachon* [39] (superb oysters), *Bayonne* [41] (visit the Bonnat Gallery), *Biarritz* [42], and *St. Jean de Luz* (tiny and delightful). You may want to sample wines in the cellars of Mouton-Rothschild in *Pauillac* or make an excursion either to the small Basque village of *Sare* or the overly commercial religious site of *Lourdes* [44].

To the east, you can take in the Toulouse-Lautrec art gallery in *Albi* [50], the medieval section of *Carcassonne* [48], and the Basilica of St. Sernin in *Toulouse* [47].

The fashionable Côte d'Azur is flower-filled and fresh, offering a superb climate, outstanding resorts, and fine dining. Its sophistication has brought in a culture-conscious set intent on studding the coastline with delightful museums filled to the brim with invaluable works of art: see the Grimaldi Museum in *Antibes*, the Maeght Foundation's art in *Saint Paul-de-Vence*, the Léger Museum of *Biot,* to name a few. In *Marseille* [56] take in the Old Port before an evening meal of *bouillabaisse* (for two), in *Aix-en-Provence* [55] try not to miss Cézanne's atelier just outside of town, and in *Avignon* [54] you'll find the Calvet Museum interesting. *Grasse* is world-famous for the fine perfumes it produces (best visited in spring), *Cannes* [62] is notorious for the spring film festival (bring business cards saying you're a film distributor), and the towns of *Arles* [53], *Nîmes* [51], and *Orange* boast well-preserved Roman amphitheatres. *St. Tropez* still swings with flesh and flash despite yearly rumors of its demise as a jet-set mecca. Just on the edge of France, you can gamble with shieks and shahs in the tiny principality of *Monaco* [64]. Off the coast is one of the roughest and most primitive islands in the Mediterranean. *Corsica* [58-61] remains natural in perfect contrast to the hothouse environment on the Continent. Be sure to take a car or rent one if you visit this island.

North of the Riviera while away sunny summer days at the resorts of *Annecy* [78] or *Aix-les-Bains* [73], ski from December to April in superb resorts such as *Chamonix* [76], *Courchevel, Mégève,* and *Val d'Isère,* and of course, eat in the great restaurants in and around *Lyon* [74].

Continue north into the heart of wine country. Weave along the wine road from *Mâcon* [79] to *Dijon* [82]. Stay in the picturesque village of *Avallon* [92] making an excursion to the shrine at *Vézelay.* See the Hôtel Dieu in *Beaune* with its fanciful coral-snake roofs and the abbey at *Cluny.*

West is the charming valley of the Loire, famed for its superb châteaux, delicious wines, and great country inns featuring delicious regional cooking. Highly recommended are the following châteaux: *Amboise, Angers* [95], *Azay-le-Rideau, Blois* [96], *Chambord, Chenonceau* [100] (a gem), *Villandry.* The abbey at *Solesmes* is also worth a detour for Benedictine singing.

The lazy Dordogne and turbulent Tarn flow through the south central region noted for superbly preserved villages such as *Sarlat, St. Cirque Lapopie,* and *Les-Eyzies-de Tayac,* nicknamed the *Capital of prehistory.* Fortified *Cahors* [113], the canyon stretching from *Le Rozier* to *Sainte Enimie,* the china in *Limoges* [105], and roquefort cheese made in *Roquefort-sur-Soulzon* are other regional attractions.

WHAT'S THE WEATHER REALLY LIKE?

The weather varies considerably by region in this large, diverse country. It's usually excellent in all regions from May to early October. Paris tends to be drizzly and cold in the off-season, with occasional snowfalls, while the Côte d'Azur is mild at this time. Mild near the Mediterranean means cool, occasionally rainy and windy, but often pleasant and sunny. Mild does not mean enjoyable swimming weather. The wine regions are best in the fall as is château country. The southwest is gorgeous in the spring. So is Brittany.

SOME SUGGESTIONS FOR A MORE ENJOYABLE TRIP

The French National Tourist Office has many free booklets on each of the regions described in this chapter. If you decide to travel to certain areas, be sure to write the office for brochures and pamphlets. It also has information on *relais de campagne*, château hotels, tiny inns, inexpensive restaurants in Paris, and sight-seeing, varying from popular tourist sights to lesser-known attractions, such as formal gardens, museums along the southern coast, and favorite fishing spots. Be sure to make reservations far ahead for travel in the peak season. France has long been one of the most popular tourist destinations in Europe. There's a room booking service in the airports and train stations of Paris. You can also dial ELY 1212 for room information. The roads are excellent throughout the country, making car trips enjoyable and highly recommended. In the peak season it can be extremely difficult to find a car to rent in Paris. A tip: take the subway to one of the suburbs and look for a local garage with the sign *voitures à louer*. Here you'll have a good chance of finding a car at a most reasonable rate. If you don't speak French, there will be a communications barrier. But you'll be able to hurdle it if you're there in person. It's always wise to make reservations for restaurants in France. You can ask the concierge in your hotel to call for you. This will save you the trouble of trying to communicate over the phone. In the more formal restaurants you should wear appropriate dress (at least a coat and tie for men and equivalent dress for women). Take advantage of public transportation whenever you can. The *bateau-mouches* in Paris are less expensive in the morning as are museums on Sundays (often crowded, however). Take trains to sights near Paris. This is easier than fighting traffic or getting lost. Many shops close in August, *the* month in France for annual vacations. In smaller towns even the bakery and butcher shop close during this month. Ski areas are packed on weekends, at Christmas, and at Easter. Try to avoid them at these times.

WHERE TO STAY

Agay [62]

Baumette   Agay   tel: 44 00 15
A fine hotel with lovely views and a great restaurant. Comfortable. Pool. Expensive. Closed mid-October to mid-March. Southwest of Cannes.

Agonac [108]

Château L'Evêque   Agonac   tel: 54 30 50
Ancient castle with twelve rooms. Nice park setting with special evening events in June. Noted for fine cuisine (truffles). Moderate to expensive. Closed January and February. North of Périgueux.

L'Aigle [20]

Hotel du Dauphin   Place de la Halle   tel: 517
Large, comfortable rooms in this hotel overlooking the main square. Excellent seafood and superb snails in the fine restaurant. Open all year. About thirty-five miles from Lisieux.

Ainhoa [42]

Argi-Eder   Aïnhoa   tel: 25 77 11
Only fifteen miles from St.-Jean-de-Luz you'll discover a picturesque town with a very fine inn. Great view. Peaceful Reasonable prices. South of Biarritz near Spain.

Aix-en-Provence [55]

Riviera Le Pigonnet   Route de Marseille   tel: 26 21 52
Just south of the city—a small luxury villa in a quiet and serene

setting. Authentic and warm. Comfortable rooms furnished in traditional manner. Fine cuisine. Lovely garden and pool. Expensive.

Mas d'Entremont   *Celony*   *tel: 26 12 04*
North of Aix. Tiny country inn with a lovely park. Charming atmosphere. Fine cuisine. Pool. Moderately expensive. Closed November to March.

Ajaccio [59]

Eden Roc   *Route des Sanguinaires*   *tel: 21 39 47*
Five miles outside of town is a fine hotel with a view of the bay. Comfortable. Very quiet. Access to a beach. Pool. Expensive. Closed in winter.

des Etrangers Hotel   *2 rue Rossi*   *tel: 21 01 26*
Small, modest hotel surrounded by lovely gardens. Comfortable rooms, most with bath. Nice view. Good regional cooking. In the inexpensive to moderate bracket.

Albi [50]

Hostellerie du Grand St. Antoine   *17 Rue St. Antoine*   *tel: 54 04 04*
A hotel with a light and airy garden atmosphere. Moderate.

Hôtel la Réserve   *Route de Cordes*   *tel: 56 79 79*
A fine country inn with a pleasant setting and comfortable rooms. Pool. Tennis. Expensive.

Alpe d'Huez [71]

Ours Blanc   *Alpe d'Huez*   *tel: 80 31 11*
The "White Bear" is just one of many fine hotels in this ski resort. It's very comfortable. Two-hour drive from Grenoble.

Amboise [97]

Auberge du Mail   *32 Quai Général de Gaulle*   *tel: 104*
On the river with comfortable rooms, but the French accent is definitely on the cooking—very fine, indeed. Reasonable prices as well. Just east of Tours.

Le Choiseul   36 Quai Viollettes   tel: 281
In a quiet park, this charming inn offers fine furnishings and
very comfortable rooms (the Duke and Duchess of Windsor slept
here). The cooking is nice, but the Auberge du Mail offers even
better meals.

Arles [53]

Le Jules César   Boulevard des Lices   tel: 96 49 76
A seventeenth-century convent converted into a fine hotel. Fine
restaurant. Open all year.

Ascain [42]

Etchola   Ascain   tel: 54 00 08
Delightful country hotel with lots of flavor and charm. Wonder-
ful cooking. Expensive, but it's worth it. Only four miles from
St.-Jean-de-Luz. South of Biarritz.

Asnieres-sur-Nouere [1]

*Hostellerie du Moulin et du Maine Brun   Asnières-sur-Nouère
tel: 97 91 11*
Stunning mill in tasteful elegance. Wonderful antiques. Idyllic
park setting on the river. Pool. Riding nearby. Extremely comfortable and luxurious. Excellent cuisine with delicious regional
specialties including snails and squab. Very expensive. Highly
recommended. About five miles northwest of Angoulême.
Closed in January.

Auvillers-les-Forges [7]

Hostellerie Lenoir   Auvillers-les-Forges   tel: 35 24 02
On the main square of town, this comfortable inn offers nice
rooms and a superb cuisine with specialties ranging from Ardennes ham to salmon or crayfish in season. Calm day trips and
walks can be taken in this peaceful area. About forty-five miles
from Laon near Rocroi.

Avallon [92]

Hostellerie de la Poste   13 Place Vauban   tel: 448
Elegant and enchanting décor full of atmosphere and charm.
Twenty-nine comfortable rooms. Peaceful garden. Delicious food
known throughout the region. Excellent wine cellar. Expensive.
Highly recommended. Closed December and January.

Moulin des Ruats   Vallée du Cousin   tel: 8 at Avallon
Small, authentic inn in quiet and peaceful surroundings. Excellent food. Moderate. Open mid-March through October.

Avignon [54]

Hôtel de l'Europe   12 Place Crillon   tel: 81 41 36
A good hotel dating back to the sixteenth century, with a very
fine restaurant. Lots of antiques. Expensive.

Le Prieuré   Villeneuve-les-Avignon   tel: 82 56 31/82 76 31
Palatial inn converted from a fourteenth century monastery with
a lovely garden—just across the Rhône from Avignon. Twenty-
five rooms. Superb cooking. Tennis and pool. Expensive. Closed
mid-November to mid-February.

Bagnoles-de-L'Orne [21]

Bois Joli   Avenue P. du Rozier   tel: 033/16 34 33
Delightful country restaurant with twenty rooms. Wood adds a
rustic touch. Expensive. Closed winters. South of Caen.

Baix [69]

La Cardinale et sa Résidence   Baix   tel: 58 88 07
Actually two spots; both hotel and separate restaurant are great.
Very comfortable. Fine food. Closed November to mid-February.
Just twenty miles from Valence.

Barbezieux [36]

La Boule d'Or   9 Avenue Gambetta   tel: 78 00 11
Twenty miles to the southwest of Angoulême you'll discover one
of the finest inns in the region. Delicious local recipes have won

its restaurant a superior reputation. The rooms are simple but comfortable. Moderate.

Barbizon [1]

Hôtellerie du Bas Bréau   222 Rue Grande   tel: 066-4005
Wonderful rustic coaching inn which was once a favorite of Robert Louis Stevenson. Extremely well known. Very calm in the middle of the week. Delightful gardens. Fine cuisine. Comfortable and spacious rooms. Only thirty-one miles south of Paris. Expensive. Closed mid-November until the end of December.

Barbotan les Thermes [43]

L'Hôtel Thermal   Barbotan les Thermes   tel: 4
Thirteenth-century building with twenty comfortable rooms. Lotus ponds, tennis, hunting. Expensive. Closed November to March. North of Pau.

Barsac [38]

Château de Rolland   Barsac   tel: 75
Monastery converted into small inn (only seven rooms). Fishing and hunting. Moderate to expensive. Closed March. About twenty-five miles from Bordeaux near Langon.

Beaulieu-sur-Mer [64]

La Réserve de Beaulieu   5 Boulevard Général LeClerc   tel: 01 00 01
Luxury accommodations and one of France's finest restaurants. Great location with gardens and lovely view. Private beach and pool. Very expensive. Southwest of Monaco.

Beaune [82]

Hôtel de la Poste   Boulevard Clemenceau   tel: 22 08 11
A fine hotel with traditional elegance and modern comforts. Small, but the excellent restaurant has a good choice in both dishes and wines. The crawfish are delicious. Expensive.

Hôtel Le Cep   27 rue Maufoux   tel: 22 35 48
Seventeenth-century building converted into luxury hotel. Comfortable visits to wine cellars arranged. Moderate to expensive. Closed December and January.

Les Baux [53]

La Cabro d'Or   Les Baux   tel: 97 33 21
Fifteen comfortable rooms in a calm setting, close to the Oustau de Baumanière (famous restaurant). Riding, tennis, and pool. Moderate to expensive. Closed January. Northeast of Arles.

Belfort [83]

Hostellerie du Château   9 Rue Général de Négrier   tel: 28 29 63
A fine inn with antiques and excellent cuisine. Expensive. Southwest of Mulhouse.

Beynac et Cazenac [112]

Hotel Bonnet   Beynac   tel: 29 50 01
From spring to fall this is a riverside favorite, where the local specialties vary from fresh fish to poultry. Only a few rooms. Reasonable. Northwest of Rocamadour via Souillac.

Les Bezards [93]

Auberge des Templiers et sa Chaumière   45 Les Bézards
tel: 01 80 01
Twenty-five elegant rooms in a peaceful setting. Rustic atmosphere and country flavor enhanced by the gardens. Heated pool. Tennis. Riding. Very fine cooking, including fresh game in the off-season. Highly recommended. Expensive. Twelve miles south of Montargis. Closed mid-January to mid-February. East of Orléans.

Biarritz [42]

Miramar   Rue Vagues   tel: 24 04 40
A deluxe hotel. Very large and comfortable. Geared to groups. Open May through September. Expensive.

Château de Brindos   Anglet   tel: 24 12 51
Only a short drive from Biarritz in a calm and very relaxed setting. Lovely lake for fishing. Charming.

Hôtel du Palais   Avenue de l'Impératrice   tel: 24 09 40
A mecca for those who can afford it. Large and luxurious in a
superb location. Gorgeous pool. Very expensive. Open from
mid-April until the beginning of October.

Billiers-Penlan [31]

Domaine de Rochevilaine   Billiers-Penlan   tel: 26 60 16
Seaside location ideal for fishermen. An exquisite fifteenth-cen-
tury estate with lovely gardens and view. Comfortable rooms.
Very expensive. Closed November. Only sixteen miles from
Vannes.

Biriatou [42]

Bakéa   Biriatou   tel: 26 76 36
Ten miles from St.-Jean-de-Luz you'll discover a superb inn
right next to Spain. View of the valley and lush countryside.
One of the finer kitchens in the region. Peaceful and pleasant.
Expensive, but great value. South of Biarritz.

Blois [96]

Hostellerie de la Loire   8 Rue de Lattre de Tassigny   tel: 78 26 60
Good hotel with reasonably comfortable rooms and reasonably
good food.

Bordeaux [38]

Aquitania   Parc des Expositions   tel: 29 73 80
A large hotel with a noncentral location—a plus in this city. Park
setting. Very fine cooking. Expensive.

Bouilland [82]

Hostellerie du Vieux Moulin   Bouilland   tel: 21 51 16
A few very comfortable rooms in this country inn with a view to

the valley. Noted for its superb dining. Near Beaune; southwest
of Dijon.

Bourg-en-Bresse [79]

Auberge Bressane   Bourg-en-Bresse   tel: 21 10 06
Southeast of Mâcon, the inn is one of the best in the region. The
cooking is marvelous. Superb poultry and frogs' legs. Highly recommended.

Bourget-du-Lac [73]

Ombremont   Bourget-du-Lac   tel: 36 00 23
High above town with a great view. Peaceful park setting. Small,
very comfortable inn with excellent cooking. Expensive. Open
spring through fall. Just six miles from Aix-les-Bains.

Bourth [3]

Auberge Chantecler   Bourth   tel: 5
The inn faces the main church in town. The rooms are quite
modest, but the restaurant is excellent. Near Verneuil-sur-Avre
about thirty-five miles from Chartres.

Bresson [71]

Chavant   Bresson   tel: 44 85 59
Lots of atmosphere in this small twelve-room inn. Fireplace for
chilly nights. Garden in warmer weather. Excellent regional
cooking. Only about four miles from Grenoble.

Brignogan-Plage [26]

Castel-Régis   Brignogan-Plage   tel: 83 06 06
Fine hotel-restaurant combination with an emphasis on the
cooking. Lovely view. Pool. Open mid-April until the end of
September. North of Brest.

Le Bugue [108]

Royal Vézère   Place H-de Ville   tel: 54 20 01
Peaceful riverside setting. View from the terrace. Calm and relaxing. Comfortable. About twenty-five miles from Périgueux.

Le Cabellou-Plage [28]

Hôtel de la Belle Etoile   Le Cabellou-Plage   tel: 97 05 73
Very comfortable hotel near the beach, with covered pool, tennis, sailing, fishing, and delicious seafood. Nice flower-filled terraces. Very expensive. Open summers only. About fifteen miles from Quimper.

Cagnes sur Mer [62]

Le Cagnard   Cagnes sur Mer   tel: 20 73 21
Ancient provincial inn, a part of the city's ramparts. Lots of atmosphere. Lovely restaurant. Unique and very expensive. North of Nice.

Calvi [60]

Le Grand Hotel de Calvi   3 Boulevard Président Wilson   tel: 5
A luxurious hotel overlooking the bay. Comfortable, with fine cooking. Expensive. Closed in the winter.

Campigny [20]

Le Petit Coq aux Champs   Campigny   tel: 41 04 30
Wonderful, tiny, and rustic inn set in small park. A few very comfortable rooms. Excellent regional restaurant. Pool. Expensive. About twenty-six miles from Lisieux near Pont-Audemer.

Cannes [62]

Hotel Canberra   12 rue d'Antibes   tel: 38 20 70
Nice central location for this comfortable and modern hotel. Twin beds. The garden side's best (ask for number 304). Parking. Use of Hotel Victoria pool. No restaurant, but good breakfasts. Moderate to expensive.

L'Embassy   8 rue de Bône   tel: 38 79 02
Good location. Quiet, comfortable, and compact rooms, some
with good view. Very pleasant and quite expensive.

Réserve Miramar Hotel   66 la Croisette   tel: 38 24 72
Small luxury hotel in good location, with easy access to the
beach. Tasteful atmosphere. Comfortable rooms, with bath and
balcony. Admittedly, a splurge.

Carcassonne [48]

Domaine d'Auriac   Carcassonne Route St. Hilaire   tel: 25 07 79
Two miles southeast of Carcassonne. A fine hotel in a park with
very quiet rooms. Traditional atmosphere. Open all year. Moderate.

Hôtel de la Cité   Place St. Nazaire   tel: 25 03 34
Medieval atmosphere in this authentic hotel with a great view.
Moderate. Open spring to fall.

Caudebec-en-Caux [18]

Hotel de la Marine   18 Quai Guilbaud   tel: 96 91 11
A modest hotel that is both comfortable and calm with a lovely
location on the Seine. Very relaxing. Tennis nearby. Open all
year. East of Le Havre.

Cazauban [43]

Château Bellevue   Cazauban   tel: 95
Modest château, with quite comfortable rooms in a lovely park
with pool. Moderate. Northeast of Pau.

La Caze [115]

Château de la Caze   La Caze   tel: 1 at La Malène
A wonderful fifteenth-century castle overlooking the Tarn. Delightful garden atmosphere. The chef can teach you how to catch
the local trout—you'll need special minnows. More sporting bait
doesn't seem to work. Great atmosphere. Ideal in the late
spring, when both bird-watching and trout-fishing are good. Expensive. Near La Malène twenty-six miles from Millau.

Chablis [92]

Hôtel de l'Etoile-Bergerand   Chablis   tel: 53 10 50
Delightful small country inn with fine food. Very reasonable. Closed mid-December to mid-February. North of Avallon.

Chalon-sur-Saone [79]

St. Georges et Terminus   32 Avenue Jean-Jaurès   tel: 48 27 05
Nice, comfortable hotel with excellent food at quite moderate prices. About thirty-five miles from Mâcon.

Chamonix [76]

Hôtel la Croix Blanche   7 Rue Vallot   tel: 53 00 11
Small inn with comfortable rooms. Moderate.

Hotel Mont Blanc   Place de l'Eglise   tel: 53 05 64
Small, traditional hotel with pleasant atmosphere. Very comfortable. Pool. Expensive.

Park Hotel   1 Avenue Majestic   tel: 53 07 58
Large, expensive hotel with a charming feeling. Well-furnished rooms. Pool. Fishing nearby. Lively.

Champagnac-de-Belair [108]

Moulin du Roc   Champagne de Belair   tel: 54 80 36
Lovely riverside mill with only five rooms. Moderate. Closed November to late December. About twenty-one miles from Périgueux near Brantôme.

Champillon [3]

Le Royal-Champagne   Champillon   tel: 51 25 06
Here's a gem only four miles from Epernay: a seventeenth-century coaching inn converted into a modern hotel with reasonably comfortable rooms and great cooking. Fabulous view. Delicious dishes. Open all year. Highly recommended.

Chartres [3]

Hotel du Grand Monarque   22 Place des Epars   tel: 21 00 72
Not far from the cathedral in the century-old part of town. Great atmosphere. Simple but excellent cooking. Cozy and comfortable rooms. A paradise in country living for those who speak French. Moderately expensive. Only sixty miles from Paris.

***Chateau-Arnoux [66]

La Bonne Etape   Château-Arnoux   tel: 9
Twenty-three rooms are available in this bright and cheerful inn, which has a fine dining room featuring excellent local recipes. Don't miss a meal here. About sixteen miles from Digne.

Chatillon-sur-Seine [82]

Hotel de la Côte d'Or   Rue Charles-Ronot   tel: 93 91 11
On the outskirts of town is an ivy-clad inn with only six charming rooms. Known for its excellent cuisine, with an emphasis on local specialties. Dining in the garden if the weather is fine. A gastronomic stop here is highly recommended. About fifty miles from Dijon.

Chaumontel [1]

Château de Chaumontel   95 Chaumontel   tel: 471-0030
An eighteenth-century hunting lodge in a lovely park only twenty miles north of Paris. Fresh and natural setting—quite romantic. A number of rooms with bath. Restful and pleasant. Fine cuisine. Expensive.

Chaumont-sur-Loire [96]

Hostellerie du Château   Chaumont-sur-Loire   tel: 79 88 04
A peaceful retreat on the glorious road through château country. Only fourteen rooms, of which four are apartments. Pleasant. Reasonably good restaurant. About eleven miles from Blois.

Chaumont-sur-Tharonne [93]

Hotel de la Croix-Blanche   41 Chaumont-sur-Tharonne   tel: 12
Charming country inn in a wonderful village on a small square.
The life here revolves around the kitchen, which produces taste-
ful local specialties. Lots of fun. About twenty-two miles from
Orléans.

Cheffes [95]

Château de Teildras   Cheffes   tel: 8
Attractive château in a pastoral setting, ten miles north of Angers. Calm and relaxed. Riding. Moderate. Closed late December
to mid-February.

Chenehutte-les-Tuffeaux [98]

Hostellerie du Prieuré   49 Chènehutte-les-Tuffeaux   tel: 51 15 31
Calm isolation in a park setting with a view of the river below. A
Renaissance manor with ultracomfortable rooms and excellent
cooking. A real charmer. Pool. Expensive. Closed January and
February. About thirty-five miles from Angers; near Saumur.

Cheronnac [105]

Château de Chéronne   Chéronnac   tel: 00 40 51
Fourteen peaceful rooms in this delightful inn surrounded by a
tranquil park. Fine food, the specialty *foie gras*. Closed in winter.
Moderate. About thirty-five miles from Limoges.

Chinon [99]

Château de Marçay   Marçay   tel: 93 03 47
Just a short drive to the south of Chinon is the château de Marçay, a fine country hotel with a wonderful atmosphere. The park
setting adds a peaceful touch to what is a comfortable and
moderately priced hotel. Pool and tennis. Closed mid-December
to mid-February.

Cluny [104]

Hôtel Moderne   near the station   tel: 18
Comfortable rooms and great food at very reasonable prices.
Closed from October through mid-November. About fifty miles
from Roanne.

Cognac [36]

Moulin de Cierzac   Cognac   tel: 83 61 32
A seven-mile drive to the south of Cognac leads you to a riverside inn with a refreshing garden atmosphere. The food is delicious and the few rooms reasonably comfortable. Moderate.
Closed in January and February. Northwest of Angoulême.

Col de la Faucille [77]

La Mainaz   Col de la Faucille   tel: 17 Mijoux
A fine hotel with a good restaurant in an Alpine setting. About
sixteen miles from Geneva; near Gex.

Collonges-la-Rouge [109]

Relais St.-Jacques de Compostelle   Collonges-la-Rouge   tel: 25 41 02
In a gem of a town—half-forgotten and wonderful. Ten comfortable, if modest, rooms. Inexpensive to moderate. Closed January
and February. About fifty-five miles from Aurillac.

Colroy la Roche

Hostellerie La Cheneaudière   Colroy la Roche   tel: 97 61 64
Small, hillside retreat with a few comfortable rooms. Charming
throughout. Good trout fishing. Moderate to expensive. Closed
December.

Compiegne [8]

Hostellerie du Royal-Lieu   Rue de Sanlis 9   tel: 440-0791
Compiègne is a delightful country town. Just outside it you'll
find the Royal-Lieu in a quiet park with superb cuisine. The
rooms are modest.

Condrieu [74]

Hôtel Beau Rivage   Condrieu   tel: 85 52 24
Overlooking a river, the hotel has a lovely view. The twenty-six rooms are comfortable. Fine restaurant. About six miles from Vienne; about twenty miles from Lyon.

Courchevel [71]

Hotel Carolina   Courchevel   tel: 08 00 30
Small, comfortable, and located near the lifts. Open winter only. Expensive. Northeast of Grenoble.

Coye-la-Foret [1]

Le Château du Regard   60 Coye-la-Forêt   tel: 457-6016
Small country inn in an idyllic and isolated forest area. Some rooms with bath. Eat in the nearby Hôtel des Etangs. Only twenty-six miles from Paris to the north.

Dampmart [1]

Auberge de Quincangrogne   77 Dampmart   tel: 430-0852
No one would normally stop in this town if it weren't for this wonderful inn. Right on the edge of Paris in a serene waterside setting. A lovely view and even better cuisine. Open all year and worth the twenty-mile drive.

Deauville [19]

Normandy   Rue Jean-Mermoz   tel: 88 09 21
Large, fine hotel. Expensive.

Dijon [82]

Chapeau Rouge   5 Rue Michelet   tel: 30 28 10
Traditional atmosphere with comfortable rooms. Excellent cuisine with lots of variety. Fine wine list. Moderate rates. Closed mid-December to mid-March.

Hôtel Central   10 Rue du Château   tel: 30 44 00
Pleasant atmosphere. Comfortable and attractive rooms. The cooking is quite good. Moderate.

Divonne-les-Bains [77]

Château de Divonne   Divonne-les-Bains   tel: 50 00 32
In an ancient mansion. Forty comfortable rooms. Park. Good cooking. Very expensive. Only ten miles from Geneva.

Dreux [3]

Auberge du Gué des Grues   Dreux   tel: 46 50 25
Idyllic riverside setting near the forest, in absolute calm. A comfortable inn with an exceptional restaurant serving game in the off-season. Open all year. About 20 miles from Chartres.

Echenevex [77]

Auberge des Chasseurs   Echenevex (Gex)   tel: 41 54 07
Known mainly as a very good restaurant, the inn also has some rooms. Garden. Expensive. About ten miles from Geneva.

L'Ecluse [49]

L'Auberge de l'Eglise   L'Ecluse   tel: 37 40 70
Follow Route 9 from Perpignan, and you'll come to this town with an inn full of atmosphere. Very French feeling in this mansion with pool, tennis, and spacious park. Open all year. Fifteen miles southwest of Perpignan.

Epernay [5]

Hotel des Berceaux   13 Rue des Berceaux   tel: 51 28 84
This reasonably comfortable traditional hotel has a fine restaurant. Moderate. Open all year.

Etables-sur-Mer [25]

La Colombière   Etables-sur-Mer   tel: 32 43 54
A hotel overlooking the sea with fine gardens and excellent

cuisine. Expensive. About fifteen miles from Paimpol to west of Dinard.

Eugénie-les-Bains [43]

Les Prés d'Eugénie   *Eugénie-les-Bains*   *tel: 58 19 01*
Wonderful, country inn with fifteen comfortable rooms, pools, and tennis courts. Known for its superb restaurant, *pot au feu*. Very expensive. Closed November to March. About thirty-three miles from Pau.

Evian-les-Bains [77]

Hotel Royal   *Plateau des Mateirons*   *tel: 400*
A fine summer hotel in a lovely park with a view of the lake. Luxurious but casual. Excellent cuisine. Pool. Tennis. Ultraexpensive. Open end of May until beginning of September.

Hotel de la Verniaz   *Route de l'Abondance*   *tel: 490*
A better choice than the Royal for many people. Sporty and nice with tennis, riding, and pool. Comfortable. Expensive but within reason.

Les Prés Fleuris sur Evian   *Evian-les-Bains*   *tel: 14 at St. Paul*
Twelve comfortable rooms. Lovely view to lake in distance. Expensive. Closed late October to late March.

Eyne [49]

Auberge d'Eyne   *Eyne*   *tel: 04 71 12*
Ancient farm with only eleven comfortable rooms. Geared to riding in summer and hunting in fall. Moderate. Closed mid-October to mid-December. Near Saillagouse, a long drive southwest into the mountains from Perpignan.

Les Eyzies-de-Tayac [108]

Hotel Cro-Magnon   *Eyzies*   *tel: 53 96 06*
A nice hotel with terraces and a pleasant garden. Regional cooking and reasonably comfortable rooms. Lots of atmosphere with fairly expensive rates. About thirty miles from Périgueux.

Eze-Bord-de-Mer [65]

Le Cap Estel   Eze-Bord-de-Mer   tel: 01 50 88/44
A luxury villa in an exotic garden. Great location and view. Pool.
Fine food. Closed in the winter. Only eleven miles from Menton.

Eze-Village [65]

Hostellerie du Château de la Chèvre d'Or   Eze-Village   tel: 01 51 16
A tiny clifftop hotel with gourmet cooking and a stunning view
of the sea below. Very comfortable. Pool. Expensive. Closed end
of October until the end of December. Only eleven miles from
Menton.

Fere-en-Tardenois [6]

Hostellerie du Château   Fere-en-Tardenois   tel: 82 21 13
An elegant sixteenth-century inn with some very seductive
suites. Wonderful woodsy flavor. Huge park surrounds the hotel
for absolute privacy and calm. The cooking is out-of-this-
world—one of the top restaurants in the region, even in the
country. Superb crayfish. Expensive. West of Reims and fourteen miles northeast of Château Thierry. Closed January and
February.

Flagy [4]

Auberge du Moulin   77 Flagy   tel: 431-6789
The tiny inn is simple and basic, converted from a thirteenth-
century mill. Delightful and comfortable. Fine regional cooking.
Fishing, hunting, and riding. Expensive. Closed midwinter.
Only fifty-three miles from Paris near Nemours, southeast of
Fontainebleau.

Fontainebleau [4]

Napoléon   9 Rue Grande   tel: 422-2039
Large, formal hotel with comfortable, attractive rooms. Fine dining. Expensive.

Fontvieille [53]

La Régalido   Rue Fréderic Mistral   tel: 97 70 17
Five miles northeast of Arles. A tiny inn converted from an ancient mill. Fun. Fine food. Nice garden. Expensive. Closed mid-March to mid-December.

La Foret Fouesnant [28]

Manoir du Stang   La Forêt Fouesnant   tel: 94 02 22
Small, charming manor at the end of a private drive. Calm park and garden setting. Gracious, antique atmosphere. Comfortable. Superb cooking. Expensive. Open mid-April through September. Ten miles from Quimper.

Gemenos [55]

Relais de la Magdaleine   Gémenos   tel: 04 40 05
Quiet and peaceful setting for a charming country inn with sixteen rooms. Pool. Very expensive. Closed January to mid-March. About twenty-five miles from Aix-en-Provence.

Gimont [47]

Château de Larroque   Gimont   tel: 06 02 20
Calm inn surrounded by park. Ten comfortable rooms. Moderate. Closed January. About thirty-five miles from Toulouse.

Gordes [54]

La Mayanelle   Gordes   tel: 72 00 28
Ancient dwelling converted into comfortable hotel with only ten rooms. Lots of atmosphere. Moderate. Closed January to mid-February. About twenty-five miles from Avignon.

La Rose d'Or   Gourdes   tel: 75 60 21
Ancient home with ten comfortable, simple rooms. Nice atmosphere. Moderate. Closed late November to early January.

Gué-des-Grues [1]

Auberge Gué-des-Grues   Gué-des-Grues   tel: 46 50 25
Comfortable country inn with a pleasant atmosphere. To the
west of Paris.

Hennebont [30]

Château de Locquénolé   Hennebont   tel: 65 20 69
Lovely estate with superb furnishings and comfortable rooms.
Park setting. Fine cuisine and wines. Worth a detour. Expensive.
Closed in January. About twenty-five miles from Quiberon.

Honfleur [20]

Ferme St. Siméon   Route A. Marais   tel: 347
An eighteenth-century Norman house with seven comfortable
and calm rooms. Lovely view and peaceful garden. Fine seafood
specialties. Of special appeal to those who love impressionist
painting—the surroundings evoke that atmosphere. Closed
January to mid-March. Twenty miles from Lisieux.

Igé [79]

Château d'Igé   Igé   tel: 02 33 99
Medieval building converted into small inn surrounded by vineyards. Calm and isolated feeling. Nice flower garden. Meals for
guests only. Moderate to expensive. Closed November to mid-
March. Northwest of Mâcon.

Ile de Re [35] (La Flotte)

Richelieu   Ile de Ré   tel: 09 60 70
Fine food and quite comfortable rooms in this nice inn. Expensive.

L'Isle-Adam [1]

Le Cabouillet   5 Quai de l'Oise   tel: 469-0090
Just outside of town you'll find a charming riverside inn with a
gorgeous dining room. The natural setting and the superior

cuisine make the thirty-minute drive from Paris seem very short. Twenty-seven miles to the northwest of the capital.

Issoudin [101]

Hotel de France et du Commerce   *3 Rue Pierre-Brossolette*
tel: 49 91 11
Reasonably comfortable rooms and fine cooking for very reasonable prices. Directly in town. Closed in February. About twenty-five miles from Bourges.

Lasalle [52]

Château de Montvaillant   Lasalle   tel: 85 22 71
A twelfth century building converted into pleasant inn near National Park. Pool. Moderate. Closed late September to late May. About forty-five miles from Nîmes.

Liffré [27]

Hôtellerie du Lion d'Or   8 route de Fougères   tel: 57 31 09
Seventeenth-century building converted into charming gourmet restaurant with a delightful garden atmosphere. Expensive. Closed Sunday evening and Monday. Only ten miles from Rennes.

Ligny [9]

Le Château de Ligny   Ligny   tel: 85 25 84
Seventeenth-century castle with authentic and elegant décor. Quite comfortable (only ten rooms). Moderate to expensive. Near Caudry, about twenty miles from St. Quentin.

Lissieu [74]

La Réserve   Lissieu   tel: 47 36 01
A luxurious hotel with a very well-known restaurant only ten minutes from Lyon. Highly recommended. Closed mid-December to mid-February.

Liverdun [89]

***Hotel des Vannes**   6 Rue Porte-Haute*   *tel: 25 75 02*
The inn· has thirteen comfortable rooms, but the French come
from many miles away to eat in the famous restaurant, one of
the best in France. The location overlooking the river is peaceful.
Only ten miles from Nancy. Closed February.

Locquénolé [26]

Hôtel Kerliviou   Locquénolé   tel: 67 21 04
Small, calm, and comfortable inn with lovely flower gardens and
good seafood specialties. Sailing and fishing. Moderate. Near
Morlaix, about thirty-seven miles from Brest.

Loué [94]

Hôtel Ricordeau   11-13 rue Libération   tel: 27 40 03
Very comfortable hotel with a fine restaurant. Fishing. Moderate
to expensive. Closed January. About seventeen miles from Le
Mans.

Luynes [97]

Domaine de Beauvois   Luynes   tel: 50 50 11
One of France's most attractive château-hotels, with quiet and
scenic surroundings. Absolutely ideal location. Sports include
tennis and fishing (in late spring). Pool. Open all year. Expensive. Highly recommended. Two and a half miles from Luynes.
Near Tours.

Maintenon [3]

Hotel de l'Aqueduc   Place de la Gare   tel: 23 00 05
Lovely château. Modest rooms. Closed January. Forty-eight
miles to the southwest of Paris. Only twelve miles from
Chartres.

Mallemort Pont-Royal [55]

Moulin de Vernègues   Mallemort Pont-Royal   tel: 57 42 33
Wonderful inn converted from a medieval mill. Comfortable. Ex-

quisite dining room. Very quiet. Riding, tennis, and pool. Open all year. Nearly twenty miles from Aix-en-Provence.

Marquay [108]

Délibie-Veyret   Marquay   tel: 10
Simple country inn with rustic rooms and no-nonsense cooking. Very reasonable. About thirty-seven miles from Périgueux.

Marseille [56]

Le Petit Nice   la Corniche   tel: 52 14 39
Lovely villa in great location with twenty comfortable, pleasant rooms. Expensive.

Mégève [78]

La Gérentìere   Mégève   tel: 21 25 01
Twelve rooms are available in this inn known for its fine cooking. Refined atmosphere. Great fresh trout. Expensive. Closed mid-November to mid-December. About forty miles from Annecy.

Menton [65]

Hotel Prince de Galles   4 Avenue Général de Gaulle   tel: 35 71 01
Comfortable and pleasant hotel only five miles from Monaco. Try to get corner rooms (number 8 and 44 recommended). Moderately expensive.

Mercuès [113]

Château de Mercuès   Mercuès   tel: 35 00 01
Five miles northwest of Cahors is a delightful hotel with lots of atmosphere and history. Breathtaking view. Large, with six apartments available. Park setting. Very calm. Superb food. Tennis. Luxurious. Expensive.

Méribel [78]

Le Grand Coeur   Méribel   tel: 08 60 03
Large, delightful mountain chalet with comfortable rooms and a good restaurant specializing in grills. Pool. Expensive. Closed spring and fall. About fifty-five miles from Annecy.

Meyrargues [55]

Château de Meyrargues   Meyrargues   tel: 24 50 32
A tiny castle overlooking the river in a natural setting. Only fourteen comfortable rooms. Excellent restaurant. Closed January and February. The inn is ten miles north of Aix-en-Provence.

Meyrueis [115]

Château d'Ayres   Meyrueis   tel: 10
A twelfth-century monastery with pool and park. Expensive. Open April to October. About twenty-five miles from Millau.

Millac par Mauzac [108]

La Métairie   Millac (Lalinde)   tel: 61 50 47
A rustic charmer in the moderate price range with pool, hunting, and only ten rooms. Ideal location in château country. Moderate. Closed late October to late March. Nearly forty miles from Périgueux.

Millau [115]

Moderne   11 Avenue Jean Jaurès   tel: 60 01 23
A modest inn with a very fine restaurant. Moderate.

Moëlan sur Mer [29]

Les Moulins du Deu   Moëlan sur Mer   tel: 96 60 73
Sixteenth-century mill in a riverside park with pool. Comfortable. Fishing. Moderate. Closed mid-January to mid-February. About fifteen miles from Lorient.

Molinons [4]

Hostellerie de Molinons   Molinons
tel: 9 at Villeneuve-l'Archevêque
A restaurant-hotel combination by the water in a park setting, with an emphasis on the fine food. Moderate. About fifteen miles from Sens, to southeast of Fontainebleau.

Molitg les Bains [49]

Château de Riell   Molitg les Bains   tel: 05 12 29
Romantic inn with lovely rooms, very comfortable and tasteful. Pool, tennis, hunting, and fishing. Very expensive. Closed November through March. Near Prades to southwest of Perpignan.

Monaco [64]

Hotel Balmoral   12 Avenue Costa   tel: 30 62 37
An old-fashioned cliff-hanger with comfortable rooms. Nice view. Friendly. Moderate to expensive.

Bristol   25 boulevard Alber ler   tel: 30 18 61
Near the harbor with bright but functional rooms. Restaurant on eleventh floor. Moderate to expensive.

Montbazon [97]

Le Château d'Artigny   37 Montbazon   tel: 06 01 77
Large and stately castle-hotel in a lovely park. Wonderful view. Pool and tennis. The most sumptuous hotel of its kind in the valley. Fine rooms and excellent cooking with an emphasis on local specialties. Closed November to mid-January. Expensive, and worth it. South of Tours.

Domaine de la Tortinière   37 Montbazon   tel: 06 00 19
A fanciful château set in an ultracalm park overlooking the valley. Ideal combination of comfort and fine cuisine. Fourteen rooms, of which six are apartments. The service and atmosphere couldn't be more pleasant. Pool. Highly recommended. Expensive. Closed December and January.

Montelimar [69]

Relais de l'Empereur .   Place Max-Dormoy   tel: 01 29 00
Peaceful stopover spot dating from the eighteenth century. Fishing and hunting nearby. Closed mid-November to mid-December. About thirty miles from Valence.

Montluçon [102]

Château St. Jean   Montluçon   tel: 05 04 65
Only eight rooms available in this ancient stone inn covered with ivy. Nice gardens and pool. Good restaurant. Moderate.

Montoire-sur-le-Loire [96]

Hotel du Cheval Rouge   1 Place Foch   tel: 82 91 11
A superb country inn on the edge of town. One of the finest in the region, with a quality restaurant that can't be beat for service and fine food. The snails are out of this world. About twenty-five miles from Blois.

Montpellier [51]

Demeure des Brousses   Montpellier   tel: 92 85 48
Eighteenth-century manor with a quiet location in a lovely park just outside of town. Open all year. Moderate.

Montpinchon [22]

Château de la Salle   Montpinchon   tel: 16
Ancient inn with only six modest rooms. Lovely park setting. Moderate. Closed November to mid-March. Nearly fifteen miles from St.-Lô. Southeast of Cherbourg.

Montreuil [11]

Château de Montreuil   4 Chaussée des Capucins   tel: 06 00 11
A British feeling in this inn with only seventeen moderately comfortable rooms. Lovely spot in a park with a fine restaurant. Closed mid-November to mid-December. About fifty miles from Arras.

Les Mousseaux [2]

Auberge de la Dauberie   Les Mousseaux   tel: 487-8057
In what was once a farm you'll now find an exquisite dining room with a warm fireplace. Spectacular gardens in late spring through early fall. Only a few modest rooms available. Closed mid-January to mid-February. To the southwest of Paris, about ten miles from Versailles.

Murbach [84]

St. Barnabé   Murbach   tel: 76 92 15
A fine hotel with good food. Nice location with garden and view to the valley. Outside of Guebwiller, about fifteen miles from Colmar.

La Muse [115]

Grand Hotel du Rozier et de la Muse   La Muse   tel: 60 60 01
A very fine inn on the River Tarn with a good view from the terrace to the surrounding woods. Peaceful atmosphere. Nice restaurant. Trout-fishing in May. Expensive. Open April to October. About fifteen miles from Millau.

Nançay [101]

Les Meaulnes   Nançay (Neuvy sur Barangeon)   tel: 51 61 15
Delightful, half-timbered retreat. Excellent restaurant with delicious game. Hunting arranged. Expensive. Closed February. About twenty miles from Bourges.

Nans les Pins [55]

Domaine de Chateauneuf   Nans les jpins   tel: 78 90 06
Eighteenth-century mansion converted into comfortable hotel with pool, tennis, and hunting. Moderate to expensive. Closed late November to mid-April. About twenty-seven miles from Aix-en-Provence.

Nemours [4]

Hotel de l'Ecu de France   3 Rue de Paris   tel: 428-1154
A comfortable fourteenth-century hotel with a restful feeling and
fine food. Moderate. Southwest of Fontainebleau.

Nice [63]

Hôtel la Pérouse   11 Quai Rauba Capeu   tel: 85 61 04
A quiet and comfortable hotel above the city (elevator to it). Terraced rooms, some with kitchenette. Garden, pool, great view.
Try for number 203. Unique. Moderate to expensive. No restaurant.

Westminster   27 Promenade des Anglais   tel: 88 29 44
Large traditional hotel near the sea. Comfortable. Moderately
expensive.

Hôtel Georges   3 Rue H. Cordier   tel: 86 23 41
Tiny authentic hotel with friendly service. Comfortable. Moderate.

Napoléon   6 Rue Grimaldi   tel: 87 70 07
Small, relatively calm and comfortable hotel. A good in-between
choice. Moderate.

Brice et Bedford   44 Rue du Maréchal Joffre   tel: 88 14 44
Friendly and pleasant budget hotel. Comfortable. Moderate.

Nieuil [105] (St. Martin-le-Faux)

La Chapelle St. Martin   Nieuil   tel: 75 80 17
Lovely white mansion with only nine comfortable rooms in a
park two miles northwest of Limoges. Moderate. Closed February.

Nieuil [36]

Château de Nieuil   Nieuil   tel: 71 34 01
Once the hunting lodge of François Ier, now a very comfortable
castle-hotel with twelve tasteful rooms. Pool, tennis. Moderate to
expensive. Closed mid-November to mid-December. About
twenty-five miles from Angoulême.

Noailles [8]

Hostellerie du Manoir de Framicourt   Noailles   tel: 446-3016
An isolated farm converted into an inn with modest rooms and a delightful dining room. Restful surroundings with a large garden. Rural flavor. Open all year. Nearly fifteen miles from Clermont to west of Compiègne.

Le Nouvion-en-Thierache [9]

Hotel Petion   Rue T. Blot   tel: 011
A modest inn with a central location. Comfortable rooms that don't match the excellence of the local specialties served in a warm small-town atmosphere. Closed mid-January to mid-February. Nearly thirteen miles from Guise to northeast of St. Quentin.

Noves [54]

Auberge de Noves   Noves   tel: 94 12 21
An extremely elegant inn with great décor. Superb cooking including delicious duck with exceptional local wines. Quite comfortable rooms with atmosphere. Pool. Ultraexpensive. Worth a long detour. Closed January. It's eight miles southeast of Avignon.

Onzain [96]

Domaine des Hauts de Loire   Onzain   tel: 79 72 57
An ivy-clad mansion with only sixteen tasteful rooms. All set in a large, calm park. Expensive. Closed mid-November to February. About ten miles from Blois.

Pacy-sur-Eure [17]

L'Etape   1 Rue Isambard   tel: 36 03 33
Very fine, if modest, country inn with a wonderful setting near the river. Good cooking. Garden and terrace in warmer weather. Open all year. About forty miles from Rouen, near Evreux.

Paimpol [25]

Le Relais Brenner   *Paimpol*   *tel: 20 11 05*
Small inn with comfortable rooms and refreshing gardens. Nice seafood specialties. Fishing. Expensive. Closed mid-November to mid-December. West of Dinard on the coast.

Paris [1]

Hôtel de l'Abbaye   *10 rue Cassette, 6è*   *tel: 548-3264*
A seventeenth-century abbey converted into charming, small hotel with its own interior courtyard. Comfortable. Moderate.

Hotel Ambassador   *16 Boulevard Haussman, 9è*   *tel: 770-6374*
Huge hotel near the Opèra. Traditional atmosphere, comfortable rooms, and reasonable service at expensive, but not exorbitant rates. Ideal for someone who wants to be in the center of the city without paying the high rates of the superdeluxe hotels.

Atala   *10 rue Châteaubriand*   *tel: 225-0162*
Fifty comfortable rooms in a modest but pleasant hotel nicely located near the Champs-Elysées. Most rooms with bath—try for number 62. Flowery gardens. You can eat in the courtyard in nice weather. Moderate.

Brighton   *218 rue de Rivoli, ler*   *tel: 073-2780/260-3003*
Quite large, but nice, hotel in good location on the right bank. Modest, yet nicely furnished, rooms with view—try for number 419. Tasteful. Moderate to expensive.

La Bourdonnais   *111 Avenue de la Bourdonnais, 7è*   *tel: 705-4542*
Sixty-five comfortable rooms in calm residential hotel not far from the Eiffel Tower. Attractive restaurant. Moderate.

Le Colbert   *7 rue de l'Hôtel, 5è*   *tel: 633-8550*
A modern hotel in seventeenth-century style tucked away in a medieval alleyway in the heart of the Latin Quarter. Modest, compact rooms (some with view of Notre Dame). Try for number 21. No restaurant. Expensive.

Hôtel de Castille   *37 rue Cambon, ler*   *tel: 073-4820*
Attractive townhouse (once owned by the Count of Castille) converted into pleasant hotel with many rooms overlooking a

lovely courtyard. Varied rooms, many with shower. Good location, near the Opera. Moderate.

Hôtel (l')   13 *Rue des Beaux-Arts, 6è*   tel: 325-2722
An offbeat gem. A horribly exclusive hotel that has tried unsuccessfully to stay out of travel guides. Exquisite rooms. Casual atmosphere. Very "in." Very expensive.

Keppler   12 *rue Keppler, 16è*   tel: 720-6505
Fifty large, modest rooms, most with bath. Good location, near the Arc de Triomphe. Not fancy. Moderate.

Lancaster   7 *Rue de Berri, 8è*   tel: 359-9043
Relatively small hotel with an intimate, yet posh, atmosphere. More relaxed than the superstars. Beautifully furnished and very comfortable. Expensive.

Montaigne   6 *Avenue Montaigne, 8è*   tel: 359-3957
Thirty-three comfortable rooms in this cute little hotel frequented by models. No restaurant. Moderate.

Quai Voltaire   19 *Quai Voltaire, 7e*   tel: 548-4291
Small and delightful hotel with modest but comfortable rooms. Appeals to select group. Moderately expensive.

Régents-Garden   6 *rue Pierre-Demours, 17è*   tel: 754-3940
Calm and charming with forty-three spacious rooms—number 1 is a gem. A lovely garden area. No restaurant. Expensive.

La Résidence du Bois   16 *rue Chalgrin, 16e*   tel: 727-4634
Small luxury hotel with a fine French flavor. Near the Place de l'Etoile. Quiet and Intimate. Fine but very expensive. No restaurant (though small meals served on demand).

Royal   33 *Avenue Friedland, 8è*   tel: 359-0814
Fifty-seven bright, tasteful rooms. Flowery and nice. Attractive restaurant. Expensive.

St. Simon   14 *Rue St. Simon, 7e*   tel: 548-3566
Small and charming with comfortable rooms. Intimate and authentic French flavor. No restaurant. Moderate.

San Régis   12 *Rue Jean-Goujon, 8è*   tel: 359-4190
Small traditional hotel with intimate and authentic atmosphere. Very comfortable. Moderate.

St. Louis   75 Rue St. Louis-en-l'Ile, 4è   tel: 033-1013
Small attractive hotel with French flavor. Compact rooms. No elevator. Ideal for young people. Moderate.

Scandinavie   27 Rue Tournon, 6è   tel: 633-4520
Small and authentic with a French flavor to its Scandinavian name. Very comfortable. A fine hotel in the moderate range. Note: no bar or restaurant. No elevator.

Terass'Hôtel   12 rue Joseph de Maistre, 18è   tel: 606-7285
Large, tasteful hotel in Montmartre. Spacious rooms and a few fancy suites. Delightful terrace with superb view. Excellent breakfasts and good dining in a country ambience. Very expensive.

Perouges [74]

Ostellerie du Vieux Pérouges   Place du Tilleul   tel: 61 00 88
An authentic inn with twenty comfortable rooms. However, it's the cooking that is outstanding. A unique restaurant with lots of atmosphere. Calm and nice. Expensive. About twenty-three miles from Lyon.

Pessac L'Alouette [38]

La Réserve   Avenue Bourgailh   tel: 45 13 28
Although five miles from Bordeaux, this is probably the best place to stay in the immediate region. The modern inn is set in vine-growing territory. Wonderful, calm setting. Extremely comfortable. The food is among the region's best. Expensive.

Le Pin-au-Haras [20]

Hostellerie du Tourne-Bride   Le Pin-au-Haras   tel: 2
Tiny Norman inn with superb antiques. Only a few rooms in the ancient building, located in wonderful wooded surroundings. The dining room, noted for its superb cooking, overlooks the garden. Riding. Closed mid-winter (usually in January and February). About twenty-five miles from Alençon to south of Lisieux.

Pléven-Plancoët [25]

Manoir du Vaumadeuc   Pléven-Plancoët   tel: 27 14 67
A fine manor set in a delightful park with fishing and hunting for residents. Golf and tennis nearby. Only nine comfortable rooms. Good cooking. Closed December to mid-April. About twenty miles from Dinard.

Poitiers [34]

Paris   123 Boulevard Grand-Cerf   tel: 41 38 01
A simple restaurant with some rooms available after a delicious and reasonably priced meal. Noted for its tasty frog's legs.

Poligny [81]

Hostellerie des Monts-de-Vaux   Poligny   tel: 82 123
Tiny, delightful inn with comfortable rooms. Expensive. Closed mid-November to mid-December. Southwest of Besançon (about fifty miles).

Pont-Audemar [20]

Auberge du Vieux Puits   6 Rue Nôtre-Dame-du Pré   tel: 41 01 48
An old Norman inn with a rustic atmosphere and superb restaurant. Garden. A few rooms—very modest. About twenty-two miles from Lisieux.

Pont L'Eveque [21]

Hostellerie Aigle d'Or   68 Rue Vancelles   tel: 141
You'll have to make reservations for this superb restaurant in a sixteenth-century inn. Expensive. About twenty-six miles from Caen.

Pornichet [32]

Fleur de Thé   Avenue Sellier   tel: 60 42 93
A fine inn with good cooking and comfortable rooms. Closed winters. Moderate. Near La Baule.

Port-en-Bessin [21]

Hostellerie du Bosq   Port-en-Bessin   tel: 92 72 81
A large, relaxing eighteenth-century castle in the country with delicious seafood on its menu. Just five miles from Bayeux, northwest of Caen.

Porticcio [59] (Golfe d'Ajaccio)

Le Maquis   Porticcio   tel: 25 00 12
Small, comfortable inn with modest rooms. Nice atmosphere. Moderate.

Pougues-les-Eaux [80]

Château de Mimont   Pougues-les-Eaux   tel: 68 22 52
Luxurious accommodations in this estate with only ten rooms. Superb furnishings and an idyllic setting. Pool. Riding, fishing, and hunting for guests, who will also enjoy the cooking. Highly recommended. Expensive. Open all year. Only six miles from Nevers.

Ramatuelle [62]

Hostellerie du Baou   Ramatuelle   tel: 97 70 48
Fifteen comfortable rooms in a hillside inn with lovely view to the sea. Moderate to expensive. Closed mid-October to mid-March. South of St. Tropez. Southwest of Cannes.

La Rémigeasse [37]

Le Grand Large   La Rémigeasse (Ile d'Oléron)   tel: 47 08 18
Small, expensive hideaway on an attractive island. Close to the beach with pool, sailing, and tennis. Fine meals (dinners only). Closed October to March. About twenty-five miles from Royan.

Riec-sur-Bélon [28]

Chez Mélanie   Riec-sur-Bélon   tel: 97 91 05
A traditional restaurant serving fine dishes in an aristocratic atmosphere including original paintings. Nice. Some rooms avail-

able. Closed December to February. Moderate to expensive. Only ten miles from Concarneau, southeast of Quimper.

Rocamadour [112]

Sainte Marie   Rocamadour   tel: 7
A good hotel and restaurant combination with a very fine view. Moderate.

Rochegude [54]

Château de Rochegude   Rochegude   tel: 04 81 88
A luxurious château surrounded by vineyards. Exceptional cooking. Comfortable rooms. Pool. Highly recommended. Closed January to mid-February. Expensive. About ten miles from Orange, to northeast of Avignon.

Rocroi [7]

Hostellerie Lenoir   Rocroi   tel: 35 24 02
Only eight miles from Rocroi you'll discover this inn with modest rooms and a fine cuisine. Truffles are its specialty. Nice, calm surroundings. Wonderful area for walks. Moderate. About fifty miles from Laon.

Roquebrune [65]

Vistaero   Roquebrune   tel: 35 01 50
Fine inn with thirty comfortable rooms. Lovely view. Pool. Not far from the sea. Expensive. Closed mid-November to late December. Only a few miles from Menton.

Les Rosiers [98]

Auberge Jeanne de Laval   49 Les Rosiers   tel: 51 91 11
Charming, comfortable inn with garden in the back. Noted for its outstanding regional cooking. Moderate to expensive.

Rouen [17]

Hôtel de la Cathédrale   *12 Rue St.-Romain*   *tel: 71 57 95*
A tiny, charming inn near the cathedral with modest but comfortable rooms. No restaurant. Moderate.

Rouffach [84]

Château d'Isenbourg   *Rouffach*   *tel: 49 63 53*
Small château in lovely park with great view. Pleasant and comfortable. Pool. Moderate to expensive. Closed January and February. Ten miles from Colmar.

St. Germain en Laye [1]

La Forestière   *1 Avenue du Président Kennedy*   *tel: 963-0893*
Calm, flower-filled oasis with twenty-three nicely furnished and very comfortable rooms. Excellent restaurant. Luxury atmosphere. Riding. Very expensive. On the outskirts of Paris.

St. Germain-Lembron [106]

La Beaugravière   *St. Germain-Lembron*   *tel: 38/96 91 11*
Thirteen comfortable rooms in a rustic, ivy-clad inn twenty miles south of Clermont-Ferrand. Very calm and peaceful in park surroundings. Moderately expensive.

St. Gervais-les-Bains [76]

Alpenrose   *St. Gervais-les-Bains*   *tel: 78 29 55*
Typical mountain inn with sports, including tennis and trout fishing, nearby. Closed from mid-October until mid-December. Fifteen miles from Chamonix, at the foot of Mt. Blanc.

St. Girons [47]

Eychenne   *8 Avenue P. Laffont*   *tel: 574*
Both the restaurant and the hotel have a fine atmosphere. Reasonable. About sixty miles from Toulouse.

St. Hilaire-du-Rozier [71]

Bouvarel   St. Hilaire-du-Rozier   tel: 2
A fine little inn with a superb restaurant. Garden. Expensive.
Worth a special trip. Near Romans-sur-Isère southwest (fifty
miles) of Grenoble.

St. Jean-Cap Ferrat [63]

La Voile d'Or   Avenue Mermoz   tel: 06 58 25
Luxurious hotel with great service and view. Comfortable and
unique rooms. Sophisticated dining. Pool. Expensive, but worth
it. Closed November through December. Only six miles from
Nice.

St.-Jean-de-Luz [42]

Hôtel de Chantaco   St.-Jean-de-Luz   tel: 26 14 76
One mile from the center of town. Superb hotel with quiet garden atmosphere. Tennis and golf. Expensive. Open April to October.

St. Lattier [71]

Le Lièvre Amoureux   St. Lattier   tel: 36 91 11 then 4 at St. Lattier
Tiny, delightful inn with a limited number of comfortable rooms.
Garden dining. Fishing and hunting. Moderate to expensive.
About forty miles from Grenoble.

St.-Nabord [84]

Claire-Fontaine   St.-Nabord   tel: 62 03 96
Fifteen delightful rooms, but the inn is noted for its fine dining
in a room with a wonderful flavor. Delicious trout. Expensive.
Near Remiremont, about fifty miles from Colmar.

St.-Nicolas-de-la-Balerme [113]

Château Saint-Philip   St.-Nicolas-de-la-Balerme   tel: 66 91 11
Only a short drive from Agen. On the River Garonne with ten-

nis, riding, and fishing. Great location. Pleasant atmosphere. Good cooking. Expensive. About fifty miles from Cahors.

St. Paul-de-Vence [63]

Auberge le Mas des Serres   *St. Paul de Vence*   *tel: 32 81 10*
Tiny luxury inn with superbly furnished rooms and excellent food. Delightful country atmosphere. Very expensive. Closed late November to late January. About twelve miles from Nice.

Hotel la Colombe d'Or   *Place des Ormeaux*   *tel: 32 80 02*
In wonderful surroundings is this small luxury inn with a worldwide reputation for comfort and excellent cooking. A charmer, well-heated in cooler periods. Outstanding private art collection. Pool. Very expensive. Closed mid-November to mid-December.

Le Mas d'Artigny   *St. Paul de Vence*   *tel: 32 84 54*
Luxury hotel with superb rooms and fine villas on a sixteen-acre estate overlooking the town. Very fine regional dishes. Tennis, pool (and individual pools for each villa). Very expensive.

St. Pons [48]

Château de Ponderach   *route de Narbonne*   *tel: 97 02 57*
A few rooms in an isolated estate, with fishing and hunting. Tennis and swimming as well. Moderate. Closed mid-October to mid-April. About forty-five miles from Carcassonne.

St.-Remy-de-Provence [54]

Hostellerie du Vallon de Valrugues   *Chemin Canto Cigalo*   *tel: 440*
Small pleasant hotel in park setting. Comfortable. Pool. Expensive. About fifteen miles from Avignon.

St. Romain de Lerps [69]

Château du Besset   *St. Romain de Lerps*   *tel: 60 32 86*
A luxurious château with unique, comfortable rooms. Lots of atmosphere. Pool, tennis. Ultraexpensive. Closed October to mid-March. Eleven miles northwest of Valence.

St. Tropez [62]

Hotel Résidence de la Pinède   St. Tropez   tel: 97 04 21
Small, very fine inn with all the trimmings for a comfortable seaside vacation. Very expensive. Open mid-April to mid-October.

Byblos   Avenue P. Signac   tel: 97 00 04
Lovely inn in provincial style with very comfortable rooms. Nice
location. Pool. Varying rates from expensive to ultraexpensive.
Closed November and December.

Samois-sur-Seine [4]

Hostellerie du Country-Club   quai République   tel: 424-6034
A relaxing, isolated inn with a calm, riverside setting. Wonderful
feeling of being in the country away from it all. Closed mid-
winter. Forty miles to the south of Paris, near Fontainebleau.

Sare [42]

Arraya   Sare   tel: 54 20 46
Nine miles from St.-Jean-de-Luz is a fascinating small hotel
loaded with antiques and serving some of the finest regional
cooking in the area. Rustic, authentic, and fresh, with a delightful garden. Reasonable. South of Biarritz.

Savignac-les-Eglises [108]

Parc Hotel   Savignac-les-Eglises   tel: 05 00 12
In a lovely park, this hotel offers comfortable rooms and fine
cooking. Charming. Serene. Expensive. Closed February. Highly
recommended. About thirteen miles from Périqueux.

Sciez-Bonnatrait [78]

Château de Coudrée   Sciez-Bonnatrait   tel: 72 62 33
A medieval castle on a lake in a pleasant park with tennis and
fishing. Charming, quiet, and lovely. The food is good. Open
end of April until mid-October. Just fifteen miles from Geneva.

Semur-en-Auxois [92]

Hotel du Lac   Semur-en-Auxois   tel: ask for Cabine Pont et Massène
A modest inn close to a lake in the country. Cozy. Fine, if simple, cooking. About twenty-five miles from Avallon.

Sept-Saulx [6]

Hôtel du Cheval-Blanc   Sept-Saul   tel: 49 46 03
Only fourteen miles from Reims. A seventeenth-century inn with superb cooking, specializing in chicken and crayfish. Nice location by a quiet stream. Garden. Very fine.

Talloires [78]

L'Abbaye   Talloires   tel: 44 70 81
Fine, very comfortable inn with terraces opening up on a lake. Sailing and fishing. Pleasant open-air restaurant. Expensive. About ten miles from Annecy.

***Auberge du Père Bise   Talloires   tel: 44 72 01
Nine miles from Annecy is one of the finest restaurants in France. Attractive rooms as well. Highly recommended. Worth any detour. Expensive. Closed November to mid-February.

Thury-Harcourt [21]

Relais de la Poste   Thury-Harcourt   tel: 80 72 12
A comfortable and very modest inn with excellent cuisine. The cooking is done by the owner, who specialises in seafood dishes. Calm and excellent. About fifteen miles from Caen.

Tonnerre [82]

Hostellerie de l'Abbaye St. Michel   Rue St. Michel   tel: 55 91 11
A tenth-century abbey just outside town. Rustic feeling. Flowers in a refreshing park. Good view. A quiet retreat, as the monks well knew. About ninety miles from Dijon; near Auxevre.

Tours [97]

Hotel Métropole   14 Place Jean Jaurès   tel: 05 40 51
Comfortable hotel with a remarkably good restaurant. A nice place to stay. Moderate.

Tourtour [54]

La Bastide   Tourtour   tel: 70 57 30
Small, attractive, and unique inn with comfortable rooms and fine view. Pool. Luxurious atmosphere. Expensive. Closed mid-October to late March. Near Salernes; about fifty miles from Aix-en-Provence.

Tremolat [108]

Vieux Logis   Trémolat   tel: 61 80 06
Trémolat is thirty-five miles south of Périgueux, approximately seven miles from Lalinde. The small inn is both fresh and lovely, with a delightful garden atmosphere. Fine food. Moderate prices. Closed January and February.

Trigance [62]

Château de Trigance   Trigance   tel: 76 91 18
Ancient fort with a great view. Only a few moderately priced rooms. Closed November to Easter. About fifty-five miles from Cannes.

Ustaritz [41]

Etchebertzea   Ustaritz   tel: 31 00 56
A family feeling in this plain, comfortable inn. Hearty home cooking. Very reasonable. Just seven miles from Bayonne.

Val d'Isère [71]

Hotel Solaise   Val d'Isère   tel: 06 08 10
Excellent mountain resort hotel. Small, with fine furnishings and comfortable rooms. Expensive. Also excellent is the tiny La Bergerie (06 03 86). Northeast of Grenoble; near Italy.

Valencay [96]

Château d'Espagne   8 Rue Château   tel: 00 00 02
Small inn with great atmosphere in any idyllic setting. Delicious regional dishes. Moderate to expensive. Closed mid-December to mid-February. About thirty-five miles from Blois.

Vallée du Cousin [92]

Moulin des Ruats   Vallée du Cousin (Avallon)   tel: 8 at Avallon
Although this waterside inn with a garden has a few rooms, you'll probably want to stop here for the restaurant. It offers good regional cooking. Just outside of Avallon.

Val Suzon [82]

Hostellerie Val Suzon   Val Suzon   tel: 35 40 25
A fine hotel and restaurant with a garden. About ten miles north of Dijon. Closed January to mid-February.

Varces [71]

***L'Escale   Place de la République   tel: 97 80 19
Wooden chalet with only seven, comfortable rooms. Superb regional cooking. Refreshing atmosphere. Moderate. Closed February. Twenty-five miles southwest of Grenoble.

Varetz [105]

Château de Castel Novel   Varetz   tel: 25 75 01
An ancient building in a park with reasonably comfortable rooms, a nice atmosphere, and superb food. Pool. Open May to November. Nearly eighty-five miles from Limoges near Brive-la-Gaillarde.

Vence [63]

Château du Domaine St. Martin   Vence   tel: 32 01 35
Very well known luxury hotel with a view to the coast. A lovely
mansion with many antiques. Aristocratic and quiet. Ask for one
of the villas. Park, pool, and tennis. Ultraexpensive. Closed December to February. Northwest of Nice.

Verdun-sur-Meuse [88]

Hotel Bellevue   Rond Point de Lattre de Tassigny   tel: 86 04 24
Near the gardens on the outskirts of town. A lovely, if large,
hotel that has some excellent seafood dishes.

Verneuil sur Avre [17]

Hostellerie du Clos   98 rue de la Ferté-Vidame   tel: 32 21 81
Agreeable and modest inn with thirteen comfortable rooms and
a very fine restaurant. Moderate to expensive. Closed mid-December to mid-January. South of Rouen.

Versailles [2]

Trianon Palace   1 Boule de la Reine   tel: 950-3412
Large traditional hotel in a lovely park. Comfortable. Fine classic
cuisine. Expensive.

Vezelay [92]

Poste et Lion d'Or   Vézelay   tel: 56
Try not to miss this hillside inn with a view to the valley. It's got
lots of character. The rooms are old-fashioned, but nice. The excellent restaurant is great with moderate prices. Reserve.

Vichy [103]

Pavillon Sévigné   52 Boulevard Kennedy   tel: 98 55 42
Once the estate belonging to Mme. de Sévigné. Lovely park surrounds it. Nice feeling. Expensive. Open from May until the end
of September.

Vieille-Toulouse [47]

La Flanerie   route de Lacroix-Falgarde   tel: 52 42 80
Some lovely, comfortable rooms in a calm location. Light meals
only. Inexpensive to moderate. South of Toulouse.

Villefranche [63]

Château de Madrid   Villefranche   tel: 01 00 88
Comfortable hotel with a superb restaurant. Lovely garden and
view. Very expensive. Three miles east of Nice.

Welcome Hotel   Quai Courbet   tel: 80 70 26
Very attractive hotel on the quai with forty comfortable rooms.
Try for number 17. Excellent breakfasts. Expensive. Closed
November and December.

Villefranque [41]

Château de Larraldia   Villefranque   tel: 5
One of France's very finest castle-hotels, set in a beautiful park.
Lots of antiques. Luxurious. Excellent cuisine. Pool. Very expen-
sive. Worth a detour. Near Bayonne.

Villeneuve de Rivière [44]

Hostellerie des Cèdres   Villeneuve de Rivière   tel: 89 12 04
Charming hotel amid ancient cedars. Comfortable and relaxed.
Moderate. Closed early January to early March. Near St.
Gaudans; about fifty miles from Lourdes.

Vironvay [20]

Les Saisons   Vironvay   tel: 40 02 56
A rural retreat with only nine rooms. Wonderful atmosphere.
Tennis and hunting. Moderate. Closed mid-January to mid-Feb-
ruary. Near Louvier; about fifty miles from Lisieux.

Vouillé [34]

Château de Périgny   Vouillé   tel: 51 80 43
Romantic castle of light stone. Comfortable with pool, tennis,

FRANCE 119

riding, and trout fishing. Moderate to expensive. Northwest of
Poitiers.

Wimereux [14]

Atlantic Hotel   Wimereux   tel: 32 41 01
Unimaginative name for a hotel with one of the finest restaurants
in the region. Although the rooms are modestly comfortable, the
food is just superb, especially the seafood dishes. Moderate.
About twenty miles from Calais.

WHERE TO EAT

Aix-en-Provence [55]

Hiely-Luccullus   5 Rue République   tel: 81 15 05
Gourmet cooking with a regional flavor. Excellent wines. Moderate.

Ajaccio [59]

D'A Mamma   Passage Guinghetta   tel: 21 39 44
Wonderful local specialties in a home-cooking atmosphere.
Reasonable.

Antibes [62]

***La Bonne Auberge   Antibes   tel: 34 06 65
Famed for its delicious bouillabaisse, this is one of the wonderful
restaurants along the coast. Superb, flower-filled atmosphere.
Fifteen-thousand-bottle wine cellar. Expensive. Just east of Cannes.

Asnieres [1]

Le Pot au Feu   50 Rue des Bas   tel: 733-0071
Just on the outskirts of Paris to the northwest. Charming, small
restaurant with excellent seasonal specialties. Rumored to be on
its way out or under new management—call ahead to be sure.
Worth a detour if still in operation.

Avallon [92]

Le Chapeau Rouge   11 Rue de Lyon   tel: 512
In an old house is a fine restaurant offering delicious duck at reasonable prices.

Le Morvan   Road to Paris   tel: 076
In a rather refined atmosphere you'll be served some delicious dishes, including the ubiquitous duck (*canard*) and simmering snails (*escargots*).

Barbizon [1]

Grand Veneur   Barbizon   tel: 437-4044
A rustic restaurant with fine local dishes. Warm fireplace. Good atmosphere.

Bayonne [41]

La Tanière   Quai des Mousseroles   tel: 25 53 42
A delightful restaurant with local specialties including thinly sliced ham—the region is famous for it. Wonderful shellfish. All at a reasonable price.

Beaune [82]

Restaurant du Marché   12 Place Carnot   tel: 22 12 00
Some rooms for rent in this inn with lots of atmosphere, but it's the food which counts—superb, as are the wines. Moderate. Southwest of Dijon.

Biarritz [42]

***Café de Paris   5 Place Bellevue   tel: 24 19 53
A luxurious restaurant with a central location. Classic *haute cuisine*. Wonderful wine cellar. Very expensive.

L'Alambic   Place Bellevue   tel: 24 53 41
Great regional dishes. Popular restaurant with fine cooking at reasonable prices.

Bordeaux [38]

Dubern   42 allées de Tourny   tel: 48 03 44
Very fine restaurant specializing in fresh seafod. Moderately expensive. Closed Sunday.

Riche   62 Rue Saint-Rémi   tel: 48 84 71
Superb and simple restaurant with extremely reasonable prices.

La Toque Blanche   245 Rue de Turenne   tel: 48 97 86
A charming restaurant with some of those Arcachon oysters on the menu. Reasonable.

Bougival [1]

Coq Hardi   16 Quai Rennequin-Sualem   tel: 969-0143
An elegant country restaurant with a garden atmosphere and fine food. Eleven miles west of Paris.

Auberge de Camelia   7 Quai George Clemenceau   tel: 969-0302
Charming retreat with a delightful restaurant specializing in duckling. Moderate. Closed August.

La Brague [62]

***La Bonne Auberge   La Brague (Antibes)   tel: 34 06 65
A fine restaurant with a flowery, airy atmosphere. Superb regional cooking. Expensive. Closed in November. Outstanding wine collection. Just east of Cannes.

Cahors [113]

La Taverne   41 Rue J. B. Delpech   tel: 35 28 66
One of the finest restaurants, if not the finest, in the area. Tasty truffles and *foie gras* are it specialties. Closed only in the last part of November. Highly recommended.

Cannes [62]

Laurent   16 Rue Macé   tel: 39 32 56
Lots of atmosphere and fine local specialties. Moderate.

Le Chapon   26 Rue Jean-Jaurès   tel: 38 42 46
Delicious fish dishes with fine wines. Nice setting. Expensive.

Au Mal Assis   16 Quai St. Pierre   tel: 39 13 38
Simple and fun, with both fish and meat dishes. Good and very reasonable.

La Coquille   65 Rue Félix-Faure   tel: 39 26 33
Fine restaurant with both seafood and meat dishes. Moderate.

La Reine Pédauque   4 Rue Maréchal Joffre   tel: 39 40 91
Excellent food and wine in a delightful restaurant. Expensive.

Carry-le-Rouet [56]

L'Escale   Promenade du Port   tel: 45 00 47
Overlooking the sea ten miles west of Marseille is a superb restaurant surrounded by lovely flowers. Wonderful setting. Expensive. Closed in the winter.

Chagny [82]

Lameloise   36 Place d'Armes   tel: 49 02 10
A fine gastronomic stop for trout. Snails are superb. The ancient home offers a few modest rooms as well. Southwest of Dijon via Beaune.

Champniers [36]

Le Feu de Bois   Champniers   tel: 95 45 10
Simple and fine grills in this country restaurant only three miles north of Angoulème. Reasonable.

Chartres [3]

Cazalis (Henri IV)   31 Rue du Soleil-d'Or   tel: 21 01 55
Both fancy and simple dishes in this superb restaurant. Expensive.

Châteauneuf-du-Pape [54]

Mule-du-Pape   Châteauneuf-du-Pape   tel: 83 50 30
Delicious cuisine with superb local wines. Very fine and expensive restaurant. Only ten miles from Avignon.

Chavoire [78]

Pavillon Ermitage   Chavoire (Annecy)   tel: 45 81 09
Although the inn offers rooms, most travelers stop at the restaurant for its superb cooking. Garden. Lake. Expensive.

Chenonceaux [100]

Hotel du Bon Laboureur   Chenonceaux   tel: 29 90 02
Delightful stop for lunch from spring to fall. Very reasonable and attractive restaurant on a visit to the valley's most beautiful château—that of Chenonceau.

Col de la Luere [74]

Mère Brazier   Col de la Luère   tel: 48 70 35
Close to Lyon is one of the finest restaurants in the region. Great view in this gorgeous location with cooking to match. Expensive.

Collonges Au Mont d'Or [74]

***Paul Bocuse   50 Quai de la Plage   tel: 47 00 14
Inkeepers since 1765, the family has come up with the "father of French cuisine." Elegant restaurant rated as tops in a country where a good chef is revered. Expensive. Five miles north of Lyon.

Condom [46]

Table des Cordeliers   Avenue Général de Gaulle   tel: 368
A fine restaurant, only twenty-four miles southwest of Agen. West of Montauban.

Dinan [24]

Marguerite   27 Place Du-Guesclin   tel: 39 21 28
Modest, old-fashioned rooms in what is a superb restaurant. Excellent regional dishes at moderate prices. South of St. Malo.

La Ferté-Sous-Jouarre [1]

Auberge de Condé   1 Avenue de Montmirail   tel: 022-0007
A charming restaurant offering regional specialties. Fun. Simple. Delicious lamb. Expensive. Closed in February. To the east of Paris (about forty miles).

La Galère [62]

Guerguy la Galere   La Galere   tel: 38 96 71
Superb restaurant with gardens and lovely view to the sea from the terrace. Near Théoule about six miles from Cannes.

Gevrey-Chambertin [82]

La Rôtisserie du Chambertin   Gevrey-Chambertin   tel: 34 33 20
The restaurant is very good, but the wine is excellent. The inn is known for its fine cellar. Expensive, but great value. A must. About eight miles from Dijon.

Gordes [54]

Les Bories   Gordes   te.: 51 Gordes
A delightful restaurant with regional specialties. Moderate. Nearly twenty-five miles from Avignon.

Grenoble [71]

Chaumière Savoyarde   27 rue Gabriel-Péri   tel: 87 29 71
Tiny little restaurant only a short walk from the central railway station, but still difficult to find. Typical cuisine of the region for a discriminating group. Geared mainly to someone who speaks French well. Moderate.

Guéthary [42]

Hotel Pereria   Guéthary   tel: 26 51 68
Fresh and airy garden atmosphere adds a special touch to the delicious regional dishes. Fine restaurant with reasonable prices. Only three miles from St.-Jean-de-Luz. South of Biarritz.

Hericy [1]

Hostellerie Le Clou   7 Avenue de Fontainebleau   tel: 423-7343
A simple but warm inn with delicious cooking. Although on the main street, there's a garden in the back. Open all year. Only forty-seven miles to the south of Paris.

Illhaeusern [84]

***Auberge de l'Ill   Rue de Collonges   tel: 47 83 23
An absolutely exquisite restaurant in a delightful garden atmosphere. Ranked as one of the best in France by most gourmets. Reservations essential. Expensive. Only ten miles from Colmar.

Lyon [74]

Nandron   26 Quai Jean-Moulin   tel: 42 03 28
Centrally located on the river in the center of Lyon, the restaurant offers excellent local specialties. Expensive. Reserve.

La Mère Guy   35 Quai Jean-Jacques Rousseau   tel: 42 42 32
A luxurious, riverside restaurant serving classic French cuisine in an exquisite flower-filled dining room. One of the region's very best. Expensive. Reserve.

Juliette   23 Rue de l'Arbre-Sec   tel: 28 64 06
If you really want to try the local dishes, this is the place to go. Very fine. Reasonable.

Leon de Lyon   1 Rue Pleney   tel: 28 11 33
Warm and wonderful. Superb. Expensive.

Chez Rose   4 Rue Rabelais   tel: 60 57 25
For the flavor of the region, try this inexpensive inn.

Mâcon [79]

Auberge Bressane   14 Rue 28 Juin 1944   tel: 38 07 42
A great regional restaurant with superb dishes and wines. Expensive.

Marseille [56]

Calypso   3 Rue des Catalans   tel: 33 10 73
One of the finest seafood restaurants along the coast. Excellent bouillabaisse. Superb fresh fish. Expensive.

Les Catalans   6 Rue des Catalans   tel: 33 99 09
Another extraordinary seafood restaurant with fresh fish and shellfish including delicious oysters. Expensive.

Mionnay [74]

***Chez La Mère Charles   Mionnay   tel: 91 82 02
Although it's possible to stay in this inn, people really come here for the cooking, some of the best in the region. Wonderful atmosphere. Expensive. Eight miles north of Lyon.

Monaco [64]

***Le Bec Rouge   12 Avenue Saint Charles   tel: 30 74 91
Small and very fine restaurant serving excellent seafood including delicious mussels. Very expensive. Reserve.

La Calanque   33 Avenue Saint Charles   tel: 30 63 19
Small seafood restaurant. Nice, but very expensive.

La Chaumière   Place du Jardin Exotique   tel: 30 77 08
Regional specialties matched by a superb view of Monaco and the coast. Very expensive.

Rampoldi   3 Avenue des Spélugues   tel: 30 70 65
Fine small restaurant with varied menu. Fun. Expensive.

Mougins [62]

***Le Moulin de Mougins   Mougins   tel: 90 03 68
Authentic sixteenth-century mill now converted into a well-known inn with lots of atmosphere and superb cooking. Only a

few rooms available. Expensive. Closed November and December. Worth any detour. Short (four-mile) drive from Cannes.

Moulins [102]

Hôtel de Paris   *21 rue de Paris*   *tel: 44 00 58*
Excellent regional specialties including delicious lamb dishes. Expensive. Northeast of Montluçon.

La Napoule-Plage [62]

***L'Oasis*   *La Napoule-Plage*   *tel: 38 95 52*
One of the finest restaurants in France, with a delightful courtyard and lovely flower-filled atmosphere. Delicious regional cooking. Expensive. Worth a detour. Closed November and December. Only five miles from Cannes.

Nersac [36]

Le Pont de la Meure   *Nersac*   *tel: 97 60 48*
Fine regional specialties and delicious wines. Moderate. South of Angoulême.

Nice [63]

La Poularde   *9 Rue Gustave Deloye*   *tel: 85 22 90*
Superb regional cooking including fine seafood and excellent poultry. Very nice. Expensive.

Paris [1]

The French have a deep appreciation for fine food, fine wine, and an August vacation. Good restaurants become national shrines in which every dish is meant to appeal to all the senses. A great meal often takes· two to three hours. Most gourmets will tell you three things before a splurge in one of the capital's finer restaurants: Eat lightly the night before, avoid hard liquor, and order a simple, relatively inexpensive wine with your meal.

Allard   *41 Rue St. André des Arts, 6e*   *tel: 326-4823*
Racine once lived in this area, and this bistro does the seventeenth-century writer justice. You'll have to make reservations a

day or two in advance to eat here. This is one of Paris's great off season restaurants—popular in winter. In the spring the specialty is stewed duck with turnips and in the fall it's woodcock (*bécasse*). Every day there's a special dish which most Parisian gourmets know quite well. Good Burgundy wines. Expensive.

André   12 Rue Marbeuf, 8è   tel: 359-7507
Very simple restaurant with a basic menu. Good and very reasonable.

Androüet   41 Rue d'Amsterdam, 8è   tel: 874-2693
This is a specialty restaurant said to have over ninety varieties of French cheeses. Moderate.

Archestrate (L')   84 Rue de Varennes, 7è   tel: 551-4733
Lovely restaurant with unusual and equally memorable dishes. Fashionable. Expensive.

Auberge des Deux Signes   46 Rue Galande, 5è   tel: 325-4656
Lovely restaurant with fine dishes in a charming atmosphere. Reasonable.

Le Berthoud   1 Rue Valette, 5è   tel: 033-3881
A late-night charmer with turn-of-the-century flavor appealing to actors and actresses. Relaxed. Lots of good-looking people. Country cooking doused with fine Beaujolais wine. Reasonable.

Bisson Etoile   63 Rue Pierre-Charron, 8è   tel: 359-7878
Seafood and grills in attractive restaurant appealing to businessmen. Expensive.

Bistro 121   121 Rue de la Convention, 15è   tel: 828-1385
Gourmet's love this simple restaurant with superb salads and lovely atmosphere. Chicken, truffles, and hare are delicious and just a small sample of the menu. Good wines. Expensive.

Le Bistrot de Paris   33 Rue de Lille, 7è   tel: 548-3244
A bit phony, but nevertheless fashionable. The rustic dishes are fine. Superb Bordeaux wines complement the tasty food. Expensive.

Les Bosquets   39 Rue d'Orsel, 18è   tel: 606-1112
Simple, rustic atmosphere. Hearty home cooking. Delicious *coq au vin*. Reasonable.

Castel   *15 Rue Princesse, 6è*   *tel: 326-9022*
A so-called private club with a dining room. No one has yet fig-
ured out the secret of getting through the door, but some people
manage. Very much the place to see and be seen. Expensive.

La Chamaille   *81 Rue Saint-Louis-en-l'Ile, 4è*   *tel: 633-3546*
Charming, intimate restaurant with fine, reasonably priced food.

Le Chambiges   *4 Rue Chambiges, 8è*   *tel: 359-1584*
A modest restaurant with the kind of cooking a hungry and
knowledgeable traveler will appreciate. Very reasonable.

Le Champ de Mars   *17 Avenue de la Motte-Picquet, 7è*
tel: 705-5799
Rustic and red (Beaujolais—that is). Fun. Reasonable.

Au Charbon de Bois   *16 Rue du Dragon, 6è*   *tel: 548-5704*
Lively and fun. Nice grills. Light prices.

La Chaumière   *35 Rue de Beaune, 7è*   *tel: 548-4664*
A very reasonable and extremely popular restaurant with fine
hearty cooking and delicious game in the off-season.

Chez Garin   *9 Rue Lagrange, 5è*   *tel: 033-1399*
Some say this is the best restaurant in Paris. Pleasant atmosphere with imaginative and superb cooking. Very expensive.

Chez les Anges   *54 Boulevard de Latour-Maubourg, 7è*
tel: 705-8986
A warm and very popular restaurant serving superb liver, fine
ham, *coq au vin*, and very good wines. Expensive.

La Chope d'Orsay   *10 Rue du Bac, 7è*   *tel: 548-1515*
Country cooking with delicious game in season. Very reasonable.

Clos des Bernardins   *14 Rue de Pontoise, 5è*   *tel: 033-7007*
Lots of atmosphere in this medieval restaurant specializing in
veal and salmon. Very good seafood. Expensive.

Le Cochon d'Or   *192 Avenue Jean-Jaurès, 19è*   *tel: 607-2313*
Superb pork and seasonal dishes washed down with the best in
Beaujolais. Excellent grills and seafood. Wonderful bistro with a
colorful atmosphere. Moderately expensive.

La Coquille   *6 Rue du Débarcadère, 17è*   *tel: 380-2595*
This is an off-season favorite for seafood aficionados. Discreet

and superb service. What shellfish! The out-of-this-world *coquilles St. Jacques* is served only from October to May. For those who like blood sausage (*boudin*) this is the place to go. Expensive.

Drouant   18 Place Gaillon, 2è   tel: 073-5372
An old-fashioned nineteenth-century literary meeting place with good cuisine and much better atmosphere. Expensive.

Le Duc   243 Boulevard Raspail, 14è   tel: 326-5959
Anyone who adores seafood should head immediately to the yachtlike dining room of Le Duc. A luxury setting for fresh fish and shellfish including oysters, crayfish, and superb mussels. Fine white wines to accompany the delicacies. Expensive.

L'Escargot Montorgueil   38 Rue Montorgueil, 1° tel: 236-8351
Wonderful nineteenth-century setting in what was once Les Halles. Full of charm and the scent of bubbling *escargots*, delicious snails, the specialty of the house. Fine fish, kidneys, and delicious wines. Romantic. Expensive.

La Falcatule   14 rue Charles V, 4è   tel: 277-9897
A fine restaurant not well-known to Americans. Small and stylish. Expensive.

La Ferme Saint-Hubert   6 Rue Cochin, 5è   tel: 326-2103
A very reasonably priced restaurant with fine cheeses and good Burgundy wines. Healthy and hearty cooking with the kitchen open into the late hours.

Le Galant Verre   12 Rue de Verneuil, 7è   tel: 222-3781
Imaginative and fine cooking with an emphasis on good steak and delicious pâtés. The dishes more than make up for the lack of atmosphere. Expensive.

Gérard   4 Rue du Mail, 2è   tel: 236-9377
Near the Place des Victoires is this simple yet sophisticated small restaurant with a mixed-bag clientèle. No pretense, but good cooking. Reasonable prices.

Au Gourmet de l'Isle   42 Rue Saint-Louis-en-l'Ilhe, 4è
tel: 326-7927
Rustic, romantic, and reasonably priced. Charming candlelit dining. Superb country cooking with generous portions. Warm and friendly.

Le Grand Véfour   *17 Rue de Beaujolais, 1°*   tel: 742-5897
In the very-best-of-France category, this restaurant (once a casino) offers wonderful classical dishes in a sumptuous décor. The shrimp and lamprey are excellent, as are nearly all of the dishes on this great restaurant's menu. Fine wines. Expensive, but worth it—a good value in the high-price area.

Chez Jamin   *32 rue Longchamp*   tel: 727-1227
Very fine specialties from the Bordeaux region, including lamprey smothered in rich sauce. Excellent lemon tarte for dessert. Great wines. Expensive. Closed Sunday.

Lascaud   *7 Rue de Mondovi, 1°*   tel: 742-3669
A colorful bistro which is usually packed with an equally colorful and chic clientèle. Country cooking and a rough atmosphere—in the good sense. Crowded. Reasonable.

Lasserre   *17 Avenue Franklin D. Roosevelt, 8è*   tel: 359-5343
This sumptuous restaurant is certainly one of the best in France. Everything is just right, from the crystal glasses to the gold-rimmed plates. Flowers in silver vases. The ultimate in chic. Lasserre serves classic French dishes in a classic French manner, with all the finesse imaginable. Excellent wines. Although it's very expensive, it's an experience not to be missed.

Ledoyen   *Carré des Champs-Elysées, 8è*   tel: 265-4782
Extremely popular gourmet cuisine on the light side—a good reason why this is a favorite at lunch. Restful atmosphere. Fine. Expensive.

Le Louis d'Or   *81 Boulevard Gouvion-Saint-Cyr, 17è*   tel: 758-1230
Nicest in warm weather. An attractive restaurant in the Hôtel Méridien with classic dishes. Expensive.

Lous Landès   *9 Rue Georges-Saché, 14è*   tel: 567-0804
A fine place to get fat on country cooking and superb wines. The brandy here tops off the delicious meal in a way even Napoleon would have envied. Expensive.

Lucas-Carton   *9 Place de la Madeleine, 8è*   tel: 265-2290
Connoisseur's favorite. Spotless and elegant restaurant where it helps to be known as well as knowing. Fine fresh sole and superb woodcock (*bécasse*) in season—November is probably the

best month. Charming atmosphere and rather relaxed service. Expensive.

Aux Lyonnais   32 rue St. Marc, 2è   tel: 742-6559
Excellent sausage and superb beaujolais. Moderate to expensive. Closed Sunday and August.

***La Marée*   1 rue Daru   tel: 924-5242
Near the Etoile. Rich and very elegant restaurant noted for excellent lamb and outstanding seafood. Very expensive. Closed Sunday and August.

Maxim's   3 Rue Royale, 8è   tel: 265-2794
Maxim's is a Parisian monument. It is the "in" place to be in the evening, especially on Friday and Tuesday nights, when evening clothes are a must. It's one of France's finest with dancing and music. Like a dinner at the Taillevent, one at Maxim's is an experience. Very expensive.

Aux Neuf Epis   18 rue Mayet, 6è   tel: 734-9161
Delicious rabbit and veal smothered in prunes. Good regional wines. Moderate. Closed Sunday and August.

L'Orangerie   28 Rue Saint-Louis-en-L'Ile, 4è   tel: 633-9398
A stylish restaurant now "in" with the young and beautiful people. Wonderful winter choice. Very romantic. Geared to the late-night set. Superb beef and lamb. Expensive.

***Le Pactole*   44 Boulevard St. Germain, 5e   tel: 326-9228
Here you'll find an artist at work producing some of the most original and imaginative dishes, all from fresh produce and meats found in the daily marketplace. Courses change with the season. Emphasis on *la nouvelle cuisine* concept geared to trim calories and to keep the original taste intact. Exceptional. Expensive. Closed February and August.

Au Petit Montmorency   26 Rue de Montmorency, 3è   tel: 272-3104
A fine restaurant with a romantic flavor. Delicious veal and game in season—try the woodcock. An offbeat location, but it's right on when it comes to cooking. Expensive.

Au Petit Riche   25 Rue Le Peletier, 9è   tel: 770-8650
Wonderful old world flavor. It's crowded at noon because it's next to the Salle Drouot, Paris's great auction house. Unless

you're going to the auction, try this restaurant at night when the mood is softer and more subdued. A charming restaurant with delicate dishes including seasonal and regional (Loire) ones. Very reasonable.

Pharamond   24 rue Grande Truanderie, 1er   tel: 231-0672
Wonderful Norman cooking with emphasis on tripes, cider, camembert, and Calvados (local drink). Moderate. Closed Sunday and July.

Pierre   10 Rue de Richelieu, 1°   tel: 742-3641
Small, fine restaurant with good food and superb wines. Although quite expensive, you get good value here. It's doubtful you'll have any complaints with such specialties as duck or delicate sweetbreads.

Prunier-Duphot   9 Rue Duphot, 1°   tel: 073-1140
An old-fashioned restaurant with a ninteenth-century ambience. It serves some of the finest seafood in France along with excellent wines. The service is great. Expensive.

Au Quai d'Orsay   49 Quai d'Orsay, 7è   tel: 551-5858
Warm, "in," and lively. Small restaurant with turn-of-the-century atmosphere. Country cooking and fine Beaujolais wines. Reasonable.

Reginskaïa   128 Rue La Boétie, 8è   tel: 256-2000
Not well known to Americans, this is a lively restaurant with lots of activity at night. The cooking is quite good.

Le Relais de la Butte   12 Rue Ravignan, 18è   tel: 606-1618
A fine old restaurant making a comeback. Very reasonable.

Restaurant du Marché   59 Rue de Dantzig, 15è   tel: 828-3155
Country cooking topped with fine wines in a Parisian bistro—expensive and very good.

***Roger Lamazère*   23 Rue de Ponthieu, 8è   tel: 359-6666
A very fine restaurant with lots of atmosphere. Owned by a onetime magician who has learned the trick of turning out some masterful dishes. The restaurant is especially famous for its truffles—the best season for these is from mid-December until the end of February. The owner is said to order this delicacy by the ton. Quite a show. Very expensive.

Le Rubis   10 rue du Marché St. Honoré   tel: None
A delightful bistro with full information on all of the best in
place to try wines *by the glass*. Hints on bistro hopping: be in
place by 11:45 a.m. or go between 5:00 p.m. and 7 p.m. Light
snacks served as well. Inexpensive.

Saint-Antoine   21 Rue des Prêtres St. Germain-l'Auxerrois, 1°
tel: 231-5012
If you can ever get through the street address and find this
friendly, small restaurant, you'll be delighted at both the simple
fine food and the reasonable check.

******Taillevent   15 Rue Lamennais, 8è   tel: 359-3994*
A townhouse setting with a quiet and serious air about it.
Superb and spacious dining with many regional specialties
mixed in with the finest Paris has to offer. Extremely stylish and
elegant clientèle who appreciate the superb cuisine and some of
France's finest wines—the cellar is said to have close to 150,000
bottles of wine. Always "in," the Taillevent hosts a festival for
160 guests, the famous La Paulée, a formal and quite fashionable
wine-tasting party held in March. It's possible with some per-
suasion well in advance to wrangle a seat. Exceptional with
prices to match.

******La Tour d'Argent   15 Quai de la Tournelle, 5è   tel: 033-2332*
One of the world's great restaurants (a few say the greatest) with
some tables looking out on Notre Dame—a good reason to come
at night. Famous for its duck dishes, especially pressed duck,
which even the owner admits is not his favorite. Near-perfect
wine list. Fascinating wine cellar. Its own *Son et Lumière* show for
those in the know. Very expensive.

La Truffière   4 Rue Blainville, 5è   tel: 633-2982
An attractive, simple restaurant with truffles and enough taste in
cooking to make it a good bet. Reasonable.

Vivarois   Avenue Victor-Hugo 192, 16è   tel: 504-0431
One of Paris's classical choices. Modern and bright décor with
warm overall feeling. Limited but superb menu which will be an
epicurean's delight. Very fine and equally expensive.

Yves et Solange   12 Rue Dauphine, 6è   tel: 033-6630
Seafood and daily specials make this a warm choice for someone
interested in a tasty meal at a reasonable price.

Pont-Aven [30]

Moulin Rosmadec   Pont-Aven   tel: 97 70 22
A wonderful mill with the authenticity of the Bretagne region. A great restaurant with delicious local specialties. Southeast of Quimper.

Pontchartrain [1]

L'Aubergade   route Nationale   tel: 489-0263
A very fine restaurant in a lovely garden setting—best from late spring through early fall. To the west of Paris.

Pont de Basseau [36]

La Marmite du Pêcheur   Pont de Basseau   tel: 95 28 65
Good country cooking in this charming restaurant. Reasonable. Three miles from Angoulème.

Les Ponts-Neufs [24]

Lorrand-Barre   Les Ponts-Neufs   tel: 32 78 71
One of the best restaurants in Bretagne, with lots of atmosphere in the rustic setting. Exquisite local specialties. Great. Expensive. Short drive from Lamballe; about thirty-five miles from St.-Malo.

Port-Royal [1]

Chez Denise   Port-Royal   tel: 052-7071
Delightful country atmosphere and gardens add to the flavor of this fine restaurant. To the southwest of Paris.

Reims [6]

La Chaumière   184 Avenue d'Epernay   tel: 47 35 97
An elegant restaurant which is a local favorite of those in the know. Truffles and snails highlight superb regional cooking, which relies on light sauces sprinkled with Champagne. A superb restaurant with prices to match.

Roanne [104]

***Troisgros*   *Place de la Gare*   *tel: 71 26 68/71 66 97*
Although a few rooms are available in this inn, it's principally
noted as one of the top restaurants in France. This is a gastronomic "tour de force." Very expensive and ultrafine.

Roquebrune   [65]

Au Grand Inquisiteur   *18 Rue du Château*   *tel: 82 95 37*
Unusual and delightful inn serving delicious regional specialties.
Lots of atmosphere. Fun. Moderate. Near Menton.

Rouen [17]

Couronne   *31 Place Vieux-Marché*   *tel: 71 40 90*
Superb food in this Norman restaurant with lots of feeling and
fine service. Moderate.

St.-Jean-de-Luz [42]

Petit Grill Basque   *2 Rue St. Jacques*   *tel: 26 03 53*
Simple and nice. Good location. Good regional specialties.
Reasonable. South of Biarritz.

La Vieille Auberge   *22 Rue Tourasse*   *tel: 26 19 61*
A favorite for fresh fish. Simple and to the point—good.
Reasonable.

St.-Malo [24]

Duchesse Anne   *5 Place Châteaubriand*   *tel: 40 85 33*
An excellent seafood restaurant closed from December to March.

St. Tropez [62]

Leï Mouscardins   *St. Tropez*   *tel: 97 01 53*
Very fine restaurant. Elegant and casual. Superb fresh fish. Expensive. Reserve. Southwest of Cannes.

Sarlat [112]

Hotel de la Madeleine   *1 Place Petite-Rigaudie*   *tel: 59 10 41*
A simple country inn with wonderful, hearty cooking. Specializes in local dishes. Reasonable prices. Northwest of Roc-Amadour via Souillac.

Sassenage [71]

Rostang   *Sassenage*   *tel: 88 50 24*
Generations of tradition have made this one of the truly outstanding restaurants in France. Superb dining in an elegant atmosphere. Large garden is delightful in warm weather. A few modest rooms are available. Highly recommended. Expensive. Reserve. On the outskirts of Grenoble.

Saulieu [82]

Côte d'Or   *2 Rue Argentine*   *tel: 018*
Here's a restaurant worth a long detour, although you may well wonder whether you'll ever make it to your room after a meal in this gastronomic temple. Expensive. Closed November. West of Dijon.

Souillac [112]

Grand Hotel Couderc   *Souillac*   *tel: 30*
Recommended for a good meal consisting of local specialties. North of Roc-Amadour.

Steinbrunn-le-Bas [83]

Moulin du Kaegy   *Steinbrunn-le-Bas*   *tel: 48 01 34*
Not far from Mulhouse one finds this attractive sixteenth-century country house with lots of atmosphere and good regional cooking.

Strasbourg [85]

Rôtisserie Aubette   31 Place Kléber   tel: 32 34 94
A very fine restaurant with a good reputation. Excellent local dishes and fine wines. Expensive.

Valentin-Sorg   6 Place de l'Homme-de-Fer   tel: 32 12 16
Lots of atmosphere and a wonderful view of the city. The food is good, the wine excellent. Expensive.

Maison des Tanneurs   42 Rue du Bain-aux-Plantes   tel: 32 79 70
Great atmosphere. A snail-fancier's find. Expensive.

***Crocodile   10 Rue de l'Outre   tel: 32 13 02*
Regional cooking at its best. Wonderful atmosphere. Gracious service. A must. Very expensive and worth every *centime*.

Thoissey [79]

Au Chapon Fin   Thoissey   tel: 49
About ten miles from Mâcon is this fine inn with eighteen comfortable rooms and one of the best restaurants in France. Frogs' legs, birds, and Beaujolais add up to a delicious meal. Expensive, but worth it. Closed January and February.

Tournus [82]

Greuze   4 Rue Albert Thibaudet   tel: 166
Lots of flavor to this wonderful inn with superb cooking. Moderate. Reserve. South of Dijon.

Tours [97]

***Barrier   101 Avenue de la Tranchée   tel: 54 20 39*
An off-season restaurant geared to discriminating tastes. One of France's very finest, with a chef dedicated to keeping this restaurant's name in the forefront of gastronomic shrines. Delicious duck and salmon. The very finest in wines. A tasteful treat. Very expensive. Closed Wednesday.

La Petite Marmite   *103 Avenue de la Tranchée*   *tel: 53 03 85*
As so often happens in France, fine restaurants spring up next to
the greatest restaurants in the country. La Petite Marmite is one
example. The food is very good, but not at all pretentious. The
prices are equally reasonable.

Valberg [63]

Les Flocons   *Valberg*   *tel: 02 50 11*
Although this is a hotel, it's known mainly for its fine food.
Wonderful scenery. Moderate. Just over fifty miles from Nice.

Valence [69]

***Pic*   *285 Avenue Victor Hugo*   *tel: 43 15 32*
Some rooms are available in this inn, which ranks in the top
from a gastronomic point of view. Fantastic cooking in an airy,
garden setting. Highly recommended. As expensive as it is fine.

Versailles [2]

Ile-de-France   *45 Rue Carnot*   *tel: 950-0528*
Plush restaurant with delicious dishes. Expensive.

Vézelay [1]

L'Esperance   *Vézelay*   *tel: 100*
A riverside restaurant in lovely park. Superb cuisine. Expensive.
Closed mid-November to mid-December. South of Paris.

Vienne [74]

***Point*   *Boulevard F. Point*   *tel: 85 00 96*
Gourmets are forever debating whether this is the best restaurant in France or not. The debate's absurd. The cooking here is
superb, as is the ambience. Whether it's number 1 or number 20,
it's still worth the high price. An experience. Make reservations
well ahead of time. Closed in November. South of Lyon.

Vonnas [79]

Chez La Mère Blanc   Vonnas   tel: 10
Twelve miles from Mâcon is another charming mecca for gourmets and gourmands. The century-old inn offers classic dishes including those featuring the best in beef. Family-owned and managed. Expensive, but worth it.

GERMANY

WEST GERMANY

DENMARK

[69] Flensburg
Schleswig
[68]
Kiel [67]
[66] Plön
Bosau [65]
[64] Travemünde
[63] Lübeck
[62] Ratzeburg

EAST GERMANY

[61] Hamburg
Lüneburg
[60]
Bremen
[59]

Celle [58]

Berlin
[70]

NETHERLANDS

[57] Hannover
Hildesheim
[56]

[55]
Osnabrück

Anholt
[53]
[50]
Essen
Duisburg[49]
Düsseldorf [48]

Münster [54]

Dortmund [51]

Goslar
[52]

REGIONS

1 — Schleswig-Holstein
2 — Hamburg
3 — Niedersachsen
4 — Bremen
5 — Berlin
6 — Nordrhein-Westfalen
7 — Hessen
8 — Rheinland-Pfalz
9 — Saarland
10 — Baden-Württemberg
11 — Bayern

Kassel [47]
Bad [46]
Wildungen

Köln [45]
[44]
Aachen Bonn
[43]
Marburg
[42]

Bad
Hersfeld
[41]

BELGIUM
[35] Bad
Schwalbach
Cochem
[39]
[34] Wiesbaden
[33] Rüdesheim
Trier
[28]
8

Koblenz
[40]

[38] Bad Nauheim
Bad Homburg [36]
Bad Orb [37]
Frankfurt [32]
Bad Soden [31]
Mainz
[29]
Darmstadt
[30]

Coburg [22]

LUX

Mannheim
[26]

Würzburg
[23]

Bayreuth
[21]

CZECHOSLOVAKIA

Saarbrücken
[27]

Heidelberg
[25]
[17] Karlsruhe
Baden-Baden [15]
Wildbad [14]
Bad Griesbach
[13]
[11]
Freiburg [12]
Bad Dürrheim
Badenweiler
[10]

Nürnberg
[20]

Rothenburg
[19]

Regensburg
[18]

10

11

Augsburg
[7]

München
[1]

AUSTRIA

FRANCE

Überlingen [9]
Konstanz
[8]
Füssen
[6]

Chiemsee
[2]

Berchtesgaden
[3]

Oberammergau [5]
Garmisch-
Partenkirchen
[4]

SWITZERLAND

0 km. 50

0 miles 50

N

ITALY

CUCL

WHAT TO SEE

Many aspects of Germany will appeal to the uncommon traveller. Nowhere will you find a wider selection of castle and romantic hotels in which to stay. You'll also be surprised by the incredible range of truly fine restaurants that make Germany one of the most interesting countries from a gastronomic point of view. Added to all of this is stunning sightseeing described briefly below.

The southern region of Germany has long been the most publicized and posterized. Many people will want to visit *Munich* [1] (München) for a few days to take in the Alte Pinakothek, Deutsches Museum (best technical museum in Europe), Residenz, Nymphenburg Palace, and the many famous beer halls that bounce to life during Oktoberfest, a yearly beer bash that begins in mid-September and runs into early October. Try to make an excursion to Schloss Herrenchiemsee at *Chiemsee* [2] (scene of Sunday night chamber concerts during the summer). The Linderhof Castle southwest of *Oberammergau* [5] (next Passion play in 1980), the fabulous and fanciful *Neuschwanstein*, the lesser-known but great *Hohenschwangau* castle, and the baroque *Pommersfelden* south of *Bamberg* are all worth a special detour. Also interesting if you have the time are the *Hohenzollern* castle south of *Hechingen* and the abbey of *Maulbronn*. The view from the Eagle's Nest at *Berchtesgaden* [3] will take your breath away, as will trips through the *Black Forest* (southwest corner of the country) and along the Romantic Road running from *Füssen* north to *Würzburg* [23] (don't miss the Residenz). The medieval towns of *Rothenburg ob der Tauber* [19] and nearby *Dinkelsbühl* are worth long detours, as is the city of *Heidelberg* [25], where you'll want to stroll through the Old Town. Lakeside *Lindau* is a relaxing resort, while *Baden-Baden* [15] is a fashionable spa noted for its active social life. The best ski area: *Garmisch-Partenkirchen* [4] (packed on weekends and during main holidays). An outstanding seasonal event is the Wagner Opera Festival in July and August at *Bayreuth* [21] (order tickets months in advance). The triangle formed between *Bayreuth*, *Nürnberg* [20], and *Coburg* [22] offers spectacular, scenic sightseeing and includes Franconian Switzerland. Drives through this region will be of particular interest to the uncommon traveller.

The most popular attractions of central Germany are the superb cathedrals of *Cologne* **[45]** (Köln) and *Worms*; the Roman remains in *Trier* **[28]**, the medieval town of *Michelstadt*; and the sights of the major cities including the Paul Klee collection in the Academy of Art in *Düsseldorf* **[48]**, the Gutenberg Press in *Mainz*, and the paintings by Rubens in the Staatliche Gemäldegalerie in *Kassel* **[47]**. Wine lovers flood *Rüdesheim* **[33]**, well known for its authentic wine taverns and frequent festivals. Other popular wine towns are *Bad Durkheim* and *Neustadt*. *Koblenz* **[40]** makes a good base for Rhine excursions, including one to the famous Loreley, while *Wiesbaden* **[34]** (at its loveliest in May) attracts gamblers on a splurge. An offbeat side trip would be to *Berlin* **[70]** to check into Checkpoint Charlie. Frankly, I'd prefer to spend my money on the delightful hidden hotels and restaurants of this region.

The northern part of Germany, not as spectacular as the south, nevertheless exudes a special charm in its smaller towns and hamlets. The atmosphere in *Celle* **[58]**, *Goslar* **[52]**, *Bosau*, and *Duderstadt* is outstanding. So are treks into the *Lüneburg Heath* (light purple in the fall) and to the island retreat of *Sylt*. The latter is extremely popular in the summer with nudists. It has typical inns that offer excellent regional cooking, including fresh fish dishes at reasonable prices. The two famous cities of the north are worth a *quick* look. *Hamburg* **[61]** offers excellent art in the Kunsthalle and some of Europe's most outlandish strip joints along the Reeperbahn while *Bremen* **[59]** is noted for the Markplatz, Schnoor District, and craft shops along Böttchergasse. Famous sights: Schloss Glücksburg, northeast of *Flensburg* **[69]**; Herrenhausen Castle of *Hannover* **[57]**; Schloss Marienburg, northwest of *Hildesheim* **[56]**; and the Wolfenbüttel Palace, south of *Braunschweig*.

WHAT'S THE WEATHER REALLY LIKE?

The weather is generally quite good from mid-May to early October. As in most of central Europe, you should expect frequent rains. Both May and September are excellent months to visit Germany if you want to avoid the summer heat and crowds. Winter begins in November stretching to early April. Winter in

the north means drizzly and cool days, while in the south it
brings frequent snowfalls to the mountainous areas.

SOME SUGGESTIONS FOR A MORE ENJOYABLE TRIP

The Romantik Hotels (and restaurants) are a chain offering excellent regional cooking, authentic atmosphere, and comfortable
accommodations at reasonable prices. They are all family-owned,
which gives them a special feeling and warmth you won't find in
larger, commercial hotels. You can get full information on these
hotels, including a very helpful road map, by writing Romantik
Hotels, D 8757 Karlstein a. Main, Freigericht Str. 5. Note that in
writing addresses in a German format that the city comes before
the street.[1] Castle hotels offer unique lodging and dining in an
atmosphere that varies from rustic to elegant. You can sleep in
two-hundred-year-old four-poster beds or dine in a stable converted into a charming country restaurant. For information on
these, contact Gast im Schloss e.V., D. 3526 Trendelburg 1. Lufthansa, the German airlines, can give you pamphlets on these
hotels as well. Both the romantic and castle hotels will call ahead
to your next destination to make a room reservation for you.
Hotel rooms are always at a premium in the peak season, especially in the larger cities. Try to make reservations well ahead of
time. If you arrive in a large city without a room reservation in
the summer, head immediately to the tourist office in the airport
or train station. For a small charge they'll find you available accommodations in the price range of your choice. Note that
Munich is packed in late September and early October during
the Oktoberfest. So are mountain resorts during major holidays
and weekends. The most convenient way to see Germany is by
car. The roads are excellent with speeds rarely controlled. You're
expected to leave the left lanes open on the *autobahns*
(superhighways). Blinking lights behind you are a sure sign that
you're in the wrong lane: move over immediately. If you rent a
car, be sure to ask for a good road map. Many of the towns
listed in this chapter will be hard to find without one. Try to
avoid city driving during rush hours, and you may want to park

1. This is changing rapidly in modern Germany with town names often following
the street.

your car to take advantage of excellent and inexpensive public
transportation in major cities. Few people give Germany credit
for its outstanding restaurants. Many of them are included in
this chapter and will give gourmets good reason to slow down.
The better restaurants have an excellent selection of wines to
choose from, and you're expected to drink wine although beer is
acceptable in the less formal regional restaurants. With
thousands of local breweries, you can't go wrong.

WHERE TO STAY

Aachen [44]

Kurhotel Quellenhof   Monheimsallee 52   tel: 48 161
Large luxury resort in lovely park. Traditional flavor. Spacious
and very comfortable rooms. Fine restaurant. Pool. Very expensive.

Anholt [53]

Park Hotel Wasserburg   Kleverstrasse   tel: 20 44
Small, charming medieval castle in a lovely park, surrounded by
a moat. Museum, gallery, and its own deer park. Nice view.
Modern rooms in what was once servants' quarters. Excellent
regional cuisine. Moderate to expensive. Near Rhine; close to
Dutch border.

Arolsen [47]

Schlosshotel Arolsen   Gr. Allee 1   tel: 30 91
Modest but reasonably comfortable castle-hotel. Pool. Moderate.
West of Kassel.

Aschaffenburg [32]

Post   Goldbacher Strasse 19-21   tel: 21 333
Attractive hotel in the center of town with comfortable rooms.
Pool. Noted for very fine regional cooking. Special gourmet
weeks organized. Parking provided in back. Very popular. Expensive. Southeast of Frankfurt.

Assmannshussen am Rhein [32]

Krone Hotel   Rheinstrasse 10   tel: 22 36
Pleasant historic riverside inn with great location and atmosphere. Comfortable rooms. Traditional flavor and service. Great restaurant with superb wines. Pool. Expensive. Closed mid-November to mid-March. Forty-five miles southwest of Frankfurt.

Attendorn [47]

Burghotel Schnellenberg   Attendorn (Biggesee)   tel: 30 31
Ancient medieval castle converted into a quiet and very comfortable hotel with a fine view. Lots of atmosphere. Good cooking. Tennis, riding, hunting, and fishing. Expensive. Closed January 15 to February 15. Just west of Kassel.

Auerbach/Oberpfalz [21]

Goldener Löwe   Unterer Markt 9   tel: 352
Modest hotel in authentic German village. Simple rooms, but delightful restaurant with many local dishes. Friendly. Moderate. South of Bayreuth.

Augsburg [7]

Palasthotel Drei Mohren   40 Maximilianstrasse   tel: 51 00 31
Large old-world hotel with pleasant atmosphere. Good dining. Quiet. Very expensive.

Baden-Baden [15]

Rebenhof   Weinstrasse 58   tel: 54 06
Charming and tiny inn with comfortable, attractive rooms. Nice atmosphere and location outside of Baden-Baden. Moderate.

Steigenberger Hotel Badischer Hof   Lange Strasse 47   tel: 22 827
Large traditional hotel classified as a national monument. Once a cloister, now a charming luxury hotel in a lovely park. Comfortable. Full of nostalgia. Very expensive.

Badenweiler [10]

Sonne   Badenweiler   tel: 50 53
Ancient inn (1620), a favorite of an older group who come to
Badenweiler to take advantage of the spa and frequent concerts.
Flowers galore. Comfortable rooms. Good dining (delicious
home-made pies). Very quiet (no cars allowed in town at night).
Packed in early spring and early fall. Relatively easy to get into
during the summer. Moderate. Good value.

Bad Friedrichshall [16]

Schloss Lehen   Hauptstrasse 2   tel: 7441
Small medieval castle with gorgeous view. Comfortable. Good
restaurant. Fine spring fishing. Moderate. Closed January. North
of Stuttgart.

Bad Godesberg [43]

Godesberg Hotel   Auf dem Berg 1   tel: 36 30 08
Pleasant inn, three miles from Bonn. Lovely view. Limited
number of comfortable rooms. Good regional cooking. Expensive.

Bad Herrenalb [15]

Mönchs Posthotel   Dobelstrasse 2   tel: 20 02
Small, attractive hotel with comfortable rooms. Well known for
its charming restaurant, serving both regional and international
dishes. Moderately expensive. Twelve miles from Baden-Baden.

Bad Hersfeld [41]

Zum Stern   Linggplatz 11   tel: 46 16
An ancient inn that has been in the family since 1874. Once used
to house guests of a nearby monastery. Excellent regional cooking served in a beamed restaurant. Rustic rooms named after
famous guests. In the center of the city.

Bad Nauheim [38]

Hilberts Park Hotel   *Kurstrasse 2-4*   *tel: 31 945*
Large old-world hotel with comfortable rooms and fine service.
Pool, tennis, and riding arranged. Expensive.

Bad Orb [37]

Weisses Ross   *Markplatz 4*   *tel: 20 91*
Half-timbered spa hotel with a tradition dating back five
hundred years. Very comfortable and surrounded by a park.
Open fireplace. Very relaxing. Moderate.

Bad Schwalbach [35]

Waffenschmiede   *Hohenstein*   *tel: 33 57*
Castle in delightful setting. Elegant atmosphere. Quite comfortable but limited number of rooms. Recommended highly for its
pleasant restaurant. Fishing arranged. Expensive. Closed
January.

Bamberg [21]

Bamberger Hof Bellevue   *4 Schönleinsplatz*   *tel: 22 216*
Small old-world hotel with quiet and comfortable rooms. Good
cooking. Expensive. West of Bayreuth.

Bayreuth [21]

Schloss Tiergarten   *Emtmannsberg*   *tel: 211*
Tiny historic inn. Comfortable rooms, but listed mainly as a dining spot. Delicious regional cooking. Lots of atmosphere. Moderate.

Bensberg [45] (Sülztal)

Schloss Georgshausen   *Bensberg*   *tel: 25 61*
Fourteenth-century manor with twelve comfortable rooms—all in
a rural setting with horses and golf. Good regional cooking. Expensive. East of Cologne (Köln).

Berchtesgaden [3]

Geiger   Berchtesgadenerstrasse 111   tel: 55 55
Small pleasant hotel, like a fine home with lovely rooms. Known
for its fine regional cooking. Expensive. Park, pools, and fishing.
Closed November.

Berlin [70]

Gehrhus Schlosshotel   Brahmsstrasse 4-10   tel: 826-2081
A palace converted into an elegant luxury hotel. Lovely park in
fashionable Grünewald. Traditional flavor and service. Small
number of very fine rooms furnished in period style. Lots of atmosphere. Candlelight dining. Tennis and pool. Noncentral location. Expensive.

Haus Franken   Hochbergplatz 7   tel: 772-4016
Tiny, charming guest house with a small number of comfortable
rooms. Moderate.

Bierhütte b. Freyung [1]

Bierhütte   Bierhütte   tel: 315
A brewery until 1916—converted recently into clean and very
comfortable inn (distinctive, regional architecture reminiscent of
nearby Czechslovakia). Ask for larger rooms on the south side
(1–5 overlook the pond). Trout fishing. Nice restaurants with interesting local specialties: fried camembert, batter-fried apples,
and fresh venison. Lovely walks in this isolated mountain area.
Also shopping for local glassware. Moderate. Northeast of
Munich, near Czech border.

Bitburg [28]

Sport Hotel Südeifel   Biersdorf   tel: 841
Five miles west of Bitburg. Large modern hotel in idyllic setting.
Ideal for walking. Very comfortable. Tennis and fishing. Expen-
sive. North of Trier.

Bochum [50]

Parkhotel Haus Bochum   *Bergstrasse 141*   *tel: 51 898*
Tiny traditional inn with comfortable rooms. Known for its fine
regional cooking. Moderately expensive. Between Essen and
Dortmund.

Boppard [40]

Bellevue Rheinhotel   *Rheinallee 41-42*   *tel: 20 81*
Large and comfortable older hotel. Nice view. Pleasant throughout. Very good restaurant. Expensive. Closed in January. South
of Koblenz.

Braunlage [52]

Weidmannsheil   *Obere Bergstrasse*   *tel: 30 81*
Large, lovely hotel with fine view. Very comfortable and attractive. Pool. Expensive. Southeast of Goslar.

Zur Tanne   *Herzog-Wilhelm-Strasse 8*   *tel: 10 34*
Modest looking from the outside, but truly a fine hotel and restaurant. Comfortable rooms; tasty lobster and steaks served from
the grill. Charming beer "room" with local flavor. Moderate.
Southeast of Goslar.

Bremen [59]

Bremer Hospiz   *Löningstrasse 16*   *tel: 32 16 68*
Large, comfortable hotel with simple rooms, some with bath.
Good central location. Not fancy. Moderate.

Brünen-Marienthal [49]

Haus Elmer   *Brünen-Marienthal*   *tel: 500*
Very simple, but charming, inn with seven comfortable rooms.
Quite good regional cuisine. Moderate. Northwest of Essen.

Buchen/Odenwald [23]

Prinz Carl   Hochstadtstrasse 1   tel: 18 77
Modest hotel dating back to 1610 with older rooms in main house and newer (immaculate) rooms in wing. Has the appeal of an aging mistress. Wine cellar and popular regional specialties in the restaurant. Try the *torte*. Moderate. Southwest of Würzburg.

Buehl [15]

Burg Windeck   Kappelwindeckstrasse 104   tel: 23 671
Tiny rustic inn with lovely view. Limited number of comfortable and quiet rooms. Very isolated. Excellent cuisine. Moderately expensive. Closed January. Near Baden-Baden (south).

Burg Rabenstein [21]

Hotel Restaurant Burg Rabenstein   Burg Rabenstein   tel: 313
Seventeen comfortable rooms in an ancient (twelfth century) building. Fishing. Moderate. Closed mid-January to mid-February. Five miles north of Behringersmühle; about thirty miles from Bayreuth.

Celle [58]

Parkhotel Fürstenhof   55-56 Hannoversche Strasse   tel: 27 051
Nice atmosphere in this charming manor converted into a pleasant hotel in quiet setting. Comfortable. Good regional cooking. Pool. Expensive.

Cleeberg [38]

Schlosshotel Burg Cleeberg   Cleeberg   tel: 401
Very comfortable and pleasant castle-hotel with a fine restaurant. Hunting, riding, tennis, and fishing. Expensive to very expensive. North of Frankfurt; about six miles from Bad Nauheim.

Cochem [39]

Alte Thorschenke Hotel   Brückenstrasse 3   tel: 70 59
Small historic inn near Mosel with lots of atmosphere and

charm. Varied, comfortable rooms. Some with four-poster beds. Fine restaurant. Ideal in the fall for anyone interested in wines and wine festivals. Very fine choice in this region. Moderately expensive. Closed from December through February.

Cologne [45] (Köln)

Park Hotel St. Georg   *Rather Mauspfad 11*   *tel: 86 12 71*
Small hotel on the outskirts of the city. Reasonably comfortable. Geared to riders. Moderate.

Darmstadt [30]

Schlosshotel Jagdschloss Kranichstein   *Kranichsteinerstrasse 261 tel: 78 626*
Tiny manor converted into lovely rustic inn surrounded by quiet park. Comfortable. Pleasant throughout. Delicious game dishes served in the off-season. Expensive.

Weinmichel Hotel   *Schleiermacherstrasse 8-10*   *tel: 26 822*
Small modest hotel with comfortable rooms—half with bath. An excellent restaurant with gourmet dining. Expensive.

Dinkelsbuhl [19]

Hotel Deutsches Haus   *Weinmarkt 3*   *tel: 23 46*
Tiny, historic inn dating from the fifteenth century. Simple but with lots of atmosphere. Antiques throughout. Excellent regional cooking. Moderately expensive. South of Rothenburg.

Goldene Rose Hotel   *Markplatz 4*   *tel: 22 76*
Small historic inn with modest rooms. Medieval atmosphere. Fishing and riding can be arranged. Expensive. Neither of these hotels is recommended for the overly demanding.

Düsseldorf [48]

Atlantic Hotel   *Fürstenplatz 3*   *tel: 37 60 56*
Small modern hotel with modest, comfortable rooms. Half with bath. Quiet location. Parking. Moderate.

Enzklösterle/Nordschwarzwald [14]

Waldhorn-Post   Wildbader Strasse 1   tel: 411
A charming hotel with a history back to 1145. Very comfortable
rooms. Tennis and swimming, as well as hunting in the area.
Good regional cooking with venison and trout on the menu. Be
sure to try the house brandy. Moderate. South of Wildbad.

Ettal [4]

Benediktenhof   Ettal   tel: 46 37
Small attractive hotel with comfortable modest rooms. Fine re-
gional restaurant with delicious cooking. Moderate. Closed
November to mid-December. North of Garmisch-Partenkirchen.

Ettlingen [17]

***Erbprinz   Rheinstrasse 1   tel: 12 071
Charming well-known luxury inn with comfortable rooms and a
superb restaurant with both French and regional cooking. For
gourmets. Very expensive. Near Karlsruhe (south).

Feuchtwangen [19]

Greifen-Post   Markplatz 8   tel: 91 33
A charming excursion from the more famous Rothenburg ob der
Tauber. A comfortable inn, in the family for three generations
(since 1855). Warm and relaxing. Moderate.

Flensburg/Oeversee [69]

Historischer Krug   Flensburg   tel: 334
Dating back to 1519, this is the oldest guest house in the region.
It's very famous in the region for superb cooking and fine wines.
Try the shellfish, smoked salmon, or special ribs. Charming and
highly recommended. Moderate.

Frankfurt am Main [32]

Gravenbruch Hotel   *Neu Isenburg 2*   *tel: 55 71*
Large and lovely luxury resort five miles east of town. An ancient hunting lodge converted into a stylish retreat set in a beautiful park. Very comfortable and tasteful rooms. Excellent dining. Tennis and pool. Very expensive. Worth the drive.

Höchster Hof Hotel   *Am Mainberg 3 (Höchst)*   *tel: 30 00 71*
Quiet and very simple hotel in noncentral location. Comfortable. Good in the moderately expensive range.

Freiburg [11]

Rappen Hotel   *Münsterplatz 13*   *tel: 31 353*
Tiny, delightful inn. Wonderful location. Very quiet and relaxing. Rustic but warm. Comfortable. Good regional cooking. Moderate. Closed February.

Schlossbergblick Hotel   *Ludwigstrasse 36*   *tel: 36 927*
Small hotel in quiet district. Good view. Modern and bright rooms. Nice. Expensive. Closed mid-December to early January.

Victoria Hotel   *Eisenbahnstrasse 54*   *tel: 33 211*
Small, comfortable hotel with modest rooms. Delicious regional cooking. Moderate.

Freudenstadt [14]

Waldhotel Stokinger   *Lauterbadstrasse*   *tel: 21 87*
Small, charming hotel in forest setting. Traditional atmosphere and service. Comfortable and very pleasant rooms. Idyllic. Moderately expensive. Closed November to mid-December. South of Wildbad.

Friedrichsruhe [16]

****Waldhotel Friedrichsruhe*   *Friedrichsruhe*   *tel: 70 78*
Lovely, eighteenth-century manor converted into an elegant

hotel in idyllic park setting. Abundant gold leaf, chandeliers, and formal gardens. Attractive and very comfortable rooms— most with bath. Excellent restaurant serving delicious regional specialties and outstanding wines. Pool, tennis, fishing. A great European hotel. Very expensive. Near Ohringen, fifteen miles from Heilbronn to north of Stuttgart.

Fulda [41]

Zum Kurfürsten   Schlosstrasse 2   tel: 70 001
Small castle converted to authentic inn. Quite comfortable. Moderately expensive. South of Bad Hersfeld.

Garmisch-Partenkirchen [4]

Alpina Hotel   Alpspitzstrasse 12   tel: 55 031
Small delightful Alpine hotel with comfortable rustic rooms. Good regional cooking. Pool. Very expensive. Closed November to mid-December.

Clausing's Posthotel   Marienplatz 12   tel: 43 55
Modernized historic inn (1639) with comfortable rooms in an idyllic setting. Wonderful view. Lots of local atmosphere, including a typical Bavarian-style restaurant with good local cuisine. Friendly and warm. Expensive.

Göppingen [16]

Hotel Hohenstaufen   Freihofstrasse 64   tel: 73 484
Small old-world hotel in fifteenth-century guild hall. Comfortable. Fine restaurant and wine cellar. Musical evenings in the off-season. Moderately expensive.

Goslar [52]

Hotel Kaiserworth   Markt 3   tel: 21 111
Small old-world hotel in fifteenth-century guild hall. Comfortable. Fine restaurant and wine cellar. Musical evenings in the off-season. Moderately expensive.

Grünwald [1]

Schlosshotel Grünwald   *1 Zeillerstrasse*   *tel: 641-1612*
Small modest lodge converted into pleasant hotel filled with antiques. Serene setting. Nice atmosphere. Good restaurant. Moderate. Near Munich (south).

Hamburg [61]

Park Hotel Beyer   *Blumenstrasse 19*   *tel: 460-4006*
Small villa converted into very comfortable hotel with quiet, spacious rooms in nice location. Attractive garden atmosphere. Moderate.

Prem Hotel   *An der Alster 9*   *tel: 24 22 11*
Larger, traditional hotel in park by the lake. Comfortable rooms, most with bath. Very pleasant throughout, with garden. Moderate to expensive.

Hammelburg [23]

Schloss Saaleck   *Hammelburg*   *tel: 24 35*
Small number of rooms available in this ancient hilltop castle surrounded by colorful vineyards. Comfortable but modest. Excellent cuisine. Moderate. North of Würzburg en route to Fulda off E70.

Hannover [57]

Georgenhof Hotel   *Herrenhäuser Kirchweg 20*   *tel: 71 22 44*
Tiny, cozy inn in lovely location. Traditional atmosphere and furnishings. Very comfortable. Good cooking. Expensive to very expensive.

Heidelberg [25]

Acor Hotel   *Friedrich-Ebert-Anlage 55*   *tel: 24 130*
Small, charming manor converted into warm and modest hotel. Moderately expensive.

Alt Heidelberg Hotel   *Rohrbacherstrasse 29*   *tel: 25 575*
Small, charming hotel with pleasant traditional atmosphere and service. Neat and nice. Moderately expensive.

Der Europäische Hof   *Friedrich-Ebert-Anlage 1A*   *tel: 27 101*
Large luxury hotel in lovely setting. Traditional atmosphere and service. Comfortable and quiet (ask for room in the main building). Lively social life. Exceptional dining. Excellent in the expensive bracket.

Parkhotel Atlantic   *Schloss Wolfsbrunnenweg 23*   *tel: 24 545*
Small villa converted into pleasant hotel with modern and comfortable rooms. Quiet location. Very expensive.

Zum Ritter   *Hauptstrasse 178*   *tel: 24 272*
Ideally located in the old town. Romantic façade gives way to pleasant public rooms, including a fine dining area, a favorite of many. Most rooms modest. A few in the front are large and nicely furnished—but noisy during the day. Moderate.

Stiftsmühle   *Heidelberger Landstrasse 129*   *tel: 50 142*
Small old mill converted into comfortable hotel in serene setting just outside of town. Fine dining. Expensive.

Heinsheim/Bad Rappenau [16]

Hotel Schloss Heinsheim   *Heinsheim*   *tel: 10 45*
Small manor converted into delightful hotel with comfortable rooms. Park setting. Pool. Fine dining. Deer-hunting arranged. Moderately expensive. Eleven miles north of Heilbronn. Closed mid-January to mid-February. North of Stuttgart.

Hilders/Rhön [37]

Engel   *Marktstrasse 12*   *tel: 71 04*
A wayside rest since the fifteenth century in one of Germany's most stunning regions. A perfect example of an uncommon and worthwhile detour for hiking, gliding, and sightseeing. A comfortable oasis away from it all. Moderate. Northeast of Bad Orb.

Hinterzarten [11]

Park Hotel Adler   *Adlerplatz*   *tel: 07 652*
Large historic resort in peaceful setting. Comfortable rooms with period pieces. Excellent cooking. Geared to the sportsman: tennis, hunting, pool, skiing, and fishing. Expensive. Closed mid-November to late December. Fifteen miles southeast of Freiburg.

Hirschhorn [25]

Schloss Hotel   *Hirschhorn*   *tel: 1373*
Small medieval castle converted into comfortable hotel with great view. Very calm. Modest but pleasant. Moderate. Closed mid-December to mid-January. Northeast of Heidelberg.

Hochhausen [16]

Schloss Hochhausen   *Hochhausen*   *tel: 31 42*
Eighteenth-century baroque castle situated along the Road of Castles. Only twelve stylish and comfortable rooms. Set in calm park. Moderate. About fifteen miles from Heilbronn to north of Stuttgart.

Hofheim [20]

Schlosshotel Bettenburg   *Hofheim*   *tel: 306*
Comfortable rooms in a fourteenth-century castle. Pool, riding, hunting, and fishing. Inexpensive. Open March to mid-January. Exit to Geroldshofen off Frankfurt-Nürnberg autobahn.

Horb [16]

Schloss Weitenburg   *Horb*   *tel: 80 51*
Small attractive eighteenth-century castle in secluded setting. Pleasantly elegant, yet rustic throughout. Comfortable rooms, some with antiques and canopied beds. Good restaurant with venison in season. Pool, riding, fishing. Moderate to expensive. Thirty-two miles south of Stuttgart via B14.

Iphofen [20]

Zehntkeller   Iphofen   tel: 33 18
Fine inn noted for its location in a wine-growing region—owns its own vineyards. Wines can be sampled by guests. Nice rooms—most with bath. Tastefully decorated. Moderate, good value. Northwest of Nürnberg; southeast of Wurzberg.

Ising am Chiemsee [2]

Zum Goldenen Pflug   Schlossterstrasse 3   tel: 421
Large authentic hotel with lots of atmosphere and calm surroundings. Comfortable rooms with antiques. Delicious regional cooking. Ideal for riding. Expensive. Closed mid-January through February.

Isny [6]

Berghotel Jägerhof   Isny   tel: 691
Small delightful chalet in a quiet setting. Comfortable and very pleasant. Fishing. Moderate. Closed in November. Northwest of Füssen.

Jagsthausen [18]

Guesthouse in the Götzenburg   Jagsthausen   tel: 22 22
Lovely traditional inn with comfortable rooms, many with antiques and canopied beds. Known for an outstanding restaurant—excellent regional cuisine and wines. Unique plays given in the courtyard during a July-and-August festival. Lovely park and fishing. Moderate. Open mid-March to October. West of Rothenburg.

Karlshafen [47]

Hotel Zum Schwan   Conradistrasse 3-4   tel: 10 44
Small castle converted into pleasant, if modest, hotel. Comfortable. Moderately expensive. Closed December and January. North of Kassel.

Karlsruhe [17]

Schloss Hotel   Bahnhofplatz 2   tel: 31 805
Large traditional hotel with comfortable old-fashioned rooms.
Good regional cooking. Expensive.

Kassel [47]

Schloss Hotel Wilhelmshöhe   Schlosspark 2   tel: 30 061
Lovely castle converted into comfortable hotel. Varied rooms,
some with antiques. Elegant dining. Very expensive.

Kettwig [48]

***Schloss Hotel Hugenpoet   August-Thyssen-Strasse 51   tel: 60 54
Charming medieval castle surrounded by moat. Black marble
staircase, sixteenth-century fireplace, and museum pieces in
many bedrooms. Private collection of paintings. Tasteful and
very comfortable. Superb cuisine and flawless service. Tennis
and fishing. Very expensive. About twelve miles from Düsseldorf.

Kiel [67]

Conti-Hansa Hotel   Schlossgarten 7   tel: 51 244
Small modern hotel with comfortable contemporary rooms.
Views of harbor and park. Very good restaurant. Expensive.

Klais [4]

Hotel Schloss Elmau   Klais   tel: 221
Large palace hotel surrounded by forest and lakes. Geared to the
sportsman with skiing in the winter. Elegant yet informal. Moderate to expensive. Near Krün; about eleven miles from Garmisch-Partenkirchen.

Koblenz [40]

Diehls Hotel   Ehrenbreitstein   tel: 72 010
Large, pleasant riverside hotel with comfortable rooms. Moderately expensive.

Königssee [3]

Königssee Hotel   Königssee   tel: 23 43
Large attractive resort with comfortable, if simple, rooms.
Geared mainly to warm weather. Fishing. Moderately expensive.
Closed late October to early December. South of Berchtesgaden.

Schiffmeister Hotel   Königssee   tel: 30 22
Small, authentic inn with modest rooms and superb view. Moderately expensive.

Konigstein im Taunus [32]

Sonnenhof Hotel   Falkensteiner Strasse 7   tel: 50 33
Baron Rothschild's villa converted into lovely hotel in beautiful
park. Elegant throughout. Very comfortable and stylish rooms.
Excellent cooking. Very expensive. West of Frankfurt.

Konstanz [8]

Steingenberger Inselhotel   Auf der Insel 1   tel: 25 011
Large monastery converted into charming island retreat. Lovely
throughout. Very comfortable. Water sports, including fishing
and sailing. Very expensive.

Kronberg [32]

Schlosshotel Kronberg   Hainstrasse 25   tel: 37 03
A gem—delightful castle converted into luxury hotel surrounded
by wonderful woods. Traditional flavor with lots of antiques, art,
and tapestries. Very comfortable and tasteful. Superb cooking.
Golf course was favorite of Ike's. Ultraexpensive and worth it.
Only a twenty-minute drive north of Frankfurt.

Kronenburg/Eifel [44]

Schlosshotel Das Burghaus   Burgberring 4   tel: 265
Limited number of rooms in converted manor. Quite comfortable
with authentic flavor. Not luxurious. Moderate. Closed mid-
November until the end of December. Close to Belgium.

Künzelsau [16]

Schloss Stetten   Künzlsau   tel: 40 77
Romantic one-thousand-year-old castle surrounded by a moat.
Simple and rustic with a fine apartment. Plain meals. Boasts its
own ghost, riding, pool, and lots of fresh air. Moderate. Closed
late January through February. Northeast of Stuttgart.

Kyllburg [28]

Fremdenheim Schloss Malberg   Kyllburg-Eifel   tel: 2208
Nineteenth-century baroque castle perched on peaceful mountaintop with lovely gardens and view. Elegant throughout. Spacious rooms. Good restaurant. Trout fishing. Five-day minimum
stay. Expensive. North of Trier via Bitburg.

Ladenburg bei Heidelberg [25]

Zum Alten Kloster   Zehnstrasse 2   tel: 53 58
Ancient inn dating back to 1398 (once a nunnery). Charming,
rustic flavor but modern amenities. Comfortable rooms with
canopied beds. Open fireplace. Good regional cooking. Moderate. North of Heidelberg.

Lauenstein bei Ludwigsstadt [56]

Burghotel Lauenstein   Lauenstein   tel: 256
Near the castle. Peaceful and reasonably comfortable rooms. Not
luxurious. Moderate. Closed in February. Southwest of Hildesheim.

Lembeck [54]

Schlosshotel Lembeck   Lembeck   tel: 72 13
Ancient castle converted into comfortable hotel with limited
number of rooms (some with four-posters). Authentic atmosphere. Inner court, moat, and swans on the pond. Excellent
cuisine. Expensive. Near Wulfen. Southwest of Münster.

Lichtenfels [22]

Schlossgasthof Banz   Lichtenfels-Oberfranken   tel: 577
Small monastery converted into lovely quiet hotel with cozy rooms and fine restaurant. Natural setting with fishing nearby. Moderate. South of Coburg.

Lindau [8]

Lindauer Hof   Seepromenade   tel: 40 64
Small and quite comfortable hotel with lovely view to the lake and surrounding mountains. Moderate. Open Easter to mid-October. East of Konstanz at tip of lake.

Lubeck [63]

Hotel Lysia   Auf der Wallbalbinsel 1   tel: 71 077
Small modern hotel in pleasant setting. Comfortable and quiet. Tennis, riding, and golf arranged. Very expensive.

***Schabbelhaus   Mengstrasse 48-50   tel: 72 011
Patrician house converted into elegant, superb regional restaurant. One of the best in Europe with varied main dishes, such as pike in raisin sauce and fine red wines. Not to be missed if you're in the area. Expensive.

Lüdenscheid [51]

Delenkrug   Lüdenscheid   tel: 75 27
Very fine and comfortable hotel with charming overall atmosphere. Wonderful view, terrace, and pool. Good regional cooking. Moderate. Southeast of Dortmund.

Lüneburg [60]

Zum Heidkrug   Am Berge 5   tel: 31 249
Half-timbered building dating back to 1455. Historical feeling throughout with charming, small beds and delightful restaurant with delicious fish dishes (try the flounder filets) and an excellent wine cellar. Moderate.

Mainz [29]

Mainz Hilton   *68 Rheinstrasse*   *tel: 10 781*
Very large modern hotel with nice view. Comfortable. Expensive.

Mannheim [26]

Steigenberger Hotel Mannheimer Hof   *Augusta-Anlage 4-8*
tel: 45 021
Very large luxury hotel with traditional atmosphere and service.
Modern comforts. Fine dining. Very expensive.

Meersburg [8]

Hotel Drei Stuben   *Winzergasse 1-3*   *tel: 60 19*
Tiny historic inn with pleasant intimate rooms. Modest but
charming. Moderately expensive. Closed end of December to
mid-February. Opposite side of lake from Konstanz.

Miltenberg [23]

Hotel Riesen   *Miltenberg*   *tel: 36 44*
Germany's oldest inn already famous in the Middle Ages. Cozy
rooms. Rustic restaurant. Breakfast served under the roof in special room. Pool. Moderate. Southwest of Würzburg.

Munchen [1] (Munich)

Adria   *Liebigstrasse 8a*   *tel: 29 30 81*
A small, modern hotel with calm and comfortable rooms, most
with bath. No restaurant. Good value in moderate bracket. Near
the English Gardens.

An der Oper   *Falkenturmstrasse 10*   *tel: 22 87 11*
Small hotel with charming flavor. Comfortable, but compact,
rooms with no view. Excellent restaurant. Parking available.
Good location, near the opera. Expensive.

Hotel Biederstein   *Keferstrasse 18*   *tel: 39 50 72*
Small, intimate hotel in Schwabing. Near a park. Try for room
numbers 54 (piano) or 46 (double with terrace). Moderate.

Carlton   Theresienstrasse 17   tel: 28 20 61
Good value in the moderate range. Comfortable and nicely located, near shopping streets and the Alte Pinakothek. Try for
room numbers 407 or 410 (the latter is quiet).

Hotel Domus   St. Anna Strasse 31   tel: 22 17 04
Small, smart, and immaculate. Only forty-five comfortable
rooms. Good restaurant. Expensive.

Englischer Garten   Liebergesellstrasse 8a   tel: 39 76 96
In the Bohemian section known as Schwabing. Flavor of a coun-
try house. Try for room number 23. Comfortable and pleasant.
Moderate.

Königshof Hotel   Karlsplatz 25   tel: 55 84 12
Large, modern, and very comfortable hotel in an ideal location in
the center of town. Truly superb restaurant with great fish and
meat dishes in a romantic setting (ask for a table by the window). Parking in nearby garage. Refined and very expensive.

Hotel Preysing   Preysingstrasse 1   tel: 48 10 11
Quiet, hillside retreat on the outskirts of town with sixty com-
fortable, attractive rooms. Very quiet. Ask for room number 407.
Expensive. Tram number 9 takes you there.

Splendid Hotel   Maximilianstrasse 54   tel: 29.66 06
Lives up to its name. Small, gracious, and very attractive with
nicely furnished rooms, some antiques. Very quiet and friendly.
Most rooms with bath. Traditional flair and residential flavor.
Moderate to expensive.

Hotel Stachus   7 Bayerstrasse   tel: 59 28 81
Quite large hotel near the central station. Modern, simply furnished, quite comfortable. Most rooms with bath. Good value in
the moderate range.

Hotel Wapler   Schwanthalerstrasse 8   tel: 59 16 64
New, cozy, and nice. Only fifty-two rooms—ask for a quiet one.
Numbers 65 and 67 recommended. Moderate.

Münster [54]

Schloss Höhenfeld   Altenroxel 8   tel: 210
Short drive west of Münster. Small lodge converted into quite

comfortable hotel with cozy rooms. Moderate.

Schloss Wilkinhege Hotel   *Steinfurterstrasse 374*   *tel: 21 30 45*
Small authentic manor converted into comfortable hotel with modern facilities. Excellent cuisine. Castle cellar. Attractive throughout. Moderately expensive.

Münster-Handorf [54]

Hof zur Linde   *Hauptstrasse 69*   *tel: 32 322*
Modest-looking farmhouse with fantastic authentic interior. Delightful restaurant with open fireplace. Hams hanging from beams. Game dishes (owner's a hunter). Charming guest house with comfortable rooms. Surrounded by linden trees. Moderate. Northeast of Münster.

Münstertal [11]

Spielweg   *Münstertal*   *tel: 218*
Black Forest mountain retreat, very popular with Germans for long stays. On the main road, so ask for quiet rooms. Good regional cooking, hearty dishes including fine sausage and fresh fish. Indoor and outdoor pool. Moderate. South of Freiburg.

Murnau [5]

Alpenhof   *Murnau*   *tel: 10 45*
Very comfortable inn at the foothills of the Alps. Lovely, pastoral setting. Pool. Excellent restaurant. Expensive. Just north of Oberammergau.

Nagold [16]

Post   *Bahnhofstrasse 2*   *tel: 40 48*
Ancient inn in the Scholl family since 1773. Warm and friendly. Comfortable rooms in modern style. Dining in authentic, old-world atmosphere. Excellent cuisine featuring saddle of hare, stuffed leg of lamb, and braised beef. Fresh asparagus in spring, game in fall. All accompanied by fine wines. Topped off with a "romantic" coffee. Superior service. In the center of town—you can't miss the two-hundred-year-old brass sign and lovely half-timbered facade. Moderate. Southwest of Stuttgart.

Neckarmühlbach [16]

Burg Guttenberg   Neckarmühlbach   tel: 228
A few rooms in a feudal castle. Modest yet comfortable.
Medieval banquets à la fifteenth-century. Falconry flights at 11:00
a.m. and 3:00 p.m. daily except Monday (call ahead). Moderate.
Closed December to mid-February. Near Hassmersheim; fifteen
miles from Heilbronn to north of Stuttgart.

Neckarzimmern [25]

Burg Hornberg   Neckarzimmern   tel: 27 58
Ancient castle converted into comfortable, if modest, hotel.
Lovely excursions in spring and fall. Riding. Moderate. Closed
January to mid-February. Thirty miles east of Heidelberg.

Neubeuern am Inn [1]

Burghotel   Marktplatz 23   tel: 2456
Tiny, delightful inn in serene setting. Comfortable and pleasant
rooms. Good regional cooking. Moderate. Closed early
November to mid-December. Near Rosenheim, about forty miles
from Munich.

Nördlingen [20]

Hotel Sonne   Marktplatz 3   tel: 40 67
Small, historic hotel (1472) with fine rooms. Not fancy, but nice.
The Apollo astronauts stayed here. Moderately expensive.
Southwest of Nürnberg.

Nörten-Hardenberg [52]

Burghotel Hardenberg   Nörten-Hardenberg   tel: 347
Small, quiet, and comfortable inn with a calm and luxurious at-
mosphere. Lovely forest setting. Excellent regional restaurant.
Hunting, fishing, riding. Closed mid-December to mid-January.
Moderate. Sixty miles southeast of Hannover. Southwest of
Goslar.

Nürnberg [20]

Grand Hotel   Bahnhofstrasse 1-3   tel: 20 36 21
At entrance to old city. Large, fine traditional hotel. Attractive throughout. Very expensive.

Oberammergau [5]

Alois Lang Hotel   Sankt-Lukas-Strasse 15   tel: 41 41
A gem. Named after the man who played Christ in the Passion play for many years. Eisenhower stayed in this delightful inn. Small, comfortable, and surrounded by pleasant gardens. Elegant dining. An attractive rustic retreat. Very expensive. Closed late October to late December.

Oberkirch/Baden [15]

Obere Linde   Hauptstrasse 25-27   tel: 30 38
Half-timbered inn (1659) directly on the main road through town. Comfortable, nice rooms. Very fine regional cooking and wines—try the trout and almond dish. Friendly service. Moderate. South of Baden-Baden.

Obernkirchen [57]

Gasthof Schütte   Eggeweg 2   tel: 423
Small, simple rural inn with comfortable rooms and very pleasant dining. Riding and fishing arranged. Moderate. Closed late November to late December. Southwest of Hannover.

Oberstdorf [6]

Alpenhof Hotel   Zweistapfenweg 6   tel: 30 95
Small charming inn in quiet location. Comfortable and attractive throughout. Pool. Good choice in the moderate range. Closed from mid-October to mid-December. Southwest of Füssen.

Weigand Hotel   Sachsenweg 11   tel: 1084
Another comfortable retreat. Moderate. Closed in November and early December.

Oberwesel [34]

Schlosshotel Auf Schönburg   Oberwesel   tel: 81 98
Tiny, ancient castle with lovely view from bluff. Lots of antiques
and nice atmosphere in idyllic vineyard setting. Very comfortable. Superb regional cooking. Moderate. Closed December
through January. Thirteen miles from Bingen. West of Wiesbaden.

Osnabrück [55]

Gastliches Ritterhaus   Osnabrück   tel: 631
Small peaceful inn in rural setting. Quite comfortable, yet modest. Moderate to expensive.

Palmberg [1] (Ampfing)

Schloss Geldern   Palmberg   tel: 474
Comfortable inn (1860 manor) with excellent regional restaurant.
Elegant, yet rustic, décor. Moderate. Excellent base to visit mad
Ludwig's castles. Only fifty miles east of Munich.

Papenburg [59]

Hilling   Hauptkanal Links 20   tel: 22 58
A stylish and charming hotel that you would not expect to find
in such a small, hidden town. Very comfortable and elegant
throughout. Excellent cuisine geared to gourmets with an emphasis on fine fish dishes. A delight to tea drinkers with
home-made sweets. Moderate. West of Bremen.

Passau [1]

Zur Laube   Im Ort 14   tel: 21 11
Tiny ancient house converted into comfortable hotel. Lovely setting and atmosphere. Good regional restaurant. Moderate.
Closed mid-January to mid-February. East of Munich; near Austrian border.

Schloss Ort   Passau   tel: 42 11
Medieval castle converted into modern inn. Comfortable and pleasant. Not luxurious. Moderate.

Petershagen [55]

Schloss Petershagen   Petershagen   tel: 346
Fourteenth-century palace converted into pleasant, comfortable hotel. Only nine rooms. Riverside setting with tennis. Moderate. Closed mid-winter. Six miles north of Minden to the east of Osnabrück.

Rendsburg [67]

Zum Landsknecht   Schleifmühlenstrasse 2   tel: 22 394
Ancient mansion dating back to 1541 converted into historic hotel with modest yet comfortable rooms. Small. Moderate.

Reutlingen [16]

Park Hotel Friedrich List   Listplatz 1   tel: 37 454
Small, attractive inn with modern rooms and fine cuisine. Moderately expensive. South of Stuttgart.

Rheda-Wiedenbrück [55]

Ratskeller-Wiedenbrück   Markt 11   tel: 84 20
A four-hundred-year-old inn in an ancient city much as it was in medieval times. Excellent regional cooking and fine beer in authentic surroundings. Will appeal to artists. New wing with comfortable rooms. Moderate. South of Osnabrück.

Riedenburg [18]

Burghotel Schloss Eggersburg   Riedenburg   tel: 14 98
Hillside home of Bavarian dukes converted into comfortable hotel with pleasant rooms, some antiques. Family-run. Restaurant specializes in game. Riding, fishing. Moderate. West of Regensburg.

Rothenburg ob der Tauber [19]

Adam   29 Burggasse   tel: 23 64
Tiny medieval inn with atmosphere and charm. Cozy and pleasant. Lots of antiques. Good regional cooking. Expensive.

Burg Hotel   Klostergasse 1-3   tel: 22 52
Small, cheerful hotel with lovely view. Lots of authentic flavor. Quiet. Expensive.

Eisenhut Hotel   3-7 Herrengasse   tel: 20 41
Large, authentic medieval inn overlooking the city. Attractive and charming throughout. Terrace and garden. Lots of antiques. Ideal in the off-season. Expensive. Worth a detour. Closed January and February.

Goldener Hirsch Hotel   Untere Schmiedgasse 16-25   tel: 20 51
Large, elegant charmer filled with history. Quiet and comfortable. Many antiques. Excellent choice in the expensive class.

Markusturm   Rödergasse 1   tel: 23 70
This unique town is a must for all visitors. The Markusturm is an attractive inn with comfortable rooms (number 20 high up with antiques, number 18 with four-poster). Some units geared to parents with children. Tasteful dining room with quite good, if straightforward, cooking. Moderate.

Rüdesheim [33]

Waldhotel Jagdschloss Niederwald   Rüdesheim   tel: 25 15
Rustic lodge converted into comfortable hotel above the town. Good regional cooking. Moderate. Open April through October. Chairlift from Assmannshausen and cable car from Rüdesheim.

Ruhpolding [3]

Sporthotel Gästehaus Am Westernberg   Wundergraben 4   tel: 17 31
Small attractive inn with comfortable rooms—some with bath. Very quiet. Riding. Moderate. Closed end of October to mid-December. Northwest of Berchtesgaden.

Sababurg [47]

Burghotel   Sababurg   tel: 10 52
Former Hessian hunting lodge converted into tiny modest hotel with medieval atmosphere. Moderate. Closed January 15 to February 15. Of Sleeping Beauty fame. North of Kassel via Münden.

St. Goar [40]

Schlosshotel auf Berg Rheinfels   St. Goar   tel: 74 55
Comfortable castle surrounded by vineyards with attractive terrace. Not far from Lorelei. Pool. Expensive. Twenty-two miles south of Koblenz.

Salzhausen/Lüneburger Heide [60]

Josthof   Am Lindenberg 1   tel: 292
A secret hideaway—rustic, stone farmhouse with three hundred years of history. Authentic interior with crackling fireplace. Very quiet and peaceful rooms. Pool, fruit trees (May), and hikes into the heath. West of Lüneburg and an ideal excursion from Hamburg.

Schieder [57]

Schlosshotel Burg Schwalenberg   Schieder   tel: 167
Modest castle converted into isolated retreat. Simple. Only a few rooms available. Moderately expensive. Closed early January to late February. Southwest of Hannover.

Schleswig [68]

Waldhotel am Schloss Gottorf   Stampfmühle 1   tel: 23 288
Secluded mansion with comfortable, if modest, rooms. Nice serene atmosphere. Good regional cooking. Expensive.

Schliersee [2]

Schliersbergalm   Schlierberg   tel: 67 21
Small, authentic chalet in spectacular location with superb view. Comfortable if rustic. Moderate to expensive. West of Chiemsee.

Schwangau [6]

Schlosshotel Lisl   Neuschwansteinstrasse 1-3   tel: 91 06
Small, modest inn with lovely view. Very quiet. Quite expensive. Closed November to mid-December. Just northeast of Füssen.

Schwetzingen [25]

Adler Post   Schlosstrasse 3   tel: 12 006
Small, modest hotel noted for its fine regional cooking. Moderately expensive. South of Heidelberg.

Seefelden/Bodensee [8]

Fischerhaus   Seefelden   tel: 85 63
For three centuries a farmer's home. Now skillfully converted into an idyllic, lakeside retreat. Limited number of small, modern, and very comfortable rooms. Lovely pool surrounded by lawn. Fine regional restaurant serving *à la carte* only. Good pike fishing. Moderate. North of Konstanz, across the lake.

Seeon [1]

Schloss Hotel Seeon   Seeon/Chiemgau near Traunstein   tel: 92 25
Medieval monastery converted into rustic inn with comfortable rooms. Lovely setting. Moderate. Southeast of Munich.

Siegburg [45]

Weinhaus auf der Arken   Mühlenstrasse 35-37   tel: 63 840
Delightful inn dating back to 1437. Known for its intimate and tiny wine restaurant with inner court and open grill. Simple and very relaxed. Moderate.

Spangenberg [47]

Schloss Spangenberg   Spangenberg   tel: 866
Delightful lodge converted into charming hotel with limited number of rooms. Great view. Comfortable. Ideal for riding and fishing. Moderate. Closed November. Southeast of Kassel.

Stolberg/Aachen [44]

Altes-Brauhaus-Burgkeller   *Klatterstrasse 12*   *tel: 27 272*
A tiny, charming inn with twelve comfortable and cozy rooms. Lots of atmosphere throughout and a delightful restaurant serving delicious local dishes. Moderate. East of Aachen. Expanding.

Stuttgart [16]

Am Schlossgarten Hotel   *Schillerstrasse 23*   *tel: 29 99 11*
Large modern hotel in central location. Comfortable. Fine dining. Very pleasant. Expensive.

Schlosshotel Solitude   *Solitude*   *tel: 69 10 91*
Small hunting lodge converted into simple, authentic inn in the woods above town. Attractive. Moderately expensive. Closed late December to early January.

Tecklenburg [55]

Parkhotel Burggraf   *Meesenhof 7*   *tel: 425*
Small modern hotel with comfortable rooms and a fine restaurant. Expensive. West of Osnabrück.

Titisee-Neustadt [11]

Adler-Post   *Hauptstrasse 16*   *tel: 50 66*
Ancient inn located on the main street. Park on the hill in back. Comfortable, straightforward rooms (ask for one with a balcony). Tiny pool indoors. Outstanding regional restaurant offering great grills, a make-your-own-salad bar, and fine regional wines. Nice atmosphere throughout. Expensive. East of Freiburg.

Todtmoos-Weg [10]

Schwarzwald Hotel   *Todtmoos-Weg*   *tel: 273*
Completely isolated high in the mountains (you'll take a narrow hairpin road past dark pine forests). A two-hundred-year-old chalet with comfortable rooms, most with balcony. View to pastureland and sounds of tinkling cowbells in the distance. Good

local cuisine. Best speak German or Italian. Trout fishing, hiking, and skiing. Moderate to expensive. East of Badenweiler.

Travemunde [64]

Kurhaus Hotel   Aussenallee 10   tel: 40 61
Elegant old-world hotel with comfortable rooms—ask for one with sea view. Good location. Expensive. Closed October through March.

Trechtingshausen [34]

Schlosshotel Burg Reichenstein   Trechtingshausen   tel: 61 01
Medieval castle with lovely view over the Rhine. Attractive in the fall with the colors in surrounding vineyards. Very comfortable (some rooms with period pieces). Closed winter. Southwest of Wiesbaden.

Tremsbüttel [47]

Schloss Tremsbüttel Hotel   Tremsbüttel   tel: 65 44
Lovely medieval castle converted into fine traditional hotel in quiet park setting. Lots of antiques. Pleasant atmosphere. Excellent cuisine and wines. Tennis. Very expensive.

Trendelburg [47]

Burghotel Trendelburg   Trendelburg   tel: 312
Medieval castle converted into comfortable hotel with many antiques. Lovely view. Quite modest. Fishing arranged (best in spring). Riding. Moderate. Closed end of November through mid-February. Twenty miles north of Kassel.

Triberg [11]

Parkhotel Wehrle   Marktplatz   tel: 40 81
Delightful Black Forest hotel in park. Spacious and very comfort-

able. Some antiques. Pleasant atmosphere. Excellent food. Pool. Fishing arranged. Moderately expensive. Northeast of Freiburg.

Trier [28]

Porta Nigra   *Porta Nigra Platz 1*   *tel: 78 161*
Small new hotel. Nicely furnished rooms with good view. Expensive.

Vellberg [19]

Schloss Vellberg   *Vellberg*   *tel: 575*
Only a few rooms in this peaceful and pleasant castle-hotel. Ask for honeymoon room in tower. Pool, hunting, fishing. Moderate. Southwest of Rothenburg.

Wahlscheid [43]

Schloss Auel Hotel   *Wahlscheid*   *tel: 20 41*
Small ancient castle converted into lovely moated hotel in quiet park. Many antiques in bedrooms (some with four-posters). Traditional flavor. Fine restaurant. Tennis, riding, pool, and fishing. Expensive. Sixteen miles east of Bonn.

Waldeck [47]

Schloss Waldeck   *Waldeck*   *tel: 53 24*
Ancient castle lying on a timbered hill with view to lake below. Twenty comfortable rooms. Good regional cooking. Moderate. Closed November to mid-March. Southwest of Kassel.

Walldorf [25] (Heidelberg)

Landgraf   *Hauptstrasse 25*   *tel: 20 87*
Rustic, half-timbered inn outside of Heidelberg with several tiny, authentic rooms upstairs above a fine regional restaurant. Rough wooden beams and stone covered with farm implements. Hearty peasant cooking. Romantic cellar for intimate occasions. Moderate.

Wangen/Allgaü [8]

Alte Post   Postplatz 2   tel: 40 14
A small, delightful hotel in the center of town, with a nearby annex on a hill (view to Alps of three different countries). Warm and comfortable. Delicious regional dishes, such as fresh fish bathed in a unique dill sauce. Good local wines. A must for a meal. Moderate to expensive. Highly recommended. East of Konstanz.

Wassenberg [44]

Hotel Burg Wassenberg   Wassenberg   tel: 22 44
Ancient castle converted into comfortable, pleasant hotel with limited number of rooms. Nice view and setting. Fishing, riding, and tennis arranged. Moderately expensive. Twenty-five miles north of Aachen.

Weinheim/Bergstrasse [26]

Fuchs'sche Mühle   Birkenauer Talstrasse 10   tel: 25 91
Small delightful inn with lots of atmosphere. Comfortable. Moderate. Northeast of Mannheim.

Zur Pfalz   Marktplatz 7   tel: 63 320
Tiny, ancient inn with modest but comfortable rooms. Delightful. Moderate.

Weissach Tegernsee [1]

Bachmair-Weissach   Tegernseestrasse 103   tel: 64 52
Superb excursion from Munich. Wonderful lake area. Authentic hotel with very comfortable rooms, nice pool, idyllic location, and fine regional cooking—hearty, peasant fare. Sunny terrace for drinks and snacks. Tennis nearby. Thirty-five miles south of Munich (exit for Tegernsee from Salzburg autobahn).

Wiesbaden [34]

Klee Hotel   Parkstrasse 4   tel: 30 50 61
Small, modern hotel in good central location. Not at all fancy,
but pleasant with compact, comfortable rooms. Good value in
the moderate range.

Wirsberg [21]

Post   Wirsberg   tel: 888
Small, family hotel in an isolated spa town. In the center near
the church. Comfortable rooms. Very fine regional restaurant.
Moderate. Good value. North of Bayreuth.

Wurzburg [23]

Rebstock   7 Neubaustrasse   tel: 50 075
Large old palace converted into comfortable hotel. Expensive.

Zell [39]

Schloss Zell   Schloss Strasse 8   tel: 40 84
Fourteenth-century castle converted into attractive hotel with
nicely furnished rooms. Wonderful in the fall with surrounding
hotel-owned vineyards. Well-known restaurant with an accent
on fresh fish and game. Expensive. Closed mid-December to
mid-January. South of Cohen.

Zweibrücken [27]

Fasanerie   Zweibrücken   tel: 40 413
Lots of atmosphere in this small (only thirty-one rooms) inn
noted for its outstanding regional cuisine. Comfortable, with a
lovely view and terrace. Pool. Moderate. East of Saarbrücken.

WHERE TO EAT

Baden-Baden [15]

***Stahlbad**   *Lichtentaler Strasse 27*   *tel: 24 569*
Extremely well-known luxury restaurant with wonderful atmosphere and delicious French dishes. Ultraexpensive.

Bad Neuenahr [43]

Weinhaus Sankt Peter   *Rheinstrasse 26*   *tel: 34 031*
Ancient inn noted for superb regional and international cuisine. Very pleasant. Moderately expensive. Closed mid-December through February. South of Bonn.

Bamberg [21]

Weinhaus Messerschmitt   *Lange Strasse 41*   *tel: 26 471*
Formal and attractive regional restaurant with wide variety of local specialties including an unusual smoked beer. Hearty, peasant-style cooking. Quiet, relaxed, stiff. Expensive.

Berlin [70]

Aben   *103 Kurfürstendamm*   *tel: 857-3036*
Traditional atmosphere and fine international cuisine. Elegant. Expensive.

Conti-Fisch Stuben   *Sybelstrasse 14*   *tel: 885-9074*
Very pleasant restaurant serving excellent fish dishes. Expensive.

Kempinski Grill   *Kurfürstendamm*   *tel: 881-0691*
An intimate and elegant restaurant with delicious grilled meats and shellfish. Scrumptuous desserts. Very expensive but worth it.

***Maître**   *Meinekestrasse 10*   *tel: 883-8485*
Well-known luxury restaurant with superb French cuisine and fine atmosphere. Ultraexpensive.

Le Paris   *211 Kurfürstendamm*   *tel: 67 08 92*
Very pleasant French restaurant with good service and wine list. Expensive.

Ritz   *Rankestrasse 26*   *tel: 24 72 50*
Gourmet cuisine, varied and delicious. Pleasant service. Expensive.

Bernkastel [28]

Alteste Weinstube   *Am Kreuz*   *tel: 86 62*
In the family for a century and a very fine regional restaurant, with such dishes as venison and fresh fish complemented with outstanding regional wines. Some rooms for overnight guests. Moderate. Northeast of Trier.

Bonn [43]

***Chez Loup*   *Oxfordstrasse*   *tel: 63 67 77*
Charming, small restaurant with a quiet elegance. Lovely dishes such as tender lamb cooked with hints of France. Excellent choice for the businessman on an expense account.

Weinhaus Maternus   *Poststrasse 3*   *tel: 36 28 51*
Fine well-known restaurant serving varied menu. Pleasant. Moderately expensive.

Wirtshaus St. Michael   *Burnnen Allee 26*   *tel: 36 47 65*
Lots of atmosphere. Good regional and international cuisine. Moderately expensive. Door is closed; just knock.

Bremen [59]

Deutsches Haus   *Am Markt 1*   *tel: 32 10 48*
Popular restaurant well-known for regional dishes. Quite expensive.

Ratskeller   *Am Markt*   *tel: 32 79 82*
Picturesque dining with emphasis on local recipes. Six hundred varieties of wine. Good in its class. Moderately expensive.

Schnoor 2   *Schnoor*   *tel: 32 12 181*
Very appealing authentic restaurant serving delicious regional dishes. Expensive.

Cologne [45] (Köln)

***Auberge de la Charrue d'Or*   *Habsburger Ring 18-20*
tel: 21 76 10
Don't judge this one by its cover. Deceptively simple with open kitchen. Very fine menu, skillfully prepared. Expensive.

***Bremer*   *Durenerstrasse 225-227 (Lindenthal)*   *tel: 44 50 33*
Simple inn with surprisingly good regional and international dishes. Moderately expensive. Highly recommended.

Die Bastei   *Konrad Adenauer Ufer 80*   *tel: 23 61 23*
Wonderful location, providing great view in clear weather. Good international cooking. Quite expensive.

***Goldenen Pflug*   *Olpener Strasse 421*   *tel: 87 18 65/89 55 09*
Attractive regional restaurant serving delicious local specialties. Moderate. Five miles east of city center.

***La Poèle d'Or*   *An St. Agatha 27*   *tel: 24 11 12*
Intimate and delightful, with outstanding French cuisine. Very expensive.

Weinhaus Im Walfisch   *Salzgasse 13*   *tel: 21 95 75*
Popular for its regional dishes and ancient atmosphere. Expensive.

Darmstadt [30]

Weinmichel   *Darmstadt*   *tel: 26 68 22*
Delightful regional restaurant. Simple and very pleasant. Excellent regional dishes. Moderate.

Deidesheim [25]

Gasthaus Zur Kanne   *Weinstrasse 31*   *tel: 396*
Excellent off-season choice. Delicious seasonal specialties in this historic inn dating from 1374. Moderately expensive. West of Heidelberg.

Dortmund [51]

Hövelpforte   *Hoher Wall 5*   *tel: 14 28 03*
Fine regional and international cooking in pleasant authentic at-

mosphere. Expensive.

Zum Ritter   *Ostenhellweg 3*   *tel: 52 79 00*
Varied international dishes well-prepared and served with taste.
Moderate.

Durbach [15]

***Gasthaus Ritter*   *Hauptstrasse*   *tel: 74 975*
An inn with exceptional regional cooking. Expensive. Not to be
missed. Northeast of Offenburg; to south of Baden-Baden.

Dusseldorf [48]

Müllers & Fest   *Königsallee 12-14*   *tel: 32 60 01*
Nice ambience and fine international cooking. Expensive.

***Walliser Stuben*   *Aderstrasse 46*   *tel: 37 47 57*
Charming in the off-season, touristy in the summer. Nice atmosphere and quite good cooking. Expensive to very expensive.

Frankfurt [32]

***Adloff*   *Hochstrasse 27*   *tel: 29 28 67*
A tiny gem with lots of rustic charm. Very tasteful in its simplicity. A surprise for many. Excellent menu and service. Expensive.

Brückenkeller   *Schützenstrasse 6*   *tel: 28 42 38*
Authentic, with romantic dining. Fine international dishes with
quite fine wines. Expensive.

Mövenpick   *6231 Post Sulzbach*   *tel: 31 00 01*
Very pleasant, well-known restaurant serving varied menu.
Good. Expensive. Autobahn exit Frankfurt-Hoechst.

Freiburg [11]

Weinstube Zur Traube   *Schusterstrasse 17*   *tel: 32 190*
Lots of atmosphere and fine international cuisine mixed with delicious local specialties. Moderately expensive. Reserve.

Göttingen [47]

Alte Krone   Weenderstrasse 13-15   tel: 56 640
Authentic and charming restaurant with delicious French and regional dishes. Expensive. Northwest of Kassel.

Hamburg [61]

Atlantic Grill   An der Alster 72   tel: 24 80 01
The Hotel Atlantic is one of the great luxury hotels of Europe, a little too expensive to be included in this guide as a small hotel of value and charm. For a splurge, though, you may want to eat here. Very fine dining. Expensive.

***Auberge Française   Rutschbahn 34   tel: 410-2532
Tiny and rustic, just the opposite of many other recommendations in this section except for the great food. Fine French overtones. A gem. Expensive.

Restaurant Haerlin   Neuer Jungfernstieg 9   tel: 34 941
You'll find this in the Hotel Vier Jahreszeiten, another truly great luxury hotel that has been omitted from this guide because of its price tag. But dining here is a recommended splurge.

Hermann Sellmer   Grosse Elbstrasse 143   tel: 38 34 43
Wonderful view matched by the tempting fish dishes. Expensive.

Jacob   401-403 Elbchaussee   tel: 82 93 52
Historic restaurant with nice view and fine fish dishes. Very expensive. Six miles west of city center.

Peter Lembcke   Holzdamm 49   tel: 24 32 90
Popular local restaurant with varied menu. Nice fish dishes. Tends to be a bit crowded. Expensive.

Mühlenkamper Fährhaus   Hans Henny Jahnnweg 1   tel: 220-6934
Ancient and very fine restaurant, with excellent game dishes in the off-season. Good selection of wines. Expensive.

Ratsweinkeller   Grosse Johannisstrasse 2   tel: 34 41 53
Excellent international and regional cooking matched by pleasant atmosphere. Moderately expensive.

Schümanns Austernkeller   *34 Jungfernstieg*   *tel: 34 53 28*
Formal restaurant serving superb international dishes. Accent on fresh fish. Expensive.

Süllberg   Blankenese-Süllberg   *tel: 86 16 86*
Ten-mile drive west of Hamburg. Lovely setting and décor. Delicious regional specialties. Best in warmer weather. Expensive.

Weinrestaurant Ehmke   Gänsemarkt 50   *tel: 35 38 71*
Fine cooking in a pleasant restaurant with good service and tempting desserts. Expensive.

Karlsruhe [17]

Onkel Paul   Amalienstrasse 89   *tel: 22 314*
Charming rustic restaurant with fine regional cooking. Moderately expensive.

Kiel [67]

Restaurant im Schloss   80 Wall   *tel: 51 727*
Formal restaurant with fine continental cuisine. Accent on delicious fish dishes. Expensive.

Konstanz [8]

***St. Stefanskeller   Am Stefansplatz 41*   *tel: 23 566*
One of the finest restaurants in Europe. Superb cooking along the *nouvelle cuisine* lines with a wide variety of delicious specialties complemented by a select choice of fine wines. Wonderfully romantic and sensual atmosphere—fresh flowers abound. Full of antiques. Friendly, gracious service. Very expensive. Not to be missed as a splurge.

Lindau [8]

Spielbank   Oskar Groll Anlagen 2   *tel: 52 00*
Pleasant casino restaurant with good regional and international cooking. Moderately expensive.

Lubeck [63]

Schabbelhaus   48-50 Mengstrasse   tel: 72 011
Lovely old-world atmosphere matched by fine cuisine. Expensive.

Mainz [29]

Haus des Deutschen Weines   Gutenbergplatz 3   tel: 28 676
Here you can sample hundreds of varieties of wines. International dishes served as well. Relaxed. Moderate.

Munchen [1] (Munich)

***Boettner   Theatinerstrasse 8   tel: 22 12 10
Tiny French restaurant with some local dishes. Pleasant. Very expensive. Delicatessen with specialties for gourmets.

Chesa Rüegg   Wurzerstrasse 18   tel: 29 71 14
Good Swiss cuisine at moderate prices.

Ewige Lampe   Residenzstrasse 15   tel: 22 09 49
Formal restaurant with varied menu. Popular with opera crowd. Expensive.

Franziskaner und Fuchsenstuben   Perusastrasse 5   tel: 22 43 79
Typical Bavarian beerhall with garden restaurant. Fine for its class. Moderate.

***Käfer-Schänke   Schumannstrasse 1   tel: 47 60 11
Consistently a winner and always worth a try. Expensive.

Hotel der Königshof   Karlsplatz 25   tel: 55 84 12
Very fine formal dining with view to streets below. Varied and nicely prepared menu. Expensive. Be sure to ask for a window table.

Schwarzwälders   Hartmannstrasse 8   tel: 22 72 16
Authentic German flavor and dishes. Good off-season choice. Quite expensive.

Tantris   *Johann-Fichte-Strasse 7*   *tel: 36 20 61*
Truly fine French cuisine in a very pleasant restaurant that will appeal to even the most demanding tastes. Elegant atmosphere. Expensive.

Zur Kanne   *Maximilianstrasse 36*   *tel: 22 12 36*
Small and intimate restaurant serving fine regional and international dishes. Moderately expensive.

zum Klösterl   *Sankt Anna Strasse*   *tel: 22 50 86*
Good regional cooking at moderate rates. Reserve an upstairs table. Closed Sunday.

Munster [54]

Ratskeller   *Prinzipalmarkt 8*   *tel: 44 226*
Lively restaurant in the town hall. Both regional and international dishes. Nothing fancy, but fun. Moderate.

Nürnberg/Grossreuth [20]

Rottner   *Winterstrasse 15*   *tel: 61 20 98*
A must stop on a tour through this region. A charming farm converted into an authentic restaurant with wonderful atmosphere. Fresh produce from their own garden. Fresh game in season and fish pulled wriggling from their own tank. Known for asparagus in spring, gosling in summer, and game birds in fall and winter. Great selection of wines. Expensive, and worth every pfennig. A gem. Go to the center of Nürnberg, follow signs toward Stuttgart. Watch for Rothenburger Strasse to your right. Take it toward Grossreuth/Schweinau. You'll come to army barracks. Take a left across from these.

Oberbergen [11]

Schwarzer Adler   *Hauptstrasse 23*   *tel: 715*
Authentic inn with outstanding regional cuisine. Superb chicken. Expensive. Northwest of Freiburg. And worth the detour.

Oeversee [69]

Historischer Krug   Bundesstrasse 76   tel: 334
Modest, historic inn six miles south of Flensburg. Simple, comfortable rooms. Small. Moderate. Closed October through March.

Rastatt [17]

***Katzenberger's Adler   Murgtalstrasse 7   tel: 32 103
One of the great restaurants in Germany with superb regional dishes accompanied by very fine wines. Lovely, authentic décor with an appropriate romantic flair. Dishes with a hint of fantasy and reminiscent of France. Try the pike, delicious venison, and the restaurant's own cake. Everything just right—worth a special detour. Very expensive, but a must. South of Karlsruhe. Closed October.

Ravensburg [8]

***Waldhorn   Marienplatz 15   tel: 23 017
Wonderful, old-world ambience in the dining room, noted nationally for its excellent cooking and fine service. Modest rooms for an overnight stay (ask for one with a view). Moderate. Northeast of Konstanz.

Rendsburg [67]

Zum Landsknecht   Schleifmühlenstrasse 2   tel: 22 394
Simple, unpretentious inn dating back four hundred years. Elegant restaurant with excellent regional cooking. West of Kiel.

Stetten im Remstal [16]

Zum Ochsen   Stetten   tel: 61 113
A superb regional restaurant with lots of atmosphere only a short drive from Stuttgart. Colorful and authentic. Hearty, peasant fare with an emphasis on fresh meat and delicious local sausages (the restaurant makes its own). Very good local wines. Expensive. Highly recommended. East of Stuttgart.

Stuttgart [16]

Alte Post *Friedrichstrasse 43* *tel: 29 30 79*
Very attractive, with both regional and international dishes. Nice atmosphere. Expensive.

Exquisit *Karlstrasse 3* *tel: 219-8222*
Fine stop for lunch on shopping spree in the Brenninger department store. Very fine dining. Expensive.

Graf Eberhard *Eberhardtstrasse 6* *tel: 24 72 71*
Fine regional restaurant. Attractive atmosphere. Moderate.

Mövenpick *Kleiner Schlossplatz 11* *tel: 22 00 34*
Good modern restaurant with excellent meat dishes. Quite expensive.

Tinnun [69] (Island of Sylt)

Landhaus Stricker *Boy-Nielsen-Strasse 10* *tel: 31 672*
An authentic Frisian farm that has been a tavern for centuries (it dates back to 1781). Outstanding fish dishes served in rustic room with open fireplace. Moderate. West of Flensburg on the island of Sylt, known for its superb bathing beaches in summer.

Ulm [16]

Zur Forelle *Fischergasse 25* *tel: 63 924*
Historic restaurant specializing in regional cooking. Very popular and well known. Quite expensive. Southeast of Stuttgart.

Wiesbaden [34]

Mutter Engel *Bärenstrasse 5* *tel: 30 10 44*
Well-known and very popular elegant restaurant serving both international and regional dishes. Expensive.

Weissenburg [20]

Rose *Rosenstrasse 6* *tel: 20 96*
Delightful town with its own little market. The Rose is a modest hotel but well known locally for fine cuisine—only fresh produce

and fruits used. Cellar available for drinks. Moderate. South of Nürnberg.

Wurzburg [23]

Schiffbäuerin   Katzengasse 7   tel: 42 487
Rustic, with delicious fish dishes and fine regional wines. Moderate. Closed late January.

GIBRALTAR

GIBRALTAR

SPAIN

● Gibraltar

MOROCCO

WHAT TO SEE

This British outpost is just a dot on the southern coast of Spain, directly across from Tangier, Morocco. Its attractions are the view from the fourteen-hundred-foot rock, the caves inside, and the pushy Barbary apes that have become this bastion's symbol. You can get great bargains in Gibraltar, a *true* duty-free port.

WHAT'S THE WEATHER REALLY LIKE?

Very mild even in the winter. Quite hot in mid-summer, although cool ocean breezes keep it fresh.

SOME SUGGESTIONS FOR A MORE ENJOYABLE TRIP

You should really think of Gibraltar as an island, since its borders are closed to Spain. You reach Gibraltar by taking a flight on a small plane from Tangier. It dips across the ocean and lands on a small field beneath the rock. Lots of fun and very scenic. The atmosphere is thoroughly English, completely the opposite of Morocco. Very calm and not at all pushy. Still, you're expected to bargain even on the already low prices offered in the shops. Firm, but polite, bargaining works. Never leave any articles lying about when meeting the Barbary apes. They love carrying off purses, cameras, hats, and sunglasses if given the chance. You're warned not to feed the apes or get close to them, although everyone does (they often jump onto people's shoulders). You're told to declare all purchases on your return to Morocco. Only a saint would. Rarely will the Moroccan authorities bother foreign tourists. No one should carry hashish back and forth between Gibraltar and Morocco, although its use is obviously tolerated in the latter country.

WHERE TO STAY

Gibraltar

Queen's Hotel   Boyd Street   tel: 34 38
Small, charming hotel with comfortable and attractive rooms. Nice view. Modern. Fishing arranged. Inexpensive to moderate. A good budget choice.

Rock Hotel   Europa Road   tel: 34 56
Very large and modern hotel in lovely park with a magnificent view. Comfortable and attractive throughout. Good restaurant and delightful open-air grill. Pool. Moderate to expensive.

GREAT BRITAIN

GREAT BRITAIN

REGIONS

1 — Northumbria
2 — Lakeland
3 — Yorkshire
4 — Northwest
5 — West Midlands
6 — East Midlands
7 — East Anglia
8 — Thames and Chilterns
9 — London
10 — Southeast England
11 — Southwest England
12 — The Channel Islands
13 — Wales
14 — Scotland

Orkney Islands [63]
Thurso [62]
Ullapool [61]
Outer Hebrides
Island of Skye [59]
Inverness [58]
Aviemore [56]
Braemar [55]
Aberdeen [57]
Fort William [53]
Island of Mull [54]
Perth [52]
St. Andrews [51]
Glasgow [50]
Edinburgh [46]
Island of Arran [49]
Prestwick [48]
Ayr [47]
[60]

NORTHERN IRELAND
Newcastle-upon-Tyne [45]
Keswick [44]
Durham [43]
Scarborough [42]
York [41]
1
2
3
IRELAND
Liverpool [39]
Llandudno [38]
Conway [37]
Bangor [36]
Caernarvon [35]
Chester [34]
Manchester [40]
4
Nottingham [33]
6
Spalding [32]
Norwich [22]
13
Leicester [30]
Coventry [29]
Stamford [31]
Stratford-upon-Avon [28]
Cambridge [21]
Broadway [27]
5
8
7
Gloucester [26]
Oxford [20]
Pembroke [23]
Bristol [25]
Cardiff [24]
Windsor [19]
9
London [1]
Bath [18]
Canterbury [2]
11
Salisbury [10]
Winchester [4]
Rye [3]
Exeter [17]
[6]
10
Brighton [5]
Plymouth [13]
Torquay [12]
Southampton
Portsmouth [7]
Isle of Wight [8]
Penzance [15]
Falmouth [14]
Bournemouth [9]
Isles of Scilly [16]
12
Channel Islands [11]
FRANCE

0 km. 50
0 miles 50

N

CUCL

WHAT TO SEE

Going into the English countryside is like stepping into a superb antique shop surrounded by a refreshing, flower-filled garden. Here you'll find the historic inns and country manors that make the ideal base for exploring nearby towns, cathedrals, gardens, and stately castles. You'll find dozens of these listed in the sections on where to stay and eat in this chapter. Whether you decide to head north to York, west into Wales, or south to curve along the magnificent coast, you'll find that these are delightful places to stop and rest. For the uncommon traveller, excursions into the countryside from London are a must.

Still, London is the starting point for most trips. Listed below are the most popular tourist sights in town. Next to each one you'll find the nearest *tube* (subway) station. The subway system is superb, allowing you to discover the city quickly, comfortably, and at low cost. Volumes of *free* information on the city's sights await you in most hotels, as well as a small map outlining the subway system. If you're at all confused about it, ask for a short explanation from your concierge.

British Museum, Great Russell Street (W.C. 1) (Holborn tube station)

Buckingham Palace (S.W. 1)—Changing of the Guard at 11:30 a.m. (Victoria Station)

Houses of Parliament (S.W. 1) (Westminster Station)

Madame Tussaud's Waxworks, Marylebone Road (N.W. 1) (Baker Street Station)

National Gallery, Trafalgar Square (W.C. 2) (Trafalgar Square Station)

National Portrait Gallery, St. Martin's Place (W.C. 2) (Trafalgar Square Station)

St. Paul's Cathedral, Ludgate Hill (E.C. 4) (St. Paul's Station)

Tate Gallery, Millbank (S.W. 1) (Pimlico Station)

Tower of London, Tower Hill (E.C. 3) (Tower Hill Station)

Victoria & Albert Museum, Cromwell Road (S.W. 7) (South Kensington Station)

Westminster Abbey, Parliament Square (S.W. 1) (Westminster Station)

For something a little more offbeat and uncommon, why not take advantage of the smaller happenings and sights London has to offer? Here are just a few suggestions:

Go to an auction—preferably at Christie's, 8 King Street (S.W.1) or at Sotheby's, 34 New Bond Street (W. 1).

See a cricket match at Lord's in St. John's Wood or at The Oval in Kennington.

Walk along Westminster Bridge at night.

Go horseback riding in Hyde Park— call 584-9474 or 235-6846 for arrangements.

Visit Guy the Gorilla at the London Zoo.

Tour some of the city's most famous and interesting pubs. Call the Pub Information Centre, 333 Vauxhall Bridge Road (S.W. 1), tel: 228-3261.

See the Ceremony of the Keys at the Tower of London each night just before 10:00 P.M. Get written permission from the Resident Governor, Constable's Office, Tower of London, London (E.C. 3).

Put yourself into the eighteenth century with an evening stroll along Barton, Cowley, Lord, and North streets only a few blocks from the Houses of Parliament.

Take a canal trip through the middle of London by calling 286-3438 for time, boarding point, and reservations.

Stretch your legs on Cheyne Walk by the Chelsea Embankment.

Watch a trial in the Magistrate's Court opposite the Royal Opera House. You'll find it in Bow Street.

Walk through the famous Kew Gardens, at their best in the spring.

Get a great view of the city from the tall tower of the new Post Office, Maple Street (W. 1).

Visit the Stock Exchange in the financial district of The City.

See a rugby match at Twickenham Stadium or in the Old Deer Park of Kew Gardens.

Read *Sporting Life* for information on steeplechases and greyhound racing—great off-season attractions.

Go to the exhibitions held at either Earl's Court or Olympia in Kensington.

Head to the northwest corner of Hyde Park at Marble Arch on Sunday to visit the famous Speaker's Corner.

Visit a great street market, such as the one along Portobello Road (W. 11) on Wednesday and Saturday.

Take one of the walking tours by Offbeat Tours of London, 66 St. Michael's Street (W. 2), tel: 262-9752.

Visit Greenwich on the outskirts of town—get there by taking a boat in warm weather.

See Hampton Court Palace, a sixteenth-century gem with exquisite gardens, at their best in May.

If your time is limited, you'll still want to make an excursion from the capital. *Cambridge* [21], the cathedral at *Canterbury* [2], *Rye* [3] (charming inns), *St. Albans* with its Roman remains and nearby Hatfield House, *Oxford* [20], *Windsor* [19]—all are excellent excursions. Try to make them an overnight.

The uncommon traveller will want to explore some of the lesser-known sights and regions of England. Following is a brief outline of each:

Southeast England: The cathedral of *Canterbury* [2] is world-famous, but also very fine are those of *Winchester* [6] and *Chichester*. So are the mosaics of *Fishbourne* within a short drive. Highly recommended are the Sissinghurst Castle near *Cranbrook*, Knole Manor at *Sevenoaks*, the Leonardslee Gardens southeast of *Horsham*, and the Petworth House east of *Midhurst*. Delightful inns abound in this garden country, the ones in *Rye* [3] and nearby *Winchelsea* ooze atmosphere.

Southwest England: A wonderful region with Dorset, Devon, and Cornwall, each presenting a picture of rural England at its best. Outstanding sights are Stonehenge, near *Amesbury*, and the Longleat House, four miles southwest of *Warminster*. The medieval inner city of *Wells* is a must as are the impressive Roman baths in *Bath* [18]. The *Dartmoor* and *Exmoor National Parks* can be stunning in warm weather and provide days of pleasant hiking. Along the coast you'll be inspired by tiny ports such as *Polperro* or *Lyme Regis*.

Channel Islands: Off the southern coast you can visit the isolated, mild, and easygoing cluster of Channel Islands. They can be reached from either *Portsmouth* [5] or *Weymouth*. *Alderney*, a tiny island, appeals to bathers in the summer months, while *Guernsey* is noted for its quiet pace and excellent food (with French accents). *Jersey* offers inviting beaches, warm weather, and outstanding hotels.

Thames and Chilterns: Charming inns line the Thames, with a history dating back hundreds of years. Stay in one of these as you visit *Oxford* [20] famed for the Bodleian Library, *Windsor Castle* [19] and its priceless collection of art, *Woburn Abbey* (southwest of *Bedford*), and the lovely Savill Gardens near *Englefield Green*.

West Midlands: The theatre season in *Stratford-upon-Avon* [28] runs from April through November—a must. Peter Scott's world-famous bird sanctuary, *Slimbridge*, should also be on your itinerary. The Roman mosaics outside *Cheltenham* and in *Cirencester* are excellent, as are the gardens of Hidcote Manor near *Chipping Campden*. You can appreciate fine porcelain where it's made in *Stoke-on-Trent*. Try to take in some of the romantic villages of this region: *Banbury, Weobley, Bibury, Burford, Castle Combe*, and *Bourton-on-the-Water*.

East Anglia: *Cambridge* [21] with its lovely colleges draws most visitors to this region. But also delightful are the villages of *Finchingfield, Lavenham*, and *Kersey*. The cathedrals of *Ely, Bury St. Edmunds*, and *Norwich* [22] are impressive.

East Midlands: This is hunt country, the land of Tom Jones. You'll find superb scenery in the *Peak District* visited by 5 million people each year. Not as well known are the tulip fields around *Spalding* [32], colorful in late April and early May. Hikers head to the *Pennine Way* (180 miles of trails). Sightseers shouldn't miss the *Lincoln* cathedral and both Chatsworth House and Haddon Hall near *Bakewell*.

Wales: Here you can take advantage of low prices and rough terrain ideally suited to the sportsman. Fishing, pony-trekking, and hiking are all great. Two of the areas you won't want to miss are *Brecon Beacons* and *Snowdonia National Park*, to the north of *Cardiff* [24]. The excursion by rail to Devil's Bridge from *Aberystwyth* is fun. Try *Betws-y-Coed* as a base for visiting the north.

Northwest: *Chester* [34] is a gem with its half-timbered houses and cathedral. Also outstanding is Tatton Park near *Knutsford* and the September-October illuminations at *Blackpool.*

Yorkshire: The city of *York* [41] exudes a medieval mood with its nearly intact walls, fine Minster Church, and ancient inns. It's worth a long detour. Northwest of town you can visit Castle Howard, worth the excursion. Nature lovers will head immediately to the *Yorkshire Dales*, basing themselves in *Richmond.* Other attractions: *Haworth*, home of the Brontë sisters; picturesque *Thornton-le-Dale*; Fountains Abbey, south of *Ripon*; and the Rievaulx Abbey, northwest of *Helmsley.*

Lakeland: The region around *Keswick* [44] has rarely been seen by Americans. Yet, it's one of the most popular among the English themselves. Stay in resorts such as *Ambleside, Grange-over-Sands* or *Windermere.* Be sure to make reservations well in advance.

Northumbria: A mysterious region with remains of Hadrian's Wall at *Chollerford, Corbridge*, and *Housesteads* (superb). Visit the sixteenth-century castle of *Bamburgh*; Seaton Delaval Hall, northeast of *Newcastle* [45], and the authentic village of *Blanchland.* You may also want to visit *Washington* (ancestral home of the first president), the forest of *Rothbury,* and the area's famous beaches.

Scotland: *Edinburgh* [46] is easy to get to know and worth the effort. The views from the castle of Holyroodhouse, the National Gallery, St. Giles' Cathedral (small but lovely), and the Royal Botanical Gardens (best in late April and May) are the city's main attractions. Drives through the *Trossachs* and through the Great Glen from *Inverness* [58] to *Fort William* [55] are spectacular. Fishing, hunting (grouse), and golfing lure sportsmen here during the season. *Carnoustie, Dornoch, Gleneagles, St. Andrews* [51], *Troon*, and *Turnberry* challenge even the finest golf pros and have become synonymous with golf at its greatest. Popular resorts include *Aviemore* [56] and *Ballater*, while the Culzean Castle southwest of *Ayr* draws in many sightseers. In *Glasgow* [50] the outstanding attraction is the Kelvingrove Art Gallery. If you travel to Scotland in September, don't miss the Royal Tattoo in *Edinburgh* and the Royal Highland Gathering in

Braemar [55] (make reservations for these events and for hotels months in advance).

WHAT'S THE WEATHER REALLY LIKE?

Quite good from May through September, with June known as the most reliable month of all. October can be a very attractive month in which to travel, since the hardwoods are changing color at that time. November tends to be cool and misty, although you'll often be surprised by clear and crisp fall days. From December to late March you'll need an umbrella and warm clothes. Snowfalls are rare, but they do occur. April is an unpredictable month, but often quite nice.

SOME SUGGESTIONS FOR A MORE ENJOYABLE TRIP

The hotels listed in this chapter are generally quite small and very popular with the English. In London, rooms are hard to get from May through October,[1] so you must make reservations far in advance. In rural areas, the most popular months are late July and August, especially along the coast. If you arrive in London without a room reservation, go to the train station, where for a small amount you can find and reserve available rooms. It's less expensive than phoning many hotels yourself. If you don't care for organized tours, why not settle for a scenic ride on a double-decker bus, which will take you by many of the most famous sights? Recommended are number 15 (from Selfridges), number 15 on Oxford Street (marked Aldgate on the panel), number 11 east from Victoria (marked Liverpool Street on the panel), and the inexpensive city sightseeing tour that starts at the south side of Piccadilly. Theatre is relatively inexpensive and easy to get into. It's best to go to the box office to buy tickets. Don't phone. It's often possible to get in as a single by waiting for the sale of tickets at the theatre just before curtain time. You can also buy theatre tickets from agencies that charge a small commission for the service (e.g., Keith Prowse in Harrod's). Avoid theatre bars

1. Inexpensive rooms are hard to find all year long.

where drinks are tiny and very expensive. Knowledgeable theat-regoers simply go to the nearest pub. Teatime is a British tradi-tion. Why not dress up and do it right at the Ritz, Savoy, Dor-chester, Hyde Park, Brown's, Royal Lancaster, or Connaught Hotels? Tea is generally served from 3:45 p.m. to 5:45 p.m. and includes delicious pastries and sandwiches at most reasonable prices. In shops and markets you can often reduce prices with polite bargaining. If you're out late at night, you can get back to your hotel either by hailing a taxi on the street or by calling a minicab listed in the phone book. The subway closes by 1:00 a.m. Naturally, cab fares go up accordingly at this time. Getting to know rural England requires a small car. Try to leave London early Sunday morning when traffic is light. You may want to pick up Ordinance Survey maps of any region you plan to visit extensively. Large-scale (one inch to the mile) sections clearly show every detail of an area and help you find enchanting back roads.

WHERE TO STAY

Abberley [28]

Elms   Abberley   tel: Great Whitley 231
Large mansion on spacious grounds. Comfortable. Fine food. On border west of Stratford-upon-Avon.

Aberdovey [36]

Trefeddian Hotel   Aberdovey   tel: 547-2213
Small "castle" hotel on spacious grounds with comfortable rooms. Golf and fishing arranged. Moderate to expensive. Closed November to March. South of Bangor on the coast.

Aberystwyth [36]

Conrah Country Hotel   Aberystwyth   tel: Aberystwyth 79 41
Small country house renovated into a fine hotel with comfortable rooms—half with bath. Good cooking. Moderate. South of Ban-gor on the coast.

Abingdon [20]

Upper Reaches Hotel   Thames Street   tel: 43 11
Small and very attractive inn on the bank of the Thames. Good restaurant. Moderate. South of Oxford.

Alfriston [4]

Star Inn   High Street   tel: 495
Five miles north of Eastbourne. Quite small inn dating from the thirteenth century, when it was a shelter for pilgrims. Very attractive half-timbered front—lots of atmosphere in this charming town. Comfortable. Good restaurant. Moderate. East of Brighton.

Alnwick [45]

Hotspur Hotel   Alnwick   tel: 29 24
Just north of Newcastle. Victorian mansion recently converted into comfortable hotel. Moderate.

Ambleside [44]

Ambleside Park Hotel   Waterhead Center   tel: 25 71
Small comfortable hotel, recently modernized. Overlooking Lake Windermere. Moderate. Southeast of Keswick.

Amesbury [10]

Antrobus Arms   Church Street   tel: 3163
Ten miles north of Salisbury. Small and delightful English inn with garden. Antiques. Portrait collection. Home cooking. Fishing arranged on the River Avon. Moderate.

Armathwaite [44]

Dukes Head Inn   Armathwaite (Cumberland)   tel: 226
Tiny simple inn which can arrange fishing on the River Eden. Both salmon and trout fishing are good in April and May. Trout fishing is also good in September. Inexpensive. Nine and a half miles southeast of Carlisle; north of Keswick via Penrith.

Arrochar [50]

Ardmay House   Arrochar   tel: 242
A one-of-a-kind small country estate near the northeast end of
Loch Long near Loch Lomond. Situated in lovely gardens with
bright flowers and many birds. Comfortable bedrooms. Antiques. Charming dining room with an emphasis on fresh
home-cooked food. A gem. Quite expensive. Northwest of Glasgow.

Arundel [5]

Norfolk Arms Hotel   High Street   tel: 88 21 01
Small Georgian inn near the castle with elegant bedrooms—
some with bath. Lots of antiques. Good grill. Moderate. East of
Portsmouth.

Aston Clinton [20]

The Bell Inn   Aston Clinton   tel: 63 02 52
Small and charming hotel built by the Duke of Buckingham.
Atmosphere (three hundred years old) and antiques. Comforta-
ble. Lovely candlelight dining. Moderate. East of Aylesbury and
Oxford.

Auchterarder [46]

Gleneagles Hotel   Auchterarder   tel: 22 31
Thirty-nine miles northwest of Edinburgh. Huge stone building
in hundreds of acres of gardens and grounds. Spacious, tastefully furnished bedrooms in luxurious atmosphere. Excellent
cooking. Geared to the sportsman—golf, fishing, shooting, tennis. Open mid-April through October. Very expensive.

Ayr [47]

Hollybush House   Ayr   tel: Dalrymple 214
At Hollybush seven miles southwest of Ayr. Delightful country
estate set in peaceful area. Rooms furnished with antiques—a
few have bath. Birdwatching and fishing on the property with its
own gardens and woods. A gem. Moderate.

Ballater [55]

Invercauld Arms   Ballater   tel: 417
Small white hotel with authentic atmosphere. Large bedrooms—half with bath. Attractive views of the River Dee and
heather to the south. Delicious home cooking. Will arrange salmon and trout fishing along a nine-mile stretch. Fishing is best
from May to August. Hunting is also arranged on nearby es-
tates—bird shooting is excellent in November. Both fishing and
hunting should be reserved months in advance. The hotel rates
are moderate. East of Braemar.

Bamburgh [45]

Lord Crewe Arms   Front Street   tel: 243
Small old-world hotel. Quite comfortable, with fine French and
English cooking. Riding and tennis. Moderate. Open March to
mid-November. North of Newcastle.

Banbury [20]

Whately Hall   Horestair   tel: 34 51
Lovely seventeenth-century hotel near Banbury Cross. Nice
rooms—most with bath. Luxury restaurant overlooking gardens.
Quite expensive. North of Oxford.

Bassenthwaite [44]

The Pheasant Inn   Bassenthwaite   tel: 234
A few miles north of Keswick. Near the lake. Four-hundred-
year-old coaching inn with fine view. Comfortable, if limited,
number of rooms—some with bath. Traditional English cooking
in beamed dining room. Inexpensive.

Bath [25]

Francis Hotel   Queen Square   tel: 24 257
Eighteenth-century hotel in center of town. Charming and elegant. Comfortable rooms and splendid restaurant. Quite expensive.

The Priory   Weston Road   tel: 21 887
Delightful country house filled to the brim with period pieces in idyllic setting. Comfortable rooms (only fifteen). Pool. Excellent restaurant specializing in lamb dishes. Moderate to expensive. Only one mile from city center.

Beaumaris [36] (Isle of Anglesey)

Bulkeley Arms Hotel   Castle Street   tel: 415
Large historic inn with comfortable and very pleasant rooms. Good food. Fishing, tennis, and golf arranged. Moderate. North of Bangor.

Wern-y-Wylan Hotel   Beaumaris   tel: 398
Tiny attractive inn several miles from town. A few rooms with bath. Good cooking. Pool. Tennis. Moderate. Open April to October.

Ye Olde Bull's Head   Beaumaris   tel: 329
Historic inn with central location. Simple rooms—several with bath. Nothing fancy, but nice. Tennis, golf, and fishing arranged. Moderately expensive.

Beddgelert [35]

Royal Goat Hotel   Beddgelert   tel: Beddgelert 224
Small and pleasant hotel with comfortable rooms. Fishing arranged on nearby lakes. Moderate. Southeast of Caernorvon near Mt. Snowdon.

Beeston [34]

Wild Boar Inn   Chester Beeston   tel: Bunbury 309
Nine miles south of Chester. Old English building with comfortable rooms and top-notch restaurant. Expensive.

Belford [45]

Black Swan   Belford   tel: 266
Small and inexpensive country inn. Pleasant. Northwest of Newcastle; near Bamburgh.

Betws-y-Coed [36]

Gwydyr   Betws-y-Coed   tel: 217
Charming small hotel with comfortable, if old-fashioned, bed-rooms. Headquarters for the local fishing association. Moderate. Southeast of Bangor.

Craig-y-Dderwen Hotel   Betws-y-Coed   tel: 293
Quiet and comfortable riverside hotel. Rooms with bath at very reasonable rates. Fishing and pony trekking. Moderate.

Beverly [41]

Beverly Arms   North Bar Within   tel: 88 52 41
Quite large Georgian hotel with comfortable rooms. Good res-taurant. Moderate. Twenty-nine miles south of York.

Bexhill-on-Sea [3]

Cooden Beach   Bexhill-on-Sea   tel: Cooden 22 81
Small seaside hotel with comfortable rooms. Close to the scene of the Battle of Hastings. Good seafood. Golf and trout fishing in the region. Moderate. On the coast southwest of Rye via Hastings.

Bibury [27] (Cotswolds)

The Swan   Bibury   tel: 204
Vine-covered coaching inn on the River Coln. Exquisite location. All rooms modernized. Gardens. Fishing on private water. Mod-erate. Nine miles south of Broadway.

Bideford [17]

Portledge Hotel   Bideford   tel: Horns Cross 262
At Fairy Cross. Small and attractive seventeenth-century manor in spacious grounds. Comfortable bedrooms—most with bath. Superbly furnished. Excellent restaurant. Expensive. Closed in the winter. Northwest of Exeter on the coast.

Blanchland [45]

Lord Crewe Arms   Blanchland   tel: 251
Medieval priory converted into a simple hotel with bar in the ancient cellar. Sports its own ghost, Dorothy, who may ask you to deliver a message to her brother. Lots of atmosphere. Good restaurant. Fly fishing. Inexpensive. Eleven miles south of Hexham. West of Newcastle.

Borrowdale [44]

Lodore Swiss Hotel   Borrowdale   tel: Borrowdale 285
Four miles south of Keswick, on Lake Derwentwater. Quite large hotel in spacious grounds. Very comfortable. Excellent Swiss cuisine. Tennis, pool, and fishing. Moderate.

Bouley Bay, Jersey [11]

Water's Edge Hotel   Bouley Bay   tel: 777
Near St. Helier. Lovely hotel with view to the bay. Comfortable rooms—most with bath. Very good food. Pool. Expensive. Open April through September.

Bournemouth [9]

Carleton Hotel   East Overcliff   tel: 22 011
Large—one of England's finest hotels with gorgeous view. Very comfortable. Excellent restaurant. Pool. Expensive.

Bourton-on-the-Water [26] (Cotswolds)

The Old New Inn   High Street   tel: 20 467
Small and delightful English inn in the "Venice of the Cotswolds." Popular miniature village in the garden. Good food. Friendly bar. Moderate. North of Bibury. About eighteen miles east of Cheltenham (which is east of Gloucester).

Bowness-on-Windermere [44]

Old England Hotel   Bowness-on-Windermere   tel: 24 44
One mile south of the town of Windermere. Renovated lakeside

hotel—now almost luxurious. Lovely gardens. Quite large, with spacious and comfortable bedrooms. Southeast of Keswick.

Bradford [40]

Victoria Hotel   Bridge Street   tel: 28 706
Quite small and comfortable hotel—most rooms with bath. Quite good cooking. Moderate. West of Leeds; northeast of Manchester.

Braemar [55]

Invercauld Arms   Aberdeen Road   tel: 605
Ancient stone hotel in lovely scenic setting. Many large bedrooms. Some excellent suites. Golf, Tennis, and fine fishing. Shooting arranged as well. Expensive.

Mar Lodge   Braemar   tel: 216
Once a hunting lodge, the hotel is still a sporting center on the River Dee. Surrounded by thousands of acres of grounds. Comfortable with many antiques. Excellent cuisine. Geared to fishing (salmon) and hunting (grouse and deer). Open June to October. Very expensive.

Brecon [24]

Castle of Brecon Hotel   The Avenue   tel: 29 42
Small hotel adjoining sixteenth-century castle with lovely view. Comfortable rooms—a few with bath. Good food and fine wine. Moderate. North of Cardiff.

Brighton [4]

The Royal Crescent   100 Marine Parade   Seafront   tel: 66 311
Fine Victorian hotel with comfortable rooms and fine dining. Expensive.

Broadway [27] (Cotswolds)

Lygon Arms   Center High Street   tel: 22 55
Sixteenth-century inn on fifteen acres of grounds. Quite large

and luxurious, with attractive rooms and antiques. Very romantic. Good international cuisine and service. Delightful fireplace. Tennis. Expensive.

Burford [20]

Bay Tree Inn   Sheep Street   tel: 31 37
Tiny and exceptionally fine four-hundred-year-old inn with refreshing garden. **Beautifully furnished bedrooms.** Excellent service. Very good cooking. Moderate. West of Oxford.

Lamb Inn   Sheep Street   tel: 31 55
Peaceful fifteenth-century stone inn with fourteen rustic bedrooms—some with bath. Oak furniture and cozy atmosphere. Good cooking. Moderate.

Bury St. Edmunds [21]

Angel Hotel   Angel Hill   tel: 39 27
Attractive ancient inn made famous by Dickens. Quite large and recently renovated. Many comfortable rooms. Good restaurant. Moderate. East of Cambridge.

Callander w50]

Roman Camp Hotel   High Street   tel: 30 003
Built on the site of a second-century Roman camp, the seventeenth-century hunting lodge with pink turrets has been converted into a superb hotel on thirty acres of grounds. Charming bedrooms with many antiques—most with bath. Famous restaurant. Good fishing. Expensive. Open April to mid-September. North of Glasgow.

Cambridge [21]

Garden House Hotel   Granta Place   tel: 63 421
Modern hotel on spacious grounds near the river. Large and very comfortable rooms. Fine restaurant with excellent wine cellar. Pool. Golf nearby. Expensive.

Canterbury [2]

Slatters Hotel   St. Margaret's Street   tel: 63 271
Older hotel recently revamped with comfortable studio rooms.
Fine cooking. Quite expensive.

Carlisle [44]

Crown & Mitre   English Street (Cumberland)   tel: 25 491
Old English hotel near the cathedral. Large and quite pleasant.
Arranges fishing on the Esk River—ask for a spot near
Longtown. Moderate. North of Keswick.

Castle Combe [25] (Cotswolds)

Manor House Hotel   Castle Combe   tel: 782-206
Attractive manor on extensive grounds. Modern rooms—most
with bath. Trout fishing. Moderate. One of the best in the region. Five and a half miles northwest of Chippenham; east of
Bristol.

Castle Donington [33]

Donington Manor   Castle Donington   tel: 81 02 53
Small elegant coaching inn near East Midlands airport. Very
comfortable. Excellent restaurant. Quite expensive. Southeast of
Nottingham.

Chagford [17]

Mill End Hotel   Sandy Park   tel: Chagford 22 82
Mill converted into comfortable hotel with moderately priced
rooms. Good value. Closed November to March. Three miles
northwest of Moreton Hampstead; southwest of Exeter.

Chapel-en-le-Frith [40]

Kings Arms   Chapel-en-le-Frith   tel: 21 05
Four-hundred-year-old inn with comfortable, but rustic, rooms.
Not fancy, but fun. Moderate. North of Buxton. Southeast of
Manchester.

Cheltenham [27] (Cotswolds)

Cotswold House   The Square   tel: 84 03 30
Tiny, delightful hotel three miles from Broadway. Charming
garden in rear. Ask for "C. Aubrey Smith" room. Moderate.

Chester-le-Street [45]

Lumley Castle Hotel   Lumley Castle   tel: 588-5326
Medieval castle not far from the Lambton Lion Park. Quite comfortable rooms with bath. Known for its "medieval banquets"—
lively. Pool. Quite expensive. South of Newcastle-upon-Tyne.

Chichester [5]

Dolphin & Anchor   West Street   tel: 85 121
Fine hotel close to the cathedral and market cross. Both new and
old rooms—ask for those in rear. Good restaurant. Moderate.
East of Portsmouth.

Chipping Norton [20]

White Hart Hotel   High Street   tel: 25 72
Tiny fourteenth-century inn on Main Street. Comfortable. Good
cooking. Moderate. Northwest of Oxford.

Churt [1]

Frensham Pond   Churt   tel: Frensham 31 75
Six miles south of Farnham. Fine small hotel overlooking pond.
Beautiful rooms. Very good restaurant. Quite expensive. South-
west of London.

Cirencester [26] (Cotswolds)

King's Head   Market Place   tel: 33 21
Large inn, some of which dates back to the seventeenth century.
Antiques. Curios. Moderate. Closed January through March.
Southeast of Gloucester.

Cockermouth [44]

Trout Hotel   Main Street (Cumberland)   tel: 35 91
Small and intimate hotel with attractive restaurant. Fishing can be arranged on the Derwent. Moderate. Northwest of Keswick.

Cornhill-on-Tweed [46]

Tillmouth Park   Cornhill   tel: Coldstream 22 55
Magnificent mansion on spacious grounds at the junction of Till and Tweed Rivers. Comfortable—Sir Walter Scott room the best. Seven miles of trout and salmon fishing. Moderate. Next to town of Coldstream. Southeast of Edinburgh near Kelso.

Corwen [34]

Owain Glyndwr   Corwen   tel: 21 15
West of Llangollen. A picturesque fourteenth-century inn once voted the Welsh Pub of the Year award. Very fine cooking. Geared to the sportsman—fishing, shooting, climbing, and so on, all arranged. Southwest of Chester.

Cullen [58]

Cullen Bay Hotel   Cullen   tel: 432
Rustic hotel east of Elgin geared to the sportsman—fishing and hunting arranged. Fine French cuisine. Nice location and view of sea. Moderate. East of Inverness on the coast.

Dalmally [50]

Dalmally Hotel   Dalmally   tel: 249
Modern hotel with small neat rooms. A great spot for fishermen since the hotel owns six and a half miles of rights. Salmon fishing on the Orchy is quite good. Trout fishing on Lake Awe. Moderate. Near Tyndrum between Glasgow and Fort William.

Dedham [21]

Maison Talbooth   Stratford Street and St. Mary Road
tel: Dedham 32 23 67
Lovely atmospheric Victorian manor on the river. Ten nicely furnished rooms. Superb food in nearby converted cottage. Expensive. Southeast of Cambridge; near Colchester.

Dedham Vale Hotel   Gun Hill   tel: 22 73
Charming home near the Stour River with lovely lawn. Pleasant bedrooms—some with bath. Good food. Moderate.

Dirleton [46]

Open Arms   Dirleton   tel: 241
Twenty-one miles east of Edinburgh. Stone cottage in the country with view to medieval castle. Quiet, charming, and thoroughly Scottish. Off the beaten track. Ideal for golfers. Moderate.

Dorking [1]

Burford Bridge   Box Hill   tel: 45 61
Two miles north of town on Highway A24. Small and famous hotel with comfortable rooms and fine restaurant. Moderate. South of London.

Dornoch [61]

Royal Golf Hotel   Grange Road   tel: 283
Traditional hotel—fully modernized. Comfortable rooms—most with bath. Good cooking. Great golfing. Lake and sea fishing. Tennis. Shooting arranged. Open April through October. Moderate. East of Ullapool on opposite coast.

Downton [10]

Bull Hotel   Downton   tel: 20 374
Eight miles south of Salisbury. Coaching inn with three centuries of history. Seventeen old-fashioned rooms—some with bath. Good English cooking. Geared to fishermen, who can try their luck in the River Avon. Moderate.

Droitwich [20]

The Chateau Impney Hotel   Droitwich   tel: 44 11
Luxurious and quite large French château on extensive grounds.
River restaurant. Tennis and riding. Expensive. South of Birmingham. West of Coventry.

Raven Hotel   St. Andrews Street   tel: 22 24
Sixteenth-century manor in a central location. Fun. Moderate.

Drymen [50]

Buchanan Arms Hotel   Drymen   tel: 588
Small, fresh country inn with charming, comfortable rooms. Excellent cooking. Moderate. A gem. Northwest of Glasgow.

Dulverton [17]

Carnarvon Arms   Dulverton   tel: 302
Comfortable old country house with some fine antiques. Trout and salmon fishing, fairly good food. Moderate. Two miles south of town on B3222. North of Exeter.

Dunkeld [52]

Dunkeld House Hotel   Dunkeld   tel: 243
Charming country mansion on the River Tay in the picturesque town of Dunkeld. Spacious grounds. Large rooms—most with bath. Ask for one on the river. Very peaceful. The corner room (Number 8) may still be the best. Good cooking. Excellent fishing for both salmon and trout. Expensive. Open January through October. Northwest of Perth.

Dunster [17]

Luttrell Arms   High Street   tel: 393
Formerly the guest house of the local monastery. Now a hotel with twenty-one rooms—lots of atmosphere. Room number 12 is one of the best. Fifteenth-century Gothic hall. Closed in the winter. North of Exeter on the coast.

Durham [43]

Royal County Hotel   *Old Elvet*   *tel: 66 821*
Large, newly modernized hotel in central location. Comfortable.
Quite expensive.

Ramside Hall   *Belmont*   *tel: 65 282*
Three miles northeast of Durham. Small nineteenth-century
home surrounded by park. Quite comfortable. Moderate.

East Grinstead [1]

Gravetye Manor Hotel   *Turners Hill*   *tel: Sharpthorne 567*
South of Godstone on Highway 22. Charming small hotel and
country club—a gem in both spring and fall because of its lovely
surroundings. Luxurious bedrooms—most with bath. Very good
restaurant. Trout fishing. Moderate to expensive. Only thirty
miles from London.

Edenhall [44]

Edenhall Hotel   *Edenhall (Cumberland)*   *tel: Langwathby 454*
Small and rustic inn, which can set up fishing on the Eden.
Moderate. Three and a half miles northeast of Penrith; north of
Keswick.

Edinburgh [46]

Ellersly House   *Ellersly Road*   *tel: 337-6888*
Noncentral location for a fine small hotel in charming mansion.
Comfortable and quiet. Good dining. Great choice in the moder-
ate class.

Minto Hotel   *17-18 Minto Street*   *tel: 667-1534*
Small, charming hotel with traditional flavor. Comfortable
and functional—noncentral location. Another fine choice in the
moderate class.

Hotel Howard   *Great King Street 32*   *tel: 556-1393*
A series of townhouses converted into a modest, little hotel with
comfortable rooms. Many antiques. Not for the stuffy, but dignified nonetheless. Moderate.

Egham [19]

Great Fosters   Stroude Road   tel: 38 22
Small hunting lodge converted into hotel in lovely garden setting. Superb atmosphere. Comfortable. Moderate. Near Windsor.

Evesham [28]

The Crown Hotel   Bridge Street   tel: 61 37
Attractive and tiny hotel geared to sportsmen—fishing, golf, pony trekking, shooting, and tennis. Moderate. Southwest of Stratford-upon-Avon.

Exeter [17]

Royal Clarence Hotel   Cathedral Yard   tel: 58 464
Large eighteenth-century hotel near the cathedral. Comfortable rooms—half with bath. Nice restaurant. Moderate.

Exford [17]

Crown Hotel   Exford   tel: 243
Sixteenth-century stone inn with comfortable rooms. Great for the sportsman—hiking, riding, and trout fishing. Moderate. Closed in the winter. Seven miles northwest of Dulverton; north of Exeter.

Falmouth [14]

Royal Duchy   Cliff Road   tel: 68 541/31 30 42
Small comfortable hotel on the seafront. Hanging gardens. Famous for fine seafood. Moderate.

Meudon Hotel   Mawnan Smith   tel: Mawnan Smith 541
Small renovated mansion with lovely subtropical gardens. Comfortable rooms with fine view. Near the beach. A charmer. Moderate.

Fordwych [2]

George & Dragon   *Fordwych*   *tel: Canterbury 71 06 61*
Tiny, picturesque village inn on the River Stour. Nice old restaurant with home cooking. Inexpensive. Three miles northeast of Canterbury.

Fort William [53]

Inverlochy Castle   *Fort William*   *tel: 21 77*
Inverlochy Castle at the foot of Ben Davis only several miles from Fort William is a dream. Built in 1863, the elegant manor has been converted into a stylish hotel with traditional flair. Near a lake in a serene setting at its best in spring when the rhododendrons are in full bloom. Inverlochy offers comfortable rooms furnished in authentic style with priceless antiques. The candlelight dining is simply out-of-this-world (Mrs. Shaw is one of England's finest cooks). The service is formal, friendly, and impeccable. This is one of Scotland's great hotels, ideal for a retreat or an overnight. Fishing and hunting can be arranged. Very expensive and worth it.

Glasgow [50]

Tinto Firs Hotel   *470 Kilmarnock Road*   *tel: 637-2353*
Small, quiet residential hotel a few miles from city center. Nice. Moderate.

Glastonbury [25]

George & Pilgrims Inn   *High Street*   *tel: 31 39*
Tiny attractive medieval inn. Good home cooking. Moderate. Book in advance. Southwest of Bristol.

Glyndyfrdwy [34]

Berwyn Arms   *Glyndyfrdwy*   *tel: 210*
Charming inn with old fashioned bedrooms. Home-cooked meals. An angler's delight on the River Dee with private stretch for salmon and trout fishing. Moderate. West of Llangollen. Southwest of Chester.

Glencoe [53]

King's House Inn   Glencoe   tel: Kingshouse 259
Small historic inn near the site of the infamous Glencoe mas-
sacre. Comfortable if rustic. Good cooking. Skiing and fishing.
Moderate. Twelve miles southeast of town. South of Ft. William.

Godstone [1]

White Hart   Godstone   tel: 25 21
Tiny inn licensed since the reign of Richard II. Only a few
rooms—Queen Victoria once stayed here. Good English food.
Moderate. Closed in the winter. South of London.

Goudhurst [3]

Star & Eagle   Goudhurst   tel: 338
Tiny fourteenth-century inn with comfortable rooms. Candlelight
dining. A gem in the spring when the orchards are in blossom.
Moderate. Eleven miles northwest of Rye.

Grange-over-Sands [44]

Grange Hotel   Grange-over-Sands   tel: 36 66
Old-fashioned homelike hotel with limited number of rooms—
some with bath. Good service. Moderate. South of Keswick on
southern coast; near Ulverston.

Grantham [32]

Angel & Royal   High Street   tel: 58 16
Medieval inn where King John held court in 1213. Rustic. Moderate. Northwest of Spalding.

Grantown-on-Spey [58]

Craiglynne Hotel   Grantown   tel: 25 97
Quite large and attractive hotel with home flavor. Comfortable—a few rooms with bath. Excellent food. Moderate. Southeast
of Inverness.

Palace Hotel   *High Street*   *tel: 27 06*
Comfortable hotel geared to fishermen—special courses given in April and May. Moderate.

Grant Arms Hotel   *The Square*   *tel: 25 26*
Traditional atmosphere in a mansion converted into a comfortable hotel on spacious grounds. Tennis, fishing, and golf in the area. Moderate. Open March through October.

Grasmere [44]

Swan Hotel   *Highway 391*   *tel: 223*
Small attractive coaching inn. Quite comfortable. Moderate. Closed mid-November to mid-March. Southeast of Keswick to northwest of Ambleside.

Michael's Nook Country House Hotel   *Grasmere*   *tel: 496*
Tiny hotel with only a few rooms and one of the better restaurants in town. Moderate.

Gullane [46]

Greywalls   *Duncur Road*   *tel: 21 44*
Eighteen miles east of Edinburgh. Superb country house with gardens. Comfortable rooms. Antiques. Golf arranged. Moderate. Open April to October.

Hamble [7]

Hamble Lodge Country Club   *Hamble Green*   *tel: 32 51*
Four miles east of town. Small attractive inn with grounds and view to the river. Comfortable. Good restaurant. Moderate. Four miles south of Southampton.

Harrogate [41]

Old Swan Hotel   *Swan Road*   *tel: 40 51*
In the town center but actually a secluded country house. Large and very attractive. Famous for its food and wine cellar since 1700. Tennis. Golf. Quite expensive. Sixteen miles west of York.

Haslemere [5]

Lythe Hill Hotel   Petworth Road   tel: 51 251
One and a quarter miles east of town on Highway B2131. Four-teenth-century farmhouse with deluxe suites. Superb French cooking. Tennis. A gem. Expensive. Northeast of Portsmouth.

Hastings [3]

Beauford Park Hotel   Battle Road   tel: 51 222
North of the battleground on Highway A2100. Small eigh-teenth-century country house with fine restaurant. Pool. Riding. Moderate. East of Brighton.

Hay-on-Wye [24]

Three Cocks   Hay-on-Wye   tel: Glasbury 215
Pleasant inn with good French cuisine and fresh produce. Mod-erate. Southwest of Hay. North of Cardiff via Brecon.

Helmsley [41]

Black Swan Hotel   Market Place   tel: 92 466
Ancient hotel with a four-hundred-year history. Quite small and pleasant. Comfortable. Tea garden. Moderate. North of York in Moors.

Henley-on-Thames [19]

Red Lion Hotel   Hart Street   tel: 21 61
Small ancient coaching inn overlooking the river. Comforta-ble—varied rooms with lovely view. Good cooking. Quite ex-pensive. West of Windsor.

Little White Hart   Henley   tel: 41 45
Tiny delightful inn overlooking the Thames. Comfortable. Fun. Moderate.

Hertingfordbury [1]

White Horse Inn   Hatfield Road   tel: 67 91
Small attractive inn two miles from town. Intimate. Comfortable.

Nice setting and fine dining. Quite expensive. One and a half miles west of Hertford to north of London.

Hexham [45]

Hadrian Hotel   Wall   tel: Humshaugh 232
Near St. Wilfred's Abbey at Hexham at Wall. Built in 1740 with the stones from Hadrian's Wall. Simple but comfortable. English menu and bar with collection of arms. Moderate. West of Newcastle.

Hindon [10]

The Lamb   Hindon   tel: 225
Fourteen homey and pleasant rooms. Compact, but comfortable. Lots of atmosphere. Very good food. Moderate. Near Salisbury.

Honiton [17]

Deer Park Hotel   Honiton   tel: 20 64
Two and a half miles west of town on A30. Small eighteenth-century manor in lovely grounds. Comfortable rooms—most with bath. Fair restaurant. Three miles of trout fishing. Moderate. Closed December to mid-March. Northeast of Exeter.

Horton-cum-Studley [20]

Studley Priory   Horton-cum-Studley   tel: Stanton St. John 203
Six miles northeast of Oxford. Benedictine convent converted into attractive manor, now a small hotel with fine bedrooms and good cooking. Moderate.

Huntly [57]

Huntly Castle Hotel   Huntly   tel: 26 96
Large gray castle with modest rooms. Geared to fishermen. Open April to October. Moderate. Northeast of Aberdeen.

Hurley [19]

Ye Olde Bull   Hurley   tel: Littlewick Green 42 44
In the center of town. Once a guest house to a Benedictine monastery. Built in 1135, it may well be the oldest inn of the country. Attractive garden atmosphere. Nine comfortable rooms. Fine restaurant. Moderate. Near Maidenhead on the Thames. Northwest of Windsor.

Ilkley [40]

Craiglands Hotel   Ilkley   tel: 35 21 81
Large old hotel with new wing set in nine acres of park and gardens. Fine cuisine and wine cellar. Quite expensive. Northwest of Leeds. Northeast of Manchester.

Instow [17]

Commodore   Marine Road   tel: 347
Very comfortable. In excellent location overlooking the estuary. Most rooms with bath. Friendly service. Very fine food. Moderate. Two and a half miles northeast of Bideford; to northwest of Exeter.

Isles of Scilly [16]

The Island Hotel   Tresco   tel: (07 204) 883
A lovely little hotel on the carless eight-hundred-acre island of Tresco. Beautiful beaches and subtropical gardens. Comfortable bedrooms with fine view. Nice restaurant with good service. Moderate.

Isle of Wight [8]

Farringford House   Isle of Wight   tel: Freshwater 2500
At Freshwater near Yarmouth. Gothic building with some cottages. Quiet. Candlelight dining. Pool, tennis, and riding. Moderate. Once the home of Tennyson. Special off-season rates for writers.

Kelso [46]

Ednam House   Bridge Street   tel: 21 68
Forty-three miles southeast of Edinburgh. Georgian manor converted into friendly inn with attractive lawns and gardens sweeping to the River Tweed. Comfortable rooms—ask for one in the Ednam wing. Good food. Friendly service. Fine early spring (February to April) and late fall (October to November) salmon fishing. Note that fishing on the upper Hendersyde water of the Tweed is considered among the best in the world.

Kendal [44]

Heaves Hotel   Kendal   tel: Sedgwick 269
Small charming country mansion four and a half miles south of Kendal. Lovely garden. Quite comfortable—limited number of rooms with bath. No bar. Moderate. Southeast of Keswick.

Keswick [44]

Keswick Hotel   Center Station Road   tel: 72 020
Old Victorian hotel with gorgeous mountain views and the lake only a half-mile away. Quite large in acres of gardens. Good Swiss cuisine. Moderately expensive.

Kildrummy [55]

Kildrummy Castle Hotel   Kildrummy   tel: Kildrummy 232
Elegant tiny hotel with traditional touches. Fine antiques. Charming garden. Moderate. Open March to October. North of Ballater and Aboyne. North of Braemar.

Kingham [20]

The Mill Hotel   Kingham   tel: Kingham 255
Five miles south of Chipping Norton. Old stone mill converted into delightful inn. Nicely furnished rooms. Fine country cooking. Fun tavern. Moderate. Northwest of Oxford.

Kingsbridge [17]

Buckland-Tout-Saints Hotel   Goveton   tel: 25 86
Small Queen Anne mansion two miles from Kingsbridge between Salcombe and Totnes. Lovely garden atmosphere. Comfortable. Good restaurant. Golf, tennis, and riding. Moderate. Open May to late October. South of Exeter.

King's Lynn [22]

Duke's Head   Market Place   tel: 49 96
Large Renaissance inn—recently renovated. Nice rooms. Moderate. West of Norwich.

Kinross [46]

Green Hotel   North Road   tel: 34 67
Small modernized coaching inn with comfortable rooms. Fishing, tennis, pool. Expensive. Northwest of Edinburgh.

Kirkoswald [44]

Featherstone Arms   Kirkoswald (Cumberland)   tel: Lazonby 284
Tiny simple inn geared to fisherman (fishing on the Eden). Inexpensive. Northeast of Penrith. Northeast of Keswick.

Kirkwall [63] (Orkney)

Queen's Hotel   Kirkwall   tel: 22 00
Tiny inn with rustic but comfortable rooms. For the way out explorer. Inexpensive.

Knaresborough [40]

The Dower House   Bond End   tel: 376-3302
Tiny historic inn with comfortable bedrooms. Very good food. Moderate. Northeast of Harrogate. Northeast of Manchester via Leeds.

Kyle of Lochalsh [59]

Lochalsh Hotel   Kyle   tel: Kyle 42 02
Attractive hotel in lovely location near ferry to Isle of Skye.
Comfortable and modern rooms. Superb food. Nice. Moderate.

Lacock [25]

Sign of the Angel   Lacock   tel: 230
In charming historic village (National Trust). Small, authentic
inn. Comfortable. Moderate. East of Bristol.

Lanreath [13]

Punch Bowl Inn   Lanreath   tel: 218
Tiny and charming sixteenth-century inn—wonderful atmosphere in this ancient Cornish village. Fourposter beds. Good regional cooking. Moderate. Four miles north of Polperro, to east
of Plymouth.

Lavenham [21]

Swan Hotel   High Street   tel: 477
Fifteenth-century inn of great character in the heart of Constable
country. Comfortable rooms. Good cooking. Winter concerts.
Quite expensive. South of Bury-St. Edmunds; east of Cambridge.

Ledbury [26]

Feathers Hotel   Town Center   tel: 26 00
Tiny ancient inn with half-timbered exterior. Inside: old beams,
copper utensils, and antiques. Comfortable in rustic way. Moderate. Northwest of Gloucester.

Lerwick [57] (Shetland Island)

Queen's Hotel   Lerwick   tel: 726
Eighteenth-century stone hotel near the sea with quite comforta-
ble rooms. Rather charming. For the explorer. Inexpensive.
North of Orkneys. Accessible from Aberdeen on eastern coast.

Lewes [4]

White Hart Hotel   High Street   tel: 46 76
Small, ancient coaching inn. Comfortable rooms—half with bath.
Very fine restaurant. Moderate. Northeast of Brighton.

Lincoln [33]

The White Hart Hotel   Lincoln Center (Bailgate)   tel: 26 222
Fine old traditional hotel near the cathedral. Comfortable rooms.
Lots of antiques. Good cooking. Quite expensive. Northeast of
Nottingham.

Llanarmon [34]

Hand Hotel   Llanarmon   tel: 666
Tiny sixteenth-century inn with rustic rooms in idyllic setting.
Fishing and pony trekking arranged. Moderate. Southeast of
Llangollen. Southwest of Chester.

Llangollen [34]

Hand Hotel   Bridge Street   tel: 77 554/86 23 03
Small and charming eighteenth-century inn overlooking the
River Dee. Comfortable rooms—some with bath. Good cooking.
Salmon and trout fishing arranged. Golf. Moderate. Southwest
of Chester.

Llanrhaeadr [38]

Bryn Morfydd Hotel   Llanrhaeadr   tel: Llanynys 280
Small country inn with spacious grounds and comfortable
rooms. Fine cooking. Will arrange tennis, golf, fishing, and
shooting. Moderate. Near Denbigh southeast of Llandudno.

Llyswen [26]

Griffin   Llyswen   tel: 241
Tiny fifteenth-century inn a few miles northeast of Brecon. Attractive and rustic rooms. Moderate. West of Gloucester.

Lochearnhead [50]

Lochearnhead Hotel   Lochearnhead   tel: 237
Delightful home converted into fine hotel overlooking the Loch Earn. Nice home cooking. Tennis, shooting, golf. Moderate. North of Glasgow.

Loch Lomond [50]

Lomond Castle   Loch Lomond   tel: Arden 247
Comfortable hotel in superb setting with fine view. Excellent country cooking. Tennis and fishing. Moderate. North of Glasgow.

Long Melford [21]

Bull Hotel   Long Melford   tel: 494
One of the great old (1450) inns of the area. Timbered bedrooms. Interesting dining room. Good food. Moderate. Northwest of Colchester; near Lavenham; to southeast of Cambridge.

London [1]

Basil Street Hotel   Basil Street (S.W. 3)   tel: 730-3411
Nice location behind Harrod's. Small, traditional hotel with comfortable rooms. English atmosphere. Good value in the expensive class. Ideal for women travellers.

Blake's   33-35 Roland Gardens (S.W. 7)   tel: 373-2364/370-6701
Tiny, informal, and charming hotel—functional and very English. Smart, quiet, and quite sophisticated. Good for businessmen who shy away from larger commercial hotels. Moderate.

Capital Hotel   22-24 Basil Street (S.W. 3)   tel: 589-5171
Nice location behind Harrod's. Small luxury hotel with very comfortable rooms. Tiny, chic, and very fine restaurant. Expensive.

Casserly Court   125-127 Gloucester Terrace (W. 2)   tel: 262-3161
Small and intimate Victorian hotel in good location. Warm, not fancy. Modest comfortable rooms. Good restaurant. Moderate.

Duke's Hotel   *35 St. James Place (S.W. 1)*   tel: 493-2366
Tiny, charming hotel. Old-fashioned. Comfortable, but small rooms. Excellent service. Good food. Formal but not stiff. A great choice in its class. Very expensive.

Durrants Hotel   *George Street (W. 1)*   tel: 935-8131
Small traditional hotel with sedate pace. Close to shopping district. Comfortable and spacious rooms. Clublike atmosphere in the dining room and bar. Good choice in the moderate range.

Ebury Court   *26 Ebury Street (S.W. 1)*   tel: 730-8147
Small cozy hotel with traditional and tasteful atmosphere. Delightful bar. Superb restaurant. Moderate—an exceptional value. Note: room number 41 has a four-poster bed.

Gore Hotel   *189 Queen's Gate (S.W. 7)*   tel: 584-6601
Small and pleasant hotel noted for its fine restaurant. Good in the moderate range.

Goring Hotel   *Grosvenor Gardens, (S.W. 1)*   tel: 834-8211
Only a short walk from Buckingham Palace. Quite large and immaculate hotel—thoroughly British with nineteenth century flavor. Very comfortable with warm service. Expensive.

Hallam   *Hallam Street (Portland Place) (W. 1)*   tel: 580-1166
Small historic inn with pleasant rooms. Early Victorian atmosphere. Breakfast only. Lively location near Soho. Good budget choice.

Hendon Hall Hotel   *Ashley Lane (Hendon-N.W. 4)*   tel: 203-3341
Georgian mansion converted into comfortable hotel on outskirts of the city. Rural flavor, with pool and golf nearby. Number 5 is the room to get. Attractive dining.

Knightsbridge Green   *159 Knightsbridge (S.W. 1)*   tel: 584-6274
Small hotel in superb location. Sparkling and clean. Lovely suites. Good moderate-class hotel.

Inverness Court   *1-9 Inverness Terrace (W. 2)*   tel: 229-1444
King Edward VII had this mansion built for Lillie Langtry. Lots of atmosphere. Spacious and comfortable rooms. Elegant Lillie Langtry suite. Moderate to expensive. One of London's great small hotels.

Number Sixteen Hotel   *16 Sumner Place (S.W. 7)*   *tel: 589-5232*
Comfortable boardinghouse that could pass as a townhouse.
Very typical and nice. Moderate.

Portobello   *22 Stanley Gardens (W. 11)*   *tel: 727-2777*
Small, zany, and somewhat exclusive hotel with comfortable and
pleasant rooms. Discreet and young. Private garden. The kind of
place where you pour your own. Informal. Moderate to expensive.

Royal Court   *Sloane Square (S.W. 1)*   *tel: 730-9191*
Good location near the theatre, with easy access to the tube. Not
at all royal, but faded and friendly. Reasonably comfortable
rooms (number 106 recommended). Conservative atmosphere.
Good restaurant with *exceptional* breakfasts. Good value in the
moderate range.

Stafford Hotel   *16 St. James's Place (W. 1)*   *tel: 493-0111*
Small, quiet, and very pleasant hotel with bright rooms. Elegant
Regency atmosphere. Good service and fine French cooking. Fun
bar. Very expensive.

Tenma   *Queensborough Terrace (W. 2)*   *tel: 229-3754*
Small new Japanese hotel included for its excellent restaurant.
Tasteful throughout. Moderate.

Westbury Hotel   *New Bond Street (W. 1)*   *tel: 629-7755*
Good American-style hotel—very large, very comfortable, and
very commercial. Excellent restaurant. Very expensive, as well.

Wilbraham Hotel   *Wilbraham Place (S.W. 1)*   *tel: 730-8296*
Good location only a short walk from Sloane Square. Small and
informal—thoroughly British. Friendly. Charming restaurant.
Nothing fancy, but a great choice in the moderate class. Try for
room numbers 8 or 21.

Winlot Investment Company Limited   *37-38 St. James's Place (S.W. 1)*
tel: 499-6771
Attractive apartments including kitchenette, for longer stays in
London. Fully equipped. Maid service. Nex to Duke's Hotel.
Very expensive.

Ludlow [20]

The Feathers Inn   Corve Street   tel: 29 19
Picturesque Elizabethan country inn with carved timber front. Thirty comfortable bedrooms—half with bath. Beamed restaurant. Crackling fireplace. Riding. Moderate. West of Coventry.

Lyme Regis [17]

High Cliff Hotel   Sidmouth Road   tel: 23 00
Early nineteenth-century country house with fourteen attractive rooms—half with bath. Fine restaurant. Moderate. Closed winters. On the coast east of Exeter.

Maidenhead [19]

Boulters Lock Inn   Boulters Lock   tel: 21 291
Tiny, authentic inn in lovely location near town. Moderate.

Skindles   Mill Lane   tel: 25 115
Large old hotel with nice atmosphere. Comfortable. Good restaurant. Moderately expensive. West of Windsor.

Mallyan Spout [42]

Mallyan Spout Hotel   Goathland (Yorkshire County)   tel: Mallyan Spout 206
Small and rustic inn. Quite comfortable. Management will set up grouse hunts. Moderate. One mile west of Goathland; north of Scarborough.

Malmesbury [18] (Cotswolds)

Old Bell Inn   Malmesbury   tel: 23 44
In the village center next to the lovely abbey. Wisteria-covered stone inn with medieval staircase. Moderate. North of Bath.

Malton [41]

Talbot Hotel   Yorkersgate   tel: 20 56
Small eighteenth-century inn on the River Derwent. Terraced gardens in rear. Moderate. Northeast of York.

Marlow [19]

Compleat Angler   High Street   tel: Marlow 44 44
Luxurious riverside hotel overlooking the River Weir. Spacious and bright bedrooms. Good restaurant with fine wine cellar. Boats for hire—lovely excursions in area. Quite expensive. Northwest of Windsor.

Matlock Bath [33]

New Bath   Derby Road   tel: 32 75
Small and attractive country house on the Derwent River. Good restaurant. Tennis. Reserve. Northwest of Nottingham in Peak district.

Melrose [46]

George & Abbotsford   Melrose   tel: 23 08
Small, delightful eighteenth-century inn. Rustic and pleasant. Geared to fishermen. Moderate. Southeast of Edinburgh on way to England.

Midhurst [7]

Spread Eagle   South Street   tel: 22 11
Small black-and-white timbered inn dating back to 1430. Comfortable—half of the rooms with bath. Timbered dining room with excellent food (candlelight dining). Moderate. North of Chichester. East of Southampton.

Minster Lovell [20]

Old Swan Hotel   Minster Lovell   tel: Ashthall Leigh 614
Tiny thirteenth-century stone inn with comfortable rooms—a few with bath. Good food (candlelight dining). Moderate. Some say the legend concerning kissing under mistletoe was invented here. West of Oxford.

Moreton Hampstead [17]

Manor House Hotel   Moreton Hampstead   tel: 355
On B3212 highway in Dartmoor. Beautiful manor in lovely gardens. Large—most rooms with bath. Nice restaurant. Golf, tennis, and riding. Moderate. Twelve miles southwest of Exeter.

Moreton-in-Marsh [28] (Cotswolds)

Manor House Hotel   Center Fosseway   tel: 50 501
Seventeenth-century manor house converted into a fine hotel. Lovely grounds. Good food. Moderate. Confirm reservations in writing.

Redesdale Arms   Main Street   tel: 50 308
Attractive old stone coaching inn—small and fun. Good cooking including home-made ice cream. Moderate. South of Stratford-upon-Avon.

Nairn [58]

Newton Hotel   Nairn   tel: 31 44
Twenty miles from Inverness. Small and elegant country house on spacious grounds. Traditional atmosphere. Attractive rooms. Excellent cooking with flowers on the table and candlelight dining. Golf, riding, skiing, tennis, and fishing arranged. A superb quiet retreat. Moderate. Open April through October.

New Milton [7]

Chewton Glen   Christchurch Road   tel: 53 41
Small and exceptionally fine seventeenth-century hotel in peaceful location. Lovely gardens and grounds. Bright and comfortable rooms. Marvelous food, farm fresh produce and fresh fish. Good wines. Quite expensive. Twenty miles southwest of Southampton.

Northampton [30]

Westone Hotel   Fir Tree Walk   tel: 42 131
Fine old manor with comfortable rooms and fine French cooking. Located several miles north of the city. Southeast of Leicester.

Norwich [22]

Maid's Head   Norwich Tombland   tel: 28 821
Fine old English inn with new wing. Attractive rooms. Good cooking. Moderate.

Oakham [31]

Crown Hotel   Oakham   tel: 36 31
Small seventeenth-century coaching inn. Recently modernized. Fine French cuisine. Moderate. West of Stamford.

Oban [53]

Alexandra   Esplanade   tel: 23 81
Small mansion converted into pleasant hotel with lovely view. Quite comfortable. Open April through October. Southwest of Ft. William on the coast.

Otterburn [45]

Tower Hotel   Otterburn   tel: 673
Interesting old country house with some rooms dating back to the thirteenth century. Spacious and comfortable, but only some rooms with bath. Cocktail lounge in what were once stables. Fun. Moderate. Fifteen miles northwest of Newcastle.

Oxford [20]

Randolph Hotel   Beaumont Street   tel: 47 481
Large comfortable hotel with quite good restaurant. Expensive.

Pant Mawr [36] (Powys)

Glansevern Arms   Pant Mawr   tel: 240
Small riverside inn with ancient atmosphere. Very relaxed and snug. Not for the stuffy. Good lamb dishes. Inexpensive. Northwest of Llangurig on A44. South of Bangor.

Peebles [46]

Cringletie House   Peebles   tel: Eddleston 233
Twenty miles southeast of Edinburgh between Peebles and
Eddleston. Country hotel on spacious grounds. Delightful rural
setting. Modest. Tennis, golf, and fishing. Moderate.

Tontine Hotel   High Street   tel: 20 892
Small, attractive hotel with pleasant rooms. Moderate. South of
Edinburgh.

Penmaenpool [36]

George III   Penmaenpool   tel: Dolgellau 422 525
Tiny seventeenth-century inn with only six rooms. Excellent
riverside restaurant specializing in seafood. Fishing arranged.
Moderate. Two miles southwest of Dolgelly; to south of Bangor.

Golden Lion Royal   Penmaenpool   tel: 683
Secluded inn with comfortable rooms and interesting Victorian
bar. Moderate.

Penshurst [1]

Leicester Arms   Penshurst   tel: 551
An attractive seventeenth-century inn with large flower garden.
Wonderful location in quaint town. Moderate. Northwest of
Tunbridge Wells. South of London.

Penrhyndeudraeth [36]

Hotel Portmeiron   Penrhyndeudraeth   tel: 228
Large and elegant cottage colony. Theatrical and very comfortable, with country flavor. Lovely view. Marvelous food with wide
choice in wines. Tennis, golf, and fishing. Expensive. South of
Caernarvon. South of Bangor.

Perth [52]

Royal George Hotel   Tay Street   tel: 24 455
Forty-three miles north of Edinburgh. Lovely old hotel in which

Queen Victoria once slept. Good food. Atmospheric bar. Moderate.

Pillaton [13]

The Weary Friar   Pillaton   tel: 238
Small twelfth-century inn with dark beams, copper, and brass—full of atmosphere. Comfortable rooms. Excellent cooking, with duckling a specialty. Fishing. Moderate. Ten miles west of Plymouth via A38.

Pitlochry [52]

Green Park Hotel   Clunie Bridge Road   tel: 25 37
Small country house on river and lake in idyllic setting. Wonderful view. Comfortable rooms—half with bath. Fishing. Open March to November. Northwest of Perth.

Pooley Bridge [44]

Sharrow Bay Country House   Pooley Bridge   tel: Pooley Bridge 301
Six miles southwest of Penrith. Lovely lakeside hotel with twenty-one beautifully furnished bedrooms. Attractive grounds and antiques. Fishing and sailing. Marvelous cuisine (one of the best in England). Superb cellar. Expensive. Reserve well in advance. East of Keswick.

Port Gaverne [13]

Port Gaverne Hotel   Port Gaverne   tel: Port Isaac 244
Attractive seventeenth-century inn with well-furnished bedrooms. Candlelight dining. Pony trekking. Arrangement for sea fishing. Moderate. Closed winter. On the Atlantic coast thirty-five miles northwest of Plymouth.

Portinscale [44]

Tower Hotel & Dungeon Club   Keswick   tel: 73 099
Small and inexpensive inn with fishing on the River Derwent. Near Keswick.

Portree [59] (Isle of Skye)

Collin Hills   Portree   tel: 3
Small attractive lodge with fine views. Comfortable rooms—half
with bath. Inexpensive.

Presteigne [24]

Radnorshire Arms Hotel   High Street   tel: 406
Tiny seventeenth-century inn with simple and colorful rooms.
Lots of atmosphere, with antiques. Moderately expensive. North
of Cardiff on the border.

Ripon [41]

Spa Hotel   North Street   tel: 21 72
Small old-fashioned hotel in attractive garden setting. Quite
good restaurant. Moderate. Fifteen miles northwest of York.

Romsey [7]

White Horse Inn   Market Place   tel: 51 24 31
Small, ancient coaching inn dating from the reign of Henry VII.
Quite comfortable. Good cooking. Moderate. North of South-
ampton towards Salisbury.

Ross-on-Wye [26]

Pengethley Hotel   Ross-on-Wye   tel: Harewood End 252
Four miles west of Ross at Harewood End. Small country house
with marvelous cooking. Moderate. West of Gloucester.

Rothesay [50] (Isle of Bute)

Glenburn   Glenburn Road   tel: 500
Large resort on spacious grounds. Comfortable rooms and fine
home cooking. Tennis. Expensive. West of Glasgow.

Rothes-on-Spey [58]

Rothes Glen Hotel   Rothes   tel: 254
Small   Victorian   hotel   on   spacious   grounds.   Comfortable

rooms—half with bath. Antiques. Good cooking. Fishing and shooting. Open March to December. Near Inverness.

Rowsley [33]

Peacock Hotel   Rowsley   tel: Darby Dale 3518
Historic inn built in 1652. Comfortable and pleasant with excellent restaurant. Owns six miles of fishing rights on the River Wye. Expensive. Reserve. Four miles east of Bakewell. Northwest of Nottingham.

Ruthin [38]

Ruthin Castle   Ruthin   tel: 26 64
Large thirteenth-century castle on spacious grounds. Lovely location on the River Clewyd. Comfortable. Special candlelight dining for medieval banquets emphasizing old Tudor recipes. Tennis, golf, fishing, and pony trekking arranged. Expensive. Southeast of Llandudno.

Rye [3]

The Mermaid Inn   Mermaid Street   tel: 30 65
Famous old smugglers' inn dating from the fifteenth century. Comfortable rooms—half with bath. Queen Elizabeth stayed in number 16 in 1573. Four-posters in many. Excellent restaurant. Friendly. Fishing. Moderate.

St. Albans [1]

Sopwell House   Cottonmill Lane   tel: 64 477
A lovely Georgian manor with attractive rooms in serene setting. Fine restaurant. Golf nearby. Moderate. North of London.

St. Michael's Manor   Fishpool Street   tel: 64 444
Old sixteenth-century manor with pleasant bedrooms—some with bath. Elegant dining room. Fine wines. Moderate.

St. Andrews [51]

Old Course Hotel   St. Andrews   tel: 43 71
Fine new hotel overlooking the seventeenth green of the golf

course. Quite large, with luxurious rooms—many with balconies. Good service and cooking. Tennis, riding, and golf. Very expensive.

St. Brelade's Bay [11] (Jersey)

Atlantic Hotel   St. Brelade's Bay   tel: 44 101
New hotel with spacious rooms. Good restaurant. Pool and golf nearby. Expensive. Closed in winter.

Hotel L'Horizon   St. Brelade's Bay   tel: 43 101
Large modern hotel with nice view. Comfortable. Varied and fine cuisine. Tennis, riding, and golf. Expensive.

St. Helier [11] (Jersey)

Beaufort Hotel   Green Street   tel: 32 471
Excellent hotel with very comfortable rooms. Fine cuisine. Moderate.

Portelet Bay Hotel   St. Helier   tel: 41 204
Five miles west of town. Large attractive hotel with quiet and comfortable rooms. Nice view. Excellent restaurant. Pool and tennis. Expensive.

Hotel de la Plage   St. Clements Bay   tel: 23 474
Large seafront hotel with comfortable rooms. Modern. Nice dining. Moderate. Open all year.

St. Ives [15]

Tregenna Castle Hotel   St. Ives   tel: 52 54
One mile east of Highway A3074. Attractive and impressive eighteenth-century manor surrounded by extensive grounds. Lovely view from the large hotel. Spacious rooms. Fine restaurant. Expensive. North of Penzance.

St. Martin's [11] (Guernsey)

St. Margaret's Lodge   St. Martin's   tel: 35 757
Small and attractive hotel with comfortable rooms. Fine food. Pool. Moderate.

St. Mawes [14]

Hotel Tresanton   St. Mawes   tel: 544
Small hotel with great sea view and atmosphere—flowery, charming, upper crusty. Very comfortable rooms, but ask for one with a view. Excellent seafood (fresh oysters). Sailing and fishing. Very expensive. Closed in winter except for Christmas. Opposite Falmouth.

St. Peter Port [11] (Guernsey)

Duke of Richmond   Cambridge Park   tel: 26 221
Large very fine hotel. Very comfortable rooms. Varied and excellent cuisine. Tennis. Expensive. Open all year.

Havelet Hotel   St. Peter Port   tel: 22 199
Charming small historic inn with country flavor. Comfortable. Fine cuisine. Inexpensive.

Old Government House   St. Ann's Place   tel: 24 921
Large historic hotel with traditional flavor. Charming location and atmosphere. Very comfortable. Good restaurant. Moderate. Open all year.

St. Saviour [11] (Jersey)

Le Manoir de Longueville   St. Saviour   tel: 25 501
Near St. Helier. Ancient Norman manor converted into luxury hotel. Calm location in lovely park. Charming flavor with warmth. Very comfortable and gracious. Exquisite dining (lobster in season). Pool. Expensive.

Salisbury [10]

Rose & Crown Hotel   Harnham Road   tel: 27 908
One mile west of town. Old riverside inn facing the cathedral. Delightful with comfortable rooms—most with bath. Good restaurant. Moderate.

The White Hart   St. John Street   tel: 27 476
Large Georgian hotel with new wing. Quite comfortable. Good restaurant. Moderate.

Scarborough [42]

Royal Hotel   St. Nicholas Street   tel: 64 333
Large Regency hotel with very comfortable rooms. Gourmet restaurant. Expensive.

Shipton-under-Wychwood [20]

The Lamb Inn   High Street   tel: 83 04 65
Tiny family-run inn with antiques and charming garden. Good food (wonderful breakfasts). Moderate. West of Oxford near Burford.

The Shaven Crown   High Street   tel: 83 03 30
Attractive sixteenth-century inn (earlier a shelter run by monks of the abbey). Thirteen comfortable rooms—half with bath. Garden. Moderate.

Shrewsbury [34]

The Lion Hotel   Shrewsbury   tel: 53 107
Large coaching inn with comfortable rooms—ask for ones in the newer extension. Moderate. South of Chester.

Skeabost Bridge [59] (Isle of Skye)

Skeabost House   Skeabost Bridge   tel: 202
Five miles from Portree. Small country hotel on lovely estate. Attractive, peaceful rooms. River and sea fishing. Shooting arranged. Open April to mid-October.

Sonning-on-Thames [19]

White Hart   Thames Street   tel: 69 22 77
Old Elizabethan inn with delightful location on the Thames. Comfortable bedrooms. Good food. Moderate. Near Reading below Henley. West of Windsor.

Southampton [7]

Polygon Hotel   Cumberland Place   tel: 26 401/28 162
Large modernized hotel with quite comfortable rooms and good

restaurant. Moderately expensive.

South Queensferry [46]

Hawes Inn   South Queensferry   tel: 331-1990
Small historic inn. Quite comfortable. Good food. Moderate. Ten miles west of Edinburgh.

South Zeal [17]

Oxenham Arms   South Zeal   tel: Sticklepath 244
On Highway A30, nineteen miles west of Exeter. Tiny old stone inn believed to have been built in the twelfth century by monks. Lovely antiques, ancient flagstones, and oak-beamed bedrooms. Good restaurant with fresh produce and grilled meats. No young children. Moderate.

Spalding [32]

White Hart Hotel   Spalding   tel: 37 42
Small historic inn dating back to fourteenth century. Low ceiling and lots of atmosphere. Quite comfortable. Moderate.

Stamford [31]

George Hotel   Stamford   tel: 21 01
Ancient historic inn rebuilt in sixteenth cenury. Quite large with bright and comfortable rooms—half with bath. Moderate.

Stirling [50]

Golden Lion Hotel   8 King Street   tel: 53 51
Famous ancient house converted into fine hotel. Comfortable rooms—many with bath. Good cooking. Moderate. Northeast of Glasgow.

Stow-on-the-Wold [20] (Cotswolds)

Talbot Hotel   Market Square   tel: 631
Small and comfortable hotel overlooking square. Friendly. Moderate. Northwest of Oxford.

Stranraer [47]

North West Castle Hotel   Royal Crescent   tel: 26 44
"Castle" converted into hotel with some modern rooms. Attractive grounds and traditional atmosphere. Comfortable. Good restaurant. Tennis, fishing, and golf. Moderate. Southwest of Ayr.

Stratford-upon-Avon [28]

Alveston Manor Hotel   Clopton Bridge   tel: 45 81
Large sixteenth-century half-timbered house with many antiques. Nice grounds. Attractive throughout. Quite expensive.

Falcon Hotel   Chapel Street   tel: 57 77
Excellent central location. Ancient building converted into charming historic inn. Comfortable rooms, most with bath. Ask for ones with antiques. Expensive.

The Haytor Hotel   Stratford-upon-Avon   tel: 34 20
Half mile east of town center. Small and very attractive. Edwardian home. Family run with a personal touch in residential area. Lovely garden. Tasteful throughout. Quite expensive.

The Shakespeare Hotel   Chapel Street   tel: 36 31
Large sixteenth-century inn—each room named after a character in one of Shakespeare's plays. Comfortable and quite expensive.

The Welcombe Hotel   Warwick Road   tel: 36 11
Nineteenth-century manor house in lovely forty-acre estate. Large and comfortable—ask for rooms in newer wing. Good restaurant with both French and English cooking. Quite expensive.

Stromness [63] (Orkney)

Stromness Hotel   Stromness   tel: 298
Large hotel with magnificent view. Comfortable—some rooms with bath. Good food. For the explorer. Inexpensive.

Sutton Benger [25]

Bell House Hotel   Sutton Benger   tel: Seagry 401
On Highway A420 at Sutton Benger, four miles north of Chip-

penham. Tiny luxury hotel with ultracomfortable rooms—ask for number 12. Restaurant with a French flair—a bit stuffy. Very nice and equally expensive. Reserve well in advance. East of Bristol.

Sullom Voe [57] (Shetland)

Voe Country House Hotel   *Sullom Voe*   *tel: 241*
Nineteenth-century home with a few rooms. Comfortable and charming. Spectacular setting. Marvelous cooking with fresh vegetables. Pour your own drinks. Moderate. Book long in advance. Open April through October. North of Orkneys. Accessible from Aberdeen.

Symonds Yat [26]

Royal Hotel   *Symonds Yat*   *tel: Symonds Yat 238*
Small hotel on the bank of the River Wye. Pleasant and homelike. Salmon fishing. Moderate. West of Gloucester.

Paddocks Hotel   *Symonds Yat West*   *tel: Symonds Yat 246*
Small and quite comfortable hotel with fishing in the spring. Moderate.

Taunton [17]

Castle Hotel   *Taunton*   *tel: 26 71*
Large ivy-clad castle with Norman garden. Comfortable rooms—ask for one on top floor. Good cuisine and fine wines. Hunting. Golf. Expensive. East of the Exmoor region. Northeast of Exeter.

Tavistock [13]

The Bedford Hotel   *Plymouth Road*   *tel: 32 21*
Eighteenth-century inn—once the home of the Duke of Bedford. Large rooms, fully modernized. Nice restaurant. Moderate. Fifteen miles north of Plymouth.

Tetbury [25] (Cotswolds)

White Hart   Market Place   tel: 436
Delightful tiny hotel in lovely setting. Modest. Inexpensive. Between Malmesbury and Stroud. Northeast of Bristol.

Thorton-le-Dale [41]

Hall Hotel   Thorton-le-Dale   tel: 14 254
Small, attractive sixteenth-century manor near Pickering. Nice new wing. Lovely gardens and grounds. Fine food. Riding. Moderate. Northeast of York on south edge of Moors.

Tintern [26]

Beaufort Hotel   Tintern   tel: 202
Medieval inn with modest, comfortable rooms across from the ruins of Tintern Abbey. Moderate. Southwest of Gloucester; near Chepstow.

Ullapool [61]

The Royal Hotel   Ullapool   tel: 21 81
Small hotel in lovely setting with comfortable rooms—some with bath. Good cooking and fine wines. Excellent fishing and hunting. Moderate.

Uphall [46]

Houstoun House   Uphall   tel: Broxbourn 38 31
Converted mansion with superb rooms and delicious cooking south of Edinburgh. Worth a detour. Moderate.

Upper Slaughter [26]

The Close   Upper Slaughter   tel: 52 272
Southwest of Stow-on-the-Wold. Sixteenth-century country inn by its own lake. Very comfortable rooms. Good cuisine. Expensive. East of Gloucester.

Watermillock [44]

Leeming House Hotel   Watermillock   tel: Pooley Bridge 444
Eight miles south of Penrith on Lake Ullswater. Country house
hotel with limited number of rooms—some with bath. Personal
and warm. Moderate. Southeast of Keswick.

Wells [25]

The Swan   Sadler Street   tel: 78 877
Small, ancient inn overlooking part of the cathedral. Half of the
rooms with bath. Fair food. Moderate. South of Bristol in a
charming medieval town.

Weobley [26]

Red Lion Hotel   Weobley   tel: Weobley 220
Fine authentic inn with fishing in the spring. Quite comfortable.
Fun. Moderate. Northwest of Hereford. Northwest of Glouces-
ter.

Westonbirt [26] (Cotswolds)

Hare & Hounds   Westonbirt   tel: Call operator at Westonbirt
Typical small inn near the Arboretum. Modest and quite inexpensive. South of Berkeley. Southwest of Gloucester.

Weston-on-Green [20]

Weston Manor   Weston-on-Green   tel: Bletchington 621
Nine miles north of Oxford on A43. Small manor—splendid atmosphere and setting. Fine restaurant. Pool. Quite expensive.

Windermere [44]

Langdale Chase   Windermere   tel: Ambleside 2201
Quite small lakeside inn between Ambleside and Windermere
with delightful location and lovely view. Excellent restaurant.
Private fishing. Quite expensive. Closed December to February.
Southeast of Keswick.

Winsford [17]

Royal Oak Inn   Winsford   tel: 232
Eight miles from Dulverton. Tiny picturesque inn from the fourteenth century with thatched roof and white exterior. On the River Exe. Trout fishing. Moderate. Closed winter. South of Exford in Exmoor region. North of Exeter.

Woburn [20]

Bedford Arms   George Street   tel: 441
Handsome eighteenth-century coaching inn with attractive rooms. Interesting restaurant and bar (where you can drink with the inn's own ghost). Hunting and fishing nearby. Moderate. Northeast of Oxford.

Woodbridge [22]

The Crown Hotel   Thorofare   tel: 42 42
Former coaching inn with a central location. Comfortable chalet bedrooms. Fine dining. Quite expensive. Northeast of Colchester near Ipswich. South of Norwich near the coast.

Woodstock [20]

Bear Hotel   Park Street   tel: 81 15 11
Small and fine old stone inn with carefully preserved interior, including sixteenth-century hallway. Well-appointed rooms—some suites. Excellent restaurant. Moderate. Eight miles from Oxford on A34.

Wotten-under-Edge [26] (Cotswolds)

The Swan Hotel   Market Street   tel: 23 29
Popular old Cotswold hotel seven miles southeast of Berkeley overlooking the River Severn. Comfortable rooms and very fine French cuisine. Moderate. Southwest of Gloucester.

Yelverton [13]

Moorland Links   Yelverton   tel: 22 45
Fine small hotel with good location in Dartmoor area. Superior English and French cooking. Moderate. Ten miles north of Plymouth.

York [41]

The Post House   Tadcaster Road   tel: 67 921
Two miles west on Tadcaster Road. Large new motor inn with bright and comfortable rooms. Nice restaurant. Moderate.

The Royal Station Hotel   Station Road   tel: 53 681
Large Victorian hotel with fine gardens overlooking the Minster. Spacious and comfortable rooms. Nice restaurant. Moderate.

Young's Hotel   High Petersgate   tel: 24 229
Charming old inn with comfortable, simple rooms and charming restaurant. The birthplace of Guy Fawkes, who tried to blow up Parliament. Moderate.

WHERE TO EAT

Aberfeldy [52]

Fortingall Hotel   Aberfeldy   tel: Aberfeldy 603
Twenty miles southwest of Pitlochry. Superb cuisine—a gourmet's delight (no smoking in the dining room). Moderate. Reserve. Northwest of Perth.

Abinger [1]

Jock & Jenny's   Abinger Common   tel: 73 07 37
Picturesque restaurant in forest setting between Guildford and Dorking. Very fine French cuisine. Popular. Moderate. Southwest of London.

Alfold [1]

Chez Jean   Alford Crossways   tel: 75 23 57
Popular French restaurant eleven miles south of Guildford on Highway 281. Excellent, warm service. Moderate. Southwest of London.

Alresford [6]

O'Rorke's   34 Pound Hill   tel: 22 93
Cozy restaurant with fine English and Continental dishes. Fun. Moderate. East of Winchester.

Bath [25]

Bruno's Restaurant   2 George Street   tel: 25 141
Attractive small restaurant with excellent Italian dishes. Moderate. Reserve.

Hole in the Wall   16 George Street   tel: 25 242
A gem. One of England's better restaurants with a homey air and skillfully prepared food. Moderate. Reserve.

Priory Hotel Restaurant   Winston Road   tel: 21 887
One of the finest restaurants in Bath. Expensive. Reserve.

Biddenden [3]

Ye Maydes   Biddenden   tel: 306
In a village on Highway 262 west of Ashford. Charming small restaurant with medieval flavor. French cooking. Moderate. Northeast of Rye.

Birmingham [30]

Plow & Harrow   Hagley Road, 15 Edgbaston   tel: 454-4111/1131
Excellent French restaurant with outstanding dishes and service. Expensive. West of Leicester.

Bolton Abbey [40]

The Devonshire Arms   Bolton Abbey   tel: 67 12 65
Excellent restaurant with fine cuisine and friendly service. Good

wine selection. Expensive. North of Ilkley in the Dales. Northeast of Manchester.

Bray-on-Thames [19]

Hind's Head Hotel Restaurant   *High Street*   *tel: 26 151*
Ancient restaurant serving fine English dishes. Lots of atmosphere. Moderate. Reserve. Near Maidenhead. West of Windsor.

Broadway [27] (Cotswolds)

Hunter's Lodge Hotel Restaurant   *High Street*   *tel: 32 47*
Imaginative French and Swiss cooking. Superb and varied dishes. Fine wine list. Expensive.

Cambridge [21]

Hotel de la Poste   *Cambridge*   *tel: Swavesey 30 241*
Ten miles northwest of the city in Swavesey via Highway A604. Georgian country house with excellent French menu and fine wine cellar. Expensive. Reserve well in advance.

Blue Boar Hotel Restaurant   *Trinity Street*   *tel: 63 121*
Right in the center of town. Quite elegant dining room with varied menu. Moderate. Reserve.

Canterbury [2]

The Castle Restaurant   *71 Castle Street*   *tel: 65658*
Family restaurant. Fun and pleasant. Quite good food. Popular. Moderate.

Trattoria Roma Antica   *9 Longport*   *tel: 63 326*
Small Italian restaurant with fine food. Popular. Moderate. Reserve.

Cardiff [24]

Le Napoleon Restaurant   *7-9 Oxford Arcade*   *tel: 37 794/38 77 94*
Charming little restaurant specializing in French cuisine. Popular. Moderate. Reserve.

Castle Donington [33]

Priest House Inn   Kings Mills   tel: 10 649
Spacious restaurant serving fine French dishes. Quite expensive.
Southeast of Nottingham.

Cheltenham [27] (Cotswolds)

Malvern View   Cleeve Hill   tel: Bishop's Cleeve 2017
A very fine restaurant high in the Malvern Hills. Family-run.
Outstanding. Expensive.

Chester [34]

Blossom's Hotel   St. John's Street   tel: 23 186
Extremely popular regional restaurant. Quite expensive.

Chichester [5]

Little London   Chichester   tel: 84 899
Small, imaginative restaurant with both English and French
cuisine. Very good. Moderate. East of Portsmouth.

Chiddingfold [1]

Crown Inn Restaurant   Chiddingfold   tel: 22 55
Elevan miles south of Guildford. Fine restaurant with both English and French menu. Charming atmosphere. Popular. Moderate. Southwest of London.

Cirencester [26] (Cotswolds)

Stratton House Restaurant   Gloucester Road   tel: 38 36
Fine restaurant in Georgian house with both English and international dishes. Quite expensive. Southeast of Gloucester.

King's Head Inn   Market Square   tel: 33 21
Wonderful atmosphere and very fine food. Quite expensive.

Colchester [1]

Red Lion   Colchester   tel: 82 401
Ancient hotel now converted into pleasant steak house. Moderate. Northeast of London.

Comrie [52]

Royal Hotel Restaurant   Comrie   tel: 200
Fine English and French dishes with delicious wines. Moderate. West of Perth.

Cafe Royal & Oyster Bar   17 West Register Street   tel: 18 84
Popular restaurant for fresh seafood. Moderate. Reserve.

Eastbourne [3]

Chez Meurice   118 Seaside Road   tel: 24 894
Small French restaurant with lots of atmosphere. Very good seafood. Moderate. Southwest of Rye.

Edinburgh [46]

Abbotsford House   3 Rore Street   tel: 778-6606
Marvelous old pub with good food. Very popular. Moderate.

Cafe Royal   17 West Register Street   tel: 556-1884
Good seafood restaurant. Expensive.

Cramond Inn   Cramond Village   tel: 336-2035
Five miles northwest of town on the Firth of Forth. Ancient tavern serving delicious country food. Moderate.

Doric Tavern   15 Market Street   tel: 225-1084
Simple family-run restaurant. Pleasant. Quite good. Moderate.

Houstoun House   Uphall   tel: Broxburn 38 31
In Uphall south of Edinburgh. One of the country's best with set menu. Superb French wines. Moderate. Reserve.

Prestonfield House   *Priestfield Road*   *tel: 667-8000*
About ten minutes from downtown. Eighteenth-century estate with country atmosphere. Large menu—excellent food. Expensive. Reserve.

Fressingfield [22]

Fox & Goose Inn   *Fressingfield*   *tel: 247*
About fifteen miles north of Woodbridge on B1116. Tiny village restaurant with very good French cuisine. Quite expensive. South of Norwich.

Fyfield [20]

White Hart Restaurant   *Fyfield*   *tel: Frilford Heath 258*
Fifteenth-century inn serving fine regional cooking. Moderate. Nine miles southwest of Oxford.

Glasgow [50]

Buttery (Shandon Bell Pub)   *654 Argyle Street*   *tel: 221-8188*
Modest restaurant serving national specialties. Quite good. Moderate.

Central Hotel   *Gordon Street*   *tel: 221-9680*
This is an exceptionally fine hotel offering superb dining in the Malmaison restaurant. It's one of Scotland's better French restaurants. Expensive.

One-O-One Restaurant   *101 Hope Street*   *tel: 221-7101*
Smart and attractive restaurant with varied menu. Moderate. Reserve.

Godstow [20]

The Trout Inn   *Godstow*   *tel: Oxford 54 485*
Riverside inn with fine garden and lovely atmosphere—fireplace and prints. Good food, including fresh trout. Moderate. Reserve. Three miles north of Oxford.

Gulworthy [13]

Horn of Plenty   Gulworthy   tel: Gunnislake 528
Three miles from Tavistock. One of the country's very best restaurants, with excellent food and wines. Lovely location. Expensive. Reserve. On A390 north of Plymouth.

Hereford [26]

Grey Friars Garden Restaurant   Hereford   tel: 67 274
Quite good restaurant with continental cuisine. Expensive. Northwest of Gloucester.

Hexham [45]

Langley Castle   Hexham   tel: 481
Five miles west of town and just southwest of Haydon Bridge. Fourteenth-century castle noted for its medieval banquets. Quite expensive. West of Newcastle.

Hornsea [42]

Promenade Private Hotel   Marine Drive   tel: 12 29 44
Lovely seafront location and one of the best restaurants in the area. Varied menu. Quite expensive. South of Scarborough on the coast.

Hurley [19]

East Arms Restaurant   Hurley   tel: Littlewick Green 4280
Luxury restaurant on highway A423. Fine menu. Expensive. Reserve. Northwest of Windsor.

Ilkley [40]

Box Tree Cottage   Church Street   tel: Ilkley 29 83
Seventeenth-century farm converted into one of the finest restaurants in England. Superb wines. Extremely popular. Expensive. Reserve well in advance. Northwest of Leeds. Northeast of Manchester.

Ilmington [28] (Cotswolds)

Howard Arms   Ilmington   tel: Ilmington 226
Near Shipston-on-Stour. Tiny, magnificent restaurant with superb cooking. Expensive. West of Banbury. South of Stratford-upon-Avon.

Ivinghoe [20]

King's Head Inn   Ivinghoe   tel: Cheddington 668-264
Near Leighton Buzzard. Charming and very good restaurant with both French and English cooking in very attractive surroundings. Moderate. Seven miles from Dunstable. Northeast of Oxford.

Knutsford [40]

Bells of Peover   Knutsford   tel: Knutsford 809
Pub with lots of atmosphere. Traditional English dishes with emphasis on excellent meat. Moderate. South of Manchester.

Lechlade-on-Thames [20]

Trout Inn   Lechlade   tel: Lechlade 313
At. St. John's Lock. Attractive restaurant with fine food—trout a specialty. Moderate. West of Abingdon. West of Oxford.

Leicester [30]

Giorgio's   77 Narborough Road   tel: 29 267
Small restaurant with fine continental cuisine. Expensive.

Liverpool [39]

Oriel Restaurant   Water Street   tel: 236-4664
Fine international cuisine. Quite expensive.

London [1]

A l'Ecu de France   111 Jermyn Street (S.W. 1)   tel: 930-2837
A stylish and well-known French restaurant. Excellent cuisine. Fine service. Expensive. Reserve.

L'Artiste Assoiffe   *306 Westbourne Grove (W. 11)*   *tel: 727-4714*
Romantic spot in Portobello Antique market. Fine French cooking. Open fire in winter. Late-night dining. Modest. Moderate.

Au Fin Bec   *100 Draycott Avenue (S.W. 3)*   *tel: 584-3600*
Small and simple with surprisingly fine French cooking. Good wines. Pleasant. Moderate.

Bastians   *Hampton Court*   *tel: 977-6074*
Warm and delightful French atmosphere with superb classic cuisine. Wonderful setting. Moderately expensive.

Bentley's Oyster Bar   *11-15 Swallow Street (W. 1)*   *tel: 734-6210*
Delicious fresh seafood in fine restaurant. Superb oysters. A great off season choice. Moderately expensive. Reserve.

The Brompton Grill   *243 Brompton Road (S.W. 3)*   *tel: 589-8005*
Large, dignified, and steady. Touches of charm. Excellent continental cuisine. Expensive.

****Capital*   *Basil Street (S.W. 3)*   *tel: 589-5171*
Outstanding hotel restaurant with excellent fish dishes and fine *vol au vent*. Good selection of wines. Charming atmosphere. Expensive.

Caprice Restaurant   *Arlington Street (S.W. 1)*   *tel: 493-5154*
Lovely décor for an elegant evening. Excellent variety of continental dishes. Quite expensive. Reserve.

****Carrier's*   *2 Camden Passage (N. 1)*   *tel: 226-5353*
Long-standing favorite of gourmets intent on a fine meal in fine surroundings. Delicious lamb chops, veal, and scallops. Good selection of wines. Expensive.

Chez Ciccio   *38 Kensington Church Street (W. 8)*   *tel: 937-2005*
Discreet and intimate Italian restaurant with excellent cooking. Quite expensive.

****Connaught*   *Carlos Place (W. 1)*   *tel: 499-7070*
The grill room in this luxury hotel offers superb cuisine in a refined, very elegant atmosphere. Rated number one by many. Very fine, very expensive. Reserve far in advance.

****Le Coq d'Or*   *Stratton Street (W. 1)*   *tel: 629-7807*
Sophisticated and sumptuous. A bit on the snobbish side. Excellent French dishes. Expensive. Reserve.

Elizabethan Rooms   *190 Queen's Gate (S.W. 7)*   tel: 584-6616
Huge hall serving medieval banquets each evening. Set price includes wine and entertainment. Moderate.

The Empress   *15 Berkeley Street (W. 1)*   tel: 629-6126
Large and luxurious, this restaurant offers a wide variety of excellent continental dishes. Expensive.

L'Etoile   *30 Charlotte Street (W. 1)*   tel: 636-7189
Among the best London has to offer—small and intimate. Excellent French dishes, superb service, friendly atmosphere, and varied wine list. Charming. A gem. Expensive. Reserve.

Fortnum & Mason   *181 Piccadilly (W. 1)*   tel: 734-8040
Many shoppers choose this as a fine department store restaurant for lunch. Opulent and smooth. Simple, very fine cooking. Expensive. Reserve.

Le Français   *259 Fulham Road (S.W. 3)*   tel: 352-4748
Small gem serving delicious French regional cooking. Seasonal dishes—superb fish. Warm. Expensive.

The Ganges   *40 Gerrard Street (W. 1)*   tel: 437-0284
Excellent Indian food—real curry dishes served with flair. Moderate. Reserve well in advance.

***Le Gavroche   *61-63 Lower Sloane Street (S.W. 1)*   tel: 730-2820
Quiet, sober, and aristocratic. Superb seasonal specialties. Creative cooking at its best. For serious gourmets. Stuffy. Very expensive.

The Guinea   *30 Bruton Place (W. 1)*   tel: 629-5613
Small and lively. Pick your own steak—charcoal-broiled to order. Expensive. Reserve.

The Hunting Lodge   *18 Lower Regent Street (S.W. 1)*   tel: 930-4222
Elaborate, somewhat baroque clublike atmosphere. Strictly English fare with excellent seasonal dishes, including fresh game. Very expensive.

Jasper's Bun in the Oven   *11 Kew Garden (Richmond)*
tel: 940-3987
Charming Georgian home converted into French restaurant with fine steaks and tempting fish dishes. Modest. Moderate. Ideal for lunch when visiting Royal Gardens at Kew in spring.

Lacy's   26 Whitfield (W. 1)   tel: 636-2323
Small, fine restaurant well-known for steady cooking. Expensive.

Mirabelle Restaurant   56 Curzon Street (W. 1)   tel: 499-4636
An "in" restaurant with an up-and-down reputation. Opulent with French cooking. Very expensive. Reserve.

Nick's Diner   88 Ifield Road (S.W. 10)   tel: 352-0930, 352-5641
Lively, informal, and fun. Hearty cooking. Moderately expensive.

Parkes Restaurant   5 Beauchamp Place (S.W. 3)   tel: 584-5971
Small, imaginative, and very fine. Varied menu. Expensive. Reserve.

Le Poulbot   45 Cheapside (E.C. 2)   tel: 236-4379
Refined and plush but charming. Underneath pub of same name. Excellent French cooking with superb fish and desserts. Expensive.

Prunier's   72 St. James's Street (S.W. 1)   tel: 493-1373
Aristocratic and often crowded. Gourmet cooking with superb fish dishes. Stylish with excellent service. Excellent spot for after-theater meal. Ultraexpensive.

The Secret Place   243 Old Brompton Road (S.W. 5)   tel: 373-1659
Delightful litle French restaurant open late at night. Good cooking. Open fire in winter. Moderate.

Simpson's   100 The Strand (W.C. 2)   tel: 836-9112
Ancient restaurant serving exceptional English food. Roast beef is delicious. Expensive.

La Terrazza   19 Romilly Street (W. 1)   tel: 437-8991
Large popular restaurant with elegant and colorful atmosphere. Fine Italian dishes made with fresh produce. Excellent wines. Expensive.

****Walton's*   121 Walton Street (S.W. 3)   tel: 584-0204
Geared to gourmets. Specialties include veal, salmon, and a delicious wine cream cake. Nice wines. Expensive.

Wheeler's   19 Old Compton Street (W. 1)   tel: 437-2706
Fine English restaurant with lots of atmosphere. Superb seafood with enormous variety in dishes. Fresh oysters. An excellent off season choice. Lively. Expensive.

Wilton's   27 Bury Street (S.W. 1)   tel: 930-8391
Plush, snobbish English restaurant serving traditional English
fare with excellent oysters and salmon. Ultraexpensive. Reserve.

Maidenhead [19]

Shoppenhanger's Manor Restaurant   Maidenhead   tel: 27 237
Attractive old manor with superb French cuisine. Terrific setting
and service. Reserve. West of Windsor.

Manchester [40]

Terrazza   14 Nicholas Street   tel: 236-4033
Excellent Italian cuisine. Expensive.

Canadian Charcoal Steakhouse   50 Princess Street   tel: 236-7697
Good steaks. Expensive.

Sinclair's Oyster Bar   195 Deansgate   tel: 834-8349
One of the better seafood restaurants in town. Excellent oysters.
Expensive.

Marlow [19]

La Chandelle   55 High Street   tel: 27 99
Small and very fine restaurant with both French and international dishes. Moderate. Northwest of Windsor.

Peacock's Restaurant   47 West Street   tel: 42 14
Superb French cooking. Quite expensive. Reserve.

Minster Lovell [20] (Cotswolds)

Old Swan   Asthall Leigh   tel: 614
Old Cotswold inn with both English and French menu—quite
good. Moderately expensive. West of Oxford.

Moreton-on-Marsh [28] (Cotswolds)

Manor House Hotel Restaurant   Moreton-on-Marsh   tel: 50 501
Good restaurant serving both English and French dishes. Quite
expensive. South of Stratford-upon-Avon.

Nantwich [34]

Churche's Mansion Restaurant   New Castle Road   tel: 65 933
Charming restaurant in historic Elizabethan home. Reserve.
Southeast of Chester.

Nottingham [33]

Moulin Rouge Restaurant   Trinity Square   tel: 42 845
Small restaurant with international cuisine—specialties in beef.
Expensive.

Oxford [20]

Restaurant Elizabeth   84 St. Aldgate's   tel: 42 230
One of the most popular restaurants in town. Small and intimate. Very good food. Reserve.

Saraceno Restaurant   15 Magdalen Street   tel: 49 171
Modern and popular Italian restaurant. Moderate.

La Sorbonne   130 A High Street   tel: 41 320
Fine French cuisine in seventeenth-century building. Good wine
list. Game in season. Expensive.

Penzance [15]

The Abbey Hotel   Abbey Street   tel: 41 11
Fine family-run restaurant with view to harbor. Good food.
Moderate.

Plush Folly [9]

Brace of Pheasants   Plush Folly   tel: Piddletrenthide 357
Intimate country inn with excellent food. Reservations a must.
Ten miles north of Dorchester. North of Bournemouth.

Plymouth [13]

Pedro's Octagon   69 Union Street   tel: Plymouth 60 417
Excellent choice for fresh seafood. Very expensive.

Priddy [25]

Miner's Arms   Priddy   tel: 217
A lively pub with its very own ale. Excellent restaurant serving at dinner and Sunday lunch such specialties as rabbit pie and simmering snails. Be sure to reserve. Expensive. Twenty-one miles south of Bristol.

Richmond [41]

Frenchgate Hotel   59-61 Frenchgate   tel: 20 87
Family-owned hotel serving excellent food. Quite expensive. Northwest of York; south of Darlington.

St. Helier [11] (Jersey)

La Capannina   67 Halett Place   tel: 34 602
Small Italian restaurant serving some French dishes as well. Fine. Moderate. Open all year.

Trattoria Bella Napoli   6 Cheapside   tel: 33 705
Varied cuisine—all very good. Moderate.

St. Mawes [14]

Rising Sun Restaurant   St. Mawes   tel: 233
On the seafront is a bright and cheery restaurant with good food. Moderate. Across the bay from Falmouth.

St. Peter Port [11] (Guernsey)

La Frégate   St. Peter Port   tel: 24 624
Charming French restaurant with excellent food and wines.

Salisbury [10]

Haunch of Venison   Minster Street   tel: 22 024
Charming old fourteenth-century inn with traditional taste and fine English cooking. Moderate.

Tudor Rose Inn   Salisbury   tel: Fordinbridge 22 27
In the town of Burgate ten miles south of Salisbury. Popular rustic inn with marvelous English cooking. Reserve.

Strachur [50]

Creggans Inn   Strachur   tel: 279
Marvelous country cooking in serene setting on Lake Fyne. Moderate. Northwest of Glasgow.

Stratford-upon-Avon [28]

Giovanni   Ely Street   tel: 35 28
Extremely fine Italian restaurant. Expensive.

Marianne Français   3 Greenhill Street   tel: 35 63
One of the finer French restaurants in the region. Expensive.

Tewkesbury [26]

Royal Hop Pole Hotel Restaurant   Church Street   tel: 32 36
Fine restaurant with open fireplace. Attractive and pleasant. Moderately expensive. North of Gloucester.

Thaxted [21]

The Recorder's House   High Street   tel: 438
Charming English country inn atmosphere with superb country cooking. Expensive. North of London to southeast of Cambridge.

Thornbury [25]

Thornbury Castle   Thornbury   tel: 41 26 47
One of England's finest restaurants specializing in superb French cuisine. Elegant sixteenth-century château with lovely furnishings and paintings. Evening dinners and Sunday lunch only. Closed Monday. Near Severn Bridge twelve miles north of Bristol.

Truro [14]

Rendezvous des Gourmets   10 Pydar Street   tel: 29 79
One of the best restaurants in England, with very fine French cuisine and wines. Expensive, but worth it. North of Falmouth.

Tunbridge Wells [1]

Elizabeth Barn Restaurant   Londale Gardens   tel: 27 469
Fine English restaurant with regional dishes. Moderate. South of London.

Royal Wells Inn   Mount Ephraim   tel: 23 414
Attractive restaurant serving both English and French dishes. Garden atmosphere. Moderate.

Tutbury [33]

Ye Olde Dog & Partridge   High Street   tel: 2162
Unusual fourteenth-century inn with fine English and French cuisine. Quite expensive. Northwest of Burton-upon-Trent; southwest of Nottingham.

Wallington [45]

Wallington Hall   Wallington   tel: 82 613
Seventeenth-century hall with fine exhibits, woods, and garden. Clock Tower restaurant twenty miles northwest of Newcastle. Open April through October.

Warwick [20]

Westgate Arms   Bowling Green Street   tel: 42 362
Excellent food in a fine traditional restaurant with superb view. Expensive. South of Coventry.

Whitley Bay [45]

Seaton Delaval   Whitley Bay   tel: 48 17 59
Elegant eighteenth-century manor with lovely Norman church nearby. Noted for its medieval banquets. Quite expensive. Ten miles east of Newcastle.

Winchelsea [3]

New Inn   Winchelsea   tel: 252
Warm, simple inn. Very modest but pleasant. Inexpensive.
Across from Rye.

Winchester [6]

Elizabethan Restaurant   18-19 Jury Street   tel: 35 66
Authentic English restaurant serving local dishes. Very popular.
Moderate.

Woodbridge [22]

The Captain's Table   7 Quay Street   tel: Woodbridge 3145
Friendly restaurant near the wharf with fresh fish dishes and
English specialties including fine grills. Moderate. South of
Norwich.

York [41]

White Rose Luncheon Restaurant   Jubbergate   tel: 538 45
Old-fashioned restaurant, with four hundred years of history, in
the city marketplace. Fine grills and fish dishes. Superb wines.
Moderate.

Young's Hotel   High Petersgate   tel: 24 229
Small and warm restaurant popular with the locals. Home
cooked food at a moderate price. Reserve.

Terry's   Helen's Square   tel: 23 528
Tea shop famous for chocolates and pastries.

Betty's   Helen's Square   tel: 22 323
Small café serving typical English fare. Quite nice. Moderate.

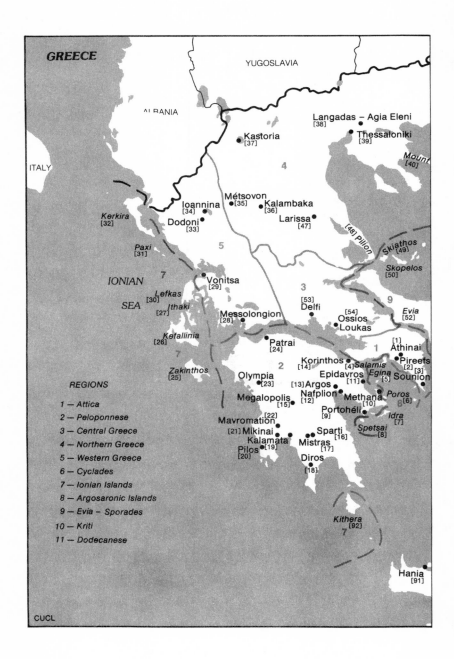

GREECE

YUGOSLAVIA

ALBANIA

ITALY

Langadas – Agia Eleni
[38]
●
●Thessaloniki
[39]

●Kastoria
[37]

4

Mount
[40]

Métsovon
●[35]
Ioannina
[34]●
●Kalambaka
[36]
Dodoni●
[33]
Larissa●
[47]

Kerkira
[32]

[48] Pilion

Paxi
[31]

5

Skiathos
[49]

IONIAN   7
Lefkas
[30]●
SEA   Ithaki
[27]●
●Vonitsa
[29]

Skopelos
[50]

9

3
[53]
Delfi
●
Evia
[52]

[54]
Ossios
●Loukas

●Messolongion
[28]

Kefallinia
[26]

●Patrai
[24]

[1]
●Athinai

7
Zakinthos
[25]

2
Korinthos
[14]●
●Salamis
[4]
Epidavros
●Argos
[13]

●Pireefs
[2][3]
Egina
[5]
Sounion

REGIONS

Olympia
●[23]

●[11]
Nafplion
[12]

Poros
6●[6]

1 — Attica
2 — Peloponnese
3 — Central Greece
4 — Northern Greece
5 — Western Greece
6 — Cyclades
7 — Ionian Islands
8 — Argosaronic Islands
9 — Evia – Sporades
10 — Kriti
11 — Dodecanese

Megalopolis●
[15]

●Methana
[10]

Mavromation
[21]Mikinai
[22]●
●
Kalamata
Pilos●[19]
[20]

●Portohéli
[9]

Idra
[7]

●Sparti
[16]
Mistras
[17]
●Diros
[18]

Spetsai
[8]

Kithera
[92]
7

Hania
[91]
●

CUCL

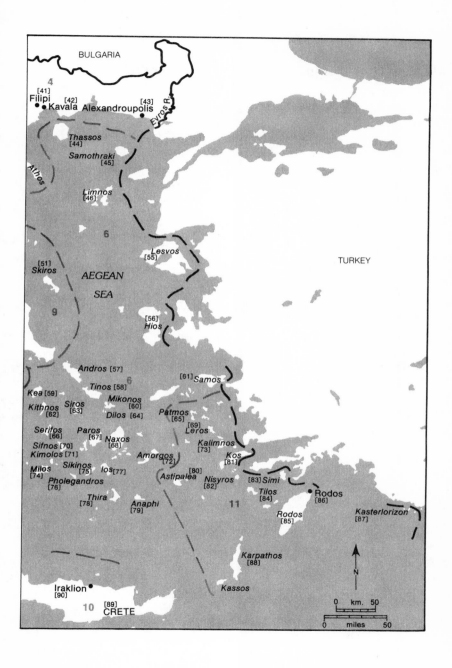

BULGARIA

4
[41]
Filipi [42]
• • Kavala   Alexandroupolis [43]
                                    Evros R.

Thassos
[44]
Samothraki
[45]

Limnos
[46]

Athos

6

Lesvos
[55]

TURKEY

[51]
Skiros

AEGEAN

SEA

9

[56]
Hios

Andros [57]

[61] Samos

Tinos [58]

6

Kea [59]
Kithnos
[62]
Siros
[63]
Mikonos
[60]
Dilos [64]
Patmos
[65]
[69]
Leros

Serifos
[66]
Paros
[67]
Naxos
[68]
Kalimnos
[73]

Sifnos [70]
Kimolos [71]
Amorgos
[72]
Kos
[81]

Milos
[74]
Sikinos
[75]
Ios[77]
[80]
Astipalea
Nisyros
[82]
[83] Simi

Pholegandros
[76]
Tilos
[84]
Rodos
[86]

Thira
[78]
Anaphi
[79]
11
Rodos
[85]
Kasterlorizon
[87]

N

Karpathos
[88]

Iraklion •
[90]
Kassos
0   km. 50

10 [89]
CRETE
0   miles   50

WHAT TO SEE

It's mild weather, archaeological sites, and the unique Greek life-style (particularly on the fourteen hundred islands) that draw most travellers to Greece. The southeastern corner of the mainland is the natural gateway into the country. *Athens* [1] (Athinai) proves captivating for several days of sight-seeing which normally includes the Acropolis, National Archaeological Museum (pay the small fee for the fabulous Santorini exhibit), and an evening at a taverna in the Plaka. Excursions to *Dafni* to see the Byzantine monastery (a wine festival is held here from July 1 to September 30) and to *Sounion* [3] for a sunset near the temple are highly recommended.

Try to visit one of the nearby islands (avoid the weekend if possible). *Egina* [5] (Aegina) offers comfortable living, interesting ruins, and delicious fresh seafood. *Idra* [7] (Hydra) has become an artists' retreat, while *Poros* [6] is more cosmopolitan, and *Salamis* [4] more Spartan (a favorite with bathers). *Spetsai* [8] (Spetse) has French and Italian accents and appeals to many.

Southwest of Athens you'll head into the mysterious Peloponese, with its ruins of many great cities. Visit *Mikinai* [21] (Mycenae), *Sparti* [16] (Sparta), *Olympia* [23], *Mistras* [17], and *Korinthos* [14] (Corinth). During the summer take in a play at the ancient theatre of *Epidavros* [11] (Epidauros) and visit the *Glyfada* cave.

Off shore are the Ionian Islands, pleasant from mid-March until late October. *Corfu* [32] (Kerkira) offers colorful island life with the kind of comfort you'd expect on the Continent. *Ithaki* [27] (Ithaca) appeals to bathers looking for isolated beaches while *Kafallinia* [26] has a harbor filled with yachts. The scented island of *Zakinthos* [25] tempts many with its easygoing yet cosmopolitan flavor. If you want to venture back onto shore, try to reach the medieval town of *Ioannina* [34].

To the north lies the perfect area for the uncommon traveller. Here you'll really be into the undiscovered Greece. Visit the monasteries of Metéora near *Kalambaka* [36] and those of *Mount Athos* [40]. The latter are open only to men. You'll see an unbelievable amount of fine Byzantine art. Hikers will head to Mount Olympus near *Larissa* [47], while travellers looking for a more typical village should seek out the hideaway of *Kastoria* [37].

Farther south you won't want to miss the temple at *Delfi* [53] (Delphi), most photogenic in the early morning or at sunset.

Off the eastern shore you'll find fascinating islands. *Evia* [52] (Euboea) has been an "in" island for a number of years and is packed during the summer since it's easily reached from Athens. *Skiros* [51] (Skyros) is more isolated, as is *Skopelos* [50] which remains rugged and rough. Seventy idyllic beaches attract many to *Skiathos* [49], more sophisticated than the other islands.

Stretching from the far north to the south you'll find the Cyclades. *Mikonos* [60] (Mykonos) continues to be the most famous drawing in an annual crowd of would-be jet-setters. Tiny *Dilos* [64] is an archaeological gem, as is *Thira* [78] (Santorini), which rises hundreds of feet from the sea (note that the famous frescoes are now in Athens). The undiscovered prize of *Limnos* [46] (Lemnos) offers sun-drenched island life in comfortable surroundings.

Rodos [85] is another in the prize category. It's warm, isolated, and very Greek (with a mixture of other cultures as well). The city of Rhodes is a kind of architectural stew. Recommended is an excursion to *Lindos* and the Valley of the Butterflies at *Petaloudes* (the latter only interesting in the summer). The weather on this island makes it an ideal off-season destination.

The weather does the same for Crete, famed for the Minoan ruins. Visit *Knossos* with its palace of Minos, *Gournia*, and *Festos* (Phaestos). The twelve-mile hike through the Samaria Gorge west of *Hania* [91] will appeal to some.

WHAT'S THE WEATHER REALLY LIKE?

From June to early September you can expect torrid and dry weather. Late September and October are lovely months in which to travel—you'll avoid the summer crowds and benefit from milder fall weather. From November to mid-March it can be quite chilly, rainy, and windy. It's still mild weather, but you won't be tempted to swim in the Mediterranean at this time. Late March, April, and May can be unpredictable but are often spectacular as the wild poppies and pomegranates burst into bloom.

SOME SUGGESTIONS FOR A MORE ENJOYABLE TRIP

Greece is one of the most affordable countries in Europe. This is one area in which you might like to splurge by staying in a luxury hotel or dining at an elegant restaurant. The bill will be surprisingly low. Less expensive hotels offer clean and comfortable accommodations but tend to be modern and somewhat sterile. Restaurants generally offer good but only rarely exceptional cooking. In some cases you'll be asked to go into the kitchen to pick out the food you'd like prepared for you. This is almost always true in the smaller villages of rural areas. Just point to the squid, fish, or chicken you'd like to eat. Many Greek wines are laced with resin. Give them a try. Then, if you don't care for the taste, ask for *aretsinoto krasi* (wines without resin). Greeks eat late by American standards: lunch from 1:00 p.m. to 4:00 p.m. and dinner from 10:00 p.m. to midnight. You should leave both the waiter and the busboy (if there is one) a small tip. Tip for the waiter goes on the plate, tip for the busboy on the table cloth (if there is one). There's often a language barrier once you get out of Athens, particularly in tiny restaurants. You'll have to communicate in sign language and simply have the waiter write the price of food on a bit of paper (carry a pencil and pad). Toilets can be a problem in some areas. You may prefer to avoid them—a good reason to carry toilet paper with you. Driving is the best way to see Greece and many times the only way. Roads are often poor. Allow much more time for driving than you normally would. Be sure to fill your tank when heading into the interior, where stations are hard to find. In town you'll find that walking and taxis are the ideal combination to get to know Athens. Taxis are great bargains (tip the driver with small change). Use the airline bus from the airport into town, however. When sightseeing, you may wish to avoid the noon-to-early-afternoon heat by relaxing in your hotel or in a cafe where pastries are delicious (Greeks have a sweet tooth). The Acropolis is best visited in early morning, late afternoon, or by moonlight (it's open when there's a full moon). The beaches to the southeast of Athens are the most popular, but the ones to the northeast are actually better. Note that beaches and roads are jammed on Sundays. If you take a cruise to some of the islands, plan ahead by bringing a food pack and air mattress with you. Be sure to include a jug of water, since you'll be terribly thirsty on the sea.* Shopping in Greece is delightful. As in southern European countries, bargaining is expected even if you already think the price is more than reasonable.

WHERE TO STAY

Aghia Galini [90] (Crete)

Akropole   4 Makariou Street   tel: 29 774
Small and simple inn. Very modest and clean rooms with balconies. No hot water and no meals. Inexpensive. Southwest of Iraklion.

Agios Nikolaos [90] (Crete)

Creta Beach Hotel   tel: 28 63 01
A large beach hotel on twenty acres of grounds. The stone bungalow hotel is a favorite of the English. Pool. Tennis. Expensive. Open mid-March through October. Near Heraklion.

Elounda Hotel   Elounda   tel: 28 461
This large and very modern hotel blends in with the setting; some say it's the nicest resort hotel in Greece. The luxury village features bungalows on the slope, with a lovely view of the sea. Pebble beach. Pool. Tennis. Sailing. Expensive. East of Iraklion.

Minos Beach Bungalows   Agios Nikolaos   tel: 22 345
Luxury accommodations in rooms facing Mirabello Bay. The cottage colony practically hangs over the water. Fresh garden atmosphere. Very comfortable rooms. Excellent for swimming and fishing. Pool. Tennis. Expensive.

Mirabello Hotel   Agios Nikolaos   tel: 28 400
A large beach hotel with an island atmosphere, simple and informal. Located only two and a half miles from town, it's quite comfortable with an accent on local taste. Some bungalows are available. Pool. Tennis. Quite expensive.

---

* Often provided but at inflated rates.

Xenia Hotel   Sofokli Benizelow   tel: 28 40 00
Quite large, comfortable hotel with lovely view. Nice regional
restaurant. Pool. Moderate.

Alexandroupolis [43]

Astir Motel   Alexandroupolis   tel: 26 448
In this out-of-the-way region you'll find a small and inexpensive
inn with comfortable and modest rooms. It's open all year and
geared to hunters who would like to shoot game-birds in the off
season.

Andros [57]

Xenia   Andros   tel: 22 270
Tiny inn with modest rooms. Comfortable. Near the beach. Inexpensive. Open April to October.

Arta [34]

Xenia   Frourion Artis   tel: 74 13
Pleasant modern hotel. Good spot for hunters and fishermen.
Tennis. Inexpensive. South of Ioannina.

Athens [1]

Athens is the bargain capital of Europe when it comes to inexpensive and clean accommodations. Even the luxury hotels are
in the affordable range, at least for a night or two. Most hotels
offer less atmosphere than you would find in other cities, but
they're comfortable and certainly excellent in value.

Amalia   10 Amalias Avenue   tel: 323-7301
Nice location for this small traditional hotel with modern
facilities. Comfortable and pleasant rooms. Quite expensive, but
good value.

Athenée Palace Hotel   1 Kolokotroni Street   tel: 323-0791
Good location. A large, deluxe hotel with a traditional flair.
Comfortable rooms—stress the fact you want a quiet one. Quite
expensive, but good value.

Athens Hilton   46 Vassilissis Sofias Avenue   tel: 73 03 01
One mile from the center of town is this huge shiny link in the Hilton chain. The plumbing is perfect in the modern and comfortable rooms—ask for one with a view of the Parthenon. Exquisite use of marble and a lovely rooftop restaurant. All the tinsel imaginable, including a pool. Lots of comfort and lots of tourists. Very expensive.

Attica Palace Hotel   6 Karageorghi Servias   tel: 322-3006
Very comfortable and tasteful hotel in the moderate price range. Nice location and lovely view from the roof garden. Air conditioned throughout. Excellent value.

Electra Palace Hotel   18 Nicodimou Street   tel: 324-1401
Comfortable hotel at the foot of the Acropolis. All rooms with bath. Rooftop pool. Air-conditioned throughout. Good value in moderate price range.

Hotel Grande Bretagne   Constitution Square   tel: 323-0251
Superb location. The huge traditional hotel, nicknamed the "GB," has become a symbol of class with great views from rooms high up on the front of the building. The hotel has been the setting for many novels and almost witnessed the assassination of Sir Winston Churchill in its hallowed halls. It's become a bit touristy recently, but it's still very fine and very expensive.

King George   Constitution Square   tel: 323-0651
Superb location. A large traditional hotel—one of the best in town, with a regal atmosphere. Comforable and attractively furnished rooms. Ask for a room on one of the top two floors. Lovely rooftop restaurant. Very expensive.

King's Palace   4 Venizelos Avenue   tel: 62 32 31
The large hotel has been recently renovated. Its plush rooms are very comfortable—ask for one high up (those with a westerly view are the quietest). Very dignified atmosphere. From the roof garden you can see the Changing of the Guards. Expensive.

Omiros Hotel   15 Apollonos Street   tel: 323-5486
Small hotel with modest, compact rooms. All with bath and air-conditioning. Roof garden. Good budget choice.

Plaka Hotel   7 Kapnikareas   tel: 322-2096
Modern, multistory building with simple, but comfortable,

rooms. Good family choice. Nice roof garden. View to the Acropolis. So-so food. Nice value in budget category.

Royal Olympic   *28-32 Diakou Street*   tel: 922-0185/922-6411
Small modern hotel geared to businessmen in a fine location. The rooms are comfortable—ask for room in the front as high up as possible. The restaurant has excellent steaks. Pool. Expensive.

St. George Lycabettus   *Kleomenous 2*   tel: 79 07 11
A large modern hotel with fine service and a good view—one to be watched. Pool. Moderate.

Corfu: See Ermones, Gouvia, Glyfada, Kerkira, Moraitika.

Corinth [14] (Korinthos)

King Saron   *Korinthos*   tel: 25 301
Luxury beach hotel about three and a half miles from the modern city. Excellent suites. Fine rooftop restaurant. Tennis. Pool. Moderate.

Crete: See Aghia Galini, Agios Nikolaos, Hania, Hersonissos, Iraklion, Mallia.

Dassia [32] (Corfu)

Castello Bimbelli   *Dassia*   tel: 28 184
Only seven miles from Corfu town, this former hunting lodge is now a delightful hotel overlooking the sea, in a twenty-five-acre park. The accommodations are simple, calm, and comfortable. The atmosphere is authentic, with some fine antiques in the public rooms. During cooler weather a log fire burns to take away the chill. Transportation to the beach one mile away. Moderately expensive.

Delfi [53]

Delfi Hotel   *Delfi*   tel: 82 350
A fine hotel overlooking the valley. One of the better in town. Moderate.

Amalia   Delfi   tel: 82 260/82 101
Large hotel with pleasant rooms. Good cooking. A bit touristy.
Moderate.

Xenia   Delfi   tel: 82 151
Small hotel with comfortable rooms and lovely view. Pleasant.
Inexpensive.

Vouzas   Delfi   tel: 82 233
New hotel offering modest rooms with a nice view. Moderate.

Egina [5]

Marisa Bay Hotel & Bungalows   Aghia Marina   tel: 32 282
Large resort with a nice location and comfortable rooms. Pool.
Tennis. Moderate to expensive. Ten miles from town.

Nafsika Hotel   21 April Boulevard No. 55 (in town)   tel: 22 333
A small bungalow complex close to the beach. Not fancy, but
comfortable. Open April to October. Moderate.

Brown Hotel   4 Toti Chatzi   tel: 22 271
Lovely hotel on the water directly in town with fine rooms—ask
for one overlooking the garden. Quiet. Moderate.

Ermones [32] (Corfu)

Ermones Beach   Ermones   tel: 94 241
Huge bungalow complex nine miles to the southwest of Corfu
town. Overlooking the sea with comfortable and simple rooms.
Pool, beach, tennis, and a bus to the golf links. Expensive. Open
April to October.

Evia Island [52]

Lucy Hotel   8 Voudouri Avenue, Chalkis   tel: 23 831
Large first-class hotel with view to the sea and its own beach.
Some bungalows. Quite comfortable. Tennis. Inexpensive.

St. Minas Beach Hotel   Chalkis   tel: 81 211
Large hotel with modern facilities and quite comfortable, if simple, rooms. Beach and garden atmosphere. Tennis. Moderate.

Aegli Hotel   Aedipsos   tel: 22 216
Small, with functional rooms and furnishings. Nice location on the sea with a relaxed atmosphere. Inexpensive.

Avra   Aedipsos   tel: 22 216
Fine beach-resort hotel with a nice restaurant. Comfortable. Inexpensive. Open April to October.

Gouvia [32] (Corfu)

Corcyra Beach Hotel & Bungalows   Gouvia   tel: 28 770
A large central building is surrounded by a lovely garden and fine bungalows. The rooms are very comfortable. The emphasis here is on water sports. Tennis. Pool. Only five miles from Corfu. Quite expensive. Open April to October.

Glyfada [1] (Athens)

Astir Hotel & Bungalows   Vas. Georgiou 11   tel: 894-6461
A large resort complex only ten miles from Athens. Lovely area with trees and flowers near the beach. Deluxe accommodations. Fine food. Water sports, tennis, and golf nearby. Ultraexpensive, but with substantial off season reductions.

Glyfada [32] (Corfu)

Glyfada Beach   Glyfada   tel: 29 390/23 012
Ten miles west of Corfu town is this large first-class hotel with a fascinating cliff backdrop. Relaxing and rather casual atmosphere. Comfortable, not luxurious rooms. Ask for one with a sea view. Pool. Expensive.

Hania [91] (Chania) (Crete)

Doma   124 Venizelou Street   tel: 21 722
This lovely old house offers very simple and quite comfortable rooms. The overall feeling is of relaxed elegance, not luxury. Moderate.

Xenia Hotel   Hania   tel: 24 561
Small, modest hotel with simple rooms. Pool. Moderate.

Hersonissos [89] (Crete)

Nora   Hersonissos   tel: 21 271
Fifteen miles from Iraklion is a large resort hotel oriented to water sports. The rooms are modest but comfortable. Pool. Moderate.

Idra [7]

Leto Hotel   Idra   tel: 52 280
A small inn with rustic but comfortable rooms. Inexpensive. Open April to October.

Miramare Beach Hotel   Idra   tel: 52 300
Bungalow complex on the beach. Geared to water sports. Quite inexpensive. Open mid-April to mid-October.

Miranda Hotel   Idra   tel: 32 230
Once a mansion, now converted into a tiny hotel with rustic rooms. Delightful. Inexpensive. Open only from April to October.

Xenia Hotel   Idra   tel: 52 217
In town. A small hotel with modest and inexpensive rooms. Open all year.

Ioannina [34]

Palladion Hotel   1 Scoumbourdi Street   tel: 25 856
Central location. A large hotel with simple and pleasant rooms. Inexpensive.

Xenia Hotel   33 King George II Street   tel: 25 087
Nice hotel with a lovely view to the lake. Comfortable. Fine garden. Moderate.

Iraklion [90] (Crete)

Astir Hotel   25th of August Street   tel: 28 22 22
The small hotel has a colonial atmosphere. Located directly in the city in a noisy and lively section. Comfortable, but not luxurious. Inexpensive.

Atlantis   *Meramvelou & Igias Streets*   *tel: 28 82 41*
The large hotel with a lovely view of the harbor offers many quiet and comfortable rooms. Not fancy, but nice. Quite expensive.

Knossos Beach Hotel and Bungalows   *Iraklion*   *tel: 28 84 50*
Seven miles from the city you'll find this large and quite modern hotel with a relaxed feeling. The rooms (mostly in bungalows) are basic and pleasant. Expensive. Open March to October.

Itea [53]

Xenia   Itéa   tel: 32 262
Only twelve miles from Delfi is a less touristy spot on the sea. A quiet and secluded motel with a quite fine restaurant.

Kalambaka [36]

Xenia Hotel   Kalambaka   tel: 23 27
Small hotel with a distinctive view. Lovely and very quiet setting. Simple and comfortable. Moderate. Open April to November.

Kastoria [37]

Xenia   Kastoria   tel: 22 565
Delightful small hotel with a unique lakeside setting. Traditional flavor. Quite comfortable. Open April to October. Inexpensive.

Kastron [46] (Limnos)

Killini Golden Beach   Kastron   tel: 37 104
Lovely new resort hotel two miles from Kastron directly on the sea. Fine cuisine. Pool. Expensive.

Kavala [42]

Tosca Beach Hotel   Kavala   tel: 50 03
Large bungalow beach-resort. Garden atmosphere. Comfortable. Moderate.

Kerkira [32] (Corfu)

Corfu Palace Hotel   *V. Konstandinou Street*   *tel: 29 485*
One of the island's leading large luxury hotels with a formal atmosphere. Lovely view to the sea. The rooms are comfortable and pleasant. Good cuisine. Delightful pool in a subtropical garden area. Casino. Sports, including tennis and sailing. Ultraexpensive.

Cavalieri   *4 Kapodistrou Street*   *tel: 29 283*
Located on the outskirts of town, this seventeenth-century mansion has been converted into a pleasant hotel. Lovely beaches and coves nearby. The rooms are both simple and comfortable—ask for one with a sea view. This way you may get a glimpse of Albania. The atmosphere is fresh and warm. Moderate.

Corfu Kanoni   *Kanoni*   *tel: 22 980/23 996*
This is a large first-class hotel with a breathtaking view of the bay. The rooms are comfortable without luxury. Oriented to business meetings. Pool. Moderate.

Kinetta [1]

Akti Kinetta Beach & Bungalows   *Kinetta Beach*   *tel: 323-2053*
The cottage colony is just a short drive from Athens. Lovely beach resort with gardens. Comfortable. Quite expensive.

Kos [81]

Alexandra Hotel   *25-31 Martiou Street*   *tel: 28 301*
Large hotel close to the beach with comfortable rooms and a fine view. Open March to November. Moderate.

Oscar   *Doris Hotel*   *59 El Venizelou Street*   *tel: 80 90*
Large hotel with quiet and comfortable rooms. Pool. Inexpensive. Open all year.

Dimitra Beach Hotel   *Aghios Fokas*   *tel: 28 581*
Secluded bungalow complex four miles from the port. Fine beach, nightlife, and restaurant. Very relaxing. Inexpensive.

Atlantis Hotel   Kos   tel: Call operator
Brand-new beach hotel which should be one of the best on the island—worth checking into.

Lagonissi [1]

Xenia Lagonissi Hotel & Bungalows   Lagonissi   tel: 895-8511
Twenty-five miles from Athens (coach service by hotel). Huge resort blending into the natural setting. Sports-oriented with beach, pool, and tennis. Good food. Expensive.

Lesvos [55]

Delphinia I Hotel   Methymna   tel: 22 627
Large hotel near the beach with modest rooms geared to families. Pool. Fishing. Moderate. Open mid-April to mid-October.

Motel Votsala   Thermi   tel: 31 231
Small inn with nicely furnished rooms. View of the sea. Ideal for families. Moderate. Open May to October.

Xenia Hotel   Lesvos   tel: 22 713
Four miles from town and on the sea. Quite nice. Moderate.

Limnos [46]

Hotel Akti Myrina   Myrina   tel: 22 681/323-0249
Large cottage colony with stone buildings in local style. Right on the sea with a pleasant garden atmosphere. The isolated bungalows have an open and airy feeling—luxurious island living. Geared to water sports. Fine local cooking. Tennis. Open May to mid-October. Expensive, but worth it.

Mallia [89] (Crete)

Akti Sirinion Hotel   Mallia   tel: 28 24 04
Very large resort hotel with a lovely location. Simple but pleasant rooms. Expensive.

Ikaros Village   Mallia   tel: 31 268
Large resort hotel with an emphasis on relaxation and informality. Simple but pleasant rooms. Water sports, beach, pool. Expensive.

Sirens   Mallia   tel: 31 231
Large resort hotel with modest and quite pleasant rooms. Secluded. Pool. Open April through October. Expensive.

Mikonos [60]

Alkistis Hotel   Mikonos   tel: 22 332
Large resort hotel with bungalows on the beach. Lovely sea view. Quite comfortable. Expensive. Open April to October.

Leto Hotel   Mikonos   tel: 22 207
Small inn near the harbor with comfortable rooms. Nice feeling. Good food for the island. Moderate. Open all year.

Xenia   Mikonos   tel: 230
Small hotel with simple but pleasant rooms. Inexpensive rates, which are a fine value for the island. Open April to October.

Moraitika [32] (Corfu)

Marbella Beach Hotel   Aghios Ioannis Peristeron   tel: 92 245
Eleven miles south of Corfu town is a large, deluxe hotel with a view to the sea. Pool. Tennis. Beach. Bus service to town. Expensive.

Miramare Beach   Moraitika   tel: 28 183
Ten miles from Corfu town is a large hotel featuring cabanas in an olive grove. Comfortable with a private beach filled with bikini-clad Scandinavians bent on sun and fun from mid-April to the end of October. Tennis. Ultraexpensive.

Nissaki Beach   Nissaki   tel: 91 232
The Nissaki Beach is one of the many huge new first-class hotels opening up to accommodate the influx of tourists in the high season. Located in an olive grove with its own beach, it offers comfortable and compact rooms. Pool. Expensive. Open April to October. Eighteen miles north of Corfu town.

Nafplion [12]

Amphitryon Hotel   Nafplion   tel: 27 366
Small hotel with nice view of the harbor and pleasant rooms.
Pool. Moderate.

Xenia   Acronafplia   tel: 27 205
On a ridge with a fine view. Small hotel with very comfortable
rooms. Inexpensive.

Olympia [23]

Miramare Olympia   Skafidia   tel: 23 601
Huge resort hotel in secluded area with comfortable rooms and
bungalows. Pool. Tennis. Open April to October. Expensive.

SPAP Hotel   Olympia   tel: 21 514
Small hotel with very comfortable rooms. Pleasant location.
Good cooking. Moderate.

Xenia Hotel   Olympia   tel: 21 510
Small, modest hotel in pleasant location. Comfortable rooms,
some with shower. Inexpensive.

Parnes [1]

Mont Parnes Hotel & Casino   Mt. Parnes   tel: 24 91 11
Twenty miles from Athens. High on a mountain with a lovely
view in a natural setting. Quite luxurious, with fine food and
service. Subdued, but still oriented to the casino crowd. Expensive.

Paros [67]

Xenia   Paros   tel: 21 394
Small hotel with modest rooms. Fishing. Inexpensive. Open April to October.

Poros [6]

New Aigli Hotel   Poros   tel: 22 372
Small hotel with simple rooms. Moderate.

Poros Hotel   Poros   tel: 22 216
Small hotel on the sea with modest accommodations. Inexpensive. Open April to October.

Rodos [85]

Europa Hotel   28th October St. No. 94   tel: 22 711
Quite large and comfortable hotel located by the sea. Very modest, but with bath and nice view. Open April to October. Inexpensive.

Astir Hotel   V. Konstandinou-Orfanidou Street   tel: 26 284/86 81
Very large hotel with good view to Turkey. Near the beach. Elegant but quite informal. Fine restaurant with both French and local specialities. Casino. Pool. Tennis. Ultraexpensive. Open all year.

Imperial Hotel   23 King Constantine St.   tel: 22 431
A modern hotel with comfortable, simple rooms—all with bath or shower. Short walk to beach. Moderate.

Olympic Hotel   12 King Pavlus Square   tel: 24 311
Small, simple hotel in quiet location, just a short distance from the beach. Modest rooms, most with bath or shower. Moderate.

Park Hotel   12 Riga Fereou St.   tel: 24 611
Quite large hotel with modern, comfortable rooms. Located in peaceful area, only short distance from sea. Nice view. Good regional restaurant. Pool. Nice. Moderately expensive.

Riviera Hotel   Miaouli Beach   tel: 22 581
Attractive beach hotel with comfortable rooms—all with bath or shower. Good view. Open April to October. Inexpensive to moderate.

Spartalis Hotel   Nic. Plastiras St.   tel: 24 371
In the center of town. Comfortable, yet modest. Very fine regional restaurant. Inexpensive.

Samos [61]

Xenia   Samos   tel: 27 463
Small hotel with modest and inexpensive rooms. Open April to October.

Skiathos Island [49]

Skiathos Palace   Koukounaries   tel: 42 242
Modern hotel with sports as main attraction: riding, sailing, swimming. Nice rooms with view to the sea. Very expensive.

Nostos   Tzaneria   tel: 42 520
Large hotel with modern facilities in a natural setting. Riding, sailing, pool. View to the bay. Moderate.

Esperides   Achladies   tel: 42 245
Large hotel on a beach. Comfortable rooms. Pool. Moderate. Open April to mid-October.

Xenia Hotel   Skiathos Island   tel: 42 041
Small, comfortable hotel near the beach. Moderate to expensive. Open May to October.

Spetsai [8]

Posidonion   Spetse   tel: 72 208
Simple inn with calm feeling. Almost as if you're outdoors. Inexpensive. Open all year.

Kasteli Hotel   Spetse   tel: 72 311
Simple, but offering bungalows for privacy. Fishing and hunting can be arranged. Moderate. Open April to October.

Thassos [44]

Makryammos Bungalows   Limin   tel: 21 202
Lovely large cottage colony in local style with view of the sea. Very comfortable. Expensive. Open April to mid-October.

Thessaloniki [39]

Hotel Mediterranean Palace   *9 V. Constantinou*   *tel: 28 521*
Large traditional hotel in a quiet but central location. Lovely view. Comfortable rooms. Moderate.

Electra Palace Hotel   *Aristotelous Square*   *tel: 32 221*
Central location. Large, comfortable hotel. Inexpensive.

Tinos [58]

Tinos Beach Hotel   *Kionia*   *tel: 22 626*
Very large hotel with modern rooms. Comfortable and quite pleasant. Moderate.

Varibobi [1]

Auberge Tatoi   *Varibobi*   *tel: 801-4537*
Tiny inn only a short drive from Athens in a natural setting. Large and comfortable rooms. Quiet and relaxing. Moderate— superb value.

Vouliagmeni [1]

Astir Palace Hotel & Bungalows   *Vouliagmeni*   *tel: 804-0211*
Huge hotel with luxury bungalows only fifteen miles from Athens. On a lovely bay with beach. Spacious and comfortable rooms. Tennis. Golf nearby. Very expensive.

Zakinthos Island [25]

Strada Marina Hotel   *16 Lomvardou Street*   *tel: 22 761*
Small and modest hotel with view of the sea. Comfortable. Inexpensive. Open all year.

WHERE TO EAT

Athens [1]

Gerofinikas   *10 Pindarou Street*   *tel: 62 27 19*
Mediterranean cuisine is served in a lovely dining room. Small, with an intimate feeling. Good service. Expensive.

Vladimiros   *12 Aristodemou Street*   *tel: 71 74 07*
A large restaurant serving Greek and Russian food in a garden atmosphere. Fine food and service. Moderate.

Costoyannis   *Zaimi Street*   *tel: Call operator*
Not at all plush, this restaurant serves Greek food in an authentic atmosphere. You're expected to trot into the kitchen to pick out your main dish. Lots of fun. Theater groups often dine here late in the evening. Quite reasonable.

Ta Papakia   *5 Iridanou Street*   *tel: 71 24 21*
A unique blend of elegance and simplicity with duckling as the specialty. Warm. Good service. Moderate.

Dionyssus   *45 Roberti Galli Street*   *tel: 91 23 91/91 37 78*
At the food of the Acropolis is a rather touristy restaurant serving quite good international and local dishes. Expensive.

Delphi   *13 Nikis Street*   *tel: 323-4869*
Fine Greek and continental cuisine. Moderately expensive.

Zonar's   *9 Panepistimiou Avenue*   *tel: 323-0336*
Excellent Greek specialities with lots of style. Very popular and centrally located. Moderate.

Balthazar   *27 Tsocha Street & Vournazou*   *tel: 644-1215*
Lively restaurant in the Kolonaki district with fine Greek dishes. Moderate.

Kifissia [1]

Bokaris   *17 Archarnon*   *tel: 801-2589*
Both the subway and the bus go to Kifissia, where you can dine in this thoroughly Greek restaurant. Food brought to you on

trays with a wide variety of appetizers—all of them Greek delicacies. Nice garden atmosphere. Moderate.

Pireefs [2]

Papakia   8 Karageorgi Servias   tel: 47 25 86
An old home converted into a restaurant serving Greek specialties, including delicious duckling. Plush but friendly. Moderate.

Zorbas   Pireefs   tel: 475-091
On the bay with a view of the fishing vessels. Trays of appetizers for seafood lovers. Fun. Moderate.

Rodos [85]

Norden   13 Kos Street   tel: 25 627
Fine European and Greek cuisine. Pleasant outdoors or in. Lobster is the specialty. Reasonable. Try too Casa Castellana, Taverna Alexis, and the Maison Fleuri (French and Greek specialties).

Tourkolimano [1] (Mikrolimano)

This delightful port is only a short taxi ride from Athens. Here you'll find a number of delicious seafood dishes served in a wide variety of restaurants. It's a great place to try baby squid or red mullet, two excellent Greek dishes. Best-known restaurants here are: *Varka, Kanaris, Kokkini, and Krana.*

ICELAND

ICELAND

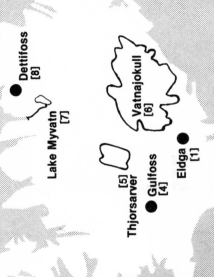

Dettifoss
[8]

Lake Myvatn
[7]

Vatnajokull
[6]

Thjorsarver
[5]

Gulfoss
[4]

Eldga
[1]

Heimaey
[2]

Eldey Rock.
[3]

WHAT TO SEE

The desolate and forbidding island of Iceland attracts offbeat travelers, who'll be rewarded with the sight of geysers, immense glaciers, hundreds of bubbling hot springs, majestic waterfalls tumbling through mile-long gashes in the earth, and birds by the thousands nesting on seaside cliffs of intriguing isolated corners or on offshore islands. The most popular sights: *Vatnajökull* [6], a glacier the size of Rhode Island and Delaware combined; the striking falls of *Dettifoss* [8] and *Gullfoss* [4] (two-hundred foot drop); *Eldey Rock* [3] with thirty thousand nesting gannets or *Thjorsarver* [5] with eleven thousand nests of pink-footed geese; the seventeen-mile chasm of *Eldga* [1], eery *Lake Myvatn* [7] in the north, and the island of *Heimaey* [2] , a modern Pompeii.

WHAT'S THE WEATHER REALLY LIKE

Most travellers venture to Iceland from May to September— during the warmer summer months there are many hours of daylight. The off-season is bleak, with heavy winds, cool temperatures, and long hours of darkness.

SOME SUGGESTIONS FOR A MORE ENJOYABLE TRIP

Icelandic Airlines offers both low-cost transatlantic flights and a special stopover package in Iceland. If the package rate seems a bit steep, ask the airlines to book a room in a small hotel or private home. They'll gladly do this free of charge. Be sure to take the airport bus to town (taxis charge a fortune for this long ride). Many tours are available to popular tourist sights, but if you prefer independent travel, be sure to book a car well in advance.

WHERE TO STAY

Reykjavik

Hotel Borg   Posthusstraeti 11   tel: 11 440
A fine small hotel in the center of town with very comfortable rooms. Elegant and popular dining room with delicious local specialties. Moderately expensive.

Hotel Loftleider   Reykjavik Airport   tel: 22 322
Very large modern commercial hotel with very comfortable rooms on the outskirts of town. Nice for an overnight stay. Expensive.

Hotel Saga   Hagatorg 1   tel: 20 600
Large modern hotel with nice view and comfortable rooms. Good in the commercial category. Very expensive.

Hotel Esja   Sudurlandsbraut 2   tel: 82 200
Large modern commercial hotel on the edge of town. Comfortable. Expensive.

Hotel Holt   Bergstadstraeti 37   tel: 21 011
Small modern hotel in central location with comfortable, if modest, rooms. Expensive.

WHERE TO EAT

Reykjavik

Hotel Borg   Posthusstraeti 11   tel: 11 440
One of the finest restaurants in town with pleasant dining room, dancing, and good service. Popular for its local specialties and international dishes. Moderate to expensive.

Naust   Vesturgata 8   tel: 17 759
Rustic bar above a pleasant restaurant in town. Quite fine food and dancing to piano music. Popular. Expensive.

IRELAND

IRELAND

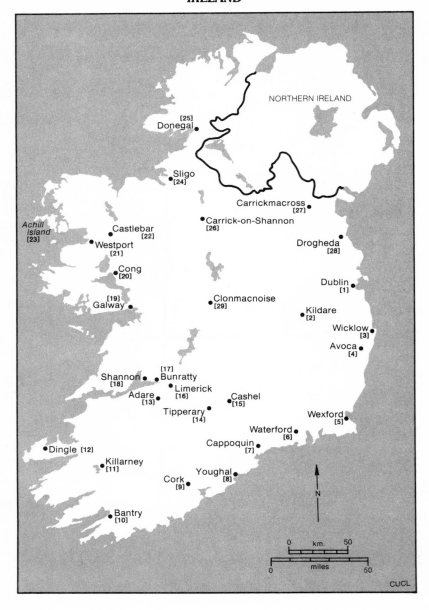

NORTHERN IRELAND

Donegal [25]

Sligo [24]

Carrickmacross [27]

Carrick-on-Shannon [26]

Achill Island [23]

Castlebar [22]

Westport [21]

Drogheda [28]

Cong [20]

Dublin [1]

Galway [19]

Clonmacnoise [29]

Kildare [2]

Wicklow [3]

Avoca [4]

Shannon [18]

Bunratty [17]

Limerick [16]

Adare [13]

Cashel [15]

Tipperary [14]

Wexford [5]

Waterford [6]

Cappoquin [7]

Dingle [12]

Killarney [11]

Cork [9]

Youghal [8]

Bantry [10]

N

0   km.   50

0   miles   50

CUCL

WHAT TO SEE

Nature lovers, sportsmen, and archaeologists are the three groups who'll find Ireland to their liking. The low prices of rooms and meals is another pleasant surprise. The *Ring of Kerry* in the southwest is a stunning drive and typical of the country's haunting beauty. Seventy salmon rivers course through the lush green hills and provide excellent fishing at low, low rates, as do the lakes famed for brown trout, which rise to the Mayfly in mid-May. Over two hundred golf courses including *Rosslare, Portmarnock, Sligo* [24], and *Bundoran* are open to the public for a modest greens fee. Archaeologists will be fascinated with the monastic ruins of *Glendalough* [3] (west of Wicklow), the Rock of *Cashel* [14], *Clonmacnoise* [29], and *Monasterboice*. And, flower lovers will head to *Birr Castle, Kildare* [2], *Glengariff*, and nearby *Garinish Island*. Sightseers will stay in *Dublin* [1] for a day or two to take in Trinity College and Christ Church Cathedral while making excursions to Howth Castle, Castletown Mansion, and the Powerscourt Demesne. A longer excursion to *Westport* [21] to see the Georgian mansion would be rewarding. Shopping is excellent, especially in the duty-free airport at *Shannon* [18], one of the few places still giving you value for your travel dollar.

WHAT'S THE WEATHER REALLY LIKE?

The overall weather in Ireland is poor, with frequent mists and a good deal of rain. May and September are the best months for sightseers who want to avoid the summer crowds and enjoy sunny days. From October through March it tends to be cool and sometimes cold, so bring a warm coat just in case. However, Ireland is swept by a branch of the Gulf Stream, which has a moderating influence on deep winter days and encourages subtropical plants to grow along the coast.

SOME SUGGESTIONS FOR A MORE ENJOYABLE TRIP

You can book a room in a hotel, guest house, farmhouse, cottage, family hotel, and so on by contacting the Central Reservations Service—Irish Tourist Board, Bord Failte, P.O. Box 273,

Stephen Green, Dublin, Ireland. Or call them at Dublin 78 12 00 (telex 33125). There's no charge for this service. They can also give you full information on car rental. You'll probably want to have a car to get off into the countryside. Allow plenty of time for scenic drives.

WHERE TO STAY

Following is a list of some of the country's finest hotels. It would be impossible to include all of the delightful boardinghouses offering great value for your travel dollar, but the local tourist office will be glad to help you find them. For the most part accommodations tend to be simple, comfortable, and clean, although they're rarely luxurious. In many of the smaller inns you'll be treated as part of the family, with warmth and personal interest.

Adare [13]

Dunraven Arms   Adare   tel: (061) 94 209
Only eighteen miles from Shannon Airport via Limerick is this dignified yet fresh country house. Lots of antiques. Spacious and well-furnished rooms. An all-in-the-family feeling. Excellent cuisine. Superb gardens in the spring. Ideal for sportsmen: fox-hunters, fishermen, and golfers. Expensive and worth it.

Ashford [3]

Hunter's Hotel   Ashford   tel: Rathnew 4106
Simple and rustic with fresh vegetables for the table. Riding. Inexpensive. Just northwest of Wicklow.

Ballina [22]

Downhill Hotel   Ballina   tel: 7
North of town towards Sligo. Quite small hotel with varied rooms. Spacious grounds. Good cooking and fine wines. Ideal for fishing (especially for salmon). Riding, tennis and pool. Expensive. Southwest of Sligo; to north of Castlebar.

Mount Falcon Castle   Ballina   tel: Ballina 146
Only eleven rooms in this guest-house near the river on spacious

grounds. Good restaurant with farm-fresh produce. Tennis, riding, and salmon fishing. Arranges deep-sea fishing as well. Quite expensive.

Ballinascarthy [10]

Ardnavaha House   Ballinascarthy   tel: (023) 49 135
Nicely modernized Georgian country house with quite fine cuisine and wine cellar. Very comfortable. Pleasant location. Riding, pool, and tennis. Expensive. East of Bantry.

Ballinasloe [19]

Hayden's Hotel   Dunlo Street   tel: 23 47
Large hotel with modern and comfortable rooms. Golf, tennis, and fishing. May is the best month for fishing, with September second-best. Good food. Quite expensive. East of Galway.

Ballymore Eustace [1]

Ardenode Hotel   Ballymore Eustace   tel: (045) 64 198
A country house set in farmland only twenty-six miles south-west of Dublin. Comfortable rooms. Family owned. Moderate.

Ballyvaughan [19]

Gregan's Castle Hotel   Ballyvaughan   tel: 5
Ancient rural manor several miles from town in idyllic setting with fine view. Limited number of fresh rooms. Lots of atmosphere with fireplace and friendly service. Fishing and riding. Moderate. Reserve well in advance—open only from April through October. On south shore of Galway Bay, twelve miles northwest of Gort.

Baltimore [10]

Baltimore House   Baltimore   tel: Baltimore 27
Family-owned seaside hotel with calm location and nice view. Quite comfortable. Good restaurant. Moderate. South of Bantry.

Bantry [10]

Ballylickey House Hotel   Bantry   tel: Bantry 71
Several miles north of town. Small and very smart mansion con-
verted into a superb hotel with comfortable rooms. Fine setting
with lawns and woods. Out-of-this-world French cooking. Pool.
Free salmon and trout fishing. Very expensive, but worth it.
Open only from April through September.

Boyle [24]

Rock House   Boyle   tel: Boyle 197
Simple inn geared to fishermen with simple tastes. Inexpensive.
Southwest of Sligo.

Cashel [15]

Cashel Palace Hotel   Main Street   tel: 61 253
Eighteenth-century Queen Anne mansion in lovely grounds.
Twenty tasteful rooms with lots of atmosphere and modern
amenities. Elegant throughout, with original paintings and
prints. Riding, hunting, fishing, and golf. Gourmet cooking.
Very expensive.

Cashel House   Cashel Bay   tel: Cashel 9
Lovely house with comfortable rooms (De Gaulle once rented it).
Flowery and nice—fuchsia abounds. Good restaurant (lobster in
season). Expensive.

Longfield House   Goold's Cross   tel: Goold's Cross 63
Fortress converted into elegant mansion with only ten comfortable rooms. Calm and scenic setting. Informal atmosphere. Fishing and hunting. Moderate to expensive.

Zetland Hotel   Cashel Bay (Connemara)   tel: Cashel 8
Small country house with nice view. Very comfortable rooms.
Home cooking. Known for outstanding sea trout fishing. Open
only Easter to mid-October. Expensive.

Castlebar [22]

Breaffy House Hotel   Castlebar   tel: 333/323
Quite large hotel several miles from town on sixty acres of

grounds. Pleasant rooms in the lovely mansion. Fresh vegetables for country cooking. Crackling fire in cool weather. Fishing and shooting.

Castledermot [1]

Kilkea Castle   Castledermot   tel: (0503) 45 156
Oldest inhabited castle in Europe (1180). Comfortable rooms with bath. Good restaurant. Many sports available. Forty miles south of Dublin. Expensive.

Clifden [20]

Clifden House Hotel   Clifden (Connemara)   tel: Clifden 34
Comfortable, family-run hotel set up for pony trekking and fishing. Moderate. West of Cong near the coast.

Abbeyglen House   Clifden (Connemara)   tel: Clifden 33
Country house with quite comfortable, modern rooms. Pool. Fishing. Moderate.

Clonmel [8]

Hotel Minella   Clonmel   tel: (052) 22 388
Nicely modernized stately home. All tasteful bedrooms with bath. Comfortable. Fishing (river flows by property). Moderate. North of Youghal.

Cong [20]

Ashford Castle Hotel   Cong   tel: Castlebar 801
Large eighteenth-century castle converted into fine hotel. Once a 3,500-acre estate (now considerably less). Still, lots of gardens and woods facing Lough Corrib. Wonderful atmosphere enhanced by antiques. Comfortable rooms—number 4 is spectacular. Delicious country cooking with excellent soup and fish dishes. Golf, tennis, riding, and "the best all around free fishing in the world." Expensive. Closed in the winter.

Connemara [20]

The Leenane Hotel   Connemara   tel: Leenane 4
Lovely old inn in idyllic setting. Quite comfortable. Set up for
lake and river fishing. Open mid-April to mid-October. Moderate. West of Cong.

Droichead Nua [1]

Hotel Keadeen   Droichead Nua   tel: (045) 31 666
Family-owned with a few bedrooms to let. All with bath. Sur-
rounded by gardens. Only one mile from Curragh racecourse.
Expensive. Southwest of Dublin.

Dromineer [16]

Sail Inn   Dromineer (Co. Tipperary)   tel: Puckane 3
Tiny and ultrasimple pub geared to fishermen seeking those fat
brown trout rising for the mayfly in mid-May. Inexpensive.
Write ahead for a boat and ghillie—reserve months in advance.
The inn is only thirty miles north of Limerick and on the water
(near Nenagh).

Dublin [1]

Fitzpatrick's Castle Hotel   Killiney Hill Road   tel: 85 15 33
Nine miles from the center of town. Small castle-hotel with eleg-
ant public rooms and pleasant bedrooms with four-poster beds.
Lovely grounds. Expensive.

Gresham Hotel   1 O'Connell Street   tel: 74 68 81
Large centrally located traditional hotel with a lovely view. Quite
elegant throughout and very comfortable. Tasteful dining. Very
expensive.

Royal Hibernian Hotel   Dawson Street   tel: 77 29 91
Large deluxe hotel in central location on quiet street. Elegant and
charming throughout with spacious rooms—all comforts. Excellent cuisine (one of Ireland's top restaurants). Gracious and very
expensive.

Sutton House Hotel   Sutton   tel: 32 26 88
Mansion converted into lovely hotel with spacious grounds.

Elegant rooms. Fine cooking. Fishing and golf in the area. Expensive. Eight miles from the center of the city.

Shelbourne Hotel   *27 St. Stephen's Green*   *tel: 76 44 01*
Large traditional hotel with superb location. Tasteful and deluxe. Spacious rooms. Fine dining. Very expensive.

Mount Herbert   *Herbert Road*   *tel: 68 43 21*
Quite large home converted pleasant and comfortable hotel in a secluded, calm location. Most rooms with bath. Moderate.

Dundalk [27]

Ballymascanlon House   *Dundalk*   *tel: (042) 71 124*
Large mansion converted into fine hotel on spacious grounds. Very comfortable. Golf, tennis, and riding. Expensive. East of Carrickmacross on the coast.

Dun Laoghaire [1]

Royal Marine Hotel   *Dun Laoghaire*   *tel: 80 19 11*
Large and comfortable seaside hotel only a short drive south from Dublin. Fine cooking. Very expensive.

Ennis [17]

Old Ground Hotel   *Ennis*   *tel: (065) 21 127*
Comfortable mansion, nicely modernized. Good restaurant and fine cellar. Only sixteen miles from Shannon Airport. Expensive. Just north of Bunratty.

Ferry Point [8] (Youghal)

Monatrea House   *Ferry Point*   *tel: (024) 42 28*
Comfortable country house on own estate—suited mainly to riders. Moderate.

Galway [19]

Ardilaun House   *Taylor's Hill*   *tel: 65 452*
Large comfortable hotel in spacious grounds—just one mile from the city center. Candlelight dining. Expensive.

Renvyle House   Galway (Connemara)   tel: Renvyle 3
Attractive hotel with comfortable rooms in two hundred acres of
grounds with lovely fuchsias and roses (Yeats spent his honeymoon here). Tennis, lake, and stables. On the Atlantic. Fine
French cuisine. Expensive.

Glenbeigh [11]

The Falcon Inn   Glenbeigh   tel: Glenbeigh 15
Comfortable country inn in lovely location. Informal and family-
run. Restaurant specializes in seafood. Moderate.

Hotel Glenbeigh   Glenbeigh   tel: Glenbeigh 4
Just a short drive east of town. Small country inn with fine view.
Charming atmosphere. Comfortable rooms. Tennis and hunting.
Superb hotel for fishermen. Exceptional salmon fishing arranged
by hotel but be sure to write ahead for details (months in advance). Guides and equipment available. Lovely horseback riding as well. Moderately expensive. Open March through October.

Towers Hotel   Glenbeigh   tel: Glenbeigh 12
Small hotel in the center of town with quite comfortable rooms
and superb cooking (mainly seafood). Moderate. Fishing. Closed
mid-October to mid-November.

Killaloe [16]

Ballyvalley Hotel   Killaloe   tel: (061) 76 187
Georgian mansion with lovely view. Comfortable rooms. Nice
public areas with fireplaces. Run by Germans. Moderate. Just
northeast of Limerick.

Killarney [11]

Dunloe Castle Hotel   Killarney   tel: 32 118
Hugh luxury hotel six miles west of town. Fine dining. All com-
forts. Riding and tennis. Very expensive. Open April through
October.

Great Southern Hotel   Killarney   tel: (064) 31 262
Hugh traditional hotel in the center of town with some new

rooms. Golf and tennis. Expensive. Open April through September.

Lake Hotel   *Killarney*   *tel: (064) 31 035*
Short drive south of town. Large lakeside hotel with fine setting. Spacious and comfortable rooms. Tennis, golf, and fishing. Moderately expensive. Open April through September.

Killiney [1]

Fitzpatrick's Castle Hotel   *Killiney*   *tel: 85 15 33*
Large, luxury castle about nine miles south of Dublin. Very comfortable with traditional atmosphere. Nice grounds. Pool. Very expensive.

The Court Hotel   *Killiney Bay*   *tel: 85 16 22*
A few luxury bedrooms available in this atmospheric hotel with view to Killiney Bay. Good restaurant. Expensive.

Kingscourt [27]

Cabra Castle   *Kingscourt*   *tel: Kingscourt 60*
Family hotel. Calm, old-world ambience. All rooms with bath. Moderate. Southwest of Carrickmacross.

Letterfrack [20]

Rosleague Manor   *Letterfrack (Connemara)*   *tel: Moyard 7*
Georgian house with nice view to the bay. Small number of comfortable rooms. Good restaurant. Moderate. West of Cong on the coast.

Newmarket-on-Fergus [18]

Clare Inn   *Newmarket-on-Fergus*   *tel: 71 161*
Near Shannon Airport. Modern luxury inn. Large, with spacious rooms. Commercial. Sports-oriented—fishing, golf, riding, etc. Expensive. Ten miles northeast of Shannon.

Dromoland Castle   *Newmarket-on-Fergus*   *tel: 71 144*
Sixteenth-century castle in fifteen hundred acres of grounds. Luxurious and elegant with lavish touches. Spacious and bright

rooms. Golf, tennis, trout-fishing, riding, and bird-shooting in an idyllic setting of woods and orchards. Fine dining. Ultraexpensive. Open April through October. Only eight miles from Shannon.

Newport [22]

Newport House   Newport   tel: Newport 12
Charming eighteenth-century house converted into delightful ivy-clad hotel surrounded by park and gardens. Superb French cuisine and fine wines. Twenty-five miles of private fishing waters—just tops for salmon and sea trout. Expensive. Closed January to April. West of Castlebar.

Oughterard [19]

Sweeney's   Oughterard   tel: (091) 82 207
Small ivy-clad country inn with comfortable rooms—most with bath. Charming village. Very good cooking. Geared to trout fishermen. Moderate. Northwest of Galway.

Parknasilla [11]

Great Southern Hotel   Parknasilla   tel: Sneem 3
Large luxury hotel—very comfortable but not extravagant. Superb location in a region with some subtropical plants. All sports, including fishing, golf, hunting, riding, and so on. Very expensive. Open April through October. Southwest of Killarney on the coast.

Rathmullan [25]

Fort Royal Hotel   Rathmullan (Letterkenny)   tel: Rathmullan 11
Peaceful, family-run hotel in extensive wooded grounds. Comfortable. Tennis, beach, ponies. Moderate. Far north of Donegal near coast.

Rathmullen House   Rathmullen   tel: 4
Quite large mansion (with only seven rooms) converted into very comfortable and tasteful hotel. Lovely lawns and flowers. Fishing, riding, sailing, tennis. Expensive. Open mid-April through September.

Rathnew [3]

Hunter's Hotel   Rathnew   tel: (0404) 41 06
Modest, family-run hotel. Gardens. Tennis. Fishing. Just northwest of Wicklow.

Stranorlar [25]

Kees' Hotel   Stranorlar   tel: Ballybofey 18
Small and reasonably comfortable inn geared to fishermen. Moderate. Sixteen miles northeast of Donegal.

Tullow [3]

Slaney Hotel   Tullow (Carlow)   tel: 51 102
Small hotel geared to pheasant hunters—shooting area nearby. Inexpensive. Write ahead for full information on the hunt and season. Nine miles east of Carlow. Southwest of Wicklow.

Upper Ballyduff [7]

Blackwater Lodge Hotel   Upper Ballyduff   tel: Ballyduff 35
Family run and quite comfortable. Has own fishing waters on the Blackwater. Some bungalows available. Moderate. West of Cappoquin.

Waterville [11]

Butler Arms Hotel   Waterville   tel: Waterville 5
Large older hotel with comfortable rooms. Can arrange both river and sea fishing. Moderate. Open May through September. On southwest coast twenty-five miles from Killarney.

WHERE TO EAT

Adare [13]

Dunraven Arms Hotel   Adare   tel: 94 209
Coaching inn surrounded by lovely grounds. Traditional atmosphere. Superb home cooking with fresh farm vegetables and delicious duckling. Quite expensive. South of Limerick.

Rathkeale Castle Matrix   Adare   tel: 31 802
Ancient castle serving gourmet dinners on special request. Fine
dining with lots of atmosphere. Expensive.

Bantry [10]

Ballylickey House   Bantry   tel: Bantry 71
Lovely country house on spacious grounds overlooking the Bay.
One of the country's finest restaurants with excellent French
cuisine. Moderate. Reserve well in advance.

Bunratty [17]

Bunratty Castle   Bunratty   tel: 61 511/61 788
Only a short drive from Shannon Airport. Elegant fifteenth-century castle serving medieval banquets. Torchlit dining, music,
and wine. Quite expensive. Reserve.

Carrigaline [9]

Chez Idawalt   Ravenswood   tel: 88 23 27
Large nineteenth-century house with tasteful dining room. Fam-
ily-run—very fine cooking, with veal the main dish. Moderate.
Reserve well in advance. Ten miles south of Cork.

Cashel [15]

Chez Hans   Cashel   tel: Cashel 25
Northwest of Waterford—a nineteenth-century church converted
into fine restaurant with excellent dishes. Both French and German cuisine. Quite expensive. Close to the Rock of Cashel. Reserve in warm weather.

Cork [9]

Blackrock Castle   Cork   tel: 33 881
Ancient castle lying on the banks of the River Lee. Authentic dining room with lovely view. Candlelight dinners. Both fine veal
and seafood as specialties. Music. Moderate. Reserve.

Arbutus Lodge Hotel   *Montenotte*   *tel: 51 237*
Fine dining with superb view of the city and river. Candlelight dinners. Specialties include both Irish and French dishes. Quite expensive. Reserve.

Dublin [1]

The Bailey   *Duke Street 2-3*   *tel: 77 37 51/77 30 55*
An ancient pub converted into a good restaurant with fine fish and Irish specialties. Quite expensive.

Connaught Restaurant   *13-14 Dame Court*   *tel: 77 08 31*
Fine budget restaurant serving local specialties including Irish stew. Simple.

Crowley's Restaurant   *10 Hill Street*   *tel: 74 14 48*
Near the city center above a pub. Recommended by the Irish as an up-and-coming small restaurant with good food at moderate prices.

Jonathan's Downstairs Restaurant   *39 Grafton Street*   *tel: 77 71 70*
Candlelight dinners with dancing—young. Moderate.

Royal Hibernian Hotel   *Dawson Street 48*   *tel: 77 29 91*
The Lafayette Restaurant is one of the country's finest. Wonderful atmosphere with superb French dishes. Top wines. Quite expensive. Reserve.

Snaffles   *47 Leeson Street*   *tel: 76 22 27*
Georgian basement converted into one of Ireland's finest restaurants serving delicious seafood and game in season. Lots of atmosphere. Expensive. Reserve well in advance.

Tandoori Room   *27 Lower Leeson Street*   *tel: 76 22 86*
Islamic décor with Northern Tandoori cuisine. Candlelight dining. Moderate. Reserve.

Dun Laoghaire [1]

Restaurant Creole   *20A Adelaide Street*   *tel: 80 67 06*
Fine basement restaurant serving excellent dishes, including duck à l'orange. Fine wines. Quite expensive. Reserve. Just south of Dublin.

Dunmore East [6]

Ocean Hotel   The Gallery   tel: 83 136
Charming coaching inn with lots of atmosphere and superb seafood. Expensive. Reserve. South of Waterford.

Glenbeigh [11]

Towers Hotel   Glenbeigh   tel: Glenbeigh 12
Excellent restaurant serving both Irish dishes and fresh seafood. Candlelight dinners. Expensive. Reserve well in advance. Closed mid-October to mid-November. Glenbeigh is west of Killarney.

Glendalough [1]

Armstrong's Barn   Annamoe   tel: 51 94
Near Glendalough south of Dublin—lovely dining room with antiques and authentic eighteenth-century prints. Regional dishes including game in season. Expensive. Reserve.

Greystones [1]

Woodlands Hotel   Greystones   tel: 87 44 23
A rising star noted for its fine dining and quiet setting south of Dublin close to the coast. Both Irish and French dishes. Quite expensive. Easy to reach from the capital.

Kilkenny [6]

Kyteler's Inn   Kieran Street   tel: 21 888
Named after the last woman in Ireland to be tried as a witch—delightful fourteenth-century building converted into a fine restaurant with delicious *coq au vin*. Quite expensive. Reserve. North of Waterford.

Kinsale [9]

The Spinnaker   Scilly   tel: 72 123
Delightful small restaurant overlooking the harbor. Candlelight dinners with an emphasis on fresh seafood, including lobster.

Expensive. Closed from November through April. Kinsale is south of Cork.

Kinvara [19]

Dunguaire Castle   Kinvara   tel: 61 511
South of Galway you'll find an authentic castle with a view to the city and bay below. Medieval banquets including wine and music. Expensive. Closed October through April.

Limerick [16]

The Merryman   5 Glenworth Street   tel: 48 738
Fine restaurant with lots of atmosphere, fireplace, and fine food. Quite expensive. Reserve.

Midleton [9]

The Yeats Room   Ballymaloe   tel: 62 531
An eighteenth-century country house on a farm—converted into one of Ireland's top restaurants, specializing in fresh fish and farm grown vegetables. Quite expensive. East of Cork.

Newbridge [1]

The Jockey Hall Inn   The Curragh near Newbridge   tel: 41 416
Authentic Georgian farmhouse converted into a fine restaurant with delicious mussels, chicken, and steak. Moderate. Reserve well in advance. Just thirty-three miles southwest of Dublin.

Red House Inn   Newbridge   tel: 31 516
Charming old coaching inn with excellent food. Specialties are fresh shellfish and chicken. Quite expensive. Reserve well in advance. Twenty-two miles southwest of Dublin.

New Ross [6]

New Ross Galley   The Quay   tel: 21 723
Combination of river cruise and dining from April through October. Buffet-style dinner. Quite expensive. Reserve. Northeast of Waterford.

Quin [18]

Knappogue Castle   Quin   tel: 61 788
Northeast of Shannon Airport—a sixteenth-century estate with medieval banquets from April through October. Meals include wine. Quite expensive. Reserve.

Rathdrum [1]

Glenwood Room   Rathdrum   tel: 61 84
Country house converted into excellent restaurant south of Dublin. Fine French cooking. Expensive. Reserve well in advance.

Robertstown [1]

Grand Canal Hotel   Robertstown   tel: 60 204
Eighteenth-century style banquets in candlelit room. Expensive. Reserve. Southwest of Dublin.

Schull [10]

O'Keeffe's Restaurant   Main Street   tel: Schull 7
Just south of Bantry—fine restaurant open from April through September. Behind the grocery shop. Fine meat, poultry, and fresh fish at moderate prices. Reserve.

ITALY

ITALY

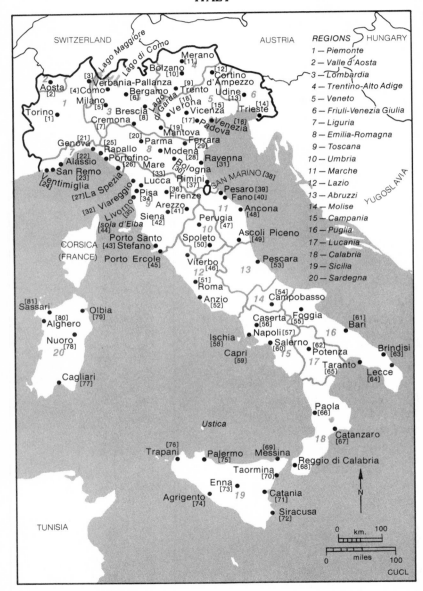

SWITZERLAND   AUSTRIA   HUNGARY

REGIONS

1 — Piemonte
2 — Valle d'Aosta
3 — Lombardia
4 — Trentino-Alto Adige
5 — Veneto
6 — Friuli-Venezia Giulia
7 — Liguria
8 — Emilia-Romagna
9 — Toscana
10 — Umbria
11 — Marche
12 — Lazio
13 — Abruzzi
14 — Molise
15 — Campania
16 — Puglia
17 — Lucania
18 — Calabria
19 — Sicilia
20 — Sardegna

YUGOSLAVIA

Lago Maggiore
Lago di Como

Merano [11]
Bolzano [10]
Cortino d'Ampezzo [12]
Aosta [2]
[3]
Verbania-Pallanza [9]
[4] Como
Bergamo [6]
Trento
Udine [13]
Milano [5]
Brescia
d/Garda
Verona [18]
Vicenza [15]
Trieste [14]
Torino [1]
3
Cremona [8]
[17]
Venezia [16]
Padova
Mantova [19]
Genova [21]
[20] Parma
Ferrara
Modena [29]
Rapallo [25]
[22] Portofino- [26]
Mare
Ravenna [31]
Alassio [23]
Bologna [30]
San Remo
Rimini [37]
SAN MARINO [38]
Ventimiglia [24]
[27] La Spezia
Lucca [36]
Pesaro [39]
Viareggio [32]
Pisa
Firenze
Fano [40]
Livorno [33]
Arezzo [41]
Ancona [48]
Isola d'Elba [44]
Siena [42]
Perugia [47]
CORSICA
Porto Santo [43]
Stefano
Spoleto [50]
Ascoli Piceno [49]
(FRANCE)
Porto Ercole [45]
Viterbo [46]
Pescara [53]
Roma [51]
Anzio [52]
Campobasso [54]
Sassari [81]
Olbia [79]
Caserta [56]
Foggia [55]
Bari [61]
Alghero [80]
Napoli [57]
Nuoro [78]
Ischia [58]
Salerno [60]
Potenza [62]
Brindisi [63]
Capri [59]
Taranto [65]
Lecce [64]
Cagliari [77]
Paola [66]
Ustica
Catanzaro [67]
Palermo [75]
Messina [69]
Trapani [76]
Reggio di Calabria [68]
Taormina [70]
Enna [73]
Catania [71]
Agrigento [74]
Siracusa [72]
TUNISIA

0   km.   100
0   miles   100

N

CUCL

WHAT TO SEE

A mild climate, an unbeatable artistic heritage, great regional cooking, varied scenery, outgoing people—all are combined in Italy, long the favorite tourist destination in Europe. Yes, prices have bounced up and down in recent years, but Italy is still affordable, particularly for those who know how to look for a bargain.

The far north of Italy is a traveller's paradise. The lovely *Borromean Islands* (best seen in May); the lakes of *Maggiore, Como, Garda*, and *Lugano* with their idyllic resorts; and the majestic mountain drives make this region a must on your itinerary. You may want to take in the Villa Taranto northwest of *Pallanza* [3], the Certosa di Pavia, a medieval monastery in *Pavia*, or either the Villa Carlotta north of *Tremezzo* or the Villa Pliniana in *Torno*. Other sights include the Palazzo Reale and the Egyptian Museum in *Torino* [1], the superb Duomo (go in the late afternoon) in *Milano* [5] (well known too for the La Scala Opera* performing from December to April), and both the Città Altà (Upper City) and the Colleoni Chapel in *Bergamo* [6]. The region offers superb skiing with deep powder conditions from December to April. Favorite resorts: *Sestriere, Breuil-Cervinia*, and *Courmayeur*. A great seasonal attraction is the fall truffle fair held in *Alba* during October. The Great Dolomite Road weaves through the mountains from *Bolzano* [10] to *Cortina d'Ampezzo* [12], a great ski resort. Other favorite resorts in this region are *Madonna di Campiglio* and *San Martino di Castrozzo*. Sightseers flock to *Venice* [16] with such sights as the Piazza San Marco, Cà d'Oro, and Grand Canal, but many miss the Scrovegni Chapel in *Padova* [17], the lovely cathedral of *Verona* [18], the Palladian palaces along the Corso Andrea Palladio in *Vicenza*, and the Piazza della Libertà in *Udine* [13]. A seasonal attraction is the fall grape harvest in *Merano* [11], best in late September and early October.

You'll find fashionable resorts long the Italian Riviera: *Rapallo* [25], *Portovenere, San Remo* [23] , and *Santa Margherita Ligure*; the "in" spots of *Porto Santo Stefano* [43] and *Porto Ercole* [45]; the inland spa of *Montecatini Terme*; the isolated island of *Elba* [44] (bring your car); the fascinating Cinqueterre with such

* *Year-round in 1978.*

village gems as *Vernazza*; and, of course, the many, many touristic sights of this famous region, including the San Lorenzo Cathedral and Villa Saluzzo in *Genova* [21], the Basilica di San Petronio in *Bologna* [30], the fabulous mosaics in the Church of San Vitale in *Ravenna* [31] (worth a long detour), and the Leaning Tower of *Pisa* [34]. But above all these stands Florence [36] (Firenze), one of the world's great small cities. Here you should park your car and wander on foot to take in the piazzas and piazzales, the Duomo, the churches and great museums, and the Tuscan villas in the surrounding hills (best seen in spring). Try to make excursions to *Certaldo* or *San Gimignano*. And, if possible, take in *Siena* [42] on your way to Rome. Siena hosts a unique horse race (the Palio) on July 2 and on August 16.

Rome [51] (Roma), one of the largest and most popular cities in Europe, demands at least a week on any itinerary. It is not a compact city, not one which can be walked about easily. You'll find a good portion of your time is taken just getting to the major sights, all of which are described in detail in *free* pamphlets distributed in most hotels. Recommended excursions* would include the Villa d'Este in *Tivoli*, the ruins in *Ostia Antica*, a short visit to *Assisi*, to the Old Town in *Gubbio*, the cathedral in *Orvieto*, and the Palazzo dei Priori in *Perugia* [48]. The view from the tiny hillside *San Marino* [38] as well as the atmosphere of the medieval town of *Todi* make both worthwhile side trips. Also of interest is the Villa Farnese, eleven miles southeast of *Viterbo* [46].

Most travellers visit the National Museum of *Naples* [57], *Vesuvius* to the east and *Pompeii*, the Amalfi Drive from *Sorrento* to *Salerno* [60], and (a short trip) the romantic island of *Capri* [59] (see the Blue Grotto in the morning). Not so well-known are the "in" island of *Ischia* [58], the superb Greek ruins at *Paestum* (better than those of Greece), timeless *Ravello*, the unique *trulli* (round, white-washed homes) near *Alberobello*, and the charms of medieval *Matera*. A seasonal attraction: the return of the swallows to *Capestrano* in late March or early April.

Sicily is well known for its superb climate and excellent archaeological sites. Try to take in the ruins of *Agrigento* [74] at sunset or in the early morning. The remains at *Selinunte* and *Siracusa* [72] are worth seeing, as are the mosaics in the

* Some of these excursions take several days.

cathedral at *Monreale*. The fine hotels and warm climate are the main attractions of *Taormina* [70]. You may want to make an excursion to *Mt. Etna*, still active.

Sardinia has become popular in recent years, thanks to the development of the *Costa Smeralda*, fifty-five miles north of *Olbia* [79]. Here you'll find luxury hotels in a primitive coastal area. A highly recommended car excursion: *Nuoro-Fonni-Lanusei-Seui-Aritzo-Desulo-Sorgono-Desulo-Fonni-Nuoro* [78].

WHAT'S THE WEATHER REALLY LIKE?

The mountainous north and the northern coasts offer mild weather from May through September. Along the Italian Riviera you can extend the season to include April and October. The central region around Florence is usually lovely from April to late October. Farther south you'll run into torrid days during July and August (also true in Florence) when many Italians head to the beach. It's especially hot on Sicily, which is better visited in the off-season. Sicily is well known for its mild winter weather. However, winter in Venice, Florence, and Rome can be cool and somewhat drab with frequent rains.

SOME SUGGESTIONS FOR A MORE ENJOYABLE TRIP

Be sure to write for or pick up three free booklets from the Italian tourist office: *A Trip to Italy; Almanacco d'Italia: Special English Edition*; and *Italy: General Information for Travellers*. You'll find detailed descriptions of regions and towns, regional maps, and information on local cooking and wines in these very fine booklets. A special museum-entrance card is available from Alitalia offices in the United States. It costs a dollar and allows you to visit all of Italy's state museums and galleries. Special gasoline coupons are available to tourists driving a car with foreign license plates (a good reason to rent a car outside of Italy if you plan extensive travel in that country). You can buy these at the border or at the Banca del Lavoro in New York. They'll cut gas costs considerably. Car travel and parking is very difficult in Italian cities, where you're advised to park the car, use public transportation, and walk to major tourist sights. Public transportation is very inexpensive. For a quick tour of Rome take the trams marked ED or

ES from the central railway station. Make hotel reservations well
in advance for the peak season, especially in Florence, Rome,
and Venice. Note that Venice is very crowded through September, while Florence is packed in May for the Music Festival.
Italian restaurants tend to be informal. Generally, you choose
the table you want by walking up to it and sitting down. You
may want to nod your head at the waiter for nonverbal agree-
ment that it's okay. Men wear open shirts in the summer without raising eyebrows. Most people choose menus *à la carte*. Often, you order the first course, eat it, then order a second or
third course. You're not expected to order the whole meal at
once. If you want half a portion, ask for *una mezza porzione*. Many
restaurants display seafood and other items by the front door. If
you have trouble explaining what you'd like to eat, point to it.
Local specialties (*la specialità della casa*) are often very inexpensive
and very good. Stick to regional wines, less expensive, and just
about as good as name brands. In Sicily drink bottled wines
(*Segesta, Marsala, Corvo Malvasia*). Once out of the restaurant and
on the road, note: the superhighways (*autostrada*) are toll roads.
They're worth the high charge if you're in a hurry, but you'll see
little of the country if you take them. If you take the car ferry to
Sicily, you can get a round-trip reduction if you stay on the island a week or more. Skiers should check into a set-price weekly
package called *settimana bianca*, which includes rooms, meals,
and lift tickets and is offered by most hotels in major ski resorts.
A final note: women out late at night are often harassed by Italian men. Take a taxi to avoid unpleasant encounters.

WHERE TO STAY

Agrigento [74]

Villa Athena   Via dei Templi   tel: 23 833
Small, comfortable hotel in pleasant setting. Main attraction of
this modest inn is the surrounding region. Quite inexpensive.

Alghero [80]

Villa las Tronas Hotel   Lungomare Valencia 1   tel: 97 53 90
Small, authentic hotel in fine garden with great view. Very quiet
and comfortable—lots of atmosphere. Pool. Expensive.

Amalfi [60]

Hotel Cappuccini Convento   Via Nazionale   tel: 87 10 08
Seventy feet above the town with a view of the sea. A fine small flower-filled retreat with cloisters still intact. Comfortable and authentic rooms. Antiques throughout. Good regional cooking. Expensive. West of Salerno.

Hotel Luna-Torre Saracena   Amalfi   tel: 87 10 02
Small medieval villa converted into lovely hotel with marvelous view to the sea. Attractive throughout. Quite comfortable in the moderate class. Nice.

Arenzano [21]

Punta San Martino Hotel   Arenzano   tel: 91 73 99
Extremely attractive hotel with superb view. Comfortable. Excellent regional cooking. Pool, tennis, and golf nearby. Moderately expensive. Closed in winter. Thirteen miles west of Genova.

Arzachena [79]

La Bisaccia   Arzachena   tel: 92 012
Near the Costa Smeralda. Sixty-two comfortable rooms with great view. Modest, but pleasant. Beach, pool, and tennis. Quite expensive. Just north of Olbia.

Asolo [16]

Hotel Villa Cipriani   Via Canova   tel: 52 166
Small delightful hotel—once a villa. Elegant and charming. Ideal location in the hills. Superb restaurant appealing to gourmets. Very expensive. Venice (northwest).

Assisi [48]

Hotel Subasio   Via Frate Elia 2   tel: 81 22 06
Delightful large hotel with modest but charming rooms. Noted for its pleasant dining on a flower-filled terrace in warmer weather. Moderate. Just east of Perugia.

Bellagio [4]

Villa Serbelloni   Bellagio   tel: 95 02 16
Very pleasant hotel with great view. Isolated on the lake. Peaceful. Swimming. Quite luxurious throughout and very expensive.

Bellaria [31]

Locanda delle Dune   Viale Panzini 223   tel: 44 296
Small, delightful hotel surrounded by large park with superb view. Very comfortable and charming. Moderate. Open April through September. Bellaria is only nine miles from Rimini. Southeast of Ravenna.

Bressanone [10]

Hotel Elefante   4 Via Rio Bianco   tel: 22 288
Small and comfortable hotel in garden setting. Quite attractive. Noted for its good food in attractive dining room. Moderately expensive. Northeast of Bolzano.

Busseto [20]

I Due Foscari   Busseto   tel: 92 337
Tiny, quiet hotel with nice atmosphere. Pleasant, comfortable rooms. Moderately expensive. Northwest of Parma.

Capri [59]

A Pazziella   4 Via Pastina   tel: 837-0642
Tiny modest inn with charming atmosphere. Attractive. Moderate.

La Pineta   6 Via Tragara   tel: 837-0141
Small, with varied rooms—all attractive and cheery. Garden atmosphere. Pool. Moderately expensive. Good value in modest class.

Luna   Viale Matteotti 3   tel: 837-7035
Small, quiet hotel with view to the sea. On a cliff with garden setting. Charming throughout. Fresh and colorful rooms. Very expensive. Open April to October.

Flora   Via Serena 26   tel: 837-0629
Small villa converted into comfortable hotel with fine flower-filled setting and great view. Quite expensive.

Castellaneta Marina [65]

Riva dei Tessali   Castellaneta Marina   tel: 64 20 27
Small hotel in lovely setting just west of Taranto. Comfortable rooms—all with bath. Pool, tennis, golf. Very quiet and relaxing. Moderate.

Cortina D'Ampezzo [12]

Corona Hotel   Via Cesare Battisti 10   tel: 32 51
Small, authentic inn with lovely view. Quiet and comfortable. Unique art collection. Nice. Geared to the sportsman. Expensive.

Elba [44]

Hotel Iselba   Marina de Campo   tel: 97 097
Small hotel only a short drive from town. Nice natural setting. Modest yet comfortable rooms. Expensive. Open May to mid-October.

Firenze [36] (Florence)

Aprile   via della Scala 6   tel: 21 62 37
Fifteenth-century palace converted into comfortable (not luxurious) and old-fashioned hotel. Garden. Try for number 3. No restaurant. Good value in moderate bracket.

Hotel Augustus   Piazza dell'Oro 5   tel: 28 30 54
Excellent location for this small modern hotel. Comfortable rooms—ask for one on top floor (avoid rooms over street). No restaurant. Moderate.

Villa Belvedere   via Benedetto Castelli 3   tel: 22 25 01
Small, intimate hotel on a hill with lovely view and location in park. Comfortable rooms with bath. Garden, pool, and tennis. Open March to November only. Moderate to expensive.

Palazzo Benci   28 Lungarno delle Grazie   tel: 29 31 31
Palace with luxury apartments. Elegant and varied rooms. Ideal for longer stays. Maid service. Excellent value in the expensive bracket.

Berchielli   Lungarno Acciaioli 14   tel: 21 15 30
Quite large, atmospheric hotel in central location. Comfortable rooms, most with bath. Quiet in the back. Ask for numbers 85 or 89. Small rooftop terrace. No restaurant. Moderate.

Villa Carlotta   via Michele di Lando 3   tel: 22 05 30
Charming, quiet, and comfortable pension with only twenty-six rooms, most with bath. Nice garden and location en route to the Piazzale Michelangelo above town. Inexpensive to moderate.

Hotel della Signoria   via delle Terme 1   tel: 24 530
Convenient central location for this small, comfortable, and pleasant hotel. A bit noisy (try for number 36). Nice roof terrace. No restaurant. Inexpensive to moderate.

Hotel de la Ville   Piazza Antinori 1   tel: 26 18 05
Quite large (seventy-one rooms) in a good, central location. Modern yet tasteful. Try for number 420. Quiet and expensive.

Pensione Hermitage   Vicolo Marzio 1   tel: 28 72 16
A pension on top of a building with only eighteen comfortable, cheerful rooms. Flowery and fresh with roof garden. Try for number 9. Simple but nice. Moderate.

Jennings Riccioli   Lungarno delle Grazie 2   tel: 23 724
Modest, reasonably comfortable hotel with sixty-seven rooms (try for numbers 21 with view or 38 with little noise). Inexpensive to moderate.

Hotel Kraft   2 Via Solferino   tel: 28 42 73
Small quiet hotel with very comfortable, simple rooms (ask for number 104). Good value in the moderate class. Restaurant with view. Pool. Quite modern.

Hotel Villa La Massa   Candeli   tel: 63 00 51
Outside of town. Lovely villa converted into stylish hotel with peaceful and very comfortable rooms. Lots of atmosphere. Idyllic in late spring. Pool and tennis nearby. Very expensive.

Hotel Lungarno   *14 Borgo San Jacopo*   *tel: 26 03 97*
Large modern hotel—comfortable and compact. Be sure to ask for a quiet room. Try for numbers 602 or 605. Good value in the moderate range.

Hotel Villa Le Rondini   *224 Via Bolognese Vecchia*   *tel: 40 02 71*
Small villa converted into delightful inn outside of town. Wonderful view. Antiques throughout. Quite comfortable. Pool and tennis. Moderate.

Pensione Monna Lisa   *Borgo Pinti 27*   *tel: 29 62 13*
Don't judge this small pension by its cover. Pleasant fourteenth-century building near the Duomo. Quite comfortable. Try for numbers 19 or 21. Inexpensive to moderate.

Hotel Principe   *Lungarno Amerigo Vespucci 34*   *tel: 28 48 48*
A contessa's townhouse converted into cozy, cute hotel with an intimate atmosphere. Authentic and traditional throughout. Comfortable rooms with bath. Try for number 34 overlooking river or number 36 over the garden. Moderate.

Rivoli   *via della Scala 33*   *tel: 21 69 88*
Charming, small hotel not far from the railway station. Modest, comfortable rooms (try for numbers 72 or 79). Nice garden and fun bar. No restaurant. Good choice for young travellers. Moderate.

Splendor   *via San Gallo*   *tel: 483-4207*
Pleasant little place with nice atmosphere and comfortable, if simple, rooms. Charming restaurant. Good value. Inexpensive to moderate.

Tornabuoni Beacci   *via Tornabuoni 3*   *tel: 27 26 45*
A fourteenth-century palace converted into a sophisticated pension. Very comfortable, most rooms with bath. Roof garden, flowers throughout, and nice atmosphere. Moderate.

Hotel Umbria   *Piazza Massimo d'Azeglio 3*   *tel: 58 76 55*
Small villa converted into cheerful, comfortable, and quiet hotel in noncentral location. Garden, garage, and good restaurant. Bright rooms with bath (try for number 6). Warm. Moderate.

Villa Park San Domenico   *via della Piazzola 55*   *tel: 57 66 97*
A convent converted into a villa-hotel with lots of atmosphere
and a great view, especially from the restaurant. Traditional atmosphere with many antiques. Comfortable rooms with bath.
Ask for canopied bed if desired. Ideal for travellers with car (it's
in noncentral location). Expensive.

Fonteblanda [42]

Corte dei Butteri Hotel   *Fonteblanda*   *tel: 88 55 47*
Large, attractive resort in peaceful setting. Wonderful view near
the sea. Very comfortable. Tennis and pool. Moderate. Open
April to mid-October. South of Siena via Grosseto on the coast.

Forte dei Marmi [27]

Astoria Garden Hotel   *10 Via Leonardo da Vinci*   *tel: 80 754*
Small, charming inn surrounded by pines. Comfortable. Delight-
ful choice in the moderate range. On the coast south of La
Spezia.

Genova [21]

Eliseo Hotel   *Via Martin Piaggio 5*   *tel: 89 20 16*
Small, simple hotel with charm and comfort at reasonable rates.
Good restaurant. A nice budget choice.

Grottaferrata [51]

Hotel Villa Florio   *25 Viale Dusmet*   *tel: 94 52 76*
Villa converted into charming hotel. Fluttering reputation. Moderate. Thirteen miles southeast of Rome.

Ischia [58]

Pensione La Villarosa   *13 Via G. Gigante*   *tel: 99 13 16*
Small, secluded villa. Comfortable and relaxed. Pool. Moderate.
Open April through October.

Maratea [60]

Hotel Santavenere   Maratea   tel: 71 60
Superb cliffside setting for this small estate converted into a
modern luxury hotel with splendid view to the sea. Elegance
matched by comfort. Topflight cooking. Very expensive. Open
from March through October. Far north of Paola on the coast.

Merano [11]

Castel Freiborg   Monte Franco   tel: 32 402
Fourteenth-century castle converted into authentic hotel four
miles from Merano. Small. Quite expensive. Closed winters.

Missiano [10]

Schloss Korb   Missiano   tel: 52 199
Large medieval castle converted into attractive hotel with pool
and tennis. Moderate. Open April to October. Only seven miles
south of Bolzano.

Mogliano [16]

Villa Condulmer   Via Zermanese   tel: 45 00 01
Ten miles northwest of Venice you'll find a delightful villa con-
verted into fine hotel. Rustic hideaway. Lovely park setting.
Tennis and pool. Moderate to expensive.

Nervi [21]

Savoia-Beeler Hotel   Via Eros da Ros 8   tel: 37 89 41
Small, pleasant hotel in nice setting. Comfortable. Attractive in
modest way. Good budget choice. East of Genova.

Olbia [79]

Sporting   Porto Rotondo   tel: 44 029
Tiny, charming beachside hotel. Relaxed. Pool. Water sports.
Very expensive. Open May through September. About seven
miles north of Olbia.

Orta [3]

Hotel San Rocco   *Via Gippini*   *tel: 90 222*
Small, charming, historic hotel near the lake with fine view and quiet setting. Rustic but comfortable. Moderate. Open April to September. South of Verbania.

Orvieto [50]

Hotel Virgilio   *5-6 Piazza Duomo*   *tel: 52 52*
Tiny hotel. Modest but modern. Inexpensive.

Ristorante La Badia   *Frazione San Martino 463*   *tel: 90 359*
A short drive from Orvieto. Tiny, charming historic inn noted for delicious local dishes and wine. Comfortable. Lots of atmosphere. Pool. Moderate. West of Spoleto.

Ospedaletti [23]

Le Rocce del Capo Hotel   *Lungomare Colombo 65*   *tel: 59 733*
Small seaside resort near San Remo. Comfortable and pleasant budget hotel. Southwest of San Remo.

Padova [17]

Le Padovanelle Hotel   *2 Strada Ippodromo*   *tel: 62 56 22*
Small country hotel with a superb restaurant. Elegant. Lots of atmosphere. Delicious local and international dishes. Pool and tennis. Expensive to moderately expensive.

Palermo [75]

Mondello Palace   *Palermo*   *tel: 45 00 01*
Large, comfortable hotel surrounded by gardens. Tasteful. Good cooking. Moderately expensive.

Villa Igiea   *Salita Belmonte 1*   *tel: 54 37 44*
Large luxury hotel in Moorish design with fine view to the bay. Surrounded by lovely gardens with subtropical plants. Extremely comfortable. Romantic dining. Tennis and pool. A superb choice in the expensive bracket.

Pisa [34]

Arno Hotel   Piazza della Repubblica   tel: 22 243
Not for the stuffy—a simple, unpretentious hotel in a town
noted for the absence of fine accommodations. Good restaurant.
For the adventuresome. Inexpensive.

Porto Cervo [79]

Hotel Cervo   Costa Smeralda   tel: 92 003
Large, fine hotel. Not luxurious but nice. Delightful location.
Charming rooms in regional style. Pool, golf, tennis, and water
sports. Very expensive.

Porto Ercole [45]

Il Pellicano   Porto Ercole   tel: 83 38 01
Small, splendid farmhouse in idyllic setting. Fresh garden atmosphere. Rustic elegance in all rooms. Good restaurant. Tennis. Pool. Very expensive. Open April through October.

Positano [60]

Hotel Miramare   25 Via Trara Gendino   tel: 87 50 02
Small, beautifully situated, and comfortable. Good restaurant.
Moderate. Open April through October. West of Salerno on the
coast.

Hotel San Pietro   Positano   tel: 87 54 54
Clifftop hotel only a half mile south of Positano. Small, modern,
and ultracomfortable. Each room has terrace offering view to the
sea. Immaculate and bright. Elegant throughout. Expensive.
Open April through October.

Albergo Le Sirenuse   30 Via Cristoforo Colombo   tel: 87 50 66
Ancient home converted into attractive inn with lovely view.
Very comfortable. Antiques throughout. Expensive.

Ravello [60]

Hotel Caruso Belvedere   52 Via Toro   tel: 87 15 27
Medieval town house converted into hotel with comfortable

rooms and excellent restaurant. Perched hundreds of feet above bay. Moderate. Only sixteen miles from Salerno.

Hotel Palumbo   34 Via Toro   tel: 87 15 41
Medieval palace converted into comfortable hotel. Wonderful view. Delightful restaurant with superb Italian dishes. Moderate.

Ravenna [31]

Bisanzio   30 Via Salara   tel: 27 111
Small, comfortable hotel in good location. Modest yet pleasant. Moderate.

Roma [51] (Rome)

Carriage Hotel   via delle Carrozze 36   tel: 679-5166
Small hotel in the thick of things—a favorite of filmmakers. Small, straightforward rooms, some with terraces. Very fine in the moderate bracket.

Centro Diffusione Spiritualità (Casa d'Ospitalità)   via dei Riari 44
tel: 654-0122/656-1296
Only forty rooms in this inn run by sisters. Simple, quiet, and delightful, with garden and perfect location in Trastevere. But not for swingers (gates close at 11:00 p.m. sharp). Meals include wine. The *bargain* in Rome if it suits your personality.

Hotel delle Legazioni   via Barberini 11   tel: 46 59 97
Large, admittedly touristy, but comfortable hotel with simple rooms with bath. Ask for one with a balcony. Good value for its kind. Moderate.

Hotel delle Muse   via Tommaso Salvini 18   tel: 87 00 95
A noncentral location, but a delightful hotel. Ancient building fully modernized in quiet area. Only forty-two rooms, most with bath. Easy parking. Fun regional restaurant. Wonderful garden open June to mid-September. Moderate.

Hotel Dinesen   18 via di Porta Pinciana   tel: 46 09 32
An older hotel with only fifty simple, but comfortable, rooms at moderate rates. Attractive garden court and pleasant location near Borghese Gardens. No restaurant.

Hotel Eliseo   30 Via di Porta Pinciana   tel: 46 05 56
Quite small, simple, and tasteful. Old-fashioned in nice sense. Comfortable, not luxurious. Moderately expensive.

Hotel Forum   25 Via Tor de'Conti   tel: 679-2446
Unique location near the Roman ruins for this fine historic hotel offering charming, if compact, rooms. Attractive throughout with good service and nice restaurant. Expensive.

Hotel d'Inghilterra   14 via Bocca di Leone   tel: 68 90 10
One of Rome's older hotels in a good location near the Spanish Steps. Quite large with a nice atmosphere. Extremely comfortable. Charming choice in the moderate range.

Quattro Fontane   via 4 Fontane 149a   tel: 475-4936
Good central location for this intimate hotel with comfortable rooms, most with bath. Good in the inexpensive to moderate bracket.

Hotel Raphaël   Largo Febo 2   tel: 65 69 05
Nice location near the Piazza Navona. Quite large and older hotel with so-so, simple rooms (ask for one with terrace and view). Nice atmosphere. Moderate to expensive.

Hotel Pensione St. Elisabetta   140 via Veneto   tel: 48 03 18
Small, quite elegant hotel with attractive rooms. English flavor. Nice in its moderate class.

Hotel Sant'Anselmo   Piazza Sant'Anselmo   tel: 57 35 47
Friendly, small hotel close to the Forum. Comfortable and reasonably quiet. Good for families. Moderate.

Pensione Scalinata di Spagna   Piazza Trinità dei Monti 17
tel: 679-3006
A tiny, fourteen-room gem, nearly perfect in its class, with a delightful garden and comfortable rooms. Bathrooms are down the hall. Ideal for single women. Moderate.

Pensione Sitea   90 Via V. E. Orlando   tel: 475-1560
A wonderful value—small and charming hotel in the moderate range. Tasteful and popular.

Hotel Valadier   via della Fontanella 15   tel: 68 69 66
Once a bordello, now a charming and comfortable hotel with antiques and traditional ambience. Some lovely rooms with bath. Good restaurant. Moderate.

San Felice Circeo [52]

Punta Rossa   San Felice Circeo   tel: 52 80 69
Delightful small hotel with comfortable rooms and lovely view.
Pool. Moderately expensive. Closed in winter. Both hotels are
about sixty miles from Rome. Southeast of Anzio.

San Gimignano [42]

Hotel La Cisterna   Piazza della Cisterna   tel: 95 328
Small, delightful hotel with very comfortable rooms matched by
the excellence of the restaurant. Idyllic setting with great view.
Great choice. Moderate. Northwest of Siena.

San Marino [38]

Grand Hotel San Marino   28 Viale Lungomonte   tel: 99 24 00
Small, fresh hotel. Most rooms have lovely view. Comfortable if
compact. Moderately expensive. Closed December and January.

Santa Margherita di Pula [77]

Is Morus   Santa Margherita   tel: 92 14 24
Small, elegant mansion in refreshing pine woods by the shore.
Great view. Very comfortable. Pool, tennis, and water sports.
Very expensive. Open Easter through October. South of Cagliari.

Santa Teresa Gallura [79]

Moresco   Santa Teresa Gallura   tel: 74 188
On northern tip of the island. Small hotel with comfortable
rooms. All with bath. Great view. Garden and beach. Open June
to September only. Moderate. North of Olbia on tip of island.

San Vigilio [11]

Berghotel Vijiloch Monte San Vigilio   San Vigilio   tel: 51 236
Small boardinghouse. Comfortable and pleasant with lovely
view. Pool. Moderate. Closed November to mid-December. Near
Lana to the south of Merano.

Sestri Levante [26]

Grand Hotel dei Castelli   26 Via della Penisola   tel: 41 044
Small castle-hotel full of nostalgia and atmosphere. Antiques
throughout. Comfortable rooms. View to sea. Fine setting with
gardens. Tennis. Very expensive. Open mid-May through September. Thirty miles southwest of Genova. Southeast of Por-
tofino.

Siena [42]

Park Hotel   Via Marciano 166   tel: 44 803
Large medieval villa converted into charming inn with attractive
rooms. Very quiet and peaceful. Good local cooking. Pool and
tennis. Moderate.

Hotel Villa Scacciapensieri   24 Via di Scacciapensieri   tel: 41 441
Converted from seventeenth-century villa. Just outside of town
in wonderful park. Quiet and comfortable. Varied rooms. Pool
and tennis. Moderate. Open mid-March through October.

Taormina [70]

San Domenico Palace   5 Piazza Domenico   tel: 23 701
Lovely, large medieval monastery converted into one of Italy's
most attractive hotels. Luxury cells with lots of antiques. Spectacular view to the sea hundreds of feet below and to Mount Etna
in the distance. Subtropical gardens. Good cooking. Pool and
tennis. Excellent off season choice. Very expensive.

Hotel Timeo   59 Via del Teatro Greco   tel: 23 801
Charming small hotel with comfortable rooms. Nice setting in
park. Wonderful view. Moderately expensive. Open only from
fall to spring—an indication of the best season on Sicily.

Torino [1]

Villa Sassi Hotel   47 Via Traforo del Pino   tel: 89 05 56
Tiny villa in wonderful park just outside of town. Quite comfortable and extremely popular for its superb restaurant, one of the
best in the area. Lots of atmosphere. A charmer in the moderate
class.

Varigotti [21]

La Giara Hotel   Via Aurelia   tel: 60 152
Small, very pleasant hotel with view of sea. Comfortable. Quite expensive. About sixteen miles from Savona; to west of Genova.

Venice [16] (Venezia)

Pensione Accademia   Fnd. Bollani, 1058-60   tel: 37 846
Calm, old-fashioned hotel on the Grand Canal. Somewhat of a country feeling. Comfortable, but not for the stuffy. Inexpensive to moderate.

Hotel Cavalletto & Doge Orseolo   1107 San Marco   tel: 70 00 95
Large, attractive hotel in convenient, central location with comfortable rooms, most with bath. Nice throughout. Moderate to expensive.

Concordia   Calle Largo San Marco 367   tel: 70 68 66
Small, pleasant hotel in good central location. Modest, yet very comfortable rooms, most with bath. Charming restaurant. Moderate to expensive.

La Fenice et Des Artistes Hotel   San Marco 1936   tel: 32 333
Small hotel with wonderful atmosphere and quite comfortable rooms, attractively furnished and with bath or shower. Next to the Opera. No restaurant. Moderate.

Flora Hotel   Calle Largo 22 Marzo 2283a   tel: 25 324
Small, old-fashioned hotel with large, comfortable rooms, half with bath or shower. Delightful garden. No restaurant. Charming in the moderate to expensive class. Closed mid-November to mid-February.

Gabrielli Sandwirth   Riva degli Schiavoni 4110   tel: 31 580
Large, historic hotel with nice traditional atmosphere and comfortable rooms, most with bath. Admittedly old-fashioned, but calm and pleasant. Expensive.

Locanda Cipriani Pensione   Torcello Island   tel: 73 01 50
Isolated island retreat about forty minutes by boat from Venice. A gem. Elegant villa converted into attractive inn with only six

comfortable rooms and an excellent restaurant. Lots of atmosphere and wonderful flower-filled surroundings. Expensive, and worth it. Closed late October to mid-March.

Monaco & Grane Canale Hotel   Calle Vallaresso   tel: 70 02 11
Quite large and tasteful hotel overlooking Grand Canal. Nice rooms with bath, ask for modern or traditional according to taste. Good in the expensive bracket.

Quattro Fontane   16 via Quattro Fontane   tel: 60 227
On the Lido. Small, modest, yet very comfortable hotel, most rooms with bath. Quite good restaurant. Open May to September only. Moderate.

Verona [18]

Albergo Due Torri   4 Piazza S. Anastasia   tel: 34 130
Large hotel loaded with antiques. Unusual atmosphere. Quite comfortable. Very calm. Expensive.

WHERE TO EAT

Acquapendente [46]

Milano   Acquapendente   tel: 71 10
Fine restaurant serving local specialties. A few rooms. Quite expensive. About thirty-two miles north of Viterbo.

Assisi [48]

Taverna dell'Arco   8 Via San Gregoria   tel: 81 23 83
Lots of atmosphere in this historic restaurant serving delicious local cuisine at moderate prices. Fun.

Bari [61]

La Pignata   9 Via Melo   tel: 23 24 81
Excellent regional restaurant serving delicious Italian dishes. Expensive.

Bazzano [30]

Della Rocca   Bazzano   tel: 83 12 17
Wonderful regional restaurant. Superb *tortellini*, unique *gran fritto misto* (must be ordered in advance), and fine wines. Expensive. Some rooms available. Closed Friday. Just west of Bologna.

Bergamo [6]

La Taverna dei Coleoni   7 Piazza Vecchia   tel: 23 25 96
Superb atmosphere and cuisine matched by first-class service. Outstanding regional dishes. Moderately expensive.

Bologna [30]

Diana   via dell'Indipendenza 24   tel: 23 13 01
One of the finest traditional restaurants in Italy. Classic Italian cuisine. Game in season, fresh fish on Thursday. Expensive. Closed Monday.

Borgomanero [3]

Pinocchio   via Matteotti 147   tel: 82 273
Delicious and varied hors d'oeuvres followed by superb veal and game in season. Great red wines. Expensive. Closed Monday. South of Verbania.

Brescia [8]

La Sosta   20 Via San Martino della Battaglia   tel: 25 603
Historic and elegant dining. Superb local specialties. Moderate.

Camogli [21]

Gay   Piazzetta Colombo   tel: 77 02 42
Tiny, delightful restaurant specializing in seafood washed down with excellent white wines. Moderate. Closed Thursday. All in a wonderful little town. Southeast of Génova on the coast.

Capri [59]

La Canzone del Mare   *93 Via Marina Piccola*   *tel: 837-0589*
The brainchild of Gracie Fields—elegant and "in." Very popular and attractive restaurant serving small portions at inflated prices. Fun for the fast and fasting. Open only from April to mid-October.

La Capannina   *14 Via Delle Botteghe*   *tel: 837-0732*
A longtime favorite serving fine local dishes. Popular and quite expensive. Closed in winter.

La Pigna   *Via Roma 30*   *tel: 837-0280*
Fine garden restaurant with excellent view. Good cuisine at moderately expensive prices. Closed in winter.

Glaco's   *Via Sella Orta 10*   *tel: 837-0662*
Simple yet popular garden restaurant. Fun. Moderate.

Comacina, Island [4]

Locanda dell'Isola   *Comacina*   *tel: None*
Wonderful location and view from this fine regional restaurant isolated on the lovely Island of Comacina. Delicious lake specialties, such as *agoni alla contrabbandiera*. Moderately expensive. Open February to October.

Cortina d'Ampezzo [12]

La Capannina   *Località Alverà*   *tel: 26 33*
Very fine restaurant with both local and international specialties. Very expensive.

Al Fogher   *12 Via Grohmann*   *tel: 27 02*
Simple but quite good restaurant. Moderate.

El Toula   *Cortina*   *tel: 33 39*
At Ronco, just outside of town. Superb regional dishes. Very popular and equally expensive. Reserve.

Firenze [36]

Al Girarrosto   Piazza Santa Maria Novella 9   tel: 27 53 87
Good regional restaurant. Simple, but tasty, dishes nicely prepared. Moderate.

Harry's Bar   22 Lungarno A. Vespucci   tel: 29 67 00
Good food—not in the same league as the "Harry's" of Venice, but still excellent. Fun. Expensive.

La Loggia   Piazzale Michelangelo 1   tel: 28 70 32
Nice view over the city. Modern but good. Best in the summer. Moderate to expensive.

Ristorante Oliviero   51 Via delle Terme   tel: 28 76 43
Small restaurant serving international dishes. Very good. Quite expensive.

Ristorante Otello   Via Orti Oricellari   tel: 29 87 69
Attractive décor and fine regional dishes. Quite expensive.

Paoli   via dei Tavolini 12r   tel: 27 62 15
Good restaurant, typical of the region. Nice. Moderate.

Ristorante 13 Gobbi   9 Via Porcellana   tel: 29 87 69
Delicious local specialties at moderate prices. Nice atmosphere.

Genova [21]

Ristorante Vittorio Al Mare   Corso Italia   tel: 31 00 85
Short drive east of town. Modern seafood restaurant with delicious fish soup. Expensive. Reserve.

Zeffirino   via Settembre 20   tel: 59 19 90
Charming, authentic restaurant with an enormous menu. Fresh pasta and game in season. Great choice. Moderate to expensive.

Imola [30]

San Domenico   via Sacchi 1   tel: 29 00
Superb, regional restaurant in charming red-brick building. Outstanding *pasta*. Excellent lamb dishes. Delicious custard cream ice cream. Expensive. Closed Wednesday. Southeast of Bologna.

Lucca [33]

Ristorante Buca di Sant'Antonio   *5 Via della Cervia*   *tel: 55 881*
Charming small restaurant serving local dishes. Fun. Moderate.
North of Pisa.

Mantova [19] (Mantua)

Ristorante Rigoletto   *Lunetta San Giorgio di Mantova*   *tel: 30 367*
Excellent regional restaurant—quite popular and moderately expensive.

Merano [11]

Ristorante Andrea   *16 Via G. Galilei*   *tel: 24 400*
Small, superb regional restaurant. Quite elegant and moderately
expensive. Reserve.

Milano [5]

Ristorante Boeucc   *2 Piazza Belgioioso*   *tel: 79 28 80*
Expensive local favorite serving classic dishes. Nice atmosphere
and good service. Expensive.

Ristorante Bagutta   *14 Via Bagutta*   *tel: 70 27 67*
Popular restaurant serving excellent Italian dishes. Colorful.
Quite expensive.

***Ristorante Giannino*   *8 Via Amatore Sciesa*   *tel: 54 29 48*
One of the better-known restaurants in Italy. Nice atmosphere
and delicious cooking. Very expensive. Reserve well in advance.

***Ristorante Savini*   *Galleria Vittorio Emanuele 11*   *tel: 89 83 43*
Excellent cuisine—superb steaks and famous ice cream. Elegant.
Expensive.

Modena [28]

***Hotel Real Fini*   *24 Largo Garibaldi*   *tel: 23 80 91*
Large hotel noted for its superb restaurant. Well-known and
popular, with delicious local dishes. Expensive.

Ristorante Oreste   Piazza Roma 31   tel: 24 33 24
Another local favorite. Excellent reputation for fine regional cooking. Expensive.

Montecchio Maggiore [17]

Giulietta e Romeo ai Castelli   Montecchio Maggiore   tel: 76 021
The old fortress has been converted into a fine restaurant only seven miles from Vicenza.

Napoli [57]

Da Ciro a Santa Brigida   71 Via Santa Brigida   tel: 23 37 71
Near the opera. Modest but good restaurant. Moderate.

Il Cantinone   56 Via San Pasquale a Chiaia   tel: 23 32 59
Rustic, with lots of atmosphere. Good regional cooking. Moderate.

Dante & Beatrice   44 Piazza Dante   tel: 34 99 05
Noisy and Neapolitan—fun. Hurried. Good cooking. Moderate.

Novi Ligure [21]

Albergo Corona Grande   11-13 Corso R. Mareno   tel: 20 19
Nice atmosphere. Varied dishes including both French and Italian specialties. Moderate. Northwest of Geneva.

Orbetello [46]

Da Egisto   Corso Italia 198   tel: 86 74 69
Typical and pleasant restaurant with good steaks. Moderate. On coast west of Viterbo.

Palermo [75]

Charleston   30 Piazzale Ungheria   tel: 20 16 66
Very fine restaurant serving fresh seafood and international dishes. Elegant and expensive.

Orvieto [50]

Ristorante Morino   *37-45 Via Garibaldi*   *tel: 51 2*
One of the better restaurants in the region. Popular for fine service and cuisine. Expensive. West of Spoleto.

Parma [20]

Ristorante Aurora   *4 Sant'Alessandro*   *tel: 33 954*
One of the most delightful restaurants in the city. Well known and well liked for delicious poultry. Moderate.

Ristorante La Filoma   *15 Via XX Marzo*   *tel: 34 269*
Nice setting. Lots of atmosphere. Good regional cooking. Moderate.

Perugia [47]

La Rosetta   *Piazza Italia 19*   *tel: 20 841*
Very fine hotel restaurant known for outstanding game and black truffles. Fresh vegetables. Excellent wines. Expensive. Closed Monday.

Pescara [53]

Ristorante Guerino   *4 Viale Riviera*   *tel: 23 065*
Attractive restaurant with view of the sea. Seafood specialties. Moderate.

Piacenza [5]

Gotico   *Piazza dei Cavalli*   *tel: None*
On historic square. Pleasant regional cooking. Moderate. Southeast of Milano.

Portofino [26]

Ristorante Il Pitosforo   *9 Molo Umberto 1*   *tel: 69 020*
Ultraexpensive luxury restaurant well-known along the coast for elegance and good cuisine. On the snobbish side.

Porto Santo Stefano [43]

Il Moresco da Valli   Porto Santo Stefano   tel: 81 29 58
Attractive regional restaurant with fine view. Good local cooking. Moderate.

Riccione [37]

Ristorante Al Pescatore   11 Viale I. Nievo   tel: 42 526
Delightful seafood restaurant noted for regional wines as well. Moderate. Just south of Rimini.

Rimini [37]

Ristorante Nello   7 Via Flavio Gioia   tel: 26 610
The Nello is a favorite for fresh seafood. Moderate.

Vecchia Rimini   Via Gambalunga 33   tel: 26 610
Another excellent seafood restaurant. Moderate.

Roma [51]

Antica Pesa   Via Garibaldi 18   tel: 580-9236
Elite-oriented. Fine, but expensive.

Ristorante Apicio   3A Via Principe Amedeo   tel: 46 14 46
An exception to the "hotel restaurant" rule—very pleasant and fine. Superb Italian dishes. Lovely wine list. Expensive.

Bolognese   1-2 Piazza del Popolo   tel: 38 02 48
A people-watcher's favorite in warm weather. Nice atmosphere and good cooking. Expensive.

Campana   18 Vicolo della Campana   tel: 65 52 73
Ancient trattoria—simple. Superb regional cooking. A must. Moderate. Closed Monday and August.

Taverna Flavia   9 Via Flavia   tel: 48 92 14
Regional cooking. Special salad in the off season. Once very "in," now a bit *démodé*. Still very good, if very expensive.

La Fontanello   86 Largo Fontanella dei Borghese   tel: 68 38 49
Good choice for game in the off-season. Some excellent steaks. Small and refined. Expensive.

George's Restaurant   7 *Via Marche*   *tel: 48 45 75*
Deluxe, soft, and subdued—a gourmet restaurant which is a winter favorite. Excellent wines. Expensive, but worth it.

Girarrosto Toscano   29 *Via Campania*   *tel: 46 42 92*
Light and relaxed. Excellent steaks draw in the late crowd. Good value. Moderately expensive.

Hostaria Giggi Fazi   22 *Via Lucullo*   *tel: 46 40 45*
Sometimes riotous. Delicious chicken. A favorite with the late, late set, including opera buffs after opening night. Expensive.

Da Meo Patacca   8 *Av. S. Michele*   *tel: 581-6198*
Rustic, Roman, and often rowdy. A late-night haunt. Moderate.

Al Moro   13 *Vicolo delle Bollette*   *tel: 678-3495*
Very well known for its fine Roman cooking. Small, quite popular. Expensive.

Restaurant da Necci (Otello er Moro)   50 *Piazza dell'Oratorio*
tel: 679-0537
An intimate, romantic, and cozy restaurant much appreciated for its gourmet cooking and superb wines. Since there's no menu, you simply follow the cook's nose. Expensive.

Hostaria dell'Orso   93 *Via di Monte Brianzo*   *tel: 56 42 50*
Stylish, elegant, extremely well known luxury restaurant.

Otello alla Concordia   81 *Via della Croce*   *tel: 679-1178*
Charming courtyard restaurant which is a disaster in the summer and delightful in the off season. Moderate.

Passetto   14 *Via Zanardelli*   *tel: 654-0569*
A classic restaurant swerving from stylish to "touristy," depending upon the season and night. At its best it's superb. Quite expensive.

Al Pompiere   38 *Via Santa Maria dei Calderari*   *tel: 656-8377*
Very large and informal—Roman all the way. Good game in the off season. Moderate.

Sans Souci   20 *Via Sicilia*   *tel: 46 04 91*
Extraelegant luxury restaurant noted for its varied and excellent French and Italian dishes. Expensive.

Tre Scalini   30-36 Piazza Navona   tel: 65 91 48
Attractive dining (especially in warm weather). Famed for its delicious desserts, including *gelato tartufo*. Many people come here just for sweets. Moderate.

Toulà di Roma   Via della Lupa 296   tel: 68 17 96
Outstanding luxury restaurant—very fashionable and formal. An occasion. Exquisite, and equally expensive dishes.

Samboseto [20]

Cantarelli   Samboseto   tel: 90 133
Excellent restaurant five miles southeast of Busseto. Northwest of Parma.

San Gimignano [42]

La Cisterna e Le Terrazze   San Gimignano   tel: 94 03 28
Delightful inn with superb regional cooking. Recommended as rural hotel as well. Moderately expensive. Northwest of Siena.

San Marino [38]

La Taverna del Pianello   Piazza della Libertà   tel: 99 11 96
Simple, authentic restaurant serving good food. Moderate. Closed December to mid-January.

San Remo [23]

***Pesce d'Oro   Corso Cavallotti 270   tel: 86 641*
One of the region's better restaurants. Good regional and international dishes. Expensive.

Siena [42]

Al Mangia   Piazza del Campo 42   tel: 28 11 21
Charming regional restaurant. Simple. Moderate.

Taormina [70]

Ciclope   Corso Umberto   tel: 23 263
Wonderful fresh seafood nicely prepared and presented in sim-

ple manner. Highly recommended. Moderate to expensive. Closed Tuesday and November through December.

Torino [1]

Al Gatto Nero   14 Corso Filippa Turati   tel: 59 04 14
Excellent restaurant serving regional specialties as well as popular international dishes. Only a short walk from the train station. Quite expensive.

Ferrero   54 Corso Vittorio Emanuele   tel: 54 60 81
Delightful and elegant charmer with delicious dishes. Expensive.

San Giorgio   Borgo Medioevale   tel: 68 21 31
Nice view from this subdued castle-restaurant. Atmosphere matched by fine local cuisine. Expensive.

Trento [9]

Castel Madruzzo   Casino di Trento   tel: 56 137
Pleasant hotel noted for fine cooking. Twelve miles west of city.

Venezia [16] (Venice)

****Antico Martini   Campo San Fontin 1983   tel: 24 121*
Historic luxury restaurant near the Opera. Palatial and grand. Excellent food and service. Very expensive.

La Caravella   Via XXII Marzo   tel: 27 995
Fine and very relaxed seafood restaurant only a short walk from St. Mark's. Expensive.

Al Graspo de Ua   tel: 70 01 50
Long-standing favorite noted for superb hors d'oeuvres. Nice atmosphere and service. Expensive.

Harry's Bar   1323 Calle Vallaresso   tel: 36 797
World-famous "American" bar-restaurant combination. Lots of atmosphere. Extremely popular, fine, and expensive.

Locanda Cipriani   Torcello   tel: 73 01 50
A small inn with a few rooms on the Island of Torcello noted for its delicious cuisine (emphasis on fish) and charming atmosphere. Quite expensive. Closed late October to mid-March.

Peoceto Risorto   *Calle Donzella 249*   *tel: 25 953*
Romantic seafood restaurant. Charming. Quite expensive.

Quadri   *Piazza San Marco*   *tel: 22 105*
Traditional restaurant noted for superb food and wines at equally high prices. Perfect location on St. Mark's Square.

Taverna La Fenice   *1938 San Marco*   *tel: 23 856*
Outstanding ancient restaurant serving delicious local recipes. Nice atmosphere. Expensive.

Trattoria Alla Colomba   *1665 San Marco*   *tel: 33 817*
Colorful, typical restaurant not far from St. Mark's. Moderate.

Verona [18]

Dodici Apostoli   *3 Vicolo Corticello San Marco*   *tel: 24 680*
Wonderful location and nice atmosphere matched by excellent regional cooking and wines. Moderately expensive.

Viareggio [32]

Tito del Molo   *Lungomolo Corrado del Greco 3*   *tel: 42 016*
Very fine regional restaurant, at its best in warmer weather. Quite expensive.

Vico Equense [57]

Capo la Gala   *Vico Equense*   *tel: 879-8278*
Small attractive inn with comfortable rooms and nice view only five miles northeast of Sorrento. Pool. Moderate. Southeast of Naples.

LIECHTENSTEIN

LIECHTENSTEIN

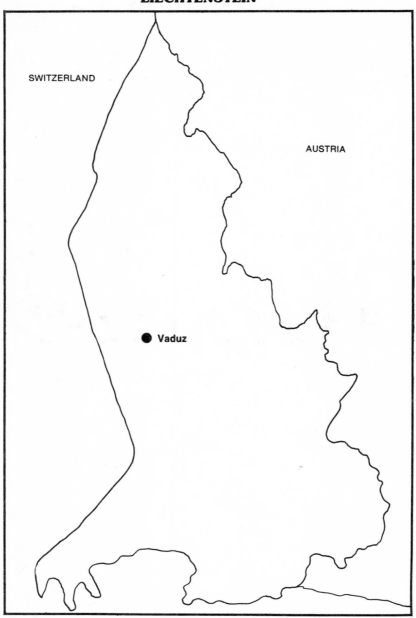

SWITZERLAND

AUSTRIA

● Vaduz

WHAT TO SEE

A tiny, taxless gem tucked into lovely mountains. The Prince's gallery with priceless masterpieces from the sixteenth and seventeenth centuries, the superb stamp museum (Liechtenstein is famous for its lovely stamps), and the scenic drive from *Vaduz* to the ski area of *Triesenberg* are highly recommended.

WHAT'S THE WEATHER REALLY LIKE?

Mild from late April to late October, but chilly and cold during the winter. Dress warmly in the off-season.

SOME SUGGESTIONS FOR A MORE ENJOYABLE TRIP

Nothing's overly complicated about Liechtenstein, but you may have trouble finding a place to stay if you don't plan ahead. Check the Switzerland chapter for nearby cities if this is the case. Note that while the stamps of this tiny country are lovely, the mail you send may take weeks to reach its destination. Even if you mark it air mail (*par avion*).

WHERE TO STAY

Vaduz

Hotel Real   Städtle 21/Rathausplatz   tel: 22 222
Tiny, delightful haven. Modest yet very comfortable rooms with lots of charm. Expensive.

Park Hotel Sonnenhof   Mareestrasse   tel: 21 192
Small, extremely comfortable hotel with delightful well-furnished rooms. Lovely location in park with great view. Excellent cuisine. Expensive. Closed last three weeks of January.

Hotel Schlössli Vaduz   Schloss Strasse 68   tel: 21 131
Small, attractive inn. Some apartments. Comfortable. Good location. Expensive.

WHERE TO EAT

Vaduz

Hôtel-Restaurant Real   *Town Center*   *tel: 22 222*
One of the very finest in Europe with both French and Swiss cuisines. Superb wine list. Excellent game in season. Very expensive. but worth it.

LUXEMBOURG

LUXEMBOURG

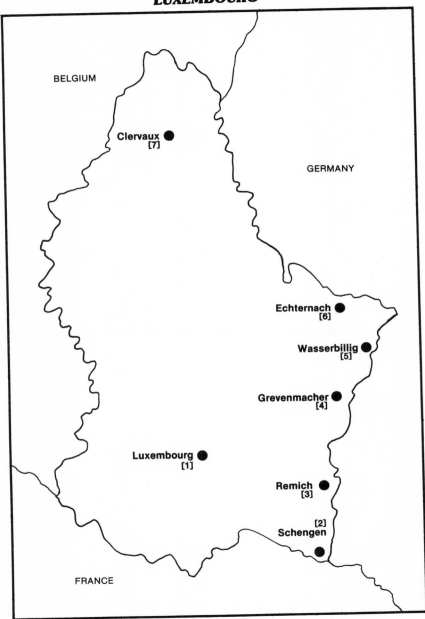

WHAT TO SEE

Most experienced travellers realize that Luxembourg is the major destination of Icelandic Airlines, which offers the lowest transatlantic fare of any scheduled airline. The tiny country's central location makes it an ideal starting point for trips to Belgium, France, Germany, and the Netherlands. The main attractions of Luxembourg are its capital, authentic country inns, wine roads, and gourmet weekends offered in many romantic retreats from late autumn to early spring. For a list of hotels offering gourmet weekends, contact the Luxembourg National Tourist Office (p. xx). Sightseers will begin with the underground passages, Grand Ducal Palace, National Museum, and Citadel de St. Esprit in *Luxembourg City*[1] before making excursions to the wine cellars at *Grevenmacher*[4] or *Remich*[3] (open Easter to mid-October), to picturesque *Echternach,*[6] or the medieval *Clervaux*[7] (note: the train trip from the capital to Clervaux is magnificent). If you arrive in Luxembourg in late September or early October, be sure to travel along the wine road from *Schengen*[2] to *Wasserbillig*[5]. Try too to visit the scenic *Ardennes* region with its many castles.

WHAT'S THE WEATHER REALLY LIKE?

The weather in Luxembourg is poor. It tends to be rainy and even snowy from the end of October through mid-April. The best time to travel is from May to early October.

SOME SUGGESTIONS FOR A MORE ENJOYABLE TRIP

Prices are steep in Luxembourg City and much lower in the country. The city itself can be seen in a day of relaxed sightseeing before travelling into rural areas. You get little value in hotel rooms, but more than you pay for at mealtime with exceptional French cuisine. Avoid the taxis at the airport and stick to the bus, which takes you to the main railway station for a song. Avoid the bars and B-girls in the capital; after all, you'll find *real* low life in Amsterdam or Paris, only a short train ride or drive away. Note that Luxembourg City is a busy little place. You should have hotel reservations before you arrive. Finally, Belgian francs are valid in Luxembourg, but Luxembourg currency is not valid in Belgium. The two currencies have the same value, so exchange any Luxembourg francs for Belgian francs before leaving the country.

WHERE TO STAY

Berdorf [6]

Bisdorff   2 Heisbich   tel: 79 208
Small hotel with lovely atmosphere. Fine restaurant. Pool. Moderate. Just west of Echternach.

L'Ermitage   44 Route de Grundhof   tel: 79 184
Tiny inn with charming atmosphere and fine restaurant. Comfortable. Pleasant setting. Moderate. Open mid-April to mid-October.

Clervaux [7]

Du Parc   1-2 Rue du Parc   tel: 91 068
Small and charming with old world flavor. Idyllic park setting. Excellent cuisine. Moderate.

Koener Hotel   14 Grand'rue   tel: 91 002
Tiny inn with modest rooms and a fine restaurant. Relaxing atmosphere. Moderate. Open mid-April to end of September.

Diekirch [6]

Hiertz   1 Rue Clairefontaine   tel: 83 562
Although the rooms are quite modest, the cooking is superb. Quite expensive. Northwest of Echternach.

Dommeldange [1]

Euro-Parc   114 Route d'Echternach   tel: 43 16 61
Small country inn with a pleasant atmosphere. Modest but comfortable rooms. Fine cuisine. Pool. Moderate. North of Luxembourg City.

Echternach [6]

Bel-Air   *1 Route de Berdorf*   *tel: 72 93 83*
Serene park setting. Comfortable rooms and excellent dining.
Trout fishing best in April. Expensive.

Grand Hotel   *27 Roue de Diekirch*   *tel: 72 078*
Beautiful old world hotel in a lovely park setting. Lots of atmosphere. Moderate.

Ehnen [3]

Simmer   *115 Quai de la Moselle*   *tel: 76 030*
Modest hotel with superb cuisine—a perfect stop along the Wine
Road. Excellent fish dishes. Expensive. North of Remich.

Larochette [6]

Du Château   *Rue de Medernach*   *tel: 87 009*
Small country inn with comfortable rooms. Delicious crayfish
and seafood. Moderate. Southwest of Echternach.

De La Poste   *11 Place Bleiche*   *tel: 87 006*
A small inn with modest rooms and a superb restaurant. Excellent cooking and wines. Expensive.

Luxembourg City [1]

Cravat   *19 Boulevard Roosevelt*   *tel: 21 975*
Small hotel with comfortable rooms in the new wing—ask for
one overlooking the valley. Very fine restaurant. Very expensive
(overpriced).

Kons   *24 Place de la Gare*   *tel: 48 60 20*
Large and pleasant hotel near the central station. Spacious and
varied rooms—not flashy, but nice. Fine service and a good restaurant. Expensive.

El Dorado   *7 Place de la Gare*   *tel: 48 10 71*
Small hotel near the central station with modern and quiet
rooms. Fairly attractive. Expensive.

Rix   20 Boulevard Royal   tel: 27 545
Small modern hotel in a quiet area with the Pavillon Royal restaurant—one of Luxembourg' better menus. Good service. Expensive.

Dauphin Hotel   42 Avenue de la Gare   tel: 48 82 82
Small, modest hotel, with compact rooms—most with bath. Not
for the stuffy. No restaurant. Moderate.

Mondorf-les-Bains [2]

Du Grand Chef   36 Avenue des Bains   tel: 68 012
Small inn surrounded by forest with comfortable rooms and a
traditional atmosphere. Superb restaurant, with crayfish as one
of the specialties. Expensive. Closed in winter. Northwest of
Schengen on French border.

Strassen [1]

Dany   72 Route d'Arlon   tel: 31 80 62
Small inn with rustic interior. Charming. Meat fondue is its specialty. Stables. Moderate. Northwest of Luxembourg City.

Vianden [6]

Heintz   55 Grand'rue   tel: 84 155
Small charming inn with lots of atmosphere. Very comfortable
and interesting. Moderate. Northwest of Echternach.

Wiltz [7]

Du Vieux Château   1 Grand'rue   tel: 96 018
Tiny, picturesque country inn with modest rooms. Moderate.
Southwest of Clervaux.

WHERE TO EAT

Gaichel [1]

La Bonne Auberge   *Gaichel (Eischen)*   *tel: 39 140*
One of the best restaurants in Luxembourg—delicious fish dishes. Expensive. Northwest of Luxembourg City on Belgian border.

Hesperange [1]

Klein   *432 Route de Thionville*   *tel: 36 177*
The restaurant is simply superb—a good stopping place on an excursion from the capital. Expensive. Southeast of Luxembourg City.

Luxembourg City [1]

Café du Commerce   *13 Place d'Armes*   *tel: 26 930*
Poor atmosphere, but excellent cuisine. Live trout taken from the tank and served with delicious cream sauce. Every dish is a masterpeice. Great value—don't judge this one by its appearance.

Au Gourmet   *8 Rue Chimay*   *tel: 25 561*
A luxurious décor in one of the city's finer restaurants with a varied menu. Excellent French cooking. Very expensive.

Rôtisserie Ardennaise   *1 Avenue du 10 Septembre*   *tel: 20 196*
One of the best values in town for fun and fine dining. Delicious regional cooking. Moderate.

Hostellerie du Grunewald   *10 Route d'Echternach*   *tel: 43 18 82*
Two and a half miles north on Highway E42. Roadside inn, with very pleasant setting, serving fresh game in season. Moderate. Some comfortable rooms available.

MALTA

MALTA

GOZO

Victoria ●

COMINO

MALTA

Valletta ●

Rabat ●

WHAT TO SEE

Malta, a British island off the southwestern toe of Italy's boot, is a relaxing retreat, as are its tiny sister islands Gozo and Comino, with their fine beaches and isolated resorts. Malta is known as an inexpensive, colorful, and pleasant Mediterranean destination, especially popular with Europeans. Outstanding sights include the Palace of the Grand Masters in *Valetta*; the underground Hypogeum Monument; the Ghar Dalam, with unique fossils; and the Ggantija prehistoric temples east of *Rabat* (Victoria) on the island of Gozo.

WHAT'S THE WEATHER REALLY LIKE?

The weather in Malta is mild from April through October, although October tends to be rainy. April and May are generally lovely, with sunny weather and relatively little rain. November can be mild enough for pleasant sailing. From December through March the weather is poor. January and February are cold, with frequent rains. The summer is generally very hot and dry.

SOME SUGGESTIONS FOR A MORE ENJOYABLE TRIP

As on most islands, you'll probably feel claustrophic unless you have a car to get to out-of-the-way spots. Have your airline reserve one for you in advance.

WHERE TO STAY

Comino Island

Comino Hotel   Comino Island   tel: 73 051
Attractive hotel with modern, comfortable rooms. Quiet setting by the sea. Pool and water sports. Inexpensive. Will provide transportation from the airport.

Gozo Island

Duke of Edinburgh Hotel   114 Racecourse Street   tel: 76 468
Ancient home converted into a small hotel with modest rooms—some with bath. Not for the stuffy. Inexpensive. Ferry to main island.

Marfa

Ramla Bay Hotel   Marfa   tel: 73 521
Small modern hotel on the northern tip of the island. Modest rooms with bath or shower. Water sports and pool. Geared to a young crowd. Inexpensive.

Mdina

Xara Palace Hotel   St. Paul's Square   tel: 74 001
Medieval palace converted into a charming hotel with comfortable rooms—all with bath. Very quiet and peaceful. Moderate.

Pieta

Sa Maison Hotel   22 Pieta Wharf   tel: 20 714
Small and very modest hotel with comfortable rooms—some with bath. Ten minutes from the sea. Good restaurant. Charming. Moderate.

St. Paul's Bay

Hyperion Hotel   Qawra   tel: 73 641
Modern hotel with typical island architecture. Modest, comfortable rooms with bath and nice view. Pool and water sports. Inexpensive to moderate.

Sliema

Imperial Hotel   Rudolph Street   tel: 30 011
Quite large, traditional hotel with hints' of elegance. Very comfortable and attractive rooms—most with bath. Pool and garden. Good restaurant. Moderate.

Valetta

Castille Hotel   *St. Paul's Street*   *tel: 23 677*
Sixteenth-century mansion converted ino charming hotel with modest, comfortable rooms. All with bath. Inexpensive.

Cumberland Hotel   *111 St. John Street*   *tel: 27 732*
Ancient palace converted into small hotel with modest rooms. All with bath. No restaurant. Moderate.

NETHERLANDS

THE NETHERLANDS

REGIONS
1 — Groningen
2 — Friesland
3 — Drenthe
4 — Overijssel
5 — Gelderland
6 — Noordholland
7 — Utrecht
8 — Zuidholland
9 — Zeeland
10 — Noordbrabant
11 — Limburg

Harlingen [21]
Leeuwarden [20]
2
Sneek [22]
Groningen [19]
Boertange [18]
Assen [17]
3
1

6

Zwolle [16]
4

Haarlem [3]
Amsterdam [1]
Aalsmeer [2]
Lisse [4]
7
Apeldoorn [15]
5
Den Haag (The Hague) [5]
8
Gouda [6]
Utrecht [14]
[12]
Arnhem [11]
s'Heerenberg
Rotterdam [7]
Tiel [13]
Nijmegen [10]

10
WEST GERMANY

Middelburg [8]
9

BELGIUM

11

N

0   km.   50

0   miles   50

[9]
Vaals

CUCL

WHAT TO SEE

Outstanding in the Netherlands are hundreds of unique museums, including tiny ones in the provinces and superstars in Amsterdam; picturesque rural inns and ancient farmhouse restaurants serving simple, yet delicious, Dutch treats; an early spring with fields of tulips blossoming in an astounding array of brilliant colors; a lively low life (one of the most explicit in Europe); and always, at every turn, the kind of hospitality that makes you feel at home.

Amsterdam [1] shines as an introduction to the Netherlands with some outstanding sightseeing. Don't miss superb museums like the Rijksmuseum, Stedelijk, and new Van Gogh Museum. Highly recommended excursions include *Aalsmeer* [2] (flower auction Monday to Saturday at 8:00 a.m.), *Alkmaar* (cheese market from end of April to mid-September each Friday from 10:00 a.m. to noon), and *Haarlem* (superb Frans Hals Museum). Also recommended are the fortified town of *Naarden*; typical *Volendam* and *Monnickendam*, and the town of *Laren*, for its handicrafts. Try too to take in the inner city of *Amersfoort* and the view from the cathedral in *Utrecht* [14]. You may also wish to be weighed on the witch scale at *Oudewater*, a lovely town in spring.

Den Haag [5] (the Hague) offers a collection of two hundred fifty Mondrians in the Gemeentemuseum, 17 Rembrandts in the Mauritshuismuseum, and Maduradam (*Holland in Miniature*) on the outskirts of town. The sixteenth- and seventeenth-century atmosphere of *Delft* makes it appealing. Try to take in the porcelain collection in the Lambert Van Meerten Museum. For authentic Delftware check into De Porceleyne Fles on Rotterdamse Weg 196. You'll find the finest assortment of windmills around *Kinderdijk*, a lively cheese market from 9:00 a.m. to noon each Thursday in *Gouda* [6], and the most fabulous display of tulips at *Keukenhof* near *Lisse* [4] from mid-March to early April. A highly recommended blossom tour: Lisse, Keukenhof, Hillegom, Treslong, Bennebroek, Linnaeushof, Noordwijk-B (to the south), Katwijk-a-Zee, Katwijk, Wassenaar, Oegstgeest (to the north), Warmond, Sassenheim, *Lisse*.

The Delta-Expo near *Stellendam* explains the enormous work of reclaiming land from the sea. You may want to spend a night in the medieval town of *Veere*. Inland, you'll want to see the living nunnery (*béguinage*) in *Breda* and the unique Evoluon Museum in

Eindhoven. Far inland in the area north of *Vaals* [9] you'll see the castles of *Eijsden* and *Kerkrade*, the charming villages of *Slenaken* and *Wessen*, and the colorful orchards around *Gulpen* (May).

Heading north you'll pass many of the castles of Gelderland. Several still remain near *Doornenburg*. In *Otterloo* you'll find Van Goghs in the Kröller-Müller Museum. The miniature town of *Bronkhorst* delights many while the ancient houses of *Buren* appeal to photographers. The following circular route takes you past blossoming orchards in April and May: *Tiel* [13], Zoelen, Ommersveld, Lienden, Kesteren, Opheusden, Randwijk, Heteren, Driel, Elden, Malburgen, Huissen, Bemmel, Ressen, Oosterhout, Herveld, Andelst, Dodewaard, Ochten, Echtelo, Ooij, Tiel.

Around *Zwolle* [16] (famed for fifteenth- to seventeenth-century houses) you'll want to visit *Giethoorn*, the Kasteel Twickel gardens in *Delden*, and the typical villages of *Staphorst* and *Rouveen* (no cars, no cameras on Sunday). Then, near *Assen* [17], don't miss the miniature gems of *Havelte* and *Orvelte*. The village of *Dwingeloo* has become an artists' retreat. In the far north you'll be entering a region noted for its beautifully preserved castles or *borgs*, such as the Borg Verhildersum in *Leens*. Also lovely is the Nienoord Estate in *Leek*. The fortress town of *Boertange* [18] looks much as it did in the sixteenth century and is worth a side trip. In *Groningen* [19] you'll find the Martinichurch and pleasant stores along the Herestraat. To the west you'll enter Friesland, a region with its own dialect and passport. Amble through the ancient streets of *Leeuwarden* [20], admire the seventeenth-century houses of *Dokkum*, visit the *Franeker* planetarium, and don't miss the unique hand-painted furniture in *Hindeloopen*.

WHAT'S THE WEATHER REALLY LIKE?

Weather is best from May to September, yet the overall climate is poor, with frequent rains from early spring until the end of fall. From November to mid-March it's cool and often cold, with occasional light snowfalls.

SOME SUGGESTIONS FOR A MORE ENJOYABLE TRIP

The tourist season in rural Holland extends from May to September although it lasts the year round in Amsterdam. The capital is packed from early March until mid-November, so be sure to reserve a room well in advance (this can be done free of charge by writing the NRC-Amsterdam, POB 3387, Amsterdam 1001, tel: (020) 21 12 11). The NRC will reserve a room in the price range you specify. Should you arrive in the capital without a room reservation, head to the VVV (tourist office) near Dam Square. They'll find you a room at a modest charge (expect an hour wait). If you drive into Amsterdam, park your car near your hotel. Then lock and leave it. Don't worry about the tickets that will accumulate on the windshield. Simply discard them at the end of your stay. Amsterdam is geared strictly to the pedestrian, not the motorist. A car is simply a hassle to deal with. Furthermore, the extensive network of trams is easy to use and very inexpensive (check into full day tickets). If you're trying to keep costs down at meals, look for an emblem with a fork on it in a restaurant window. This means that the restaurant offers a set-price touristic menu. Over six hundred restaurants offer such a menu in Holland. By all means splurge on a *rijsttafel*, an Indonesian import consisting of dozens of different dishes laid out on a table in front of you. It's expensive, but worth every florin. KLM, the Dutch airline, publishes a series of free books on Holland, all of which are excellent and detailed. The shopping and museum guides are particularly superb. You can get these books by writing to the New York office (p. xxiii.) Be sure to include twenty-five cents for each book requested (postage) and allow several weeks for delivery. The books: *Surprising Amsterdam, Happy Holland, Shopping Guide to Holland, On Foot in Surprising Amsterdam, Funlovers Guide to Holland*, and *Guide to Holland's Museums*. Note that most Amsterdammers speak some English, although communication can be more difficult in the provinces. The best way to see the country is by car, which allows you to get into the hidden villages. Since distances are short and roads very fine, travel by car is neither tiring nor overly expensive.

WHERE TO STAY

Amersfoort [14]

Witte de   *2 Utrechtseweg*   *tel: 14 142*
Small and very comfortable inn with fine French cooking. Moderate. Northeast of Utrecht.

Amsterdam [1]

Ambassade Hotel   *Herengracht 341*   *tel: 23 28 61*
Seventeenth-century buildings converted into cozy, smart hotel on canal. Only thirty-four rooms—most with bath. Try for number 24. Moderate.

American   *97 Leidsekeide*   *tel: 24 53 22*
A lively location near the concert house and Leidseplein, one of the main night life areas. Very comfortable. The dining room's a national shrine—the place to meet people at any time of day. Very expensive.

Amstel   *1 Prof. Tulpplein*   *tel: 22 60 60*
Classic atmosphere with a slant towards elegance and sophistication. Some of the rooms excellent, others so-so. Worth a gamble if you can choose your room. Ultraexpensive.

Amster Centre   *Herengracht 255*   *tel: 22 17 27*
Seventeenth-century buildings converted into nice, comfortable hotel. All rooms with bath. Try for number 422 or 482. Expensive.

AMS Hotel Holland   *P.C. Hooftstraat 162-168*   *tel: 73 39 18*
Excellent location on shopping street. Functional and comfortable. Some rooms with bath. Moderate.

Atlas Hotel   *Van Eeghenstraat 64*   *tel: 76 63 36*
Ancient red-brick building modernized throughout. Comfortable, if small, rooms. Fresh flowery feeling. Moderate.

Hotel Concorde   *Willemsparkweg 104/131*   *tel: 76 34 55*
Both modern and more elegant styled rooms. All with bath. Good value in moderate bracket.

Eden Hotel   *Amstel 142-144*   *tel: 24 17 83*
Comfortable, if compact rooms (with showers) in ancient, canal-side hotel. Moderate.

Estherêa   *Singel 305-307*   *tel: 24 51 46*
Tidy canal hotel near the Dam. Agreeable, but compact, rooms—half with bath. Good restaurant. Moderate.

Grand Hotel Krasnapolsky   *9 Dam*   *tel: 63 163*
Excellent location in the middle of the city on the main square. Tasteful and very comfortable rooms. Refined. Nice dining area. The breakfasts can be described as a happening. Very expensive.

Hotel de Haas   *Tesselschadestraat 23-29*   *tel: 12 68 76*
Townhouses converted into comfortable hotel. Only eighteen rooms with bath. Both Dutch specialties and *rijsttafel* in the restaurant. Moderate.

Hotel Jan Luyken   *Jan Luykenstraat 54-58*   *tel: 76 41 11*
Pronounced Lowken, this is a centrally located hotel. Small and nice, with quite comfortable rooms. All with bath. No restaurant. Moderate to expensive.

Owl Hotel   *Roemer Visscherstraat 1-3*   *tel: 18 94 84*
Only thirty-one cheerful rooms with bath. Comfortable. Good breakfasts. Moderate to expensive.

Pulitzer   *315-331 Prinsengracht*   *tel: 22 83 33*
Restored seventeenth-century town houses. Combination of charming canal-side atmosphere and luxury. Large and very expensive.

Hotel Roemer Visscher   *Roemer Visscherstraat 10*   *tel: 14 23 24*
Quiet, private hotel with rooms onto courtyard garden. Most rooms with shower and fold-up beds. Candlelight dining. Moderate to expensive.

Hotel Trianon   *J. W. Brouwersstraat 3-7*   *tel: 73 39 18*
Good location with simple, comfortable rooms—a few with bath. Cozy, typical restaurant. Modest. Moderate.

Hotel Wiechman   *Prinsengracht 328*   *tel: 22 54 10*
Thirty comfortable rooms in this pleasant hotel. Nice. Nothing fancy. Good restaurant. Moderate.

Apeldoorn [15]

Keizerskroon de   7 Koningstraat   tel: 21 77 44
Country setting. A fine hotel with spacious and comfortable rooms. Stylish dining. Moderate to expensive.

Arnhem [12]

Rijnhotel   10 Onderlangs   tel: 43 46 42
Small, quiet hotel on the water with comfortable rooms. Moderate to expensive.

Groot Warnsborn   277 Bakenbergseweg   tel: 45 57 51
Small, quiet hotel with modern comfort and relaxed atmosphere. Fishing. Expensive to very expensive.

Baarn [14]

Kasteel De Hooge Vuursche   14 Hilversumsestraatweg   tel: 12 541
In a wooded seventy-acre setting, this mansion converted into a luxury hotel is one of Holland's gems—only thirty miles from Amsterdam. Traditional elegance in both the public and private rooms. Extremely comfortable and tasteful throughout. The dining here has a countrywide reputation. Pool. Riding. Worth a detour. Expensive. Just north of Utrecht.

Beetsterzwaag [20]

Lauswolt   10 van Harinxmaweg   tel: 12 45
Nice country inn with a rural flavor. Very comfortable. Superb international cuisine. Tennis. Fine wooded golf course. Expensive. Southeast of Leeuwarden.

Berg en Dal [10]

Parkhotel Val Monte   5 Oude Holleweg   tel: 17 04
Large, attractive rural hotel with traditional flair. Expensive. Just southeast of Nijmegen.

Boekelo [15]

Boekelo   203 Oude Deldenerweg   tel: 14 44
Modern and comfortable rooms. Garden in the back. Peaceful.

Very expensive. Far east of Apeldoorn; near the border south of Enschede.

Borger [19]

Hotel Bieze   21 Hoofdstraat   tel: 43 21
A modest modern hotel with a fine restaurant offering delicious Dutch specialties. Moderately expensive. Southeast of Groningen.

Breda [7]

Mastbosch   20 Burg Kerstenslaan   tel: 65 00 50
Fine hotel in lovely wooded area. Traditional flavor. Quite comfortable and quite expensive. Southeast of Rotterdam.

Domburg [8]

Badhotel   3-7 Domburgseweg   tel: 12 41
Stately mansion in nicely kept gardens. One of the best hotels on the island of Walcheren. Fine cuisine. Geared to families. Rather expensive for the region. Open June to mid-September. Just northwest of Middelburg.

Gieten [19]

Braams   7 Brink   tel: 12 41
A traditional hotel with a lovely location. Modest but nice. Excellent coffee served in old Dutch *kraantjespot*. Moderate to expensive. Southeast of Groningen.

Gouda [6]

Hotel de Zalm   34 Markt   el: 12 344
Historic hotel with modest rooms. Antiques. Moderate.

Groningen [19]

Helvetia   Hereplein 51   tel: 13 73 96
Small, comfortable hotel in the center of town. Fairly nice. Moderately expensive.

Euromotel   Expositielaan   tel: 25 84 00
Very modern hotel adjoining the congress center, with studio
rooms and suites. Very comfortable. Cozy bar. Moderately expensive.

Gulpen [9]

Kasteel Neubourg   1 Rijksweg   tel: 12 22
Stylish castle with ancient furnishings, family paintings, and
enormous fireplace. Spacious rooms. Excellent cuisine with trout
as the specialty (the castle is next to a trout hatchery). Quite expensive. Just northwest of Vaals.

Heerlen [9]

Grand Hotel   17 Wilhelminaplein   tel: 71 38 46
Large, with rather rustic atmosphere. Comfortable and quite expensive. North of Vaals.

Hilversum [14]

Hof van Holland het   1-7 Kerkbrink   tel: 46 141
Located in the center of town, with both modern and comfortable rooms. Moderate. Just north of Utrecht.

Kampen [16]

Hotel de Stadsherberg   Ijsselkade 48   tel: 26 45
Modest hotel with view over the River Ijssel. Quite comfortable.
Good regional cooking. Moderate to expensive. Just west of
Zwolle.

Leeuwarden [20]

Oranje Hotel   4 Stationsweg   tel: 26 241
A fine traditional hotel offering modest but comfortable rooms.
Moderately expensive.

Leuvenum

Hotel Het Roode Koper   *82 C. J. Sandbergweg*   *tel: 73 93*
Once a patrician manor, this hotel rests in the middle of a beautiful forest. Modest rooms. Excellent cooking. Friendly atmosphere. Gardens, tennis, and riding. Moderate to expensive.

Mook [10]

Plasmolen de   *170 Rijksweg*   *tel: 14 44*
Small inn with a wonderful country flavor and garden atmosphere. Pool. Tennis. Moderate. South of Nijmegen.

Noordwijk Aan Zee [3]

Palace   *3 Kon. Wilhelminaboulevard*   *tel: 19 231*
Large, traditional hotel offering comfortable rooms and fine dining. Expensive. Just south of Haarlem.

Oosterbeek [12]

Bilderberg de   *261 Utrechtseweg*   *tel: 33 30 60*
A fine country hotel with a fresh feeling. Comfortable. Moderate. North of Arnhem.

Paterswolde [19]

Familiehotel Paterswolde   *19 Groningerweg*   *tel: 18 31*
Although large, the hotel has a warm country atmosphere with modest rooms. Expensive. South of Groningen.

Sneek [22]

Wijnberg de   *23 Marktstraat*   *tel: 24 21*
In the town of "Snake" you'll find this delightful Dutch hotel offering delicious breakfasts. Very simple with a warm atmosphere. Moderate.

Utrecht [14]

Hotel des Pays Bas   *10 Janskerkhof*   *tel: 33 33 21*
Quite small serene hotel in the center of town. Comfortable.
Well known for fine cooking. Expensive.

Valkenburg [9]

***Prinses Juliana   *11 Broekhem*   *tel: 12 244*
Excellent hotel with superb dining in the "Dutch Alps." Quite
expensive. Northwest of Vaals.

Veere [8]

Hotel de Campveerse Toren   *2 Kade*   *tel: 291*
Unique inn fitted into the old harbor tower. Informal and very
relaxed atmosphere. North of Middelburg. Picturesque view.
Moderate.

Hotel de Walvis   *Vrouwenpolder*   *tel: 17 91*
Both rooms and apartments in this comfortable hotel near the
large Veere lake. Quite expensive.

Vierhouten [15]

Mallejan de   *70 Nunspeterweg*   *tel: 241*
Comfortable hotel in a delightful forest setting. Tennis. Riding.
Moderate to expensive. North of Apeldoorn.

Vlaardingen [7]

Delta Hotel   *15 Maasboulevard*   *tel: 34 54 77*
A lovely hotel by the river with very comfortable rooms and excellent food. Expensive. Eight miles from Rotterdam (west).

Vlissingen [8]

Grand Hotel Britannia   *4 Boulevard Evertsen*   *tel: 13 255*
Located near the beach is this large and somewhat commercial
hotel offering comfortable rooms and fine service. Expensive.
Just south of Middelburg.

Vreeland [1] (on the Vecht)

Hotel de Nederlanden   3 Duinkerken   tel: 15 76
Only fifteen miles from Amsterdam. Seventeenth-century farmhouse converted into comfortable hotel. Only a few rooms,
some with bath. Moderate to expensive. Southeast of Amsterdam.

Wassenaar [5]

Auberge de Kieviet   Stoeplaan 27   tel: 79 403
An exquisite mansion with only six rooms. Noted mainly for its
excellent restaurant. Superb chàteaubriand. Expensive.

Zeist [14]

Figi   3 Het Rond   tel: 17 211
A fine hotel offering traditional service and atmosphere. Moderate to expensive. Just east of Utrecht.

Zwolle [16]

Wientjes   7 Stationsweg   tel: 11 200
Small mansion converted into pleasant hotel with spacious
rooms. Moderate to expensive.

WHERE TO EAT

Amsterdam [1]

Bali   95 Leidsestraat   tel: 22 78 78
An Indonesian restaurant offering the famous *riijstafel,* a series of
delicious dishes laid out along the table as an enjoyable feast. It
is customary to have a drink at the bar before being seated at the
table in Indonesian restaurants. The Bali is well known and
slightly overpriced. Quite elegant. Reserve.

***De Boerderij**   *69 Korte Leidsedwarsstraat*   *tel: 23 69 29*
A fun restaurant with a charming and authentic farm flavor. Excellent international dishes. Quite expensive. Reserve.

***Dikker en Thijs**   *Prinsengracht 444*   *tel: 26 77 21*
Formal and elegant, this restaurant specializes in fine French cuisine. Nice atmosphere. Quite expensive. Reserve.

Samo Sebo   *P. C. Hooftstraat 27*   *tel: 72 81 46*
Not as "in" as the Bali, but the *riijstafel* is better, making this a real value in Indonesian cooking. Quite expensive and worth it.

't Swarte Schaep   *24 Korte Leidsedwarsstraat*   *tel: 22 30 21*
Charming and well-known restaurant with centuries of history. Quite expensive. Reserve.

Dorrius   *Nieuwe Zijds Voorburgwal 342*   *tel: 23 52 45*
Very modest restaurant serving Dutch specialties at very reasonable prices. Not in the least luxurious.

Apeldoorn [15]

Bistro Le Philosophe   *P. Krugerstraat 6*   *tel: 21 78 13*
Very tasteful international cuisine. Be sure to ask the manager to sing and play the piano. Delightful. Moderately expensive.

Arnhem [12] (Schaarsbergen)

Rijzenburg   *17 Koningsweg*   *tel: 43 67 33*
Tiny restaurant specializing in game dishes during the off-season.

Delft [5]

De Prinsenkelder   *11 Schoolstraat*   *tel: 12 18 60*
Charming restaurant in old cellar. Moderate. Just southeast of the Hague.

Den Haag [5]

Boerderij de Hoogwerf   *Zijdelaan 20*   *tel: 85 01 23*
Delightful Dutch cooking in an old farm converted into a charming restaurant.

Garoeda   *18 A Kneuterdijk*   *tel: 46 53 19*
Indonesian restaurant specializing in the delicious riijstafel.

In Den Kleynen Leckerbeck   *Noordwal 1/130 Prinsestraat*   *tel: 46 19 08*
Tiny, cozy. Authentic flavor. Good food.

In 't Gemeste Schaap   *9 Raam-straat*   *tel: 63 95 72*
Both international and Dutch dishes served in this rustic restaurant with great décor. Moderate. Reserve.

't Goude Hooft   *13 Groenmarkt*   *tel: 18 50 55*
Dutch specialties in this fine restaurant. Moderate. Reserve.

***House of Lords*   *4 Hofstraat*   *tel: 64 47 71*
Elegant décor. An emphasis on French cuisine. Excellent service. Background music. Expensive. Reserve.

Meer en Bosch   *Heliltrooplaan 5*   *tel: 25 77 84*
A converted farm in a woodsy setting. Intimate and nice.

Royal   *44 Lange Voorhout*   *tel: 60 07 72*
Formal restaurant with excellent food and service. Prices to match. Reserve.

***Saur*   *47 Lange Voorhout*   *tel: 46 92 22*
A formal seafood restaurant. Exclusive and very well known. Expensive.

Enter [15]

De Twentse Hoeve   *Langevoortseweg 12*   *tel: (05408) 441*
A rustic restaurant with an old Saxon farm interior. Delightful. Very simple. Reserve. East of Apeldoorn; north of Goor.

Geesteren [15]

Erve Booymans   *Denekamperweg 14*   *tel: (05492) 393*
This Twente farm has been converted into a restaurant with an authentic interior. Very simple. East of Apeldorn to north of Almelo.

Gulpen [9]

La Truite d'Or   *Euverum 5a*   *tel: 15 00*
Delicious fresh trout in a pleasant restaurant. Moderate.

Lattrop [16]

Gerrie Hoeve   Ottershagenweg 35   tel: 93 33
Eighteenth-century Saxon farm with an authentic interior. Converted into a simple rustic restaurant. Far east of Zwolle on border near Nordhorn.

Leiden [5]

Auberge De Witte Singel   93 Witte Singel   tel: 34 343
Modest rooms. Elegant and intimate dining room with excellent cooking. Moderate. Northeast of the Hague.

Oudt Leyden   51-53 Steenstraat   tel: 33 144
Delicious regional specialties in a charming riverside restaurant. Quite expensive.

Leeuwarden [20]

Herberg de Waag   Nieuwestad 148B   tel: (05100) 37 250
This old weigh house has been converted into a restaurant with wine and cheese dishes.

Losser [15]

Erve Leusink   Leusinkweg 3   tel: (05423) 1599
Dating back to 1827, this historic farm is now a regional restaurant. Simple. East of Apeldoorn near border.

Maastricht [9]

Au Coin des Bons Enfants   4 Ezelmarkt   tel: 12 359
Excellent food in authentic surroundings. Expensive. Northwest of Vaals.

****Château Neercanne   60 Cannerweg   tel: 13 046*
Superb French cuisine in castle outside of town. Very expensive, but worth it.

Markelo [16]

In de Kop'ren Smore   Holterweg 18   tel: (05476) 1344
Ancient Saxon farm with regional specialties and lots of atmosphere. Simple. Southeast of Zwolle.

Monnickendam [1]

Stuttenburgh   Havenstraat 20   tel: 1582
A unique restaurant with a collection of music boxes and musical instruments. Just north of Amsterdam.

Oegstgeest [5]

De Beukenhof   Terweeweg 2   tel: 15 31 88
One of the best restaurants in the country, with prices to match. Delicious cuisine. Good service. Northeast of the Hague near Leiden.

Ootmarsum [16]

De Wanne   Stobben kamp 2   tel: (05419) 1270
Saxon farm converted into a restaurant with regional specialties. Simple. Southeast of Zwolle.

Pesse [17]

Het Oude Jachthuis   Eursinee 12   tel: 333
Traditional small farmhouse converted into one of the best restaurants in Holland. Elaborate lunch and dinner. Home-grown vegetables and herbs. Superb wine list. Expensive. Southwest of Assen.

Rotterdam [7]

Chalet Suisse   31 Kievietslaan   tel: 36 50 62
International cooking in Swiss atmosphere. Moderate.

Coq d'Or   25 *van Vollenhovenstraat*   *tel: 36 64 05*
Superb wines and French cuisine in romantic restaurant with prices to match.

Euromast   *20 Parkhaven*   *tel: 36 34 36*
Dining with a superb view of the surrounding city. Nearly four hundred feet high. Moderate.

In Den Rust Wat   *Honingerdijk 96*   *tel: 13 41 10*
Charming restaurant serving regional specialties in a small cottage.

Kota Radja   *Matheussenplein 13*   *tel: 23 49 80*
One of the better Indonesian restaurants in the city. Quite expensive.

Old Dutch Restaurant   *Rochussenstraat 20*   *tel: 36 05 21*
Traditional atmosphere in a delightful Dutch restaurant. Quite expensive.

Het Witte Paard   *Groenezoom 245*   *tel: 19 20 20*
Authentic country hotel with a superb restaurant. Quite expensive.

S'Hertogenbosch [13]

Chalet Royal   *Wilhelminapark 1*   *tel: 35 071*
Excellent restaurant in pleasant atmosphere. Fine service. Expensive. Reserve. South of Tiel.

Scherpenzeel [14]

De Witte Holevoet   *282 Holevoetplein*   *tel: 13 36*
Delightful inn with superb French cooking. Modest rooms. Attractive dining. Quite expensive. Reserve. East of Utrecht.

Vasse [16]

De Liskoel   *Hooidijk 26*   *tel: (05418) 253*
Twente farm, now a regional restaurant. Simple. Far east of Zwolle near border to northeast of Almelo.

Vollenhove [16]

Hotel Seidel   Vollenhove   tel: 12 62
Once the town hall, this hotel dating back to 1621 offers modest rooms in old Dutch style and superb cuisine and wine cellar. Moderate. North of Zwolle.

Weerselo [16]

Stiftschuur   Het Stift 8   tel: 428
Twente interior in a farm converted into a regional restaurant. Simple. Southeast of Zwolle to east of Almelo.

NORWAY

NORWAY

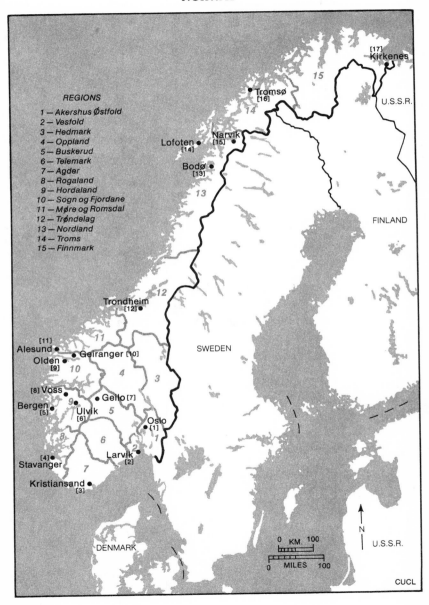

REGIONS

1 — Akershus Østfold
2 — Vesfold
3 — Hedmark
4 — Oppland
5 — Buskerud
6 — Telemark
7 — Agder
8 — Rogaland
9 — Hordaland
10 — Sogn og Fjordane
11 — Møre og Romsdal
12 — Trøndelag
13 — Nordland
14 — Troms
15 — Finnmark

U.S.S.R.

FINLAND

SWEDEN

DENMARK

U.S.S.R.

Kirkenes [17]

Tromsø [16]

Narvik [15]

Lofoten [14]

Bodø [13]

Trondheim [12]

Alesund [11]

Geiranger [10]

Olden [9]

Voss [8]

Gello [7]

Bergen [5]

Ulvik [6]

Oslo [1]

Larvik [2]

Stavanger [4]

Kristiansand [3]

0 KM. 100

0 MILES 100

N

CUCL

WHAT TO SEE

Both *Oslo* [1] and *Bergen* [5] are excellent gateways into this country famous for its fabulous fjords, such as the one at *Geiranger* [10]; superb trout fishing (try Lake *Svela* in mid-June); unique railroad trips, such as the *Bergensbanen* from Oslo to Bergen, the Midnight Sun at *Kirkenes* [17] from late May to late July, and the twelve-hundred-mile coastal trip along an incomparable shoreline (contact Bergen Line, 505 Fifth Avenue, New York, N.Y. 10017); skiing in delightful resorts, such as *Voss* [8] or *Geilo* [7], well-preserved stave churches with an outstanding one at *Heddal*; the Jostedalsbreen Glacier near *Olden* [9]; the unique Alpine *Lofoten Islands* [14] with enormous bird sanctuaries; apple-blossom time in late May at *Ulvik* [6]; eighteen-hundred-foot Pulpit Rock east of *Stavanger* [4]; the waterfalls at *Fossli*; the world's most powerful maelstrom at Bodø [13], and the sights of *Oslo,* including the Munch Museum, Vigeland's work in Frogner Park, Akershus Slott, and the Viking Ship Museum. Try too to take in Gamle Bergen in *Bergen* and both the Nidaros Cathedral and Ringve Music Museum in *Trondheim* [12].

WHAT'S THE WEATHER REALLY LIKE?

Most sight-seeing takes place from mid-May until mid-September during the long, bright days of summer. The weather is usually very good at this time, although you can expect occasional rains. It starts to get cool by October. First snows are expected in November and last through March. April is still cool, and most tourist sights are closed until May.

SOME SUGGESTIONS FOR A MORE ENJOYABLE TRIP

Hotels fill up quickly during the peak summer months, and you must make reservations far in advance. This is just as true in the fjord hotels as in those of Oslo. If you arrive in Oslo without a room, you can find one through a booking service in the central railway station. There's a small charge, but it's worth it. You may have to be satisfied with a small, clean room in a student hostel or dormitory. Off-season travellers should always check ahead to make sure that hotels are open in out-of-the-way locations. Many of them close from mid-September to mid-May. In many offbeat areas you can find simple and very inexpensive rooms in fishing shanties, mountain chalets, summer cottages, and so on. For a list of these, contact the Norwegian National Tourist Office in New York (p. 00). Campers are allowed to camp anywhere for one night as long as they ask for permission from the landowner first. Fires are not permitted. When you're travelling long distances by train or car, I'd suggest that you pack a picnic lunch. As for meals, you'll generally stop at one of the hotels listed unless you're making your own. Food generally is simple yet very good in home-cooking fashion. Alcohol is extremely expensive, and you'll want to bring in a bottle with you. Please note that penalties for drinking and driving are stiff in Norway. You can end up in the clink for a month if convicted of drunken driving (one drink can qualify you for this in Scandinavia). Car travel combined with air travel (for those long northern treks) is the best way to see this country. Get the best map you can find! You'll need it if you plan extensive travel. Skiers should avoid Norway at Easter when all rooms have been booked months ahead of time. Travellers heading into the Land of the Midnight Sun might want to take a mask with them to help in getting to sleep. If you plan to take the coastal voyage north from Bergen, note that it fills up months ahead of time in the summer but not quite so fast in spring or fall (it's available for adventurers as well in winter).

WHERE TO STAY

Balestrand [5]

Kvikne's Hotel   Balestrand   tel: 1
Very large traditional hotel with tasteful décor and comfortable rooms. Idyllic setting. Expensive. Open mid-May to mid-September. North of Bergen on the Sognefjord.

Beitostolen [7]

Beito Mountain Hotel   Beito   tel: Heggenes 650
Large modern hotel with simple comfortable rooms. Good regional cooking. Pleasant skiing. Pool. Expensive.

Beitostolen Mountain Hotel   Beito   tel: Heggenes 628
Quite small traditional hotel with cabins available. Fully modernized. Riding, skiing, and trout fishing. Warm. Moderate.

Bristol Hotel   2 Markeveien   tel: 23 26 00
Large traditional hotel with some superb suites. Other rooms vary. Good location near the harbor. Good restaurant and lively bar. Very expensive.

Bergen [5]

Neptun Hotel   Walckendorffsgate 8   tel: 23 20 15
Small commercial hotel with comfortable rooms and convenient location. Modest yet pleasant. Moderate.

Hotel Norge   4 Ole Bulls Plass   tel: 23 30 00
Large luxury hotel in central location with superb view. Modern and comfortable rooms. Excellent service. The hub of Bergen's social scene. Good restaurant. Dinner-dancing. Very expensive.

Orion Hotel   3 Bradbenken   tel: 23 16 10
Large hotel with lovely view of the harbor and town. Modern and modest rooms. Quite comfortable. Good in the moderate class.

Rosenkrantz   Rosenkrantzgaton 7   tel: 23 23 00
Small traditional hotel with old-world ambience. Quite comfortable. Good restaurant. Lively. Moderate.

Bergen [5] (Os)

Solstrand Fjord Hotel   Os   tel: 27 70 55
Quite large and lovely hotel in secluded setting near the Hardangerfjord. Comfortable rooms, most with bath. Pool, tennis, riding. Expensive.

Bodo [13]

SAS Royal Hotel   Storgaten 2   tel: 24 100
Very large, modern hotel on the harbor with excellent view.
Comfortable. Good restaurant. Expensive.

Boverdalen [9]

Roisheim Hotel   Boverdalen   tel: 24 31
Small charming inn in lovely town with rural setting. Geared to
sportsmen with fishing and hunting. Moderate. Open from June
to mid-September. Far east and inland from Olden.

Bulken [5]

Lilands Hotel   Bulken   tel: Voss 14 258
Small modest inn with fine view and good salmon fishing. Mod-
erate. Open May to mid-September. On Bergen railroad route.
Northeast of Bergen.

Drammen [1]

Park Hotel   Gamle Kirkeplass 1   tel: 83 82 80
Small, comfortable hotel with quiet rooms and fine restaurant.
Moderate. Short drive southwest of Oslo.

Espedal [1]

Dalseter Hoifjellshotell   Espedal   tel: Vinstra 33 13
Large, pleasant ski hotel with modern rooms. Black tie required
at evening meals in the winter. Skiing and riding. Moderate.
Closed late spring and late fall. Twenty miles west of Vinstra
north of Lillehammer. Far north of Oslo.

Fagernes [7]

Fagernes Hotel   Fagernes   tel: 16 00
Small, comfortable hotel with lovely view. Pool. Expensive.
North of Oslo.

Sanderstolen Hoyfjellshotell   Fagernes   tel: 337
Large, fine hotel with very comfortable rooms. Expensive.

Flam [6]

Fretheim Hotel   Flam   tel: Flam 3
Quite large, modern hotel at Aurlandsfjord. Comfortable rooms, half with bath. Pool. Open May to September. Expensive. Northeast of Ulvik.

Follebu [1]

Skeikampen Hoifjeljshotell   Tretten   tel: Follebu 823
Large ski hotel below Mount Skeikampen in lovely setting. Comfortable and warm. Good restaurant. Basement bar with fine wines. Black-tie dining three times a week in winter. Pool and tennis. Expensive. Ten miles northwest of Tretten north of Lillehammer (far north of Oslo).

Gausdal Hoifjellshotell   Tretten   tel: Follebu 28 500
Large old hotel with relaxing atmosphere and comfortable rooms. Thoroughly modernized. Fine dining. Ballroom. Pool and tennis. Black tie required for dining in winter. Expensive.

Forde [5]

Sunnfjord Hotel   Forde   tel: 21 433/21 622
Large, comfortable hotel set up for fishing. Has its own school for trout and salmon fishing which is best from late June through August. Pool. Expensive. Eighty-three miles north of Bergen.

Fredrikstad [1]

City Hotel   Fredrikstad Nygardsgate 44-46   tel: 17 750
Small modern hotel with comfortable and pleasant rooms. Very good restaurant. Moderate. Southeast of Oslo on the coast.

Geilo [7]

Bardola Mountain Hotel   Geilo   tel: 184
Large resort with very comfortable rooms. Formal dining in the winter. Riding, fishing, and hunting. Expensive.

Holms Hotel   Geilo   tel: 3/2
Large scenic hotel with comfortable rooms. Very pleasant
throughout. Good cooking. Colorful. Moderate to expensive.

Geiranger [10]

Geiranger Hotel   Geiranger   tel: Eidsal 618
Quite large, modern hotel by the famous fjord. Comfortable
rooms, some with bath. Nice view. Moderate. Open May
through September.

Union Tourist Hotel   Geiranger   tel: Geiranger 610
Large, lovely hotel with superb view. Comfortable rooms, half
with bath. Pool. Expensive. Open May through September.

Gol [7]

Hesla Hotel   Gol   tel: 12
Tiny, modest ski hotel with pleasant rooms. Trout fishing as
well. Moderate. Northeast of Geilo.

Pers Hotel   Gol   tel: 71
Large attractive hotel with chalets. Quite comfortable. Pool.
Moderate to expensive.

Granvin [5]

Maelands Hotel   Granvin   tel: 25 106
Small, modest hotel in rural setting with lovely view. Geared to
fishermen. Inexpensive to moderate. Northeast of Bergen.

Harpefoss [1]

Gola Hoifjellshotell   Vinstra   tel: Golå 1432
Log-cabin-style but luxurious ski resort oriented to families.
Lovely view in idyllic setting. Good food with special luncheon
buffet. Orchestra. Tennis, pool, and trout fishing. Formal dress
for dining in the winter. Closed late spring and fall. Expensive.
Far north of Oslo past Lillehammer.

Wadahl Mountain Hotel   Harpefoss   tel: Vinstra 1446
Large, pleasant ski hotel with modest yet comfortable rooms.
Superb location. Fine dining with black tie required twice a week

in winter. Ballroom. Pool, tennis, and trout-fishing. Closed late spring and late fall. Expensive. Ten miles southwest of Vinstra north of Lillehammer.

Hermansverk [5]

Sognefjord Tourist Hotel   Harmansverk   tel: Leikanger 54 31
Large, modern hotel with view to fjord. Comfortable. Pool. Moderate. Northeast of Bergen; on northern edge of Sognefjord near Leikanger.

Hjelledalen [9]

Hjelle Hotel   Hjelledalen   tel: Stryn 11 50
Small, comfortable hotel. Most rooms with bath. Moderate. Open late May to late September. Northeast of Olden.

Hovden [4]

Hovden Mountain Hotel   Hovden   tel: 59 100
Quite large, attractive hotel in scenic setting. Comfortable rooms with bath. Pool and sports. Expensive. Northeast of Stavanger.

Kinsarvik [6]

Kinsarvik Fjord Hotel   Kinsarvik   tel: Lofthus 21 82
Large, attractive hotel with lovely view to fjord. Comfortable rooms with bath. Expensive. East of Bergen to south of Ulvik.

Kirkenes [17]

Kirkenes Turisthotell   Kirkenes   tel: 91 491
Small modern hotel with reasonably comfortable rooms. Book well in advance. Moderate.

Kongsberg [1]

Grand Hotel   Augustsgr. 2   tel: 32 029
Small, comfortable hotel with compact rooms. Very expensive. Southwest of Oslo via Drammen.

Leikanger [5]

Leikanger Fjord Hotel   Leikanger   tel: 52 00
Small hotel with comfortable rooms and friendly feeling. Great
location and view. Moderate. Northeast of Bergen; on northern
edge of Sognefjord.

Lillehammer [1]

Lillehammer Turisthotell   Lillehammer   tel: 50 065
Small, modern hotel in lovely park setting. Comfortable. Skiing,
riding, and pool. Moderate to expensive. North of Oslo.

Nevra Mountain Hotel   Lillehammer   tel: 64 001
Large resort in lovely setting. Comfortable rooms—most with
bath. Fishing, skiing, riding, tennis, and pool. Moderate. Open
December through April and in the summer.

Victoria Hotel   82 Storgatan   tel: 50 049
Modernized hotel in central location with neat if compact rooms.
Lively Christmas season. Moderate.

Rustad Fjellstue   2612 Sjusjøen   tel: 63 408
Small rustic lodge one half hour drive from Lillehammer. Pleas-
ant if modest rooms. Good country cooking. Young. Moderate.
Closed October to December.

Loen [5]

Hotel Alexandra   Loen   tel: 15 60
Large modern hotel in lovely setting. Very smart and comfortable. Expensive. Open Easter through October. Far north of Bergen; northeast of Förde.

Lofthus [6]

Hotel Ullensvang   Lufthus   tel: 11 06
Large comfortable hotel with fine regional dishes. Good smörgasbord at noon. Expensive. Open from mid-April to mid-October. Best in late May. Southwest of Ulvik.

Nordfjordeid [11]

Nordfjord Hotel   Nordfjordeid   tel: Nordfjord 445
Comfortable hotel with nice view. Geared to the sportsman. Expensive. South of Alesund.

Norheimsund [6]

Norheimsund Fjord Hotel   Norheimsund   tel: Norheimsund 15 25
Tiny, modern hotel by the fjord. Comfortable rooms, with bath. Moderate. Open late April through September. West of Ulvik on northern side of Hardangerfjord.

Sandven Hotel   Norheimsund   tel: 15 11
Tiny mountain inn with pleasant and simple rooms. Geared to skiing and fishing. Open mid-January to mid-December. Moderate.

Oeystese [5]

Oeystese Fjord Hotel   Oeystese   tel: Norheimsund 600
Modest hotel with comfortable rooms and great view. Moderate.

Olden [9]

Olden Fjord Hotel   Olden   tel: Stryn 17 77
Small, modern hotel with comfortable, functional rooms. Nice location. Expensive.

Yris Hotel   Olden   tel: 343-1740
Large resort with lovely view. Quite comfortable. Excellent regional cooking. Special excursions to nearby glacier. Moderate to expensive. Open May to September.

Orsta [11]

Viking Fjordhotel   Orsta   tel: 480
Small modern hotel with fine view. Quite comfortable. Fishing. Expensive. On coast, to south of Alesund.

Oslo [1]

Hotel Ambassadeur   Camilla Collettsvei 15   tel: 44 18 35
Tiny exclusive residential hotel. Richly furnished, spacious, and comfortable. Intimate and quite friendly. Noncentral location. Expensive.

Gabelshus Hotel   Gabelsgate 16   tel: 56 25 90
Small charming residential hotel with pleasant casual atmosphere. Some antiques. Expensive.

Holmenkollen Hotel   Kongeveien 26   tel: 14 60 90
Small noncentral hotel with superb view. Varied rooms. Quite expensive.

K.N.A. Hotel   Parkveien 68   tel: 56 26 90
Quite large, nodern hotel with comfortable rooms, all with bath or shower. Close to Royal Palace. Nice. Very expensive.

Hotel Nobel   Karl Johansgate 33   tel: 33 71 90
Small old world hotel with charming, if modest, accommodations. A bit homey. Expensive.

Norum   Bygdoy Allé 53   tel: 44 79 90
Small, comfortable old-fashioned hotel in noncentral location. Casual. Expensive.

Smestad Hotel   Sorkedalsveien 93   tel: 14 64 90
Small, noncentral residential hotel. Comfortable and pleasant. Moderate.

Rosendal [5]

Rosendal Fjord Hotel   Rosendal   tel: Kvinnherad 81 511
Tiny, modern hotel in great location by the fjord. Very comfortable. Expensive. Southern edge of Hardangerfjord southeast of Bergen.

Sandefjord [1]

Park Hotel   Sandefjord   tel: 65 550
Very large luxury hotel—one of the best in Norway. Tasteful throughout. Very modern and comfortable rooms. Pleasant bar and restaurant. Park and pool. Expensive. A delightful resort

about two hours drive from Oslo to the southwest.

Saudasjoeen [4]

Sauda Fjord Hotel   Saudasjoeen   tel: 52 177
Tiny mansion converted into comfortable hotel, some rooms
with bath and shower. Calm. Moderate. North of Stavanger;
near Sauda.

Skanevik [4]

Skanevik Fjord Hotel   Skanevik   tel: Skanevik 155
Small, modern hotel near the water. All rooms with bath or
shower. Moderate to expensive. Open April to September. On
the coast halfway between Stavanger and Bergen.

Sogndal [5]

Sogndal Hotel   Sogndal   tel: Sogndal 302
Large, lovely resort hotel on Norway's large fjord. Superb setting and view. Quite comfortable. Fine restaurant. Pool and
fishing. Expensive. Northeast of Bergen.

Solfonn [6]

Solfonn Hotel   Solfonn   tel: 45 122
Very fine mountain hotel in idyllic location. Comfortable rooms
and nice atmosphere throughout. Good restaurant serving local
specialties. Moderate. South of Ulvik.

Stavanger [4]

Alstor Hotel   P.O. Box 259   tel: 27 020
Small, attractive hotel on outskirts of town. Comfortable, most
rooms with bath. Expensive.

Royal Atlantic   1 Jernbanevejen   tel: 27 520
Large, very fine hotel in excellent location. Modern and very
comfortable rooms. Excellent restaurant. Very expensive and
worth it.

Strandå [13]

Storfjord Hotel   Stranda   tel: Stranda 2
Quite large, modern hotel near the water. Peaceful. Most rooms with bath. Moderate. North of Bodo near the coast; southeast of Alesund.

Surnadal [12]

Surnadal Hotell   Surnadal   tel: Surnadal 51/61 195
Hotel geared to fishing for salmon on the Surna river. Small and modest. Best fishing from June 20 to August 10. Moderate to expensive. Southwest of Trondheim (eighty miles).

Tonsberg [2]

Klubben Hotel   Storgt 48   tel: 15 111
Large modern hotel with comfortable rooms. Attractive throughout with lovely view. Very expensive. Off the beaten track. Northeast of Larvik.

Tromso [16]

SAS Royal Hotel   10 Fr. Langesgate   tel: 83.606
Very large, modernized hotel. Comfortable. Good restaurant. Expensive.

Trondheim [12]

Ambassadeur Hotel   Elvegt. 18   tel: 27 134
Tiny, modern hotel with tasteful, intimate rooms. Ask for ones with view and fireplace. Very expensive.

Hotel Britannia   Dronningensgaten 5   tel: 30 040
Large traditional hotel with old-fashioned flavor. Quite pleasant but not fancy. Expensive.

Larssens Hotell   Thomas Angellsgaten 10B   tel: 28 857
Small charming hotel geared to budget travelers. Moderate.

Hotel Prinsen   Kongensgaten 30   tel: 30 650
Small modern hotel with comfortable rooms. Quite warm. Good in the commercial class. Expensive.

Ulvik [6]

Brakanes Hotel   Ulvik   tel: 5
Large century-old fjord hotel at its very best in apple blossom time in mid-May. Resting on water. Attractive throughout. Modern and very comfortable rooms. Fine dining. Tennis and fishing. Moderate. Open May to September. Reserve months in advance.

Vinstra [10]

Fefor Høifjellshotell   Vinstra   tel: Vinstra 35
Large old mountain ski resort with charming new wing. Great view. Black tie required on party nights in winter. Orchestra. Tennis and trout fishing. Pool. Closed late spring and late fall. Moderate. Just west of Vinstra to north of Lillehammer. North of Oslo en route to Geiranger.

Voss [8]

Park Hotel Liland   Voss   tel: 11 322
Small modern resort with compact yet comfortable rooms. Skiing and fishing. Moderate to expensive.

WHERE TO EAT

Bergen [5]

Bellevue   Bellevuebakken 9   tel: 31 03 33/21 18 75
Hillside setting overlooking the city. Fine Norwegian and international dishes. Well known. Expensive.

Bristol Hotel   2 Markeveien   tel: 23 26 00
Elegant restaurant with superb smorgasbord at lunch. Both French and Norwegian specialties. Dancing. Expensive.

Bryggen Tracteursted   Bryggen 6   tel: 21 38 57/21 89 20
Buy your own fish at the fish market on the harbor, bring them here, and have them cooked to order. A unique culinary experience. Offbeat. Moderate.

Hotel Norge   4 Ole Bulls Plass   tel: 23 30 00
Excellent hotel grill with international cuisine. Delicious fish and reindeer. Fine wines. Expensive.

Oslo [1]

Blom   Karl Johansgate 41   tel: 33 09 56
Famous artists' restaurant with walls and ceiling covered with colorful plaques and portraits. Good international cuisine. A bit touristy, but nice. Expensive.

Carlton Hotel   Parkveien 78   tel: 56 30 90
Good hotel restaurant specializing in fresh fish dishes, including oysters. Expensive.

Continental Hotel   Stortingsgatan 24-26   tel: 41 70 60
Elegant hotel restaurant with superb French cuisine. Very popular. Expensive.

Cossack Restaurant   Kongensgate 6   tel: 42 33 57
Russian décor and cuisine with fine fresh caviar. Expensive.

Dronningen Restaurant   Royal Yacht Club (Bygdoy)   tel: 55 91 95
Exclusive and fine restaurant serving international cuisine. Expensive. May through September.

Engebret's Cafe   Bankplassen 8   tel: 42 12 62
Ancient restaurant with great atmosphere. Good Norwegian cooking. Moderate to expensive.

Frognersaeteren   Holmenkollen   tel: 14 37 36
Superb view and fine international cuisine with some Norwegian dishes. Lots of atmosphere. Expensive.

Frascati   20 Stortinsgaten   tel: 41 68 76
Elegant yet relaxed restaurant serving fine international cuisine. Expensive.

Grand Hotel   Karl Johansgate 31   tel: 33 48 70
Excellent Grill Room with fine reputation for international cuisine. Quite expensive.

Holmenkollen Restaurant   Holmenkollen   tel: 14 62 26
Lovely view and fine Continental cuisine with some delicious Norwegian dishes. Expensive.

La Belle Sole   *Observatoriegata 2B*   *tel: 44 19 38*
Fine restaurant with excellent fish dishes. Pleasant atmosphere.
Expensive.

Najaden   *Bydoynesvejen 37*   *tel: 55 44 90*
Well-known restaurant in the Maritime Museum. Fine international menu. Excellent at lunch. Expensive.

Restaurant   *14 Damstredet*   *tel: 20 79 89*
A hunting lodge converted into unique restaurant specializing in
Norwegian dishes. You must be invited by Norwegian host since
service is only for ten or more. Expensive.

Tre Kokker   *30 Drammensveien*   *tel: 55 12 69*
Modern restaurant with fine Norwegian and international dishes. Moderate to expensive.

PORTUGAL

PORTUGAL

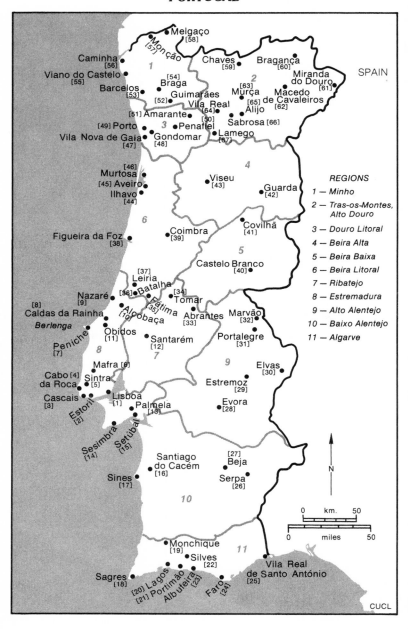

SPAIN

REGIONS

1 — Minho

2 — Tras-os-Montes, Alto Douro

3 — Douro Litoral

4 — Beira Alta

5 — Beira Baixa

6 — Beira Litoral

7 — Ribatejo

8 — Estremadura

9 — Alto Alentejo

10 — Baixo Alentejo

11 — Algarve

Melgaço [58]

Monção [57]

Caminha [56]

Viano do Castelo [55]

Chaves [59]

Bragança [60]

Barcelos [53]

Braga [54]

Miranda do Douro [61]

Guimarães [52]

Murça [63]

Macedo de Cavaleiros [62]

Vila Real [64]

Alijo [65]

Amarante [51]

Porto [49]

Penafiel [50]

Sabrosa [66]

Vila Nova de Gaia [47]

Gondomar [48]

Lamego [67]

Murtosa [46]

Aveiro [45]

Viseu [43]

Guarda [42]

Ilhavo [44]

Covilhã [41]

Figueira da Foz [38]

Coimbra [39]

Castelo Branco [40]

Leiria [37]

Batalha [36]

Tomar [34]

Nazaré [9]

Fátima [35]

Marvão [32]

Caldas da Rainha

Alcobaça [10]

Abrantes [33]

Berlenga

Obidos [11]

Santarém [12]

Portalegre [31]

Peniche [7]

Mafra [6]

Elvas [30]

Cabo da Roca [4]

Sintra [5]

Estremoz [29]

Cascais [3]

Lisboa [1]

Palmela [13]

Evora [28]

Estoril [2]

Sesimbra [14]

Setúbal [15]

Santiago do Cacém [16]

Beja [27]

Sines [17]

Serpa [26]

N

Monchique [19]

Silves [22]

Vila Real de Santo António [25]

Sagres [18]

Lagos [20]

Portimão [21]

Albufeira [23]

Faro [24]

0   km.   50

0   miles   50

CUCL

WHAT TO SEE

Portugal, an ancient land, blends an eventful past with an exciting present. Its soul, variety, and color make it an unforgettable travel experience. Its location as a balcony overlooking Morocco appeals to travellers looking for sun-drenched vacations by the sea at incredibly *low* prices.

Lisbon [1] (Lisboa) deserves two or three days on any traveller's itinerary. Outstanding are the Coach Museum, the Madre de Deus church (hard to find so take an inexpensive taxi), the Torre de Belém, and the Mosteiro dos Jéronimos. Daily life is best typified in the Alfama and the morning market near the river (go early to catch the action). Excursions from the capital into the surrounding region are fabulous. The Quinta da Bacalhoa in *Azeitão* is a lovely restored villa, a must for serious art lovers. The nearly perfect medieval city of *Obidos* [11]; the pink palace of *Queluz*; the churches of *Alcobaça* [10], *Batalha* [36], and *Mafra* [6]; the castles of *Sesimbra* [14], *Setubal* [15], and *Palmela* [13]; and the varied sights of *Sintra* [5], Byron's glorious Eden, or those of *Nazaré* [9] with its melon-rind boats—all make the discovery of this region so memorable.

On your way south to the Algarve, stop off at *Sines* [17] to take in the morning fish market. The "in" spot along the southern coast is *Albufeira* [23] with trendy boutiques and a nice beach. But more appealing to many is *Praia da Rocha* [21] with clifftop hotels, warmer weather, and protected sandy coves for isolated bathing. Other gems are *Carvoeiro* [23] and *Praia da Luz* [20]. The latter lies just west of *Lagos* [20] where you'll want to see the Chapel of St. Anthony. The drive to *Sagres* [18] where Henry the Navigator charted the seas will interest historians. The finest view along the Algarve is from *Foia* on a winding mountain road above *Monchique* [19]. In *Portimão* [21] you can go out with the sardine fleet for a fourteen-hour trip that may be one of the most memorable experiences of your vacation. Be sure to pick up a copy of the free travel pamphlet *The Algarve: The Traveler's Paradise* by Frank Cook. It's distributed in most hotels and restaurants.

Farther north and inland, three well-preserved cities stand out: *Elvas* [30], *Estremoz* [29], and *Evora* [28]. All offer comfortable rooms in local *pousadas*, the Portuguese equivalent of Spain's *paradores*—state-owned inns. *Marvão* [32] is a fascinating side trip.

It's an ancient town perched high on a mountaintop like an eagle's nest. Continuing north, you'll find the Almourol Castle eleven miles west of *Abrantes* [33]. It's accessible by boat throughout the summer. The bullfights in June at *Santarém* [12] shine (no slaughter, just fancy footwork by horses trained in the art of *dressage*). Outstanding Manueline architecture draws most travellers to *Tomar* [34]. If you want to take in the *Grutas* (Grottoes) *de Santo Antonio*, be sure to do so on a weekday. Otherwise, the place is a madhouse.

The library in *Coimbra* [39] is world-famous as is the unending beach at *Figueira da Foz* [38]. The mosaics at *Conimbriga* hardly match those of Pompeii, but they're still worth the short drive from Coimbra. If you're interested in Vista Alegre porcelain, don't miss the factory and showroom in *Ilhavo* [44]. The procession at *Fátima* [35] on the eve of May 13 and October 13 may well be the most impressive in Europe (expect to sleep in your car). During the summer months you may still catch a glimpse of nets being pulled into shore by oxen at *Mira*. Inland, the typical town of *Monsanto* will appeal to dedicated explorers braving this relatively undiscovered region. Don't miss the Museu do Grão Vasco and the twelfth-century cathedral in *Viseu* [43]. You may also take in *Caramulo*, an out-of-the-way spa. Recommended is a short stay in *Porto* [49] with an excursion across the river to *Vila Nova de Gaia* [47] to visit the entrepôts for Port wine (free sampling of thirty-year-old Tawnies).

The scented pines and fresh sea breeze make the far north very popular with foreign tourists throughout the summer. You may want to stay in the *pousada* at *Valença do Minho* [57] and visit Bom Jesus do Monte, a pilgrimage site outside of *Braga* [54]. To the northeast is an area that hums with activity during the grape harvest in late September and early October. Truly a spectacle on the steep, terraced slopes. Of interest at any time of year but at its best in spring is the Mateus estate just outside of *Vila Real* [64].

The lush, yet rugged, Portuguese island of *Madeira* lies like a shattered lobster claw several hundred miles off the coast of Morocco. Its isolation and mild weather make it particularly appealing, especially to the British who pack the hotels during the Christmas and New Year's season. You can take in Madeira as a stopover en route to Lisbon. The approach to the runway is thrilling. Equally so are the drives that curve around mountainsides with the sea hundreds of feet below. Note: you should take out a full insurance policy on any rented car or work out a daily rate with one of the many taxis for an excursion around the island. Note too that swimming from the rocky shore is ill-advised. Since most hotels have pools, it's also unnecessary.

The group of nine islands known as the *Açores* lies eight hundred miles to the west of Portugal. The islands are not lush and tropical; instead, they offer a somewhat bleak, pastoral setting in which the tinkling of cowbells and the fresh, nearly perfumed air are the major attractions. The most popular island is *São Miguel* with a striking coastline and two lovely lakes in the interior. *Terceira* is a favorite with travellers seeking isolation and a modicum of personal comfort. The other seven islands offer unusual attractions but are rarely visited: *Corvo* (archaeological remains), *Faial* (view from extinct volcano), *Flores* (fishing and flowers), *Graciosa* (spa and sulfur caves), *Pico* (whaling and lovely view from central peak), *São Jorge* (views), *Santa Maria* (mills).

WHAT'S THE WEATHER REALLY LIKE?

The most popular months in a country noted for its five hundred miles of varied coastline are July and August, when it's hard to tell where the sand ends and the sea begins. Actually, the sea is warmer in September and October—a wonderful time, if not the best, to visit the country. Comfortable bathing takes place from mid-April until the end of October. You'll find that in the winter months the weather is mild but still cool even in the south. November is one of the poorest months, often with cool spells and heavy winds. January is also cool, but it is attractive to many foreign visitors when the millions of almond trees burst into bloom along the Algarve. February, the second worst month, is occasionally quite mild, but many foreign residents leave Portugal at this time because they know the odds are against them. March is another iffy month, but you'll often find that this month marks the beginning of Portugal's glorious spring, when wildflowers and fruit trees burst into bloom. Note that even in the worst month you'll have *some* shirt-sleeve weather. The time to visit the Açores is in the summer when the hydrangeas and wildflowers cover the hills with pink, blue, and yellow blossoms, but *the off-season is unbelievably dreary*. Not the case with Madeira. It has mild winter weather and is an excellent choice in the off-season.

SOME SUGGESTIONS FOR A MORE ENJOYABLE TRIP

The most charming hotels in Lisbon fill up fast at any time of year. Be sure to reserve a room well in advance. If you have trouble getting a room in the capital, think of staying in Cascais, Estoril, or Sintra—just twenty-to-thirty minute drives away. Outside of the capital in all of Portugal's fascinating regions you'll find delightful inns geared to travellers exploring the country by car. These inns, known as *pousadas*, have a country atmosphere and are beautifully furnished in the local style. Pousadas are such an exceptional travel value that you're limited to a five-day stay in each one. All of Portugal's pousadas are described in this chapter. Prices for car rentals vary enormously, and you can often find substantial savings by going with a local firm. This would be risky in the peak months of July and August but worth the gamble in other months. In every hotel you'll find a special pamphlet on Portugal with more than enough information on the capital to last you a month. And it's *free*! One of the most sought-after items in Portugal is cigarette lighters, so if you have a friend or hope to make one during your stay, why not import extra lighters?

Flying to, from, or within the Azores can be as complicated as a jigsaw puzzle, so be sure to work out your itinerary with a travel agent or airlines before arriving in the islands. Trying to make a reservation here is as easy as filling out your income-tax forms. Visas are no longer required.

Spear fishing is fantastic throughout the year in the islands, but you have to bring your own gear. The isolation of the islands is their major attraction. The hotels reflect the off-the-beaten-track location, which means they're comfortable without the slightest hint of luxury. There are no good restaurants, and at certain times of the year it can be hard to find vegetables or an egg. The Azores are for uncommon travellers, not tourists.

WHERE TO STAY

Albufeira [23]

Hotel Sol e Mar   Rua Jose Bernadino de Sousa   tel: 52 121
Don't judge this large hotel in the center of town from the outside. Beautiful location with rooms and balconies overlooking the sea. Sailing and fishing nearby. Has its own nightclub. Moderate to expensive.

Quinta da Saudade   Rua da Pera   tel: 56 182
Five miles west of Albufeira. A half mile from the nearest beach. Riding ranch with twenty villas. Nice view, maid, pools. Family-oriented. Expensive riding.

Alfeizerão [8]

Pousada de São Martinho   Alfeizerão   tel: 98 106
Between Caldas da Rainha and Alcobaça. Small, simple, and rustic inn. About two and a half miles from São Martinho do Porto. Directly on the main road with a magnificent view. A better place to stop for lunch than to stay for the night, since it can be noisy with traffic. Note that this inn may still be closed for repairs.

Alijo [65]

Pousada Barão de Forrester   Alijo   tel: 62 215
About thirty miles from Vila Real. One of Portugal's oldest state-owned inns with a flavor closely resembling that of a youth hostel. Named after the man who set up the legal limits to the Douro region producing Port wine. The best time to visit this area is at the end of September and beginning of October to see the grape harvest. Very friendly with log fire burning in the cold nights, but don't expect too much comfort. Now being modernized. Inexpensive.

Aljubarrota [10]

Estalagem do Cruzeiro   Estrada Nacional No. 1   tel: 42 112
Near Alcobaça off the main highway. Small, rustic country inn

with a good restaurant specializing in local dishes. Very convenient for a trip to Batalha with its famous monastery. Moderate.

Amarante [51]

Pousada de São Gonçalo   Amarante   tel: 46 113
In the Serra do Marão at an altitude of three thousand feet. A roadside inn on one of the many curves between Amarante and Vila Real (about fifteen miles from both cities). A good stop-off point in an area where beds are hard to find. A bit noisy at night, but comfortable, pleasant, and convenient. Fair food. Inexpensive.

Armacão de Pera [24]

Hotel do Garbe   Armacão de Pera   tel: 55 187
One of the few really good hotels between Faro and Praia da Rocha. Medium-sized, with good view from the balconies. Beach, boats, and water-skiing nearby. Expensive, but worth it.

Vilalara   Praia das Gaivotas   tel: 55 333/55 334/55 335
Luxurious development with private club-condominium set-up. Fully furnished one- to three-bedroom apartments with verandas overlooking the sea. Thirty-two units available now, 145 planned. Excellent location with restaurant, boíte, maid service, utilities, pool, and tennis. Expensive.

Azeitão [1]

Estalagem Quinta das Torres   Quinta das Torres   tel: 22 80 01
An isolated sixteenth-century inn recently revamped to bring it into the twentieth century. The old estate set in an olive grove has priceless furniture, a pool, and a good restaurant. Moderate to expensive. Always a good value. Within commuting distance to Lisbon.

Barcelos [53]

Albergaria Condes de Barcelos   Rua Arq. Antonio Borges Vinagre   tel: 82 061
A luxury hotel where you'd least expect to find one. Modern, spacious rooms with copies of antique furniture in the local

style. The restaurant emphasizes local specialties. Moderate.

Batalha [36]

Estalagem do Mestre Afonso Domingues   Batalha   *tel: 96 260*
A very fine inn with an excellent restaurant. Comfortable. Moderate.

Berlenga [7]

Abrigo para Pescadores   Berlenga Island   *tel: 1*
In the fortress of São João Baptista on the island eight miles from the rocky coastline of Peniche. It takes about an hour to reach by boat. The pousada, previously a sixteenth-century monastery, was repeatedly sacked by coastal pirates. As the name of the inn implies, the area is known for its fishing. Very calm, with a good restaurant and beach nearby. Closed in the winter. Inexpensive.

Bragança [60]

Pousada de São Bartolomeu   Bragança   *tel: 379*
On the road winding up the hill which overlooks the city. Clean, modern, without a great deal of atmosphere, but very convenient, since it's near the Spanish border. The rooms are comfortable. It's the only decent place to eat in the area. Inexpensive.

Buçaco [39]

Palace Hotel do Buçaco   Mata do Buçaco   *tel: 93 101*
A *manueline*-style luxury hotel in a four-hundred-year-old cyprus forest. Good view and cellar. So-so restaurant. Room number 1 the best. Expensive. Recommended as a French Relais de Campagne member. Northwest of Coimbra.

Burgau [20]

Casa Grande   Burgau   *tel: Call the Burgau operator*
Country house converted into very pleasant inn with popular Portuguese restaurant. Sample of each item on the menu served as an appetizer to help you decide on what to order. Pleasant atmosphere. Limited number of rooms. West of Lagos.

Caniçada [54]

Pousada de São Bento   Caniçada   tel: 57 190
Wisteria climbs the walls of a modern, Swiss-chalet pousada with an incredible view over the valley and dam below. Tennis, pool, good service, excellent food, and an atmosphere which makes this off-the-beaten-track inn the best possible value for your money. About twenty miles from Braga in a desolate, mountain region. Inexpensive.

Caramulo [43]

Estalagem de São Jeronimo   Caramulo   tel: 86 291
A modern inn on the main road leading to the mountain town. A beautiful view of the plains below. Pool, gardens, comfortable rooms. Expensive. Southwest of Viseu.

Carrapateira [18]

Casa Fajara   Carrapateira (Aljezur)   tel: None
A four-bedroom guest house with pool and Cordon Bleu cooking. Just north of the town take right at the fishing sign (a left goes to the beach) passing palm trees on the way to the boarding house. Expensive. North of Sagres; near the coast road.

Carvoeiro [23]

Guest House Von Baselli   Carvoeiro   tel: 57 159
Only a few rooms in this guest house that overlooks the bay and town below. Beautiful location. A family feeling. Breakfast only. Moderately expensive.

Cascais [3]

Estalagem Albatroz   Rua Frederico Arouca 100-102   tel: 28 28 21
This villa once belonging to a marquis has been converted into a small, expensive inn with a view of the bay and a very private feeling. Right on the sea. Try for room number 1. Nice, even outstanding.

Estalagem Solar Dom Carlos   *Rua Latino Coelho 8*   *tel: 28 09 61*
An eighteenth-century manor house once owned by the Magellan family with walled-in gardens and Portuguese cooking. Not on the beach. Run by an English couple. Quiet, small, moderate to expensive. Room number 7 is the best.

Elvas [30]

Pousada de Santa Luzia   *Elvas*   *tel: 194*
Only a few blocks from the large arches outside this interesting walled-in city. Touristy and sterile, lacking some of the charm of other pousadas, but convenient and good value. For people interested in a little more luxury, there's the pousada at Estremoz, which is just a short drive from Elvas.

Estoril [2]

Hotel das Arcadas   *Arcadas Parque*   *tel: 26 27 91*
Medium-size, moderately priced hotel with pool and a good location. Rooms with balconies. Can't go wrong here.

Estalagem Casa Lennox   *Rua Eng. Avaro Pedro de Sousa 5*
tel: 26 04 24
Small inn with pool, gardens, and wide range of prices. Quiet and very nice. Ideal for golfers. The kind of place where you pour your own drinks.

Estalagem Belvedere   *Rua Dr. Antonio Martins 8*   *tel: 26 27 16*
A small, moderately priced inn. Intimate bar with fireplace. Harbor in distance. Nicely furnished.

Estremoz [29]

Pousada da Rainha Santa Isabel   *Estremoz*   *tel: 648*
This converted castle is one of the most beautiful pousadas in Portugal appealing to travelers who like a touch of sophistication on their trip. The inn has a gorgeous view, luxury atmosphere, a plush dining room, which specializes in regional dishes, and warm friendly service once you get past the front desk. The approach on a winding, cobblestone street is marked from the center of town. Expensive.

Evora [28]

Pousada dos Loios   Evora   tel: 24 051
Next to the Temple of Diana in the middle of the city. A converted fifteenth-century convent with a dining room skirting a central garden. Very nice atmosphere with its antiques and friendly service. A good place to eat even if you can't get a room. Inexpensive.

Faro [24]

Residencia Casa Lumena   Faro   tel: 22 028
A charming private mansion converted into small, comfortable hotel. Only twelve rooms with bath. Good location near the port. Moderate.

Funchal (Madeira Island)

Quinta de Penha de Franca   Rua da Penha de Franca   tel: 29 087
In the boardinghouse class, with antiques and breakfast by the pool. Villa-like, with its own small garden. Compact and comfortable rooms—all pleasant and airy. No restaurant. For people with simple but excellent taste. Within walking distance of Funchal. Moderate.

Pensão Vila Belo Mar   191 Estrada Monumental   tel: 20 732
Tiny hotel with a clublike atmosphere. Comfortable and warm. Attractive dining. Moderate. Taxi drive from town.

Ilhavo [44]

Estalagem Arimar   Av. Marechal Carmona 113   tel: 22 879
A very modern, comfortable hotel which has excellent food. Only a short drive from the Vista Alegre porcelain factory.

Lagos [20]

*Albergaria Casa de São Gonçalo   Rua Candido dos Reis 73
tel: 62 171*
Topflight reputation for a small inn with moderately expensive rates. Eighteenth-century atmosphere. Only ten rooms with bath.

Lisbon [1]

Albergaria Residencia Inglesa (York House)   *Rua das Janelas Verdes 32-1*
tel: 66 24 35
Tops for a boarding house even with its unusual location. Artists seem to hover around this sixteenth-century convent with a view of the Tagus River below. Its unusual furnishings give it a special flavor. Including the annex there are a limited number of rooms available. The popular inn fills up well in advance. Moderate prices. Exceptional value.

Hotel Principe Real   *Rua da Alegria 53*   *tel: 30 116*
Very nice, small hotel with moderate prices and an intimate feeling. The antiques in the main rooms are especially attractive as is the small bar. The rooms are simple and elegant. You can't go wrong here. Be sure to take all your baggage and belongings out of your car. Moderate to expensive.

Macedo de Cavaleiros [62]

Estalagem do Caçador   *Largo Pinto de Azevedo*   *tel: 56*
Only three miles off the main road with a country hunting-lodge atmosphere. Moderately comfortable rooms in an area where beds can be hard tt find. An interesting restaurant. Inexpensive.

Marvão [32]

Pousada de Santa Maria   *Marvão*   *tel: 93 201*
In the mist-filled mountains of Marvão with an incredible view from the walled city. The same eerie, windy feeling as in Les Baux, outside Arles in southern France, which attracts artists or people after the silence and calm of an eagle's nest. Only a few rooms. Small, attractive, and inexpensive. Out of the way.

Miranda do Douro [61]

Pousada de Santa Catarina   *Miranda do Douro*   *tel: 55*
Near the fortified city overlooking the cliffs and water backed up by the local dam hundreds of feet below. Donkeys wander through the hills under hawks circling overhead. The inn is modern, but the smoky smell from the fireplace is a little thick and permeates the rooms. Fair food. Way out of the way in a

desolate, windy, and cold region known for its murders (not of tourists). Inexpensive.

Monchique [19]

Estalagem Abrigo da Montanha   *Estrada da Foia*   *tel: 92 131*
A very small, beautiful inn with a good restaurant and a view from the hills to the plains below. Moderately priced and often full. Quiet and isolated with a spa nearby.

Monte dos Flores [28]

Estalagem Monte dos Flores   *Monte dos Flores*   *tel: 25 490*
A deluxe country inn located inside a charming farm. Very comfortable. Nice restaurant. Moderate. Southeast of Evora.

Mourisca do Vouga [39]

Pousada de Santo Antonio   *Mourisca do Vouga*   *tel: 52 230*
Thirty-three miles north of Coimbra just off the road leading to Porto. The simple pink building is close to the road with a view of the countryside. Far enough from the traffic not to be too noisy. Pleasant. Inexpensive. Very convenient for an overnight stop.

Murtosa [46]

Pousada da Ria   *Murtosa (Bico do Muranzel)*   *tel: 46 132*
On a spit of sand known as the Bico do Muranzel only two and a quarter miles from the Torreira beach. Outside of Aveiro via Estarreja and Murtosa. The area is far more interesting than the modern pousada, with a dining room overlooking a bay where boats harvest seawood as they glide by with luffing sails. The area is worth visiting. Inexpensive.

Obidos [11]

Estalagem do Convento   *Rua Dr. João de Ornelas*   *tel: 95 217*
Second place to the pousada is this twelfth-century convent. Small, with its own night club. Good. Moderate prices. Often full.

Pousada do Castelo   *Obidos*   *tel: 95 105*
One of Portugal's most famous inns. Beautiful view of surrounding farmland with mills in the distance. The city with its
walls intact takes you back to medieval times. The pousada, a
converted twelfth-century castle, is booked months in advance.
Although the city is now a bit touristy, it's not bad considering
what this town offers. Worth getting into for a day or two with
some advance planning.

Portinho da Arrabida [15]

Estalagem de Santa Maria da Arrabida   *Estrada Nacional*
tel: 22 89 27
Very small, inexpensive, and attractive inn with a good location
right on the sea in a reconverted fort. Terrace for outside dining
with nice view. Closed in the winter. Only eight miles from
Setúbal.

Porto [49]

Hotel São João   *Rua do Bomjardim 120*   *tel: 21662*
Tiny hotel in the center of the city offering excellent service and
charging low rates. Modest but quite comfortable.

Albergaria Miradouro   *Rua da Alegria 598*   *tel: 27 861*
Small hotel near the Castor Hotel with fine service. Modest and
comfortable, with lovely view of the city and river below.

Povoa das Quartas [39]

Pousada de Santa Barbara   *Povoa das Quartas*   *tel: 52 252*
On Highway 17 from Coimbra to Celonico da Beira. Only about
six miles from Seia. This new pousada overlooks pine-covered
mountains and is a convenient stop-off point. Very modern with
stone exterior visible from the main road. Quiet, comfortable,
good value. Not luxurious, but comfortable. Inexpensive.

Praia da Rocha [21]

Hotel de Bela Vista   *Avenida Tomás Cabreira*   *tel: 24 055*
One of the original hotels in the area. Right on the cliffs above
the recently enlarged beach. An excellent view from most of the

rooms. Tiled interior and antiques. The rooms are fairly comfortable. A place for people interested more in atmosphere than luxury. Moderate.

Estalagem Alcala   Avenida Tomás Cabreira   tel: 24 062
Good location near the beach. Nice rooms (only twenty) with bath. Not glamorous, but good value. Moderate.

Sagres [18]

Pousada do Infante   Sagres   tel: 64 222
In the Algarve on the southwesternmost tip of Europe. The tiny inn hangs on the cliffs overlooking the sea which is alive with ships passing at all times of day. Only a few rooms. The inn is isolated, comfortable, and very popular considering the windy location. A beach is just a few minutes walk away. Moderate.

São Braz de Alportel [24]

Pousada de São Braz   São Braz de Alportel   tel: 42 305
In the Caldeirão mountain range of the Algarve. A stop off point coming from or going to Faro. The inn with painted Welcome signs on your approach up the hill is a little touristy, but perfectly nice. Great view. Friendly and comfortable. Inexpensive.

Santa Clara A Velha [19]

Pousada de Santa Clara   Santa Clara A. Velha   tel: 53
The modern inn with little atmosphere overlooks the lakes created by the new dam meant to help out this isolated farming region. Barren except for a few pines and eucalyptus, which are being planted by the forestry department. A calm spot with comfortable rooms. Not exciting and out ot-the-way, which is emphasized by the gas pump near the parking lot. North of Monchique.

Santiago do Cacém [16]

Pousada de São Tiago   Santiago do Cacém   tel: 22 459
On the main highway leading to the Algarve from Lisbon. A very convenient place to stop for lunch or for an overnight stop.

Just off the main road in a clump of trees on the hill outside of town. The unusual red building is quiet, simple, nice. Beautiful view of the sea miles away. Pool, gardens, and a terrace for people who like to eat outside under wisteria-covered trellises. Good value. Inexpensive.

Serpa [26]

Pousada de São Gens   Serpa   tel: 52 327
In the hot hills of the Alentejo. About three quarters of a mile outside of town. Well-marked with signs. The best place to eat or stay in this outback farm region good for goats and grain. Simple and nice. Inexpensive.

Serra da Estrela [42]

Pousada de São Lourenço   Serra da Estrela   tel: 47 150
On the road connecting Manteigas to Gouveia in a rocky mountainous area. Completely off the tourist track. One of the only snow-covered areas in Portugal during the winter. A place for people wanting peace. Be sure to check your gas. Inexpensive.

Sesimbra [14]

Hotel do Mar   Bairron Dom Henrique   tel: 22 93 26
Large, modern, and expensive hotel with its own nightclub and pool. Overlooks the bay. Rooms with verandas. Plenty of extras for water sports. Unusual hillside location.

Hotel Espadarte   Esplanada do Atlântico   tel: 22 91 89
A large, simple hotel on the sea with special appeal for fishermen since this is the headquarters of a local fishing club.

Pensão Nautico   Rua A   tel: 22 92 33
Beautiful view from this ultrasmall boardinghouse, which appeals to athletes who don't mind the walk up to it. Inexpensive.

Setubal [15]

Pousada de São Filipe   Castelo de São Filipe   tel: 23 844
Converted castle with a beautiful view. Small, topflight inn. Good restaurant. Moderate to expensive.

Sintra [5]

Hotel Palacio dos Seteais   8 Rua Barbosa du Bocage   tel: 98 06 81
A small, government-owned luxury hotel that dates from the eighteenth century. Not to be missed. With its trimmed gardens, antiques, and perfect view of the sea, it's one of Europe's most attractive hotels. Named after the treaty with the defeated French who were allowed to return home with their booty. Seteais means "seven sighs." The Portuguese sighed with disgust at the terms of the treaty. Expensive.

Tomar [34]

Estalagem de Santa Iria   Parque do Mouchão   tel: 32 427
On an island in the town park is this small, good, and relatively inexpensive inn.

Urgeiriça [43]

Hotel de Urgeiriça   Urgeiriça   tel: 67 267
Sir Anthony Eden spent his 1952 honeymoon here. The medium-size hotel with a good view to the mountains has its own pool, tennis, and golf. Quiet, peaceful, friendly. Regional furniture. Farm nearby. Beautiful grounds with some cottages available. Wide range in prices. Only fifteen miles from Viseu; near Nelas.

Valença do Minho [57]

Pousada de São Teotonio   Valença do Minho   tel: 22 52
Built into the fortified walls surrounding the small town near the Spanish frontier a half-mile away. Much the same feeling as Obidos. The inn overlooks the valley and the Minho River below. The modern stone pousada has antique reproductions, comfortable rooms, and a pleasant dining room. Often crowded. Inexpensive. West of Monção.

Vila Nova de Milfontes [16]

Castelo de Milfontes   Vila Nova de Milfontes   tel: 8
A unique fort which the owner has rebuilt over the past forty years. Its vine-covered façade with the sea in the background is

worth seeing. Beautiful view from the terrace. Not quite as interesting inside as out, but friendly and open. The kind of place
where you pour your own drinks. The town itself is drab. Isolated, quiet, and worth a detour. Southwest of Santiago do
Cacém on the coast.

Viseu [43]

Hotel Grão Vasco   Rua Gaspar Barreiros   tel: 23 511
In the center of town surrounded by lawns and gardens, with its
own pool. Moderate to very expensive room prices.

WHERE TO EAT

Albufeira [23]

Alfredo   Rua 5 Outubro 9-11   tel: 52 059
An attractive upstairs restaurant serving Portuguese and international dishes. Both the atmosphere and food are good. Conveniently located in the center of town. Expensive.

Borda d'Agua   Praia da Oura   tel: 52 045
This by-the-sea restaurant is outside of town, but worth the trip.
An airy, clean feeling from the dining room with a good view of
the ocean. Professional service and food. Specializes in seafood.
Call ahead for reservations. Moderate.

La Cigale   Praia Olhos d'Agua   tel: 52 607
British-run beach restaurant that specializes in grills. Was serving suppers only. Reservations required. Closed Monday. Go
eight tenths of a mile past the Hotel Balaia, which is several
miles from Albufeira and well-marked from the center of town.
Turn to the right down the small hill which leads to a shabby
town. Walk out to the beach where you'll see the hideous multicolored exterior of the restaurant. Don't judge it by its cover.

Azoia [4]

Pão de Trigo   Estrada Cabo da Roca   tel: 29 90 34
On the lefthand side of the road coming into the small town of
Azoia, from the direction of Sintra, on your way to Cabo da
Roca. It's practically unmarked. The converted farmhouse with

grill and the smell of smoked meat is very popular. Lots of local atmosphere (not luxury), good food, and fun. Just knock at the door, which is often locked.

Carcavelos [2]

Fateixa   Estrada Marginal   tel: 247-0240
The restaurant is right on the sea on the coast road leading to Estoril from Lisbon. There are no signs, just an awning which you can see from the road. Roast pigs and lobsters on the main table. A clean-cut look in this modern restaurant with a good selection of grills. Beautiful view. Airy. Nice. Expensive.

Carvoeiro [23]

O Patio   Praia de Carvoeiro   tel: 57 115
An interesting restaurant with its large kegs set into the white-washed walls. Directly on the beautiful Carvoeiro beach with a famous discothèque just several minutes away in town. Recently redecorated, it has a great atmosphere. Well known for its fish and steaks. Expensive.

Togi   Algar Seco   tel: 57 107
A fairly simple restaurant set on the hill overlooking the sea, town, and beach below. Mainly French and local dishes at moderate prices. Nothing luxurious, but good. Closed Mondays.

Cascais [3]

Aos 3 Porquinhos   Av. Frederico Ulrich 7   tel: 28 23 54
An intimate and expensive restaurant right on the roundabout as you come into town from the direction of Lisbon. An excellent spot for lunch. Unfortunately, it has an up-and-down reputation.

Bar John Bull (Britania)   Praça Costa Pinto 31   tel: 28 33 19
A saloon atmosphere with plush, soft chairs and restaurant upstairs in the English tradition. Specializes in steaks. The two entrances lead to the same bar and bull.

O Batel   Tra. dos Flores 4   *tel: 28 02 15*
Clean and airy with a good feeling for a moderate-priced restaurant. Seafood and regional dishes. Simple. Opposite the fish market.

Fim do Mundo   Av. Valbom 26   *tel: 28 02 00*
A restaurant with a topflight reputation which it intends to keep. The small dining room is simple without all the show so many luxury restaurants like to put on. Both international and Portuguese cooking. Excellent. Expensive.

Taberna Gil Vincente   Rua dos Navegantes 22-30   *tel: 28 20 32*
A small, hard-to-find restaurant on the hill. Vines clinging to the outside windows give it away. Intimate. Moderate. Nice.

O Pipas   Rua das Flores 16   *tel: 28 45 01*
Shellfish and regional dishes are served in this somewhat glossy restaurant with wine kegs in the wall. Claims its seafood is always fresh. Moderate prices.

Restaurante da Marinha (Tasco)   Quinta da Marinha   *tel: 28 90 32*
Outside of Cascais with a pool and an on-the-farm layout. Very nice, especially downstairs in the Tasco. Varied menu. Expensive. A taxi is in order.

Caxias [2]

Monaco   Rua Direita 9   *tel: 243-2339*
On the main road to Estoril from Lisbon. A luxury restaurant with a varied menu emphasizing seafood specialties. It sets a most attractive table and is ultraconvenient for a side trip along the coast.

Costa de Caparica [1]

Faisão   Rua M. Agra Ferreira 33   *tel: 240-0259*
A luxury restaurant near Lisbon across the Tagus Bridge in Caparica. There you'll find a battery of signs leading you to the old mansion converted into a topflight restaurant.

Estremoz [29]

Aguias d'Ouro   Rossio Marques Pombal 27-1   tel: 36
A second floor restaurant attractive in its simplicity and clean look. In the center of town on the main square. Good food at a moderate price. Excellent value.

Faro [24]

Al Faghar   Rua Tenente Valadim 30   tel: 23 740
A large room with beamed ceiling sets off the candlelit tables. Portuguese and international dishes. Good food at reasonable prices. It is not the best restaurant on the Algarve, as posted outside, but it's good. They're especially proud of their *cataplana*.

Lagosta (Faro Ski Club)   Faro Beach   tel: 24 365
This small and very simple restaurant has a light touch and a bit of fish fantasy on the walls. It's only a short drive from Faro to the beach. After crossing the narrow bridge, take a left. The restaurant is on the left a short distance down the road. Simple fare at moderate prices.

Figueira da Foz [38]

Covil do Caçador   Marraceira   tel: 22 264
To the left of a bridge which crosses the lagoon from Figueira da Foz. A fisherman's hut. Very smoky, busy, and popular. Local dishes.

Funchal (Madeira Island)

A Seta   Estrada do Livramento/Monte   tel: 20 306
This is the best local restaurant, with characteristic table wine, fresh rough bread hot from the oven, and a choice of four specialties including codfish and chicken. Good salad. Very rustic and ultrasimple. Moderate. Best take a taxi to get there.

Lagos [20]

O Alpendre   Rua Antonio Barbosa Viana 17   tel: 62 705
This crowded, often noisy, Portuguese restaurant is a great place

to go for seafood. The *carabineiros* are worth a try. The atmosphere is good, with a small patio in the back for a before-dinner drink. Call for reservations. This is a very popular place.

Leiria [37]

Verde Pino   Rua Almirante Almeida Henriques   tel: 22 626
Off the main road near the intersection leading in all directions including Marinha Grande. A basement restaurant with little atmosphere but good value. Hearty, simple cooking. Excellent rough bread. Worth stopping for. Inexpensive.

Lisboa [1] (Lisbon)

The crowded, noisy, varied, and totally Portuguese Rua das Portas de Santo Antão behind the central post office on the Praça dos Restauradores is a fascinating eating street which no European city can quite match. Here you'll find some of the best restaurants in the city as well as snack bars, chicken houses, and an incredible variety of small restaurants. The equally alive Rua dos Correeiros is another street frequented by hundreds of Portuguese during their lunch break. The restaurants on this street cater to simple tastes.

Pabe   rua Duque de Palmela, 27a   tel: 53 56 75
The "pub's" a cozy luxury restaurant with both Portuguese and international dishes. New and very nice. Expensive.

A Gondola   Av. da Berna 64   tel: 77 04 26
Near the Gulbenkian Museum on the outskirts of town. Good food and mood with an emphasis on Italian dishes. Small terrace covered with wisteria. You can eat outside in nice weather. A bit noisy with main road nearby. Expensive. Closed Sundays. Best take a taxi.

A Parreirinha da Alfama   Beco do Espirito Santo 1   tel: 86 82 09
Worth going to at night for the walk through the Alfama and the good food. Fairly expensive. Nice.

Escorial   Rua das Portas de Santo Antão 47   tel: 33 758/32 50 78
One of Lisbon's top restaurants in a very plush, American way. Good seafood and local dishes. Expensive.

Gambrinus   *Rua das Portas de Santo Anfão 23*   *tel: 32 14 66*
Another top restaurant with excellent seafood. Worth taking a look at. There are two entrances. Expensive.

Tavares Rico   *Rua da Misericordia 35-37*   *tel: 32 11 12*
Sumptuous in a European "lots of show" way. Up-and-down five-star food and service that is worth the gamble. Very expensive.

Varanda do Chanceler   *Largo do Chanceler 7A*   *tel: 87 15 59*
A good place for seafood and folk music. Partially recommended because it's in the Alfama, which you should see at night. Fairly expensive.

Aviz   *Rua Serpa Pinto 12B*   *tel: 32 83 91*
One of the very best restaurants in Lisbon. Five-star food and service with price attached. Make reservations. Closed Sundays.

Belcanto   *Largo de São Carlos 10*   *tel: 32 06 07*
Elegant and expensive. Lively social scene.

Bonjardim   *7 Tra. de Santo Anfão*   *tel: 32 43 89*
The best grilled-chicken spot in town. Noisy, crowded, popular, and inexpensive. This is the kind of place the average Portuguese loves. The lines prove it.

Solmar   *Rua das Portas de Santa Anfão 106*   *tel: 32 33 71/30 010*
Noisy, touristy, popular, overpriced, and huge. Offers live lobsters crawling around in a large tank in the middle of the room. They're as expensive as gold.

Cervejaria Ribadouro   *Av. da Liberdade 155*   *tel: 49 411*
A very crowded, popular beer and shellfish spot with moderate prices.

Chocalho   *86 Rua Santos-O Velho*   *tel: 66 81 27*
Blood sausage, lamprey, and other local specialties in a small restaurant popular with people who really like Portuguese cooking. Best take a taxi to get there.

Lorde   *Rua Victor Cordon 14A*   *tel: 32 30 98*
A restaurant that tries to live up to its name. Elegant clientèle. Expensive.

Numero 1   44 D. Francisco M. de Melo   tel: 68 43 26
One of Lisbon's steak houses that appeals to tourists looking for
a good slab of beef. Flickering candles, good service, and moderate prices.

Monchique [19]

Estalagem Abrigo da Montanha   Estrada do Foia   tel: 92 131
A small dining room with a rustic feeling. It's on the mountain
heading up to the beautiful view from Foia. Good food at a
moderate price.

Rouxinol   Estrada Nacional   tel: 92 215
Although it's changed hands recently, it still seems to be good.
Excellent, very quiet location near the Caldas de Monchique. Has
a nice view and is very romantic. Closed Tuesdays.

Obidos [11]

Alcaide   Rua Direita   tel: 95 220
Not first-class, but good. Portuguese cooking topped off with a
superb view. Chirping birds add to the rural flavor. Worth a try
for lunch. Moderate.

Porches [21]

O Leão de Porches   Porches   tel: 52 384
A new restaurant which does not yet have a set reputation.
Should be good since it's run by the Coles, who once had the
Rouxinol in Monchique. Simple, converted farmhouse just be-
hind the church. Good food at moderate prices. Closed Tuesday.

Portimao [21]

Alfredos   Rua da Pe da Cruz 10-12   tel: 24 289
Newly decorated, it has a good atmosphere with its red-chec-
kered tablecloths and whitewashed walls. Serves international
and local dishes. Very good service. Popular. Moderately expensive.

Cascata   Rua dos Reis 14   tel: 22 938
The best moderate-class restaurant on the Algarve. Very simple
menu with good, inexpensive local dishes. The best crème
caramel I've ever eaten. The place is filled with Portuguese who
know a good thing. Hope the present owner stays.

Sete Mares (Seven Seas)   Rua Judice Biker 10   tel: 24 031
A little touristy with its fish tank, but the food is good.
Specializes in steaks and French cooking. Good service. One of
the few places where the meat is tender. Right across from the
back entrance to the Cascata. Expensive, but good value.

Porto [49]

Portucale   Rua da Alegria 598   tel: 27 861
Named after the original Roman settlement which gave Portugal
its name. This luxury restaurant on the thirteenth floor of the
multicolored building has an excellent view of the city with its
red-tiled roofs. Good. Expensive.

*Le Chien Qui Fume (Cão Que Fuma)   Rua do Almada 405   tel:
being installed*
Small place with some color. Open kitchen. Low prices for regional dishes including baked goat and the good local vinho
verdes. Not far from the Praça do Municipio.

Escondidinho   Rua de Passos Manuel 144   tel: 21 079
Tiled exterior with flower boxes, leather chairs upright and
waiting, flowered pottery on ledges jutting out from the walls,
good atmosphere on the dark side, varied menu, and luxury
prices make this one of Porto's best-known restaurants.

Praia da Luz [20]

A Forteleza   Praia da Luz   tel: Call the Luz operator
An historic sixteenth-century fort directly on the sea in a superb
location. One of the few buildings in Portugal to survive the
1755 quake. Converted by an American couple into an eating
club full of charm and atmosphere. Terrace overlooking the
ocean, salad bar, and fine fish specialities.

Queluz [1]

Cozinha Velha   *Palacio Nacional*   tel: 95 02 32
Wicker chairs, copper on the wall, flowers on every table, and
an excellent menu all served in the pink palace of Queluz which
is just a short drive from Lisbon. Expensive, but worth making a
detour if only for the atmosphere. Always make reservations.

Quinta do Lago [23]

Casa Velha   *Quinta do Lago*   tel: 94 272
One of the Algarve's finest restaurants. Rustic and regal at the
same time with whitewashed walls, fine cooking and superb
service. The three-century-old farmhouse was recently enlarged
and decorated in a truly Portuguese manner. Not to be missed.
Only ten miles from Faro. Close to Vale do Lobo.

Romeu [60]

Maria Rita   *Romeu*   tel: 4
Rustic furniture, copper, pewter, beam ceiling, stone hearth,
added to a very good regional menu which varies from cod to
tripe. You serve yourself from dishes the waitress leaves on the
table. Wine is included in the moderate price. About six miles
from Mirandela on the way to Bragança. A mile off the main
road. Well marked. Inexpensive.

Setubal [15]

Naval Setubalense   *Av. Louisa Todi 300-1*   tel: 23 674
A funny little place. Good value with an amazing number of
hors d'oeuvres (*acepipes*) ranging from razorback clams to pickled
beets. Follow the sign leading up the stairs. You'll eventually
hear the noise of clinking glasses or the thump of the waiter's
wooden leg.

Viana do Castelo [55]

Central Jorge   *Rua Candido dos Reis 11A*   tel: 23 186
Tries to make you feel wanted with its regional dishes and good
service. Conveniently located in the center of town. Moderate.

SPAIN

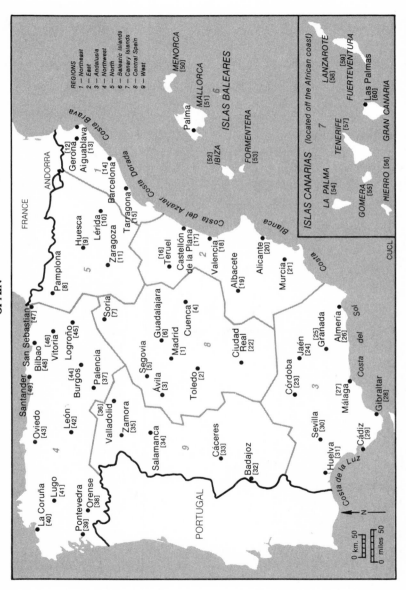

SPAIN

FRANCE

ANDORRA

PORTUGAL

REGIONS
1 — Northeast
2 — East
3 — Andalusia
4 — Northwest
5 — North
6 — Balearic Islands
7 — Canary Islands
8 — Central Spain
9 — West

ISLAS CANARIAS (located off the African coast)

ISLAS BALEARES

MENORCA [50]
MALLORCA [51]
Palma
IBIZA [52]
FORMENTERA [53]

LA PALMA [54]
GOMERA [55]
HIERRO [56]
TENERIFE [57]
GRAN CANARIA
LANZAROTE [58]
FUERTEVENTURA [59]
Las Palmas [60]

La Coruña [40]
Lugo [41]
Pontevedra [39]
Orense [38]
Oviedo [43]
León [42]
Santander [49]
San Sebastián [47]
Bilbao [48]
Vitoria [46]
Logroño [45]
Pamplona [8]
Burgos [44]
Palencia [37]
Valladolid [36]
Zamora [35]
Salamanca [34]
Ávila [3]
Segovia [5]
Soria [7]
Huesca [9]
Lérida [10]
Zaragoza [11]
Gerona [12]
Aiguablava [13]
Barcelona [14]
Tarragona [15]
Teruel [16]
Castellón de la Plana [17]
Valencia [18]
Albacete [19]
Alicante [20]
Murcia [21]
Cuenca [4]
Guadalajara [6]
Madrid [1]
Toledo [2]
Ciudad Real [22]
Cáceres [33]
Badajoz [32]
Córdoba [23]
Jaén [24]
Granada [25]
Almería [26]
Málaga [27]
Gibraltar [28]
Cádiz [29]
Sevilla [30]
Huelva [31]

Costa Brava
Costa Dorada
Costa del Azahar
Costa Blanca
Costa del Sol
Costa de la Luz

0 km 50
0 miles 50

N

CUCL

WHAT TO SEE

Low prices continue to be one of Spain's great drawing cards, but others include fabulous beaches, outstanding art galleries and museums, picture-postcard towns much as they were centuries ago, and one of the mildest climates on the Continent. *Paradores*, state supported inns, are located in towns of historic and artistic interest. They provide rooms and meals at modest rates. All of these *paradores* have been listed in this chapter with brief comments on each.

The Prado, Palacio Real, Plaza Mayor, and Fabrica Real de Tapices stand out as attractions in *Madrid* **[1]**. Be sure to make an excursion to *Toledo* **[2]** (spend two days there) to see this marvelous sixteenth-century town much as it was in the days of El Greco. The thirteenth-century cathedral is superb. Try too to take in the castle of *Aranjuez*, medieval *Avila* **[3]**, the *El Escorial*, clifftop *Cuenca* **[4]**, the well-preserved Roman aqueduct at *Segovia* **[5]**, and the Spanish Versailles at *La Granja*.

In the beginning of July you may want to visit *Pamplona* **[8]** for the Corrida de Toros (women should avoid the streets at night). The cathedral at *Zaragoza* **[11]** stands out in an admittedly austere region. Farther east you'll come to sprawling *Barcelona* **[14]**, best viewed from Tibidabo Mount. In town you'll visit the Barrio Gótico, stroll along Las Ramblas, and see the paintings in the Picasso Museum. The cathedral at *Tarragona* **[15]** and the picturesque Thursday market in *Figueras* are worth the detour.

Resorts rapidly replace the orange groves that curl down to the sea in eastern Spain. *Benidorm*, with a young group of year-round swingers, is one of the better known. If you're near *Valencia* **[18]** on March 19, see the enormous bonfires in the celebration of *Las Fallas*. Farther south is the *great* touristic region of Spain. The Gothic Cathedral of *Seville* **[30]**, the Great Mosque in *Córdoba* **[23]**, and the Alhambra of *Granada* **[25]** stand out. Fall visitors should rush to *Jerez de la Frontera* during the grape harvest (usually in September). Resorts in Andalusia are household words: *Marbella* with its jet set, *Torremolinos* with a mixture of tea drinkers and touts, and *Fuengirola* with tens upon tens of tennis twosomes. The uncommon traveller may wish to avoid them all; soaking up instead the tiny vilages that make this region so colorful and photogenic.

The western section of Spain is of limited interest. You'll travel through it on your way north. It does have interesting Romanesque buildings around *Zamora* [35]; a well-preserved medieval town, *Cáceres* [33]; and Roman ruins in *Mérida*. However, the northwest is magnificent. Take in the monastery-town of *Santiago de Compostela*, the medieval *Santillana del Mar* and nearby *Altamira Caves*, and the Cartuja de Miraflores three miles east of inland *Burgos* [33] (well known for its cathedral). Note that this region is packed with Spaniards during the summer, which extends into September. Try to come here in April, May, or October if you want to avoid the crowds. If that's impossible, sight-see in the middle of the week.

Majorca [51], *Ibiza* [52], and *Menorca* [50] are the best known of the dozen or more islands known as the Balearics. Majorca offers a warm climate, attractive beaches, and relatively low prices in its many hotels. It's particularly popular as an off-season destination among penny pinchers. Ibiza, the warmest of the main islands, has become a refuge for hippies and escapists while the appeal of Menorca lies in its lovely, isolated beaches at their best from June to early September. The islands are cool, windy, and often rainy from late October to mid-April.

All of the Canary Islands offer winter sun at low, low rates which explains much of their appeal to northern Europeans. Yet each of the Canaries has its own distinctive personality. Arid and desolate *Fuerteventura* [59] suits nudists; tiny and untouched *La Gomera* [55] appeals to escapists; while *Hierro* [56], no more than a dusty crater, appeals to few. Three hundred volcanic craters cover *Lanzarote* [58], an island known to have gone without rain for up to seven years. Then there's lush and lovely *La Palma* [54], rarely visited by a soul. The two most popular islands? *Gran Canaria* [60] and *Tenerife* [57]. Both are suited to heavy tourist trade with a number of fine, modern hotels. Gran Canaria offers better beaches, while Tenerife seems to have more soul and a rich variety of plant life typified by the 8 million banana trees spilling through the Orotava Valley. But most of the swimming on Tenerife must be done in pools, since the rocky shoreline discourages bathing. All in all, the Canaries are unique, but no one should expect the clear water, dazzling night life, or subtle charm of the Bahamas.

WHAT'S THE WEATHER REALLY LIKE?

Madrid, like much of the country, is lovely from April to late October. Spring and fall are the two most attractive seasons. Summers are often extremely hot; winters can be cold and windy, although they're often mild in Andalusia. Mild along the Mediterranean means cool, sometimes windy, often sunny. It does not mean you'll want to go swimming in the sea.

SOME SUGGESTIONS FOR A MORE ENJOYABLE TRIP

Paradores are such bargains that they often fill up far in advance in major tourist destinations. Off-the-beaten-path inns are rarely booked far in advance. Still, you should always call ahead and make reservations whenever possible. Shopping for leather goods and regional handicrafts is excellent in Spain. Bargaining is always expected. Driving is difficult, particularly along the coastal roads. Don't expect to drive long distances quickly. Plan on an average of forty miles per hour. The second class in local trains would be third class in other countries. If you're travelling by train, you might want to splurge on first-class tickets. Bullfights are a popular tourist attraction. If you buy tickets through the hotel, you'll pay many times what you'd pay at the ring. Buy *Sol e Sombra* seats close to the action (*asientos de barrera*)—a little more expensive) and be sure to bring something soft to sit on (a cushion or newspaper). If you're in the mood for a snack rather than a full meal, try the *tapas* sold in small bars and cafes. Popular are shellfish washed down with beer. Meal hours are long and late. Dinner really begins at 10:00 p.m. Siestas are common during the summer. Shops often close from noon to 4:00 p.m. Spaniards often take late-night walks, especially in smaller towns. However, in large cities women are advised to take taxis at night. Noise is a problem in all large cities. Try to book a room in a quiet part of the hotel and as high up as possible. During the off-season agree to pay the *minimo* price that should be posted in the room.

WHERE TO STAY

S'Agaró [14]

Hostal de la Gavina   Plaza de la Rosaleda   tel: 32 11 00
Perhaps the finest luxury hotel on the Mediterranean with every-thing perfect. Must be seen to be appreciated. Very expensive, and worth it. Sixty-eight miles northeast of Barcelona.

Alarcón [4]

Parador Nacional Marqués de Villena   Avenida Amigos Castillos
tel: 31 13 50
Sixty miles south of Cuenca—a Moorish castle converted into a small and intimate hotel in a stunning location. Out of the way. Inexpensive.

Albacete [19]

Los Llanos   9 Gobernador R. Acosta   tel: 22 37 50
Newer hotel with view to the park in a central location. Quite comfortable. Good food and service. Pool.

Parador Nacional de La Mancha   Albacete   tel: 21 42 90
Three miles southeast of the city. Quiet, rustic retreat. Pool. Tennis. Moderate.

Alcañiz [11]

Parador Nacional la Concordia   Castillo de los Calatravos
tel: 13 04 00
Small eighteenth century castle converted into a recently reno-vated inn with comfortable rooms. Local atmosphere. Regional specialties. Moderate. Southeast of Zaragoza.

Alicante [20]

Carlton   Rambla Mendez Nunez 1   tel: 21 63 00
Near the palm groves. A large and very comfortable hotel. Eleg-ant throughout. Excellent restaurant. Moderate.

Palas Hotel   *Cervantes 5*   *tel: 21 79 06*
Charming, simple inn with modest, but attractive, rooms. Inexpensive.

Arcos de la Frontera [29]

Parador Nacional Casa del Corregidor   *5 Plaza de España*   *tel: 362*
Fifty miles from Cadiz you'll find an old mansion converted into a modern hotel with comfortable rooms in local style. Fine food. Although it's off the beaten track, reserve a room. Moderate. Northeast of Cadiz.

Avila [3]

Parador Nacional Raimundo de Borgoña   *Marqués de Canales y Chozas 16*   *tel: 21 13 40*
Tiny delightful inn constructed from former sixteenth-century palace. Lovely rooms in local style. Good regional cooking. Lots of atmosphere. Inexpensive.

Ayamonte [31]

Parador Nacional Costa de la Luz   *El Castillito*   *tel: 32 07 00*
Modern hotel at the Portuguese border with lovely view from the hillside. Spacious, bright, and rustic rooms. Fine cuisine. Pool. Garden. Moderate. West of Huelva.

Bagur [12]

Parador Nacional Costa Brava   *Aiguablava*   *tel: 31 21 62*
Two miles from town. Small, tasteful inn overlooking the ocean on a cliff. Quiet and secluded. Quite comfortable. Pool. Tennis. Moderate. East of Gerona.

Barcelona [14]

Hotel Colón   *Avenida de la Catedral 9*   *tel: 207-1404/222-8707*
Large traditional hotel recently renovated with a lovely location in the Gothic Quarter next to the cathedral. Elegant and authentic. Comfortable. Moderate.

Gaudi Hotel   Conde del Asalto 12   tel: 222-4422
Small hotel in the old section of town with simple but comfortable rooms. Quite inexpensive.

Gran Via Hotel   Avenida José Antonio 642   tel: 221-1407
Small traditional hotel with antiques in modest but comfortable rooms. Moderate.

Hotel Manila   Rambla de les Estudios 111   tel: 232-0409
Large, tasteful hotel with view of the Gothic Quarter. Comfortable yet simple rooms. Popular roof-garden restaurant with excellent view and fine food. Moderately expensive.

La Masia Hotel   Cumbre del Tibidabo   tel: 247-5687
Small, modest hotel with authentic Spanish atmosphere. Inexpensive.

Oriente Hotel   45 Ramblas   tel: 221-4151
Large traditional hotel near the Teatro del Liceo. Comfortable. Ask for room in front. On Sundays after Mass you may see the colorful *sardana* danced in the streets. Moderate.

Bayona [39]

Parador Nacional Conde de Gondomar   Bayona   tel: 142
Twenty-one miles southwest of Vigo is a fine inn converted from a castle in a medieval setting. Tasteful public and private rooms. Very comfortable. Pool. Tennis. Ideal stop on the way to Portugal. Moderate. South of Pontevedra.

Benavente [35]

Parador Nacional Rey Fernando II de León   Benavente   tel: 63 03 00
Small, delightful castle converted into hotel with local architecture and furnishings. Spacious rooms. Charming restaurant serving local specialties. Moderate. North of Zamora.

Bendinat [51] (Majorca Island)

Bendinat   Avenida Bendinat   tel: 23 19 47
Six miles west of Palma. Small, authentic cottage colony with lovely clifftop location and garden atmosphere. Very quiet and

secluded. Cottage number 3 is very nice. Good dining. Swimming off the rocks. Tennis. Moderate. Great value.

Benidorm [20]

Corregidor Real   Avenida de Filipinas 7   tel: 85 01 03/36 01 03
Small luxury hotel decorated in sixteenth-century style with some lovely antiques. Tasteful rooms. Good cooking. Pool. Garden. It's suffering an up-and-down reputation at the moment. Northeast of Alicante on coast.

Benicarló [18]

Parador Nacional Benicarló   Benicarló   tel: 47 01 00
Small, modern inn. Very comfortable. Moderate. Northeast of Castellón on the coast.

Bielsa [9]

Parador Nacional Monte Perdido   Valle de Pineta   tel: 24
Nice modern building set in the Pyrenees near the French border. Spectacular views. Spacious and nicely furnished rooms. Good local cooking. Moderate. Northeast of Huesca.

Burgos [44]

Landa Palace   Burgos   tel: 20 63 43
Tiny luxury hotel on the road to Madrid to the south of the city. A fifteenth-century castle converted into a tasteful and quiet retreat. Rooms in wonderful period furnishings. Excellent restaurant. Pool. Garden. Expensive.

Calahorra [8]

Parador Nacional Fabio Quintiliano   Calahorra   tel: 67
Attractive inn with regional character. Comfortable and pleasant throughout. Moderate. Southwest of Pamplona.

Cambados [39]

Parador Nacional de Albariño   *Paseo Cervantes*   *tel: 171*
Sixteen miles northwest of Pontevedra on the coast. Small and intimate inn with local furnishings. Large rooms open up on the ocean.

Cardona [10]

Parador Nacional Duques de Cardona   *Cardona*   *tel: 869-1275*
Castle converted into comfortable hotel. Very nice. Moderate. Northeast of Lérida.

Carmona [30]

Parador Nacional Rey Don Pedro 1   *Carmona*   *tel: 536*
Castle converted into comfortable and attractive hotel. Moderate. Northeast of Seville.

Cazorla [25]

Parador Nacional El Adelantado   *Cazorla*   *tel: 295*
Eighteen miles from Cazorla is a small modernized castle with comfortable rooms. Regional cooking. Northeast of Granada.

Cervera de Pisuerga [49]

Parador Nacional Fuentes Carrionas   *Cervera*   *tel: 87 00 75*
Quite large, modern inn with comfortable rooms. Moderate. Southwest of Santander.

Ciudad Rodrigo [34]

Parador Nacional Enrique II   *Plaza del Castillo 1*   *tel: 46 01 50*
Small rustic inn from converted thirteenth-century castle inside walls of town with view to the river. Comfortable. Inexpensive. Southwest of Salamanca.

Córdoba [23]

Parador Nacional la Arruzafa   *Avenida de la Arruzafa*   *tel: 27 59 00*
About two miles north of Córdoba. Small hillside hotel with

view of town. Elegant. Spacious rooms. Fine dining. Pool. Tennis. Moderate. Reserve in advance.

Residencia Marisa   Cardenal Herrero 6   tel: 22 63 17
Tiny hotel behind the mosque with rustic, very comfortable rooms. Inexpensive. A gem.

El Ferrol del Caudillo [40]

Parador Nacional   Almirante Vierha   tel: 35 34 00
Forty-two miles northeast of La Coruña you'll find this modern hotel in a beautiful location on the Atlantic. Simple but comfortable.

El Saler [18]

Parador Nacional Luis Vives   El Saler   tel: 23 68 50
Six miles from Valencia. Modern building on the coast with spacious bedrooms and a lovely dining room serving fine food. Golf. Pool. Inexpensive to moderate.

Fuente Dé [49]

Parador Nacional Río Deva   Fuente Dé   tel : 7
Two miles from Espinama is a modern inn high in the Pico de Europa mountains. Very comfortable small hotel in a scenic setting. Some fishing and mountain-climbing. Moderate.

Fuenterrabia [47]

Parador Nacional El Emperador   Plaza Armas del Castillo
tel: 64 21 40
A delightful inn. Converted twelfth-century castle on a hill just across the border from France. Intimate atmosphere. Large rooms with local furnishings. Basque cooking. East of San Sebastian.

Gijón [43]

Parador Nacional Molino Viejo   Parque de Isabel la Catolica
tel: 35 49 45
Just seventeen miles north of Oviedo near the sea. Modern and

charming hotel in a lovely park. Spacious and well-decorated rooms. Fine local specialties from the kitchen.

Granada [25]

Parador Nacional San Francisco   *Alhambra*   *tel: 22 14 92*
Once an Arab mosque converted into popular inn on the mountainside within the walls of the Alhambra. Nicely furnished in Moorish style—some of the rooms in original cells. Ask for room on sunny side *not* overlooking the entrance. Rare art pieces. Quite good food. A gem. Moderate. Reserve well in advance.

Hotel Kenia   *Molinos 59*   *tel: 22 75 06*
Modest hotel with comfortable rooms. Relaxed and friendly. Inexpensive.

Guadalupe   *Avenida de los Alijares*   *tel: 22 34 23*
Fine service and food in this small hotel with a lovely view. Modest. Inexpensive.

Parador Nacional Sierra Nevada   *twenty miles from Granada*
tel: 48 02 00
Spectacular mountain resort with a remarkable view. Spacious, if rustic, rooms. Very comfortable. Reached along Europe's highest mountain road. Geared to skiing and mountain climbing. Inexpensive. In Monachil.

Guadalupe

Parador Nacional Zurbaran   *Marques de la Romana 10*   *tel: 142*
Tiny hotel in converted sixteenth-century building with comfortable and rustic rooms. Lovely setting. Pool. Inexpensive.

Jaen [24]

Parador Nacional de Santa Catalina   *Jaén*   *tel: 23 22 87*
Tiny castle converted into fine inn about three miles from town. Superb setting on cliff with magnificent view. Rustic and very comfortable rooms. Huge halls. Exquisite dining room with excellent cooking. Inexpensive. A gem.

Jarandilla de la Vera [33]

Parador Nacional Carlos V   Jarandilla de la Vera   tel: 98
Tiny inn converted from fourteenth-century castle. On the edge
of a valley with beautiful view. Local furnishings and flavor.
Comfortable. Good regional cooking. Inexpensive. Northeast of
Cáceres.

Jávea [20]

Parador Nacional Costa Blanca   Jávea   tel: 79 02 00
About three miles from Jávea east of Gata. Modern hotel with
view to the ocean. Quiet and scenic location. Comfortable
rooms. Good restaurant. Pool. Moderate. Northeast of Alicante
on coast.

Jerez de la Frontera [29]

Jerez   Avenida A. Alvaro Domecq   tel: 34 19 81
A small hotel slightly east of the city center. Modern rooms. An-
dalusian atmosphere. Nice dining. Pool. Expensive. North of
Cadiz.

Las Palmas [60] (Gran Canaria Island)

Hotel Santa Catalina   Parque Doramas   tel: 24 31 40
Very large deluxe hotel with a traditional Spanish flavor. Comfortable and tasteful rooms with some apartments for rent. Elegant throughout. Park setting with refreshing gardens. Tennis.
Pool. Expensive.

Sansofe Hotel   Portugal 62   tel: 26 47 58
Good location by the beach. Modern and very comfortable. All
rooms with bath. Excellent choice in the moderate bracket.

Lloret de Mar [14]

San Marcos de Venezia   Lloret de Mar   tel: 33 47 27
Small, charming hotel with lovely view and quite comfortable
rooms. Excellent cuisine and fine wines. Inexpensive. Open
mid-April through October. Between Barcelona and Aiguablava.

Madrid [1]

Bretón   Bretón de los Herreros 29   tel: 254-7400
Small hotel with comfortable, clean, bright rooms. Fully air conditioned. Good value in moderate bracket.

Casón del Tormes   Calle del Río 7   Tel: 241-9745
Quite nice hotel with comfortable, if functional rooms. Pleasant. Good value in moderate bracket.

*Don Quijote   Avenida D. Federico Rubio y Galí 145
tel: 459-2100*
Quite large hotel with comfortable rooms. Nice terrace with pool. Moderate.

El Coloso   Calle de Leganitos 13   tel: 248-7600
Small hotel with simple, comfortable rooms (try for number 105). Moderate.

Grand Hotel Victoria   Plaza del Angel 7   tel: 231-4500
Offbeat and authentic. A favorite of bullfighters. Ask for an outside room (number 403 is recommended). Excellent service. Good restaurant. Moderate.

Hostal Lisboa   Ventura de la Vega 17   tel: 222-8345
Wonderful location in Old Madrid. Large rooms, some with brass beds. Surrounded by delightful, tiny restaurants serving typical Spanish fare. Moderate. No English spoken.

Lope de Vega   Avenida Jose Antonio   tel: 247-7000
Small, attractive hotel with a traditional flavor. Comfortable and modest rooms. Pleasant. Inexpensive.

Reyes Catolicos   Calle De Calatrava 32/Angel 18   tel: 265-8600
Small hotel with cozy, functional rooms. Good value in moderate bracket.

Sanvy   Calle Goya 3   tel: 276-0800
Comfortable, large hotel (over one hundred rooms). Dancing on terrace in summer. Pool. Garage. So-so restaurant. Moderate.

Serrano   Marqués de Villamejor 8   tel: 225-7564
Small gem with only twenty-four rooms and four suites. Calm, fashionable, warm. Moderate to expensive. No dining room.

Málaga [27]

Parador Nacional de Gibralfaro   Málaga   tel: 22 19 02
About two miles from town you'll find a wonderful and cozy inn decorated in the local style. Nice view. Attractive and spacious rooms. Great value. Inexpensive. A gem.

Marbella [27]

Artola   Marbella   tel: 83 13 90
Small hotel with lovely grounds eight miles from the city, but a half-mile from the sea. Calm. Simple. Pool. Tennis. Inexpensive. Southwest of Málaga.

Marbella Club Hotel   Marbella   tel: 82 35 93
Small and charming with gardens and pool. Comfortable and pleasant. Tennis. Quite expensive.

Mataro [14]

Castell de Mata   Carretera de Francia   tel: 284-1681/390-3744
Small, charming seaside hotel about twenty miles from Barcelona. Quiet and secluded, in nice setting. Spacious rooms. Marvelous atmosphere with excellent cuisine and wines. Inexpensive. Open March to November.

Melilla [27] (Africa)

Parador Nacional Don Pedro de Estopiñán   Melilla   tel: 68 49 40
Modern building with comfortable rooms. Nice view to the sea. Pool. Moderate. Accessible by ferry from Almeria or Málaga.

Mérida [32]

Parador Nacional Via de la Plata   Plaza de Queipo de Llano 3 tel: 30 15 40
Small hotel in a converted monastery. Wonderful medieval atmosphere retained in superb reconstruction with emphasis on local style. Comfortable vaulted bedrooms. Fine regional cooking. Moderate. East of Badajoz.

Mojácar [26]

Parador Nacional Reyes Católicos   Mojácar   tel: 26
About one and a half miles from the city. Modern hotel with
view to the ocean. Rustic but roomy. Very quiet and pleasant.
Good cooking. Geared to the sportsman. Moderate. North of
Almeria on the coast.

Monachil [25]

Parador Nacional Sierra Nevada   Monachil   tel: 48 02 00
Twenty miles from Granada. Beautiful mountain hotel with
modern facilities—ideal for skiers and sportsmen. Quite comfortable and spacious. Fine cuisine.

Montseny [14]

San Bernat   Montana Finca El Clot   tel: 8
About twelve miles southeast of Vich. A tiny mountain hotel
noted for its fine cuisine and atmosphere. Intimate, with lots of
atmosphere. Geared to riders. Some hunting. Expensive. North
of Barcelona.

Monzon de Campos [37]

Parador Nacional Castillo de Monzon   Monzon   tel: 51
Attractive castle with limited number of comfortable rooms. Nice
atmosphere. Moderate. North of Palencia.

Nerja [27]

Parador Nacional   Nerja   tel: 52 00 50
Small modern building with view to the ocean in delightful setting only three miles from town. Comfortable and stylish. Spacious, tasteful rooms. Excellent dining. Pool. Beach. Moderate.
East of Málaga.

Ojen [27]

Parador Nacional de Juanar   *Ojen*   *tel: 82 60 71/82 61 40*
About seven miles from Ojen. Simple lodge geared to hunting in
the hills. North of Marbella.

Olite [8]

Parador Nacional Príncipe de Viana   *Plaza de San Francisco*
tel: 74 00 00
Charming and authentic castle-hotel to the south of Pamplona in
the foothills of the Pyrennes. Small, with scenic setting. Fine
local specialties from the kitchen. Inexpensive.

Oropesa [2]

Parador Nacional Virrey de Toledo   *Plaza del Palacio 1*   *tel: 172*
A fourteenth-century castle converted into a fine inn with lots of
atmosphere. Antiques abound. Airy and fresh rooms. Lovely
suites. Convenient on way to Portugal. Reserve well in advance.
Moderate. West of Toledo.

Pajares [43]

Parador Nacional Puerto de Pajares   *Pajares*   *tel: 47 36 25*
About three miles from town in the Cantabrian mountains, thirty
miles from Oviedo. Typical inn with modest rooms and excellent
local food. Inexpensive.

Palma de Majorca [51] (Majorca Island)

Hotel Maricel   *Palma de Majorca*   *tel: 23 12 40*
Small and very charming traditional hotel with a lovely location
and delightful garden. Majorcan flavor—very tasteful. Spacious
rooms and individual bungalows. Fine cooking. Pool. Tennis.
Moderately expensive. Great value.

Pontevedra [39]

Parador Nacional del Barón   *21 Calle Maceda*   *tel: 85 58 00*
Twenty miles from Vigo—a grand old seventeenth-century palace near the river. Roomy and plush with an old world atmosphere. Good restaurant. Inexpensive.

Puerto del Rosario [59] (Fuerteventura Island)

Parador Nacional   Puerto del Rosario   tel: 85 00 75
Small, remote hotel built in the local style by the sea. Nice and cozy rooms. Very simple and rustic. Pool. Inexpensive.

Puertomarín [38]

Parador Nacional   Puertomarín   tel: 20
Modern inn fifteen miles from town in an isolated area. Just a few nice rooms geared to fishermen who want to try their luck in the spring. Inexpensive. North of Orense.

Puzol [18]

Monte Picayo   Valencia-Puzol   tel: 25 31 59
Luxury hotel twelve miles northeast of Valencia. In spacious grounds with impressive view to sea and orange groves. Beautiful rooms including charming villas. Superb cooking. Pool, tennis, riding, and hunting. Very expensive.

Ribadeo [43]

Parador Nacional   Amador Fernandez   tel: 11 08 25
Modern hotel on the coast in a lovely scenic setting. Fine modern rooms with excellent dining. Best in both spring and fall. Moderate. On the coast west of Oviedo.

San Cristobal [50] (Menorca Island)

Santo Tomas   San Cristobal   tel: 25
Small, secluded hotel near the beach. Comfortable and very pleasant. Fine cuisine. Pool. Moderate. Open April to October only.

San Miguel [52] (Ibiza Island)

Hacienda   Na Xamena   tel: 33 30 46
Small, authentic hotel furnished in local style. Lots of atmosphere. Tasteful and spacious rooms. View of the rocky coast. Fishing, tennis, and riding. Expensive. Open only April to October.

San Sebastian de Gomera [55] (Gomera Island)

Parador Nacional de Gomera   San Sebastián de Gomera   tel: 87 11 00
Small, simple inn with comfortable rustic rooms. Moderate.

Santa Cruz de la Palma [54] (La Palma Island)

*Parador Nacional Santa Cruz de la Palma   Avenida Blas Pérez Gonzales 34
tel: 31 23 40*
Small regional inn with rustic and comfortable rooms. Inexpensive.

Santiago de Compostela [39]

Los Reyes Catolicos   Plaza de Espana 1   tel: 58 22 00
Not to be missed. Fifteenth-century ambience brought into the luxury class. Lovely rooms. Elegant and authentic atmosphere. Excellent cooking. A masterpiece in its class. Moderate. North of Pontevedra.

Santillana del Mar [49]

Parador Nacional Gil Blas   Plaza Ramon Pelayo 8-11   tel: 116
Twenty miles west of Santander and only one mile from the Altamira caves is a four-hundred-year-old mansion converted into a fine inn with creaky yet charming old halls. Wonderfully furnished. Large dining hall with good food. Reserve well in advance.

Santo Domingo de la Calzada [45]

Parador Nacional   Plaza del Santo 3   tel: 596
Twenty-seven miles from Logroño is a converted monastery, now a small inn with comfortable and modest rooms.

Segovia [5]

Gran Hotel   Juan Bravo 30   tel: 41 18 97
Small hotel with a superb location. Comfortable. Inexpensive.

Sierra de Gredos [3]

Parador Nacional de Gredos   near Navarredonda   tel: Sierra de Gredos
Forty miles southwest of Avila. Comfortable hotel in a former hunting lodge. Scenic retreat in the mountains. Geared to sportsmen: fishing, hunting, mountain climbing. Rustic. Inexpensive.

Sevilla [30]

Doña María   Don Remondo 19   tel: 22 49 90
Quite small hotel with a central location next to the cathedral. A few nicely decorated rooms with antiques. Intimate. No restaurant. Charming and a gem—in its category.

Montecarlo   Gavina no. 51   tel: 21 75 01
Very small traditional hotel near the railroad station. Moorish flavor. Old-world feeling. Inexpensive. Not for the stuffy.

Sitges [14]

Galeón   San Francisco 44-46   tel: 894-0612
Not on the beach, but a small and charming hotel with fine furnishings and an intimate atmosphere. Quite simple. Inexpensive. Southwest of Barcelona.

Antemare Hotel   Avenida Tercio Nostra Senora de Montserrat
tel: 894-1908
Small hotel with pleasant ambience. Good food. Rather modest overall, but nice. Pool. Moderately expensive.

Soria [7]

Parador Nacional Antonio Machado   Parque del Castillo   tel: 21 34 45
A converted mansion with only a few comfortable rooms decorated in the local style. Inexpensive.

Sos del Rey Catolico [8]

Parador Nacional Fernando de Aragon   *Sos del Rey*   *tel: 96*
Modern inn with comfortable rooms at moderate rates southeast
of Pamplona.

Teruel [16]

Parador Nacional de Teruel   *Teruel*   *tel: 60 18 00*
One mile north of town. A modern building in lovely grounds.
Very pleasant. Spacious rooms. Quite inexpensive.

Toledo [2]

Parador Nacional Conde de Orgaz   *Paseo de los Cigarrales*   *tel:*
22 18 50
Just south of town is a charming inn with a delightful riverside
location. Magnificent views from the cliff. Spacious and elegant
rooms in local style. Lots of atmosphere. Good regional cooking.
Moderate.

Alfonso VI   *General Moscardo 2*   *tel: 22 26 00*
Small and pleasant inn with a colorful atmosphere. Quite comfortable and compact rooms. Moderate.

Hostal del Cardenal   *24 Paseo de Recaredo*   *tel: 22 49 00*
Small inn next to the city walls with lovely setting. Comfortable
rooms. Superb restaurant serving excellent regional specialties.
Moderate.

La Almazara   *Carretera Piedra Buena 47*   *tel: 22 62 10*
Only three miles from Toledo you'll find a monastery converted
into a delightful inn with a farm atmosphere. Lovely views from
outside rooms (number 9 is a good choice). Spectacular sunsets.
Candlelight dining on request. Modest, but nice.

Tordesillas [36]

Parador Nacional Tordesillas   *Tordesillas*   *tel: 514*
Quite large modern inn with very comfortable rooms. Moderate.
Southwest of Valladolid.

Torremolinos [27]

Parador Nacional del Golf   Málaga   tel: 38 11 20
Eight miles from Málaga and quite close to Torremolinos. Small hotel decorated in local style with large and comfortable rooms. Near golf. Private beach. Moderate, but good value.

Tuy [39]

Parador Nacional San Telmo   Tuy   tel: 296
Modern hotel of Galician design with a riverside setting near the Portuguese border. Quiet and comfortable. Nice regional dishes. Pool. South of Pontevedra.

Ubeda [23]

Parador Nacional Condestable Dávalos   Plaza Vazquez Molina tel: 75 03 45
Small sixteenth-century mansion converted into beautiful hotel with plaza, patios, garden, and so on. Spacious rooms—ask for one in the older section. Elegant throughout, with some antiques. Excellent restaurant in charming dining room. Fine wines. Inexpensive. East of Córdoba.

Valencia [18]

Astoria Palace   Plaza Rodrigo Botet 5   tel: 22 95 90
Large new hotel with fine décor and atmosphere. Quiet and comfortable. Fine food. Lively bar. Moderately expensive.

Reina Victoria   Barcas 4   tel: 21 13 60
Large traditional hotel with simple but comfortable rooms. Casual and warm atmosphere. Good cooking. Moderate.

Verin [38]

Parador Nacional de Monterrey   Verin   tel: 41 00 75
Two miles north of Verin. A modern hotel with local style and flavor. Lovely mountain atmosphere with a fifteenth-century castle nearby. Spacious rooms. Quiet. Pool. Good spring fishing. Midway between Orense and the Portuguese border.

Vich [14]

Parador Nacional   Vich   tel: 241
About ten miles north of town you'll find a lovely hotel perched on a rock with a view to the lake below. Historical flavor. Comfortable. Moderate. North of Barcelona.

Viella [10]

Parador Nacional de Arán   near Viella   tel: 108
A modern hotel in a mountain setting only ten miles from France. Lovely garden. Comfortable rooms with some superb suites. Pool, mountain climbing, and fishing; also winter sports. North of Lérida.

Villafranca del Bierzo [42]

Parador Nacional Villafranca del Bierzo   Villafranca   tel: 54 02 79
Attractive modern hotel with comfortable rooms. Moderate. West of León.

Villalba [41]

Parador Nacional de Villalba   Valeriano Valdesuso   tel: 296
A castle converted into a hotel twenty-three miles north of Lugo. Lush setting for a small inn (only six doubles). Fine food in a fascinating local restaurant.

Zafra [32]

Parador Nacional Hernán Cortés   Plaza de María Cristina
tel: 55 02 00
Tiny inn constructed from fifteenth-century castle. Large and comfortable rooms in local style. Fine regional cooking. A nice surprise in a bleak region. Moderate. Southeast of Badajoz.

Zamora [35]

Parador Nacional de Alba y Aliste   Plaza de Canovas   tel: 51 44 97
A lovely sixteenth-century palace converted into a small inn with comfortable rooms decorated in local style with wooden beams. Lots of atmosphere. Fine regional cooking. Pool. Inexpensive.

WHERE TO EAT

Alcala de Henares [1]

Hosteriá del Estudiante   5 Calle Colegios   tel: 293-0330
Ancient student hall converted into atmospheric restaurant. East of Madrid.

Barcelona [14]

Agut-d'Avignon   Calle Avino/Trinidad 3   tel: 231-8155
A delightful hard-to-find restaurant with a romantic and rather Bohemian air about it. Picasso lived in the area. Regional cooking. Moderate.

Restaurante Amaya   20 Rambla Santa Mónica   tel: 231-5934
Anything from *tapas*, ("hors d'oeuvres,") to tops in dining. The upstairs restaurant is superb. Excellent seafood. Moderately expensive.

Los Caracoles   Calle Escudillers 14   tel: 231-7914
Traditional restaurant in the Gothic Quarter with fish as the specialty. Moderate.

***Carballeira   Reina Cristina 3   tel: 310-5392
Very attractive and fine restaurant specializing in superb fish dishes. Excellent shellfish. Expensive.

Finisterre Franco   Generalisimo 469   tel: 230-9114/239-5576
Excellent regional cooking in a traditional restaurant with fine service. Quite expensive.

El Paraguas   2 Paso de la Ensenanga   tel: 243-1321
A favorite among artists and writers who appreciate good steaks.

Petit Soley   4 Plaza Villa de Madrid   tel: 232-3135
Small restaurant serving both delicious regional and French dishes. Moderate.

Quo Vadis   7 Calle del Carmen   tel: 231-7989
Basic, but delicious, cooking with an emphasis on game and seafood. Moderate.

***Reno   Tuset 27   tel: 277-3821
Elegant and classic restaurant serving both excellent and international cuisine in an intimate dining room. Expensive. Reserve.

Via Veneto   10-12 Calle Ganduxer   tel: 250-3100
Lovely turn-of-the-century décor for a luxury restaurant serving excellent international dishes. Expensive.

Bilbao [48]

Artagón   34 Plaza Virgen de Begoña   tel: 24 41 11/47
Elegant restaurant serving both French and regional specialties. Expensive.

Cáceres [33]

Hostería Nacional del Comendador   6 Calle Ancha   tel: 21 30 12
Elegant medieval palace garden, turned into a classical restaurant with superb regional and international dishes.

Cambrils [15] (Tarragona)

Casa Gatell   Paseo Miramar 26   tel: 36 00 57
Picturesque restaurant serving seafood specialties. Very pleasant. Expensive.

Figueras [12] (Gerona)

Durán   Lasauca 5   tel: 24 18 00
Small inn with modest rooms but excellent cooking.

Ampurdán   near Figueras   tel: 24 13 57
Small hotel with modest rooms but superb restaurant. Quite reasonable.

Madrid [1]

Balthasar   Juan Ramon Jiménez 8   tel: 457-9191
An elegant, deluxe restaurant with a classic menu. Many superb Castilian specialties. Intimate atmosphere. Expensive.

La Barraca   *29-31 Reina*   *tel: 232-7154*
The specialty here is paella, a delicious rice-and-fish dish soaked in saffron.

La Brasserie   *General Oraa 5*   *tel: 276-4897*
Some of the best French cuisine in Madrid. Delicious beef and lobster.

Casa Botin   *Cuchilleros 17*   *tel: 277-1983/266-4217*
Eighteenth-century ambience in a restaurant made famous by Hemingway and the bullfighters who frequented it. Fine local specialties. Enjoyable, if touristy, atmosphere.

Casa Paco   *11 Puerta Cerrada*   *tel: 231-5108*
Charcoal steaks are the specialty here.

***Club 31   *Alcala 58*   *tel: 231-0092*
A modern and very elegant restaurant—popular and lively. Excellent cooking with a vast menu. Very expensive.

El Bodegón   *Paseo de la Castellana 51*   *tel: 410-0006*
Elegant favorite of socialites who go for its rustic decor. Fine international cuisine.

Escuadrón   *Tamayo y Baus 8*   *tel: 419-2830*
Small exclusive restaurant with superb service and impeccable cuisine. Expensive.

****Horcher's*   *6 Alfonso XII*   *tel: 222-073/232-3596*
One of Spain's finest restaurants—small and intimate with a formal atmosphere. Exceptional service and cuisine with superb grills. Both Spanish and French recipes. Excellent game. Very expensive. Reserve well in advance.

***Jockey Club   *Amador de los Rios 6*   *tel: 419-1003/419-2435*
One of the most exclusive and expensive restaurants in Spain, with an international clientèle. Small, with exceptional service and international cuisine. Very fine wine list. Reserve well in advance.

Lanzas (Las)   *Espalter 8-10*   *tel: 230-5079/228-0077*
Near the Prado is a modern and very tasteful restaurant serving excellent seafood, game, and Spanish specialties.

Ostreria (la)   *Alcala 145*   *tel: 226-1780*
Known for its northern Spanish cooking, including Basque dishes. The seafood and paella are great. Lively.

O'Pazo   *Reina Mercedes 6*   *tel: 253-2333*
Antique ambience for a superb restaurant with delicious seafood and beef. Moderate.

O'Xeito   *55 Paseo de la Castellana*   *tel: 257-2200*
Superb fish is served in this small restaurant. Moderate.

Pavillon   *Parque del Retiro*   *tel: 226-1693*
Elegant and expensive, with a fine Continental menu and good selection of wines. Seafood and Spanish dishes are excellent.

Puerta de Moros   *Calle Don Pedro 10*   *tel: 226-2781/265-7777*
Eighteenth-century palace converted into an elegant restaurant. Lots of atmosphere.

Tres Encinas   *Preciados 33*   *tel: 221-2207*
Seafood is the specialty of this small restaurant. Moderate.

Valentin   *San Alberto 3*   *tel: 231-0035/231-5063*
Popular among bullfighters is this masculine place noted for fine Spanish cuisine and lots of it. Informal.

Murcia [21]

Rincón de Pepe   *34 Calle Apostoles/Sancho 1*   *tel: 21 22 49*
Rustic restaurant with excellent regional and international dishes. Expensive.

Oviedo [43]

Casa Fermín   *Avenida del Cristo*   *tel: 21 24 59*
Tripe and fresh fish are the specialties here. Expensive.

San Sebastian [47]

Casa Nicolasa   *Aldamar 4*   *tel: 41 14 76*
An intimate restaurant with Basque cuisine. Squid and fresh crab are its specialties. Lovely red wines. Expensive.

Aiti Mari   *Puerto 23*   *tel: 41 57 26*
Another delightful restaurant with excellent Basque cuisine. Emphasis on seafood. Moderate.

Salduba   *Pescaderia 6*   *tel: 41 88 16*
Similar in many ways to the Aita Mari. Seafood dishes are delicious. Moderate.

Arzac   *Alto de Miracruz 21*   *tel: 35 11 63*
Basque cuisine with an emphasis on fresh fish. Moderate.

Pamplona [8]

Hostal del Rey Noble   *6-8 Paseo de Sarasate*   *tel: 21 17 29*
Elegant restaurant serving fine local and international dishes. Moderate. Reserve.

Josetxo   *Estafeta 73*   *tel: 22 20 97*
Both Spanish and international cuisine. Superb dining in large area. Expensive.

Santander [49]

Del Puerto   *Hernán Cortés 63*   *tel: 27 10 00*
Fish is the dish here. Excellent. Expensive.

Segovia [5]

Mesón de Candido   *5 Plaza Azoguejo*   *tel: 41 30 10*
Wonderful medieval atmosphere and superb regional cooking. Expensive.

Sevilla [30]

Hotel Inglaterra   *Plaza Nueva 11*   *tel: 22 49 70*
Fine dining in the restaurant.

Burladero (Hotel Colón)   *Canalejas 1*   *tel: 22 29 00*
Lots of atmosphere. Gourmet dining in the restaurant.

Tarragona [15]

Sol Ric   Via Augusta 227   tel: 20 32 01
Charming country restaurant just over a mile north of Tarragona. Fine regional cooking in delightful setting, with delicious scallions in the spring. Moderate.

Toledo [2]

Venta del Aire   Circo Romano 19   tel: 22 05 45
Nice restaurant with fresh atmosphere. Game birds in season. Expensive.

Valladolid [36]

Mesón la Fragua   Paseo de Zorrilla   tel: 23 20 08
Superb fish in a fine restaurant noted for regional specialties. Expensive.

Viella [10]

Hosteria Nacional Gaspar de Portola   Viella   tel: 2
Fine food, with both trout and pheasant as specialties in season. Moderate. North of Lérida.

Vitoria [46]

El Portalón   151 Calle Correria   tel: 22 49 89
Fifteenth-century timber building with unique atmosphere. Fine French and regional cooking.

Zaragoza [11]

Savoy   Calle Coso 42   tel: 22 49 16
Elegant restaurant serving excellent international and local dishes. Expensive. Reserve.

SWEDEN

SWEDEN

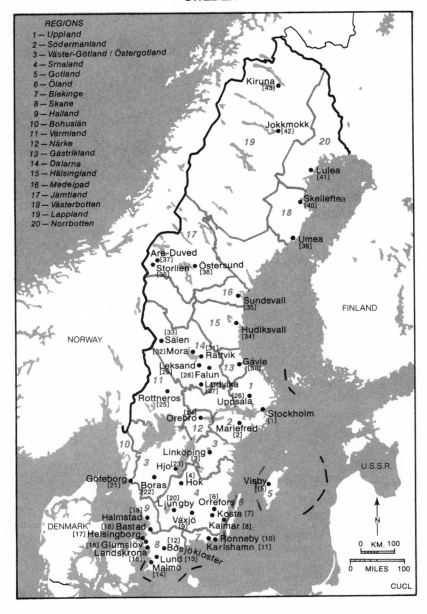

REGIONS
1 — Uppland
2 — Södermanland
3 — Väster-Götland / Östergotland
4 — Smaland
5 — Gotland
6 — Öland
7 — Blekinge
8 — Skane
9 — Halland
10 — Bohuslän
11 — Värmland
12 — Närke
13 — Gästrikland
14 — Dalarna
15 — Hälsingland
16 — Medelpad
17 — Jämtland
18 — Västerbotten
19 — Lappland
20 — Norrbotten

Kiruna [43]

Jokkmokk [42]

19

20

Lulea [41]

Skelleftea [40]

18

Umea [39]

NORWAY

Are-Duved [37]
Storlien [36]
Östersund [38]

17

16
Sundsvall [35]

FINLAND

15

Hudiksvall [34]

[33]
Sälen
[32] Mora
14 [31]
Rättvik
Leksand [29]
[28] Falun
Ludvika [27]
13
Gävle [30]

11
Rottneros [25]

1
[26]
Uppsala

[24]
Örebro
2
Mariefred [2]

12

Stockholm [1]

10

Linköping [3]
3

3

Hjo [23]

Göteborg [21]
Boras [22]

[4]
Hok

4

[20]
Ljungby
Orrefors
[6]
6

Visby [5]

5

U.S.S.R.

[19]
9
Halmstad
Växjö [9]
Kosta [7]
Kalmar [8]

DENMARK
[18] Bastad
[17] Helsingborg
[16] Glumslöv
Landskrona [15]
Lund [13]
Malmö [14]

8
Bösjökloster
Ronneby [10]
Karlshamn [11]

7

N

0   KM. 100

0   MILES   100

CUCL

WHAT TO SEE

Stockholm [1], with its rich cultural season and varied night life, is the main tourist destination for many. Main sights include the Wasa Museum, Royal Palace, and Old Town. Try to take in opera at the Drottningholm Court Theatre. A favorite excursion from mid-May through August is the boat trip on the Göta Canal, running from *Göteborg* [21] to Stockholm. The castles of *Kalmar* [8] and *Helsingborg* [17], the Gripsholm Manor at *Mariefred* [2], the Bosjökloster near *Hoor* [12], the university library in *Uppsala* [26], and the medieval town of *Visby* [5] on Gotland are popular attractions in the south, as are the glassworks in *Orrefors* [6] and *Växjö* [9].

In the central region visit the mine at *Falun* [28], the resorts of *Mora* [32] or *Rättvik* [31] on lovely Lake Siljan, and *Sälen* [33] or *Åre-Duved* [37] (fine ski resorts in the off-season).

The far north is known for Lapps, northern lights, and the midnight sun. *Lulea* [41] is a good place to see the latter from late May to mid-August. In this region you can ski twenty-four hours a day in late May at *Riksgränsen*.

WHAT'S THE WEATHER REALLY LIKE?

Lovely from May through September, the months when all sights are open to the public. In the off-season it's cold and often snowy, but this is the time when Stockholm swings with active night life.

SOME SUGGESTIONS FOR A MORE ENJOYABLE TRIP

Stockholm is packed from June through September; the latter is *the* month for conventions. You can stay with a family if you'll go to the booking office in the central railway station. There's a small charge for this service. It often proves delightful. Food is excellent throughout Sweden with an emphasis on fish dishes. Note that liquor is outrageously expensive. You'll want to bring in a bottle of your favorite booze. Beer is a poor buy, while some wines are quite reasonable. Most travellers to Sweden have their cocktails in their room rather than in a hotel or restaurant bar. In the rural areas you'll find many warm inns. If you prefer, you can camp out or stay in a youth hostel. The latter are open to all age groups and offer substantial savings over normal hotel rates. Camping is allowed anywhere for one night (no fires). You must have the landowner's permission. Distances, as in Norway, are long. You may want to combine air and car travel if you plan to go into the Land of the Midnight Sun (late May to late July). Car travel is particularly pleasant in the south, an area of 100,000 lakes. Ferry travel can be a headache if you don't make reservations well in advance. Do so especially for Finland and Germany. The night ferry to Finland has become famous recently for its swinging nightlife. Note that the alphabet in Sweden ends with three letters not in the English alphabet (two forms of A and one of O, all accented). So, if you're having trouble locating a person or place, perhaps you haven't taken this into account?

WHERE TO STAY

Abisko [43]

Abisko Turiststation   Abisko   tel: 40 000
Large mountain hotel with modest rooms—some with bath. Moderate. Open mid-March to September. East of Narvik (Norway) and southwest of Kiruna.

Are [37]

Tott Hotel Nordenskiölds   Are   tel: 50 270
Small comfortable inn with pleasant rooms—most with bath. Tennis and fishing. Moderate. Closed October to mid-November.

Hotel Grand-Aregarden   Are   tel: 50 265
Large hotel complex with varied rooms—some with bath. Specify whether you'd like a modern or traditional room. Nice park. Tennis. Expensive. Open December through April.

Bäckaskog [14]

Bäckaskog Hotel   Bäckaskog   tel: 53 250
Hotel-restaurant combination suited to visitors taking in the nearby ancient castle. Moderate. Sixty miles north of Malmö.

Boras [22]

Stadehotellet   Osterlanggatan 12   tel: 12 79 50
Small commercial hotel in central location. Attractive modern rooms. Good restaurant. Moderate.

Eskilstuna [1]

Sundbyholms Slott e Kursgard   Eskilstuna   tel: 96 285
Large seventeenth-century villa with comfortable rooms—most with shower. Nice setting. Delicious Swedish dishes and smörgåsbord. Moderate. West of Stockholm.

Falkenberg

Grand Hotel   Falkenberg   tel: 14 450
Small, comfortable hotel with lovely view. Very pleasant. Modest. Moderate.

Falun [28]

Grand Hotel   Falun   tel: 18 700
Large traditional hotel in good location. Very comfortable. Moderate.

Filipstad [24]

Hennickehammars Herrgard   Filipstad   tel: 12 565
Small manor converted into comfortable hotel oriented to family vacations. Tennis, golf, fishing, and hunting. Moderate. Just outside the charming town. Northwest of Örebro.

Gavle [30]

Grand Central Hotel   Nygatan 45   tel: 12 90 60
Very large modern hotel. Tasteful and sophisticated. Good restaurant. Moderate.

Glumslov [16]

Örenäs Slott   Glumslöv   tel: 70 250
Large castle converted into comfortable hotel with cottages available. Traditional atmosphere. Moderate.

Goteborg [21]

Palace Hotel   Södra Hamngatan 2   tel: 17 42 40
Small old-world hotel (once a castle). Traditional flavor. Varied rooms, all comfortable and pleasant. Fine restaurant with delicious Swedish specialties. Moderate.

Granna [3]

Gyllene Yttern   Gränna   tel: 10 800
A gem in the simple class. Small family-oriented resort with lovely cottages. Nice view. Serene. Fine regional cooking. Open May to September. Moderate. Near Västanå castle (open June to August. Southwest of Linköping en route to Jönköping.

Halmstad [19]

Hallandia Hotel   Radhusgatan 4   tel: 11 88 00
Small modern hotel with relaxed atmosphere. In the center of the city. Good restaurant. Expensive.

Helsingborg [17]

Grand Hotel   Stortorget 8-12   tel: 12 01 70
Large hotel in central location. Modest but very pleasant rooms. Traditional flavor. Expensive.

Villa Vingard   Sehlstedtsgatan 1   tel: 11 45 94
Small mansion converted into pleasant traditional hotel in residential area. Nice view. Quite modest. Moderate.

Hjo [23]

Bellevue Hotel   *Hjo*   *tel: 12 000*
Small resort with traditional villas. Comfortable and relaxed. Moderate.

Hok [4]

Hooksherrgård   *Hok*   *tel: 32 10 80*
Quite large and lovely eighteenth-century manor converted into calm and comfortable hotel. On the border of a lake with pool. Surrounded by woods. Smörgasbord. Pool. Sports, including golf, fishing, tennis, and hunting. Twenty miles southeast of Jönköping; about halfway between Stockholm and Malmö. Expensive.

Hudiksvall [34]

Hudiksvalls Stadshotellet   *Storgatan 36*   *tel: 15 060*
Large, picturesque hotel with comfortable rooms. Fishing. Moderate.

Jonkoping [3]

Stora Hotellet   *Hotellplan 1*   *tel: 11 93 00*
Large traditional hotel set on the water. Attractive throughout. Good view. Fine regional cooking. Moderate. Southwest of Linköping.

Käll [38]

Kallgardens Hotel   *Käll*   *tel: 41 084*
Small, charming hotel with lovely view and idyllic setting. Very casual and quite comfortable. Geared to sportsmen, with skiing and fishing. Moderate. Just east of Sollefteå; to east of Östersund.

Kalmar [8]

Stadshotellet   *Stortorget 14*   *tel: 15 180*
Large traditional hotel with modern comforts. Modest yet pleasant. Lovely dining room with fine cuisine. Moderate.

Karlshamn [11]

Stadshotellet   Kyrkogatan 23   tel: 14 260
Small, modern, with traditional flavor. Quite modest. Good regional cooking, with salmon a specialty. Mörrum river close by. Moderate.

Karlstad [24]

Stadshotellet   Kungsgatan 22   tel: 11 52 20
Large traditional hotel with attractive and varied rooms. Quite comfortable. Fine dining. Moderate. West of Örebro on the lake.

Kiruna [43]

Ferrum   Köpmangatan 1   tel: 18 600
Large modern hotel with simple compact rooms. Moderate.

Kungalv [21]

Hotel Fars Hatt   Torget   tel: 10 970
Large modern riverside resort near Göteborg. Comfortable. Geared to the sportsman with pool, fishing, golf, tennis, and riding. Expensive. North of Göteborg.

Landskrona [15]

Hotell Oresund   Kungsgatan 15   tel: 16 315
Small, pleasant hotel with comfortable rooms—half with bath. Nice atmosphere. Expensive.

Lekeryd [22]

Sunds Manor   Lekeryd   tel: 82 006
Attractive manor at Lake Nätarn. Nice setting. Comfortable rooms. Moderate. East of Jönköping to east of Borås.

Linkoping [3]

Frimurarehotellet   S:t. Larsgaten 14   tel: 12 91 80
Large centrally located hotel with varied rooms—some tradi-

tional. Quite comfortable. Good restaurant. Expensive.

Ljungby [20]

Hotel Terraza   Storatorget 1   tel: 13 560
Large hotel in central location. Comfortable, if compact, modern rooms. Fishing nearby for salmon and trout in Lake Bolmen. Moderate.

Ludvika [27]

Star Hotel Elektra   Eriksgatan 6   tel: 18 220
Small modern hotel in central location. Tavern-like atmosphere. Quite comfortable. Moderate.

Luleå [41]

Lulea Stadshotellet   Storgatan 15   tel: 10 410
Large modernized hotel in the land of the midnight sun. Quite comfortable. Sauna. Moderate.

Lund [13]

Grand Hotel   Bamtorget 1   tel: 11 70 10
Large traditional hotel in the city center. Pleasant if modest rooms. Moderate.

Lundia   Knut den Storesgata 2   tel: 12 41 40
Small modern hotel with pleasant rooms. Expensive.

Malmo [14]

Hotel Kramer   Stortorget 7   tel: 70 120
Large château converted into elegant and very comfortable hotel. Quiet and charming throughout. Excellent restaurant. Moderate.

Savoy Hotel   Norra Vallgatan 62   tel: 407-0230
Large old-world hotel with tasteful rooms. Some lovely suites. Famous French restaurant—one of the finest in Sweden. Expensive.

Mariefred [2]

Gripsholms Vårdshus   Mariefred   tel: 10 040
Sweden's most ancient inn near Mariefred. Tiny and pleasant.
Delicious smörgåsbord. Near the castle (open March to October).

Mariestad [24]

Stadshotellet   Nygatan 10   tel: 13 930
Small mansion converted into traditional hotel with comfortable
rooms—most with bath. Moderate. Southwest of Örebro.

Mora [32]

Mora Hotell   Strandgatan 12   tel: 11 750
Small hotel with nice view. Modest but comfortable rooms. Expensive. The Vasa Ski Race ends in Mora.

Morrum

Fiske & Golf Hotel Valhalla   Mörrum   tel: 50 044
Small, modest inn geared to sportsman. Arranges salmon fishing, best in April and May. Moderate.

Örebro [24]

Stora Hotellet   Drottninggatan 1   tel: 12 43 60
Large modern hotel in nice location. Pleasant and very comfortable. Fine dining. Expensive.

Rattvik [31]

Siljansborg   Rättvik   tel: 11 040
Small hotel in nice park setting. Comfortable rooms. Tennis and
skiing. Moderate.

Persborg   Rättvik   tel: 11 030
Small hotel on lovely grounds with fine view. Comfortable.
Good restaurant. Tennis and skiing. Moderate.

Riksgransen [43]

Sporthotell   Riksgränsen   tel: 43 120
Large modern hotel with comfortable rooms. Good restaurant.
Close to ski lifts. Moderate. Open March to early September. On
the Norwegian border. East of Narvik (Norway) to southwest of
Kiruna.

Ronneby [10]

Ronneby Brunn   Ronneby   tel: 12 750
Very large holiday resort with comfortable rooms. Nice scenic
setting. Some villas available. Pool, golf, tennis, riding, and
fishing. Good regional cooking. Nice choice. Moderate.

Salen [33]

Wärdshuset Gammelgarden   Sälen   tel: 21 035
Ancient inn with lots of atmosphere and a fine regional restau-
rant. Modest rooms. Moderate. Open mid-December through
April.

Högfjällshotellet   Sälen   tel: 21 100
Large modern resort with comfortable rooms. Quite informal.
Good restaurant. Moderate. Open late December through April.

Saltsjöbaden [1]

Grand Hotel Saltsjöbaden   Saltsjöbaden   tel: 717-0020
Large, elegant traditional resort with fine view. Comfortable and
nicely furnished. Delicious smörgasbord (especially Sunday
lunch). Golf, tennis, fishing. Expensive. Thirty-minute train ride
to southeast of Stockholm.

Sjöbo [3]

Snogeholms Slott   Sjöbo   tel: 16 080
Comfortable hotel in idyllic setting at Lake Snogeholmssjön.
Dates back to 1868. Moderate. Southwest of Linköping.

Simrishamn [14]

Hotel Kockska Garden   Simrishamn   tel: 11 755
Delightful inn. Pleasant stopover en route to Bornholm. Moderate. On the eastern coast opposite Malmö.

Skara [24]

Stadshotell   5 Järnvägsgatan   tel: 13 000
Small attractive inn with comfortable rooms. Moderate. Southwest of Örebro past Mariestad.

Skokloster [26]

Skokloster Wärdshus   Skokloster   tel: 38 61 00
Lovely white castle in beautiful setting with fine collection of art and arms. Good regional cuisine served in the old stable as well as comfortable rooms in modern hotel on the grounds. Moderate. South of Uppsala.

Skurup [14]

Svaneholms Slottsgästegiveri   Skurup   tel: 40 982
Both an inn and a museum housed in an ancient (sixteenth-century) building. Comfortable. Boating and fishing. Moderate. Southeast of Malmö.

Stockholm [1]

Hotel prices are astronomical here. You can avoid them during the summer by staying with a family. Reservations can be made at the Hotellcentralen in the central railway station. During the off-season you should get discounts from regular prices, but they'll still seem high.

Hotel Foresta   Herserudsvägen 22 (Lidingö)   tel: 765-2700
Very large modern hotel in a country setting fifteen minutes from the center of town. Quiet, comfortable, and serene. Ideal for someone with a car. Best in spring and fall. Pool and golf. Moderate to expensive.

Hotel Reisen   Skeppsbron 12-14   tel: 22 32 60
Large old-world hotel with lovely view of the water. Nice atmosphere. Elegant and comfortable. Excellent restaurant. Expensive.

Storlien [36]

Storliens Högfjällshotell   Storlien   tel: 70 170
Huge, comfortable hotel in lovely setting. Fine restaurant. Geared to the sportsman with skiing, tennis, riding, and fishing. Moderate.

Sundsvall [35]

Hotel Knaust   Storgatan 13   tel: 15 56 10
Large traditional hotel in central location. Elegant, with lots of atmosphere. Very comfortable. Expensive.

Sunne [25]

Länsmansgården   Sunne   tel: 10 301
Delightful old manor converted into attractive hotel only three hundred yards from its own beach on Fryken Lake. Tasteful and comfortable. Known for good regional cooking. Moderate to expensive.

Svarta [24]

Svarta Herrgård   Svarta   tel: 50 003
Tiny eighteenth-century manor converted into pleasant lake-side hotel with comfortable rooms—most with bath. Skiing, fishing, and tennis. Moderate to expensive. Southwest of Örebro.

Tallberg [31]

Hotell Langbersgarden   Tällberg   tel: 50 290
Rustic inn with cabins available. Striking view and setting. Farm flavor. Moderate. South of Rättvik.

Green Hotel   Tällberg   tel: 50 250
Small, charming hotel with lovely view. Good restaurant. Fishing, pool, and tennis. Moderate.

Tanumshede [21]

Tanumshede Gestgifveri   Tanumshede   tel: 20 018
Tiny nine-room inn with comfortable rooms and fine regional restaurant specializing in fresh fish dishes. Expensive. North of Göteborg near the coast.

Umea [39]

Hotell Bla Avenue   Radhusplatsen 14   tel: 13 23 00
Large modern hotel in convenient location. Good regional restaurant. Moderate.

Vadstena [3]

Broby Estate   Vadstena
Lovely estate with nicely furnished rooms and idyllic setting in farm country. Pool and golf nearby. Rooms let by the week only. Expensive. Contact Inter Holiday, Lilla Kungsgatan 1, S-411 08 Göteborg, Sweden. West of Linköping.

Vadstena Klosters Gästhem   Torggatan   tel: 11 530
Small convent in lovely location. Converted into delightful and comfortable inn. Fresh and friendly. Expensive. Closed in last two weeks of December.

Wärdshuset Kungs Starby   Vadstena   tel: 11 420
Tiny ancient inn with pleasant, if modest, rooms. Tasty smörgasbord at noon. Moderate.

Vagnhärad [1]

Tullgarns Värdshus   Vagnhärad   tel: 72 026
Attractive inn near the Tullgarn Castle (fine art collection). Pleasant and comfortable rooms. Moderate. Southwest of Stockholm near the coast.

Visby [5]

Visby Hotel   Strandgatan 6   tel: 11 925
Comfortable with traditional atmosphere. Pleasant and simple. Charming dining. Expensive.

Tofta Strandpensionat   Visby   tel: 65 009
Small modest inn eleven miles south of town. Arranges fishing.
Open May through September. Moderate.

Vittaryd [20]

Toftaholms Herrgårdspensionat   Vittaryd   tel: 44 032
Manor house dating back to 1870 with comfortable rooms. Moderate. North of Ljungby.

WHERE TO EAT

Bosjökloster [12] (Hoor)

Bosjökloster Castle   Bosjökloster   tel: 25 048
Fascinating castle with its own restaurant. Lovely location and view. Moderate. Open April to October from 10 a.m.-5:30 p.m.

Göteborg [21]

Henriksberg   Stigbergsliden 7   tel: 12 48 75
Elegant hilltop restaurant with superb seafood and excellent international cuisine. Very popular. Expensive.

Gamle Port   O. Larmgatan 18   tel: 11 80 27
Lively and intimate with fine continental cuisine. Moderate.

Victoria   Viktoriagatan 3   tel: 11 91 70
A favorite with artists. Pleasant atmosphere. Good regional cooking. Moderate.

Halmstad [19]

Norre Kavaljeren   Storgatan 36   tel: 11 11 69
Good regional restaurant with varied and fine cooking. Moderate.

Katrineholm [24]

Stora Djulö   Katrineholm   tel: 10 002
Lovely manor house dating back to early fourteenth-century.

Meals must be booked in advance. Expensive. Southeast of Örebro.

Lövestad [13]

Christinehof's Castle   Lövestad   tel: 26 104
Lovely restaurant in a pink building dating back to 1740 and surrounded by idyllic park and wandering sheep. Moderate. Open May through August only. East of Lund.

Malmö [14]

Kochska Krogen   Frans Suellsgatan 3   tel: 70 320
Cozy cellar restaurant with fine atmosphere and very good international cuisine. Moderate to expensive.

Kronprinsen   Mariedalsvagan 32   tel: 77 240
Varied menu with both French and Swedish dishes. Entertainment. Expensive.

Norrköping [3]

Löfstad Slott   Norrköping   tel: 35 000
Dating back to 1750, this castle houses an interesting museum and has a cafeteria in the smithy and meals at the Restaurant Slottsgården. Moderate. Open mid-May through September. Ten miles west of Norrköping. Northeast of Linköping.

Nyköping [1]

Tovastugans Vårdshus   Nyköping   tel: 17 191
Seventeenth-century manor with its own restaurant near the Nyköpingshus, castle-like building dating back to Middle Ages. Moderate. Open year round. Southwest of Stockholm on the coast.

Skanör [14]

Skanörs Gästgifvaregard   Mellangatan 13   tel: 47 02 20
Mansion converted into very pleasant restaurant, at its best from May through September. Moderate to expensive. A gem. South of Malmö on the coast in "Village of Geese."

Stockholm [1]

Aurora   Munkbron 11   tel: 21 93 59
Charming cellar restaurant with international cuisine and delicious Swedish dishes. Very popular. Expensive.

Berns Salonger   Näckströmsgatan 8   tel: 22 06 00
Both fine French and Swedish cuisine. Gambling as well. Expensive.

Djurgardsbrunns Wärdshus   Djurgardsbrunnsvagen 68   tel: 67 90 95
Old inn serving fine French cuisine. Lots of atmosphere. Best in warm weather. Expensive.

Fem Sma Hus   Nygränd 10   tel: 10 87 75
Five small houses converted into delightful restaurant with fine international cuisine and excellent fish dishes. Very popular. Moderate.

Källaren Diana   Brunnsgatan 2   tel: 10 73 10
Seventeenth-century wine cellar. Moderate.

***Operakällaren   Gustav Adolfs Torg   tel: 11 11 25
The most famous restaurant in the capital and possibly Sweden's best. View of harbor and Royal Palace from its lovely location in the opera house. Elegant nineteenth-century oak-paneled room. Very formal. Gourmet dishes. Superb service. Excellent wine list. Delicious smörgasbord at lunch. Very expensive and worth it.

Ostermalmskällaren   Storgatan 3   tel: 67 74 21
Pleasant restaurant well-known for fine fish dishes. Moderate to expensive.

Hotel Reisen   Skeppsbron 12-14   tel: 22 32 60
Excellent hotel restaurant with delightful Swedish and continental cuisine. Superb fish dishes. Excellent wines. Expensive.

Riche   Birger Jarlsgaten 5   tel: 10 70 22
Elegant dining with an accent on French cuisine. Well known and very fine. Expensive.

Solliden   Djurgarden   tel: 60 10 55
Fine restaurant in Skansen Park. Pleasant stop after or before a visit to the open-air museum. Best in warm weather from May to mid-September. Moderate.

Ulriksdals Wårdshus   Pa Solna   tel: 85 08 15
A seventeenth-century building converted into an attractive res-
taurant. Fun wine cellar atmosphere. Delicious smörgasbord.
Moderate.

Victoria   Kungstädgarden   tel: 10 10 85
Very fine international dishes in this well-known gathering spot
for the "in" set. Expensive.

Wårdshuset Stallmästaregarden   Haga Park   tel: 33 79 15
Seventeenth-century inn with garden atmosphere and fine charcoal grill. Superb smörgasbord at noon. Lots of atmosphere.
Dress up at night. Expensive. Outside of town near the air ter-
minal at Haga Park.

Västerås [1]

Tidö Vårdshus   Vàsteràs   tel: 53 043
Delightful inn (once gardener's cottage) next to main estate dating from seventeenth century. Pleasant restaurant open May to
September. Moderate. Closed Mondays. On lake Màlaren seven
miles from town. Northwest of Stockholm.

Engsö Castle   Vàsteràs   tel: 44 012
Simple cafeteria in interesting old castle, open Sundays only
(noon to 6:00 p.m.) May to September. Inexpensive.

SWITZERLAND

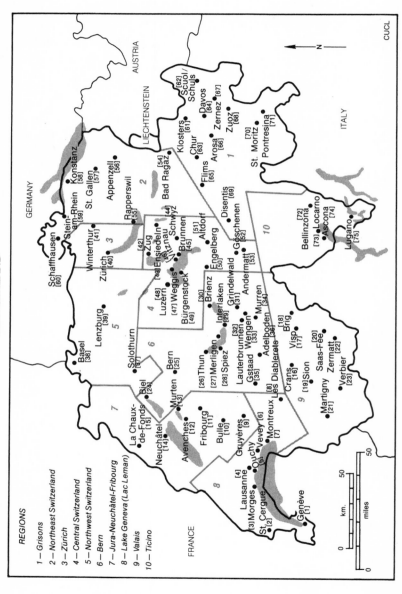

SWITZERLAND

REGIONS

1 – Grisons
2 – Northeast Switzerland
3 – Zürich
4 – Central Switzerland
5 – Northwest Switzerland
6 – Bern
7 – Jura-Neuchâtel-Fribourg
8 – Lake Geneva (Lac Leman)
9 – Valais
10 – Ticino

GERMANY
AUSTRIA
LIECHTENSTEIN
ITALY
FRANCE

Schaffhausen [60]
Stein-am-Rhein [59]
Konstanz [58]
St. Gallen [57]
Appenzell [56]
Rapperswil [55]
Bad Ragaz [54]
Klosters [61]
Scuol/Schuls [62]
Davos [64]
Chur [63]
Arosa [66]
Zernez [67]
Zuoz [68]
St. Moritz [70]
Pontresina [71]
Flims [65]
Disentis [69]

Winterthur [41]
Zürich [40]
Zug [42]
Schwyz [44]
Einsiedeln [43]
Vitznau [46]
Brunnen [45]
Altdorf
Engelberg [50]
Göschenen [52]
Andermatt [53]
Bellinzona [72]
Locarno [74]
Ascona [73]
Lugano [75]

Basel [38]
Lenzburg [39]
Solothurn [37]
Luzern [48]
Weggis [47]
Bürgenstock [49]
Brienz
Interlaken [29]
Grindelwald [31]
Murren [34]
Brig [18]
Visp [177]

Biel [24]
Bern [25]
Thun [26]
Merligen [27]
Spiez [28]
Lauterbrunnen [32]
Wengen [33]
Gstaad [35]
Adelboden [36]
Les Diablerets [8]
Crans [16]
Sion [19]
Saas-Fée [20]
Zermatt [22]
Verbier [23]
Martigny [21]

Murten [13]
La Chaux-de-Fonds [15]
Neuchâtel [14]
Avenches [12]
Fribourg [11]
Bulle [10]
Gruyères [9]
Montreux [7]
Vevey [6]
Ouchy [5]

Lausanne [4]
Morges [3]
St. Cergue [2]
Genève [1]

km. 0 50 50
miles 0

N

CUCL

WHAT TO SEE

Considered by many to be the most scenic country in Europe, Switzerland is equally famous for magnificent ski areas, unique shops, delightful country inns, and elegant resorts, not to mention some of the finest restaurants in Europe.

Geneva [1] (Genève) is one of the main gateways into this scenic land and boasts an idyllic lake-side setting, fine hotels, excellent shops, and gourmet restaurants. You'll find *free* pamphlets describing the city's sights in most hotels. Plan to spend two days here, at least. Recommended excursions include *Montreux* [7] and the nearby Château de Chillon, *St. Cergue* [2] for its view, and *Morges* [3] in the fall during regional wine festivals. All travellers will find *Gruyères* [9] worth a special detour. Many will be delighted with the old sections of *Fribourg* [11] and *Neuchâtel* [14]. And a few people will want to take in the Roman ruins at *Avenches* [12]. To the south, the *Matterhorn* dominates Valais, world-famous for its ski resorts, including *Zermatt* [22], *Saas-Fee* [20], *Verbier* [23], and *Crans* [16]. In central Switzerland, you'll find *Bern*'s [25] a delightful town with arcaded streets for rainproof shopping, a fine collection of Klees in the art museum, and authentic wine taverns for evening relaxation. *Gstaad* [35] and *Interlaken* [29] need little introduction since both are showplaces. The falls at *Lauterbrunnen* [32] are quite dramatic, but the major attraction remains the fabulous mountain *Jungfrau* (give yourself a full day to take it in).

In the north, you might be interested in the spa of *Baden*, the medieval section of *Basel* [38], along with the many works of Holbein in the city's museums, and the castles near *Lenzburg* [39]. The city of *Zürich* [40] is the second main gateway into Switzerland and is crowded much of the year. Try to make an excursion to medieval *Regensberg*. Stay in charming *Gottlieben* or *Stein-am-Rhein* [59] for atmosphere. Take in the falls of *Schaffhausen* [60] and the view from *Säntis*. And travel through *Appenzell* [56] for a glimpse of rural Switzerland at its best.

Head south into a region famous for its lakes. It's very popular in July and August. This is the region around *Luzern* [48] (its Swiss Transport Museum is the best of its kind in Europe). The view from *Pilatus* is outstanding. In Grisons, the land of 150 valleys, you'll find famous ski resorts: *Davos* [64], *St. Moritz* [70], *Klosters* [61], *Arosa* [66], and *Flims* [65]. You may want to visit the National Park at *Zernez* [67] if you come to this region in the summer. In the *Samnaun Valley* you can shop duty-free. A recommended drive: Chur-Landquart-Davos-Lenzerheide-*Chur* [63]. And a delightful, authentic village: *Zuoz* [68].

Far south, you'll find surprisingly mild weather, which explains the profusion of subtropical flowers in the poetic region of Ticino. It's known for its peaceful lakes as well. Sightseers will enjoy an excursion to the Villa Favorita near *Lugano* [75] (open weekends only from mid-March to mid-November) and a quick stop at the Madonna del Sasso in *Locarno* [73].

WHAT'S THE WEATHER REALLY LIKE?

The two main seasons in Switzerland are winter and summer. Skiing is excellent from December through April in most ski resorts. The summer in the lively lake resorts is warm, sunny—and packed. For those who prefer a more sedate and less hectic vacation, late April, May, late September, and early October are attractive and warm months to visit the resorts, which are often closed in early spring and late fall. Naturally, the wine districts are most colorful and lively in the fall, a time when you're expected to sample the new wine (and keep the glasses as well—a Swiss tradition in many wine festivals). But come prepared with a warm coat and rain gear for occasional wet spells and chills. Note that Ticino has particularly mild weather in early spring and late fall and is a favorite *off-season* destination.

SOME SUGGESTIONS FOR A MORE ENJOYABLE TRIP

The best way to appreciate Switzerland is by car. Although trains combined wtih Swiss Postal Buses can get you almost anywhere, you'll appreciate the freedom a car offers, because it allows you to get off the beaten path to take in the magnificent scenery for which this country is justly famous. Furthermore, many of the country inns and romantic hotels oozing history are only accessible by car. These are much less expensive than hotels in the major cities and in many cases more enjoyable. Costs are high in Switzerland, and you may have to give up such amenities as a private bath or toilet to keep your travel expenses down. Major cities and resorts are packed from late May to early September. Be sure to make reservations far in advance. This is also true in Swiss ski resorts during annual vacations of Christmas and Easter. If you can travel in the off-months of spring and fall, you'll find lower price and less hassle getting rooms. Switzerland is a multilingual country, and many people speak English, so communication is quite easy *in general*. Roads are excellent, but be sure to check ahead for information on passes if you travel in the winter (you must have chains if you plan to travel in mountains at this time). Skiers: you can get up-to-date snow reports in the United States by calling (212) 757-6336 from December 15 to March 15.

WHERE TO STAY

Adelboden [28]

Hotel Nevada and Tavern   Adelboden   tel: 73 21 31
A combination of an elegant hotel and authentic tavern first opened in 1628. The tavern has fine food. The hotel offers comfortable lodging, an orchestra, pool, tennis, and skiing just outside the door. Expensive. South of Spiez on highway 72/73.

Amsteg [48]

Hostellerie Stern und Post   Amsteg   tel: (044) 64 190
Delightful roadside inn southeast of Lucerne, known for a good restaurant with fresh trout and high quality beef. Moderate.

Andeer [63]

Hôtel Fravi   Andeer   tel: 61 11 51
This is a spa with a history dating back to the early 1800s. Long a favorite of kings and queens. Simple. Moderate. Twenty-four miles south of Chur.

Ascona [73]

Castello del Sole   Ascona   tel: 35 11 65
An eighteenth-century house typical of the region. Large park

on private beach. Fifty comfortable rooms. Pool. Tennis. Very expensive. Near Locarno.

Casa Tamaro   Ascona   tel: (093) 35 39 39
A patrician house on the Piazza. Elegant and stylish. Courtyard and vaulted ceilings. Charming atmosphere. Excellent cuisine. Tennis. Expensive.

Astano [75]

Albergo della Posta   Astano   tel: 73 18 81
Seven miles west of Lugano you'll discover an old patrician house combining regional atmosphere with reasonably comfortable rooms. Subtropical plants in the courtyard. Arcades covered with vines. Pool. Moderate to expensive.

Bad Ragaz [54]

Schloss Ragaz   Bad Ragaz   tel: (085) 92 355
Castle-hotel in park with pool. Forty-eight rooms with bath. Moderate to expensive.

Basel [38]

Ascot Hotel   Bachtelenweg 3   tel: 67 39 51
Near Basel in village of Riehen. Small, comfortable inn with antiques. Rooms with bath. Expensive.

Drei Könige Hotel   Blumenrain 8-10   tel: 25 52 52
One of Europe's finest historic inns. It's Switzerland's oldest, dating back to 1026. With an ideal riverside location, it exudes atmosphere and charm. The Three Kings hotel matches the fame of its guests (including Napoleon) with fine food and service. A luxury hotel. Worth a detour, if just to sit on the terrace. Ultraexpensive.

Bellelay [24]

Hôtel de l'Ours   Bellelay   tel: (032) 91 91 04
Medieval hostelry with eight rooms—four with shower. Good restaurant. Riding. Moderate. Closed November. Northwest of Biel.

Bernina-Suot [71]

Bernina Haus   Bernina   tel: (082) 66 405
Twenty-two modest rooms in a building dating back to 1515 and
located near the Bernina Pass. It has a dormitory too. Intricately
carved wood in the dining room. Not for the stuffy. Known for
summer skiing. Moderate. Closed May, October, and November.
Southeast of Pontresina.

Bex [7]

St. Christophe   Bex   tel: (025) 36 777
Fifteen rooms in eighteenth-century inn. Comfortable. Good
grills. Moderate. Southeast of Montreux off highway E2.

Bottighofen [58]

Schlössli Bottighofen   Bottighofen   tel: (072) 82 048
A bishop's summer residence converted into modest hotel with
only seven rooms (without baths). Park. Fishing. Good restaurant. Moderate. Suburb of Kreuzlingen near Konstanz.

Brienz [30]

Hôtel Kreuz   Lake Brienz   tel: 57 17 81
A country inn dating back to the seventeenth century. Visited by
Byron and Goethe. Rustic rooms at reasonable prices in a garden
atmosphere. The inn prides itself in preparing superb fish dishes.

Brigels [65]

Casa Fausta Capaul   Brigels   tel: (086) 41 358
Delightful mountain village. Ten modest rooms in a seven-
teenth-century building. Fishing and skiing. Moderate. Between
Flims and Disentis.

Brunnen [45]

Parkhotel   Brunnen   tel: 31 16 81
A large inn built into the walls of a fortress dating back to the
thirteenth century. Park. Spa. Tennis. Expensive.

Seehotel Waldstätterhof   Brunnen   tel: (043) 33 11 33
A quiet lakeside hotel with over one hundred rooms—a few
apartments with period furnishings. Lovely view. Pool. Tennis.
Very expensive.

Weisses Rössli   Brunnen   tel: (043) 31 10 22
Historic inn with thirty comfortable rooms—some with bath. On
the village square. Boat trips arranged. Moderate.

Burgdorf [37]

Stadthaus Burgdorf   Burgdorf   tel: (034) 22 35 55
Twenty-four comfortable rooms with bath in eighteenth-century
building. Pool, fishing, riding. Moderate. Southeast of Solothurn.

Château d'Oex [35]

Chalet du Bon Accueil   Château d'Oex   tel: 46 320
Near Gstaad. A lovely inn with a history going back to the mid-
dle of the eighteenth century. Old world flavor. Quiet location.
Thirty comfortable beds.

Chur [63]

Hôtel Stern   Reichgasse 11   tel: (081) 22 35 55
Dating back to 1677 this small hotel offers comfortable, small
rooms, all recently remodeled and panelled with plain wood. On
the top floor are several cozy rooms with their own balcony. The
restaurant, a favorite of local politicians (who have their own table) and artists. By all means try the *probierbrettli*—a delightful
way to sample local wines. Moderate.

Churwalden [63]

Posthotel   Churwalden   tel: 35 11 09
Five miles south of Chur on way to Lenzerheide. Thirty rooms
in sixteenth-century patrician home. Rich decorations and carvings. Corridors are vaulted to the third floor. Modern facilities.
Comfortable. Simple. Moderate.

Corseray [11]

Relais du Vieux Moulin   Corseray   tel: (037) 30 14 44
Millhouse (1840) converted into pleasant hotel with fifteen rooms. Moderate. West of Fribourg off highway 79.

Cully [4]

Auberge du Raisin   Cully   tel: 99 21 31
Tiny, superb inn that is just a short drive from Lausanne. Ideal for vineyard vacations in the fall. Delightful. Moderately expensive.

Davos [64]

Derby   Davos   tel: 61 116
Modern, comfortable, and quiet. Well-appointed for serious skiers. Moderate to expensive.

Escholzmatt [25]

Hotel Löwen   Escholzmatt   tel: (041) 77 12 06
Seventeen rooms in an inn dating from late sixteenth century. Offbeat skiing in winter. Special folkloric events arranged on demand. Moderate. Between Berne and Lucerne.

Fribourg [11]

Hôtel Duc Bertold   112 rue des Bouchers   tel: (037) 23 47 33
A nineteenth-century mansion near the church. Forty comfortable rooms. Good view of the Old Town. Fine regional restaurant. Moderately expensive. Closed mid-January through February.

Hôtel de la Rose   Place Notre Dame 179   tel: (037) 22 06 67
Seventeenth-century mansion near the church. Eighty rooms—some with period furnishings. Good French cuisine. Moderately expensive.

Geneva [1] (Genève)

Hôtel d'Alleves   Passage Kléber 13   tel: 32 15 30
A gem. A private château converted into a charming hotel.
Lovely rooms with period pieces and modern comforts, including bath. A few with balcony. Outstanding restaurant—try the
steak béarnaise. Expensive, but worth every penny.

Arbalète   3 Tour Maitresse   tel: 28 41 55
Modern, small, deluxe. Very comfortable, with a restaurant
specializing in local dishes. Expensive.

Hôtel Le Chandelier   23 Grand'Rue   tel: 21 56 88
The only hotel in the Old Town with nice view to lake and
mountains. Some rooms with kitchenettes. Cozy. Moderate.

Hôtel Le Clos Voltaire   rue de Lyon 45b   tel: 44 70 14
Voltaire's old home. Unique, charming, and quiet. In a park only
ten minutes from the city center. Functional rooms on the modest side. Moderate.

Hôtel Excelsior   34 rue Jean-Jacques Rousseau   tel: 32 09 45
Good central location for this comfortable and calm hotel. Rooms
with bath. Friendly. Expensive.

Hôtel St. Gervais Garni   20 rue des Corps Saints   tel: 32 45 72
A "Swiss chalet" with historic atmosphere. Very simple, but
comfortable. Toilets down the hall. Not for the stuffy. Moderate.

Hôtel Grand Pré   35 Rue du Grand Pré   tel: 33 91 50
Although the hotel has no restaurant and is in an offbeat location, it's highly recommended for its attractive, comfortable
rooms, really a great value at the moment. Moderate.

Hôtel du Jet d'Eau   15 rue du Simplon   tel: 36 25 60
Very modest, but relaxed and pleasant. A good budget choice.

Hôtel La Réserve   301 Route de Lausanne   tel: 74 17 41
A deluxe resort hotel outside of town in a garden setting by the
lake. The estate is quiet and secluded offering swimming, boating, and tennis to its guests. Fine cuisine. An absolute must in
the spring when the gardens are in bloom. Expensive.

Hôtel La Résidence   11 route de Florissant   tel: 46 18 33
Located in a quiet residential area with a garden atmosphere.
About ten minutes from city center. Large, turn-of-the-century

hotel with pool, tennis, view, and quite good French cuisine. Spacious and comfortable rooms. Geared to families and to people staying for some time in the city. Expensive.

Hôtel de Strasbourg et Univers   *10 rue Pradier*   *tel: 31 29 20*
An old-fashioned place with quite comfortable rooms. Cozy dining area. Moderate.

Hôtel Touring-Balance   *13 Place Longemalle*   *tel: 28 71 22*
Good location in city center near shopping. Old-fashioned but comfortable. Attractive dining. Moderate to expensive.

Hôtel de Vincennes   *18 rue Muzy*   *tel: 35 31 45*
Alpine flavor in this haven with a great view. Some rooms with kitchenettes. Moderate.

Gerzensee [25]

Hôtel Restaurant Goldenes Kreuz (Croix d'Or)   *Gerzensee*   *tel: 92 88 36*
Fifteen miles southeast of Bern you'll discover this tiny country inn, which was reconstructed in 1963 after a fire destroyed the original building dating back to the Middle Ages. Great Alpine view and good food. Wonderful setting and extremely comfortable. Only a dozen rooms. Expensive.

Glion [7]

Hôtel Victoria   *Glion*   *tel: (021) 62 51 21*
Lovely and calm hotel northeast of Montreux. Forty rooms, all comfortable. Pool and tennis. Expensive.

Gottlieben [58]

Hotel Drachenburg   *Lake Constance*   *tel: 96 203*
A thirteenth-century inn with superb furnishings. This fantastic hotel is built within inches of the Rhine. Picturesque. Great value. Only four miles west of Kreuzlingen. Worth a detour.

Hotel Krone   *Lake Constance*   *tel: 96 130*
Small, peaceful hotel in a town that will appeal to poets and those seeking quiet retreats. Overlooks an estuary, a tiny arm from Lake Konstanz. Comfortable rooms—most are modern, but a few up front are filled with antiques and atmosphere. The di-

ning is sensational, a gourmet's delight. Expensive, worth every franc.

Grindelwald [31]

Grand Hôtel Regina   Grindelwald   tel: 54 54 55
A large white resort hotel dating back to the nineteenth century. Wonderful view of the mountains. Comfortable rooms—ask for one with southern exposure. Pool. Tennis. Very expensive.

Grüsch [63]

Hôtel Krone   Grüsch   tel: (081) 51 11 16
A modest little place dating back to 1676 with ornate decorations and vaulted passageways. Good jumping off point for long distance skiing. Moderate. North of Chur off highway E61.

Gruyères [9]

Hostellerie St. Georges   Gruyères   tel: 62 246
Seventeenth-century rustic inn with a delightful terrace. Comfortable rooms. The back of the hotel has view to Gstaad ski territory. Room number 1 may be the best. The inn is known for its superb regional cooking. Worth the detour.

Fleur-de-Lys   Gruyères   tel: (029) 62 108
Six modest rooms in rustic retreat (1653) noted for its fun regional restaurant in the medieval town. Closed February. Moderate.

Hagenwil [41]

Schloss Hagenwil   Hagenwil   tel: (071) 67 19 13
Thirteenth-century moated castle in the country with quite good restaurant and only three rooms. Comfortable. Moderate. A nice excursion from Winterthur.

Interlaken [29]

Hôtel du Lac   Hoheweg 225   tel: 22 29 22
Fine tourist hotel dating back to the late nineteenth century. Not at all fancy, but pleasant. Moderately expensive.

Gasthaus zum Hirschen   *Matten-Interlaken*   *tel: 22 15 45*
An eighteenth-century inn known for its fine food. Simple accommodations. Great value.

Kleine Scheidegg [31]

Scheidegg-Hotels   Kleine Scheidegg   tel: 55 12 12
Isolated nineteenth-century inn, which can only be reached by a mountain railroad from either Lauterbrunnen or Grindelwald. Simple, rustic living in tranquil surroundings. Reasonable.

Klosters [61]

Chesa Grischuna Hotel & Restaurant   Klosters   tel: 42 222
A rustic charmer with comfortable rooms and wonderful regional cooking. Not for the stuffy, but still very tasteful. Antiques abound. Expensive.

Grand Hotel Vereina   Klosters   tel: 41 161
Fine large hotel with attractive rooms. Pool. Tennis. Expensive. Great location.

Silvretta   Klosters   tel: 41 353
Large, cultivated, tasteful. Lots of color and local atmosphere. Wonderful. Lively. Expensive.

Kussnacht [48]

Hotel Engel   Küssnacht   tel: 81 10 57
Only twenty rooms in this fifteenth-century palace. Exquisite façade and wood-carved interior. It's been in the same family for four centuries. Moderate. The inn is nine miles east of Luzern.

Küsnacht [40]

Ermitage au Lac   Küsnacht   tel: (01) 90 44 41
Thirty comfortable rooms in an ancient inn only ten miles from Zürich airport. Good restaurant specializing in lamb. Lake swimming and sailing. Moderate to expensive. Closed December to February.

Hotel Hirschen   Küssnacht   tel: (041) 81 10 27
A family-owned inn near the church with lovely painted façade.

Dates back to 1640, but rooms are modern and comfortable—most with bath. Nice woodsy location. Pool, tennis, riding. Good regional restaurant and pastry shop. Moderate to expensive.

La Cibourg [15]

La Balance   Cibourg   tel: (039) 22 58 47
Nineteenth-century changing post. Five rooms with shower. Good grills and seafood in restaurant. Riding and skiing. Inexpensive.

La Neuveville [24]

Hôtel Jean-Jacques Rousseau   La Neuveville   tel: 51 36 51
Charming country inn with an all-in-the-family atmosphere. Only seventeen simple rooms. Delightful lakefront location in one of Switzerland's most picturesque towns. Ten miles west of Biel (Bienne).

Langnau [25]

Hotel Hirschen   Langnau   tel: 21. 517
Twenty miles east of Bern on the way to Luzern. A wine tavern in the fifteenth century. Simple inn with eighteen rooms. Moderate.

Lausanne [4]

Hôtel Château d'Ouchy   Lausanne-Ouchy   tel: 26 74 51
A twelfth-century castle-hotel with antiques. Superb eight-hundred-year-old Hall of the Knights. Lovely lakeside location. Simple, tasteful rooms. Fine restaurant. Moderate to expensive.

Hôtel La Résidence   15 Place du Général Guisan   tel: 27 77 11
A renovated mansion in an ideal location. Antiques blend with modern touches for comfort. Calm, compact rooms—very nice. Moderate.

Locarno [73]

Schlosshotel   Locarno   tel: (093) 31 23 61
Comfortable hotel with thirty-five rooms—most with bath. Gar-

den. No restaurant. Moderately expensive. Near Visconti Castle.

Lucelle [38]

Auberge de Lucelle   Lucelle   tel: (066) 72 24 52
Seventeenth-century inn near the abbey on the lake. Twenty rooms with bath. Riding (trekking). Moderate. Only six miles from Delémont to the southwest of Basel.

Lugano [75]

Hotel Patio   via Motta 7A   tel: (091) 23 032
Charming inn (1552) with lovely courtyard. Twenty-four rooms with bath. Italian cuisine. Expensive.

Luzern [48]

Hôtel Château Gutsch   Kanonenstrasse   tel: 23 38 83
A magnificent small inn built on the foundations of a thirteenth-century fortress. It overlooks the city and is accessible by cable car. The blend of antique furnishings and modern facilities makes this a prize. Romantic couples should ask for the honeymoon suite. The terrace and view are magnificent. Candlelit dining in the charming dining room. Exclusive, but great value. Make reservations long in advance. Expensive.

Hotel Wilden Mann   Bahnhofstrasse 30   tel: (041) 23 16 66
In the heart of the historic town only five hundred yards from the lake. Comfortable rooms throughout. Number 91, with its terrace and quiet location high up in the hotel, is a favorite. Popular French and Swiss restaurants—the latter better value. Free use of Château-Gütsch pool and lift. Delightful cocktail bar on first floor. Moderate to expensive.

Magliaso [75]

Villa Magliasina   Magliaso   tel: 71 34 71
Comfortable rooms overlooking golf course. Pool and gardens. Family flavor. Very expensive. Closed December to February. West of Lugano.

Maienfeld [63]

Landgasthof Falknis   Maienfeld   tel: 91 818
Fifteen miles north of Chur. Twenty beds in a historic inn geared
to riders. Special riding weeks available. Comfortable. Moderate.

Malans [63]

Landgasthof Krone   Malans   tel: (081) 51 14 55
Centuries-old inn with six rooms (two with shower). Modest.
Fun restaurant specializing in game and fresh produce. Own
wine press. Unique excursion to Fada in spring to see daffodils
in bloom. Moderate. North of Chur off E61.

Matten-Interlaken

Gasthof Hirschen   Matten-Interlaken   tel: (036) 22 15 45
A 1666 farmhouse with twenty-five rooms (none with bath). Fine
regional specialties. Pool and tennis. Moderately expensive.
Closed mid-October through November.

Melide [75]

Hotel La Romantica   Melide   tel: 68 75 21
Just south of Lugano is a residence built for the kings of Savoy
in the eighteenth century. Subtropical gardens bordering quiet
beach. Ten delightful, reasonably priced rooms. Atmospheric
restaurant. Of interest in town is a "Switzerland in Miniature"
exhibition. Just south of Lugano.

Merlischachen [48]

Swiss Chalet   Merlischachen   tel: (041) 37 12 47
Centuries-old country inn with twenty comfortable rooms—six
with bath. Good steaks in restaurant. Moderate to expensive.
Closed January. Short excursion from Luzern.

Meyriez-Murten [13]

Le Vieux Manoir   Meyriez-Murten   tel: 71 12 83
Exquisite design and furnishings. Gorgeous park and beach on
Lake Murten. The nearby town is considered one of the most au-

thentic in Switzerland. Comfortable rooms (ask for room 11 or 24). Fine dining in both French and Swiss tradition. Expensive. Worth a detour. Sixteen miles west of Bern. Closed January and February.

Montreux [7]

Hôtel Excelsior   21 Rue Bon Port   tel: 61 33 05
Attractive, reasonably priced hotel with a reputation as a good place to eat.

Nyon

Hôtel du Clos de Sadex   route de Lausanne   tel: 61 28 31
Elegant lakeside home converted into comfortable hotel. Lovely view. Good regional restaurant. Very relaxing. Expensive to very expensive. North of Geneva.

Oberaach [57]

Zum Goldenen Löwen   Oberaach   tel: 69 11 22
Northwest of St. Gallen. A charming inn in a historic setting. Fine restaurant. Moderate.

Le Pas-de-L'Echelle [1]

Hôtel Restaurant P. Pittet   Le Pas-de-L'Echelle (France)   tel: 38 81 22
Very small, modest hotel twenty minutes by bus from Geneva to France. Good for those who'd prefer to be outside the capital. Clean and comfortable. Delicious cooking with such dishes as *escargots* and fresh fish. Inexpensive to moderate. Closed September.

Pontresina [71]

Hotel Weisses Kreuz   Pontresina   tel: 66 306
An inn since 1850—the oldest in this skiing village. Roentgen, who stayed here, is quoted as saying, "Four weeks of Pontresina prolonged my life by one year." The inn offers more atmosphere than comfort. Moderately expensive.

Schlosshotel   Pontresina   tel: 66 451
Large, distinguished hotel in quiet setting. Elegant and tasteful throughout, with many antiques. Wonderful view. Fine cuisine. Pool. Tennis. Riding. Fine for families. Closed late spring and late fall. Very expensive.

Poschiavo [71]

Albrici & Posta   Poschiavo   tel: (082) 50 173
Twelve rooms without bath in seventeenth-century mansion. Antiques and paintings. Tennis. Moderate. South of Pontresina off highway 29.

Rapperswil [55]

Hotel Schwanen   Rapperswil   tel: 27 77 77
A small inn built on what was once a monastery. Next to a thirteenth-century castle. Lots of atmosphere. Reasonable rates. Good value.

Regensberg [40]

Rote Rose Regensberg   Regensberg   tel: 94 10 13
Two small apartments in an inn featuring original watercolors of roses by Lotte Günthart. Medieval banquet room. Lots of antiques. Wonderful rural setting in a picturesque village. Fantastic. Expensive.

Reichenbach 1/Kandertal [28]

Gasthof Bären   Reichenbach   tel: 76 12 51
A sixteenth-century inn thirty miles southeast of Bern on the Loetschberg-Simplon railway line. Known for its fine cuisine and variety of wines. Twenty-five beds available. Inexpensive. Just south of Spiez.

Roggenburg [24]

Auberge de Moulin Neuf   Roggenburg   tel: (066) 31 13 50
Ancient mill (1692) converted into informal hotel with five rooms

(showers). Fish specialties. Fishing. Moderate. South of Basel off highway 18 en route to Delémont.

Romanshorn [58]

Hôtel Restaurant Schloss   Romanshorn   tel: (071) 63 10 27
Fourteenth-century castle with twenty-one comfortable rooms (only four with bath). Restaurant specializing in fish dishes. Moderately expensive. East of Konstanz on the lake.

Rorbas [40]

Gasthof Adler   Rorbas   tel: 96 21 12
Cozy, rustic inn dating back to 1748. Comfortable in modest way. Delightful candlelight dining. Quite expensive. Closed Tuesday. North of Zürich.

Rossinière [4]

Hôtel Le Grand-Chalet   Rossinìere   tel: 46 544
Twenty-five miles east of Lausanne. Unique eighteenth-century inn with classic mountain-farm flavor. Both Victor Hugo and Gambetta spent a night here. Moderate.

Sachseln [48]

Hôtel Kreuz   Sachseln   tel: 66 14 66
A historic inn eighteen miles south of Luzern. Park and beach on the lake. Very reasonable. Moderate.

St. Moritz [70]

Carlton Hotel   St. Moritz   tel: 21 141
Large, deluxe château-hotel with elegant public rooms, spacious and comfortable private ones. Fine cuisine. Expensive.

Hôtel Suvretta House   St. Moritz   tel: 21 121
Another great European hotel. This huge castle offers a wide variety in accommodations. Plush atmosphere. Excellent cuisine. Pool. Tennis. Ideal for families. Very expensive.

Santa Maria [70]

Hôtel Chasa Capol   Santa Maria   tel: 85 264
The property here has a history dating back to the twelfth century. This rustic, authentic inn oozes atmosphere with its wooden beams and country flavor. Simple. Fine. Great value. Santa Maria is forty-two miles east of St. Moritz, between the Umbrail and Ofen Pass.

Crusch Alba   Santa Maria   tel: (082) 85 106
Only four rooms (two with bath) in a small private hotel dating from 1600. A unique dining room and private museum. Modest. Moderate. Closed November to mid-December.

Schinznach [39]

Kurhaus Bad Schinznach and Park Hotel   Schinznach   tel: 43 11 11
A large hotel built for royalty in the seventeenth century. Rooms are like those in a castle. Formal gardens. The hotel is on the River Aare between Aarau and Baden, north of Lenzburg.

Schwyz [44]

Hotel Drei Könige   Schwyz   tel: 21 24 10
A simple country inn. One of the only buildings to escape the disastrous fire in the seventeenth century. Very inexpensive.

Seengen [48]

Hotel Schloss Brestenberg   Seengen   tel: 54 11 31
A small, spacious manor house built in the early seventeenth century. Lovely gardens overlooking the lake. On Lake Hallwil, twenty-five miles north of Luzern. Fine, but with an unstable reputation. Moderate to expensive.

Sils-Maria [70]

Waldhaus   Sils-Maria   tel: 45 331
A castlelike hotel and relaxing location described by Nietzsche as the "loveliest spot on earth." Comfortable rooms. An idyllic vacation spot for the sportsman. Not for the stuffy. Candlelight dining and concerts. South of St. Moritz. Very expensive.

Soglio [70]

Hôtel Palazzo Salis   Soglio   tel: (082) 41 208
In a picturesque town. Twenty modest rooms in sixteenth-century mountain dwelling. Fun restaurant specializing in game. Open mid-March to mid-November at moderate rates. South of St. Moritz on highway 3.

Solothurn [25]

Hôtel Krone   Hauptgasse 64   tel: 22 44 12
A delightful town for this wonderful inn built in the thirteenth century. Once the residence of the ambassador of France. Near the cathedral. Comfortable rooms with period furnishings. Ask for number 22, a great double. Expensive. Twenty-one miles north of Bern on the River Aare.

Splügen [63]

Posthotel Bodenhaus   Splügen   tel: 62 11 21
A large, popular patrician house with a long history. Napoleon and countless celebrities and kings have stayed in this inn. Fine location on the Splügen and San Bernardino Pass. Moderate to expensive. South of Chur on highway E61.

Stansstad [48]

Hotel Winkelried   Stansstad   tel: 61 26 22
Seven miles south of Luzern. An inn with history, tennis, and a beach. Moderate to expensive.

Thalwil [40]

Hôtel Alexander am See   182 Seestrasse   tel: 720-9701
Small, delightful, fresh and comfortable. Pleasant atmosphere and furnishings. Candlelight dining on request. Expensive. Non-central location, but lakefront setting. Southeast of Zürich.

Thun [26]

Hôtel Falken   Bällizstrasse 46   tel: 26 121
Country inn overlooking the River Aare. Although very old, it's

quite comfortable. Impressive dining room. Moderate rates. Located seventeen miles south of Bern.

Unterwasser [40]

Hotel Säntis   Unterwasser   tel: 52 141
A fine rustic inn. Very quiet. Good cooking. Geared to trout fishermen. Moderate. East of Zürich near Liechtenstein.

Vevey [6]

Hôtel Le Mirador   Mont-Pelerin   tel: 51 35 35
Recently brought up to date. Fine small mountain hotel a short drive from Vevey. Worth staying in just for the view. Expensive.

Hotel des Trois Couroones   Rue d'Italie   tel: 51 30 05
A charmer with comfort and character. Calm and spacious. Tasteful. Delightful terrace and restaurant. Expensive.

Villars-sur-Ollon [7]

La Renardière   Villars-sur-Ollon   tel: (025) 32 592
A rustic mountain retreat. Very isolated and calm. Only twenty-six rooms. Good restaurant. Moderate. Closed late spring and early fall. Southeast of Montreux.

Villeneuve [6]

Hotel "Le Château"   Villeneuve   tel: 60 13 57
Eighteen beds available to travelers interested in spending a night in a lovely seventeenth-century building that once belonged to the Bouvier family. Moderate. On the eastern end of Lake Geneva. Short drive from Vevey.

Weinfelden [58]

Zum Trauben   Rathausstrasse   tel: (072) 52 141
Ten rooms (most with bath) in a hotel dating back to 1648. A restaurant with fine wood carvings. Moderate. Closed July. South of Konstanz.

Weissbad [56]

Kurhaus Weissbad   Weissbad   tel: (071) 88 11 61
Quiet retreat with a lovely view. Most rooms with bath. Centuries old. Tennis. Expensive. Closed November to March. South of Appenzell.

Worb [25]

Gasthof Zum Löwen   Worb   tel: (031) 83 23 03
Ancient mansion (1375) near the church. Only six rooms (two with bath). Vaulted cellar. Moderate. Closed June. East of Bern.

Zermatt [22]

Alex   Zermatt   tel: 77 691
Rustic hotel with family atmosphere. Spacious rooms. Warm and sunny. Fine food. Great value. Moderate.

Hôtel Mont Cervin/Seilerhaus   Bahnhofstrasse   tel: 77 150
Once a tiny inn for mountain-climbers, the Mont Cervin is now one of Zermatt's finest large hotels with authentic atmosphere and an ideal central location. Comfortable rooms. Friendly service. Indoor pool. Delightful restaurant. Very expensive.

Hôtel Monte Rosa   Bahnhofstrasse   tel: 77 708
Another of Zermatt's small, authentic hotels with nineteenth-century flavor and twentieth-century comfort. Perfectly suited for mountain climbers and avid skiers. Indoor pool. Lots of fun. Expensive.

Tenne   Zermatt   tel: 77 823
A picturesque inn with colorful use of wood inside and out. Secluded. Swiss flavor through and through. Charming and excellent restaurant. A great choice. Expensive.

Zürich [40]

Hôtel Florhof   Florhofgasse 4   tel: 47 44 70
An eighteenth-century patrician house in the center of town. Lots of atmosphere. Reasonably comfortable. Only thirty-four rooms. Expensive.

Hôtel Franziskaner   *Stüssihofstatt 1*   *tel: 34 01 20*
An inn dating back to 1357. Once a monastery and a Bavarian-style beer hall. Swiss through and through. Comfortable and modern where it counts. Charming, bright. Only eighteen rooms. Not for the stuffy. Reasonable.

Hôtel Zum Storchen   *2 Weinplatz*   *tel: 211-5510*
Small traditional hotel with all the comfort of a modern one. Charming and very attractive. Excellent cuisine. Central location in the old part of town. Moderate to expensive.

WHERE TO EAT

Aarau [38]

Chez Jeannette   *Vordere Vorstadt 17*   *tel: (064) 22 77 88*
Popular local restaurant in the center of the old city. Trout, sea-food in season, and game when available. Moderate. Closed Sunday. Far to southeast of Basel.

Arbon [58]

Zum Römerhof   *Arbon*   *tel: (071) 46 17 08*
Half-timbered building at a corner of the old town wall. Dates back to early sixteenth century. Trips arranged to Lake Constance. Moderate. Southeast of Konstanz on the lake.

Basel [38] (Bàle)

Restaurant à la Fine Bouche   *Weidengasse 19*   *tel: (061) 41 39 43*
Formal regional restaurant with dining al fresco in mild, warm weather. Chef owned. Nice sole and veal. Expensive. Closed Sunday.

Bern [25]

Ermitage   *Markgasse 15*   *tel: 22 35 42*
Fine French food. Nice atmosphere. Expensive.

Kornhauskeller   *7 Kornhausplatz*   *tel: 22 11 33*
Both cereals and wine were stored in this huge cellar dating back

to 1716. One wine vat is said to have held 100,000 gallons of wine for winter "emergencies." Colorful and a bit touristy, but still fun. Fine wine and local specialties.

Kursaal Carreau Rouge   *71-77 Schänzlistrasse*   *tel: 42 54 66*
Lovely views from this fine restaurant serving French cuisine. Moderate.

Mistral   *Kramgasse 42*   *tel: 22 82 77*
Authentic cellar with romantic atmosphere serving French dishes. Music.

Restaurant du Théâtre   *Place du Théâtre 7*   *tel: (031) 22 71 77*
Quite nice in the moderate category. Perch, veal, steak—all well prepared. Closed mid-July to mid-August.

Schultheissenstube   *Bahnhofplatz 11*   *tel: 22 45 01*
Some say that the grill room in the Hotel Schweizerhof is the best restaurant in town, with cooking geared to gourmets. Intimate atmosphere. Expensive. Reserve.

Biel [24] (Bienne)

Hôtel Continental   *Rue d'Aarberg 29*   *tel: (032) 22 32 55*
Popular with the locals. Kidneys, beef, and rösti are favorites. Moderate.

Binningen [38]

Restaurant Schloss   *Binningen*   *tel: (061) 47 20 55*
A gourmet menu served in a thirteenth-century castle reached by tram number 7 from Basel. Expensive.

Brione s/Minusio [73] (Locarno)

Hôtel Dellavelle   *Brione*   *tel: (093) 33 13 21*
Simple vaulted dining area. Local specialties include fondue for two and Italian dishes. Moderate.

Brissago [73]

****Ristorante Giardino*   *Brissago*   *tel: (093) 65 13 41*
Fifteenth-century patrician house converted into elegant restau-

rant. Expensive. Closed in January. Open for lunch only on Saturday. Closed Sunday and Monday. Reserve. Southwest of Ascona.

Buchillon [4]

Auberge des Grands-Bois   Route Lausanne-Geneva (Genève)
tel: (021) 76 30 49
Simple, but very good, local restaurant noted for its fish dishes. Moderate. Nice terrace for fine-weather dining. Closed Monday. Closed January and first two weeks of September.

Buchs [56]

Restaurant Chez Fritz   Buchs (Hotel Bahnhof)   tel: (085) 61 377
Simple local restaurant. Fresh game in season. Moderate. Closed Sunday evening and Monday. South of Appenzell; near Liechtenstein.

Champéry [21]

Hôtel des Alpes   Champéry   tel: (025) 84 222
Charming hotel with a simple, fine restaurant noted for fresh trout and veal dishes. Closed May, October, and November. Moderate prices. Northwest of Martigny.

Chur [63] (Choire)

Hôtel Stern   Reichsgasse 11   tel: (061) 22 35 55
Delightful regional restaurant specializing in local cuisine and wines. Wonderful chance to sample wines by the glass. One romantic room open on request for that special night out. Moderate. Open every day.

Cologny [1]

***Auberge du Lion-d'Or   Rampe de Cologny 31   tel: (022) 36 44 32
Extremely fine restaurant with superb view and delightful lakeside terrace. Delicious duckling and croûte Landaise. Expensive. Closed Tuesday. Just northeast of Geneva.

Coppet [1]

Hôtel du Lac–Rôtisserie   *Coppet*   *tel: (022) 76 15 21*
Wonderful fresh atmosphere. Delightful garden and terrace. Formal dining. Nice grills and fish dishes. Expensive. North of Geneva en route to Nyon.

Crissier [4]

***Hôtel-de-Ville   *Crissier*   *tel: (021) 34 15 14*
Quite elegant and popular. Specialties vary with season. Closed Sunday evening and Wednesday. Closed in July and August. Northwest of Lausanne.

Fribourg [11]

Le Vieux Chêne   *Route de Tavel*   *tel: (037) 22 07 33*
Attractive country inn. Overlooks the town. Fine fowl and meat dishes as well as fresh trout. Moderate. Closed Monday.

Geneva [1] (Genève)

Les Armures   *1 Puits-St. Pierre*   *tel: 24 99 39*
Snuggled into the walls of the city, this restuarant offers Swiss specialties, including *raclette*.

Auberge de Confignon   *6 Place de l'Eglise*   *tel: 57 19 44*
You'll need a cab to get to Confignon, a small village on the out-skirts of Geneva. An offbeat inn with good steaks and delightful game dishes in the off-season.

Au Fin Bec   *55 Rue de Berne*   *tel: 32 29 19*
Fine French cuisine with excellent service. Moderate. Reserve.

Auberge de la Mère Royaume   *9 Rue des Corps Saints*   *tel: 32 70 08*
Full of atmosphere. Dedicated to the woman who threw the soup in the enemy's face to save the city. Good food. Expensive.

La Béarn   *4 Quai de la Poste*   *tel: 21 00 28*
A wonderful, small, intimate restaurant serving fine French cuisine. Elegant ambience. Very fine and equally expensive.

Buffet de la Gare de Cornavin   *town center (railroad station)*   *tel:* (022) 32 43 06
Try the Grill Room. Good cassoulet and oysters in season. Don't judge this one by its cover. Moderate.

***Le Chat Botté   *13 Quai du Mont Blanc*   *tel: 31 02 21*
A splurge restaurant in the Hôtel Beau Rivage. Refined and very formal with an excellent menu and wines. Very expensive, but worth it.

Le Gentilhomme   *Jardin Brunswick*   *tel: 31 14 00*
Elegant and quite expensive dining room of the Hotel Richemond. Subdued and quiet atmosphere. Expensive.

Le Mazot   *16 Rue du Cendrier*   *tel: 32 15 30*
The grill in the Hotel d'Allèves—nice atmosphere with fine food. Expensive.

L'Or du Rhône   *19 Boulevard Georges-Favon*   *tel: 24 55 76*
Wonderful grills, steaks, and chicken with delightful candlelit dining. Expensive. Reserve.

****Parc des Eaux-Vives*   *Quai Gustave-Ador 82*   *tel: 35 41 40*
Formal, elegant dining in a lovely park setting. Excellent menu and fine wines. Superb local fish (*omble chevalier*) dishes. Very expensive, but worth it as a splurge. Closed Monday. Closed January to mid-February.

La Perle du Lac   *128 Rue de Lausanne*   *tel: 31 35 04*
Great lakeside park setting. Fine food. Expensive. Geared to warm-weather dining.

La Pescaille   *Avenue Henri-Dunant 15*   *tel: 29 71 60*
Specializes in seafood, especially shellfish, available in the months with an "r." A great off season favorite.

Restaurant Roberto   *13 rue de la Madeleine*   *tel: (022) 21 80 33*
Good Italian dishes in pleasant, relaxing restaurant. Osso buco and other entrées complemented with wide variety of Italian wines including popular Valpolicella. Moderate. Closed Saturday evening and Sunday.

Hemiswil [25]

Gasthof Löwen *Hemiswil* *tel: 23 206*
A simple country inn with over six centuries of history. Superb local dishes from antique recipes kept in the family. The inn is twenty miles east of Bern.

Interlaken [29]

Grand Hôtel Euler *near the central station* *tel: (061) 23 45 00*
Impressive and fine with varied menu, including coquille St. Jacques, truffles, salmon, and kidneys. Expensive.

Locanda *34 Marketplatz* *tel: 25 39 30*
A comfortable, quiet, intimate restaurant with a local flavor. Fine French and regional dishes. Reserve a table.

Rôtisserie Le Mazot *Bahnhofplatz 35* *tel: (036) 22 66 55*
Quite good hotel restaurant in popular tourist town. Good steaks and kidneys. Moderate.

Schützenhaus *56 Schützenmattstrasse* *tel: 23 67 70*
Delightful restaurant with both French and local dishes. Nice atmosphere. Expensive.

Klosters [61]

Chesa Grischuna *Klosters* *tel: (083) 42 222*
A rustic charmer with local specialties. Game in season and fresh trout. Moderate. Open all year.

Langenbruck [38]

Gasthof Bären *Langenbruck* *tel: (962) 60 14 14*
Quite elegant restaurant housed in sixteenth-century building. Fine regional specialties. Moderate. Closed July and August. South of Basel en route to Bern.

Lauerz [44] (Island of Schwanau)

Island Restaurant Insel   Lauerz   tel: (043) 21 17 57
Rustic, isolated restaurant in wooded area in castle ruins. Accessible by motorboat. Moderate. Open mid-March to mid-November. West of Schwyz.

Lausanne [4]

Châlet Suisse   Signal de Sauvabelin   tel: 22 23 12
Superb Swiss cuisine in wonderful setting with great view. Moderate.

La Chaumière   23 Rue Centrale   tel: 23 53 64
Small, rustic restaurant with American-style food. Moderate.

La Voile d'Or   Avenue de Rhodonie   tel: 27 80 11
Wonderful setting and view in this French restaurant with moderate prices.

La Grappe d'Or   3 Cheneau-de-Bourg   tel: (021) 23 07 60
Very fine and expensive with good ambience. Varied menu including beef Wellington, duckling, and local specialties. Expensive. Closed Sunday.

Le Locle [15]

Hôtel des Trois-Rois   center of town   tel: (039) 31 65 55
Good local restaurant with an emphasis on beef. Simple, but pleasant. Moderate. Southwest of La Chaux-de-Fonds.

Les Geneveys-sur-Coffrane [14]

Hôtel des Communes   Les Geneveys   tel: (038) 57 13 20
Delightful, rustic restaurant. Game in season. Trout and duckling fine. Moderate. Closed Sunday evening and Monday, as well as July. Near Neuchâtel.

Locarno [73]

La Palma au Lac   Locarno   tel: (093) 33 67 71
Lovely luxury hotel with very fine restaurant. Try the varied hors d'oeuvres for two. Good rack of lamb for two. Expensive.

Lugano

Bianchi   3 Via Passina   tel: 22 302
Charming and elegant. Superb international and Italian dishes.
Moderate. Make reservations.

Luzern [48] (Lucerne)

Old Swiss House   near Lion Monument   tel: (041) 36 37 38
Elegant and authentic. Varied menu with veal and duck out-
standing. All complemented with fine French wines. Expensive.
Closed Monday. Closed from mid-November to mid-March.

Palace Hôtel Grill-Room Mignon   on the lake   tel: (041) 22 19 01
Formal dining. Nice lamb served for couples. You may want to
try the local dish *sabayon* (not for everyone). Expensive. Closed
November through March.

Schwanen   4 Schwanenplatz   tel: 22 21 01
Close to the lake. In the modern category this is one of the better restaurants. Moderate.

Wilden Mann   30 Bahnhofstrasse   tel: 23 16 66
Sixteenth-century inn with authentic local ·dishes. Quite expensive.

Merligen [27]

Hôtel Beatus   Merligen   tel: (033) 51 21 21
Nice lakeside hotel with quite good cuisine. Steak, veal, and
lamb dishes specially prepared for couples. Moderate to expensive. Closed December to mid-April.

Morat-Meyriez [13] (Murten)

Le Vieux Manoir   Morat-Meyriez   tel: (037) 71 12 83
A gem—with a lovely terrace. Very elegant and fine, with an
outstanding menu. Trout in a cream sauce, perch filets, scampi,
and lamb the main specialties. Expensive. Closed January 10 to
February 10.

Näfels [55]

Romantic Hôtel Schwert   Näfels   tel: (058) 34 17 22
Across from the Freuler Palace (don't miss it). Simple, but very fine, regional cooking and French cuisine. Excellent trout, chicken curry, and roast goat (spring). Game in season. Moderate to expensive. Open every day. East of Rapperswil.

Neuchâtel [14]

Maison des Halles   Place du Marché   tel: (038) 24 31 41
Fine formal restaurant with varied menu offering a good selection of regional dishes. Expensive.

Nyon [3]

Restaurant Le Léman   on the lake   tel: (022) 61 22 41
Good, straightforward cooking at moderate prices. Try the local fish *l'omble*. Closed Tuesday. Closed mid-December to late January. Between Geneva and Morges.

Péry-Reuchenette s/Bienne [24]

Hôtel-Restaurant de la Truite   Péry-Reuchenette   tel: (032) 96 14 10
Simple, old-style. Nice trout, sole, scampi. Moderate. Closed Tuesday. North of Biel (Bienne).

Pontresina [71]

Hôtel Schweizerhof   Pontresina   tel: (082) 66 412
Large hotel with fine dining, offering trout and Italian specialties, including ravioli. Moderate.

Regensberg [40]

Restaurant Krone Regensberg   Regensberg   tel: (01) 94 11 35
A must—if only to take in the charming twelfth-century town. Near the château. Rustic, very fine. Offering outstanding steak and veal. A gem. A twenty-minute drive from Zürich. Closed Monday. Closed the last and first week of the year.

Saint-Blaise/Neuchâtel [14]

Au Boccalino   Saint-Blaise   tel: (038) 33 36 80
Excellent and elegant regional restaurant. Offers superb game in
October, delicious truffles in November, and outstanding Italian
specialties in March. Expensive. Just north of Neuchâtel.

Saint-Imier [15]

Hôtel des XIII-Cantons   St. Imier   tel: (039) 41 25 46
Simple, regional restaurant noted for game in season, frogs legs,
bouillabaisse, trout, and veal. Moderate. Closed Sunday afternoon and Monday. Northeast of La Chaux-de-Fonds.

St. Moritz [70]

Chesa Veglia   St. Moritz   tel: 34 596/91 734/33 596
Wonderful, authentic Swiss restaurant with superb cuisine.
Housed in 1750 mansion (a farmhouse). Expensive. Make reser-
vations.

Rôtisserie des Chevaliers   St. Moritz   tel: 21 151
This restaurant in the Kulm Hotel is excellent, with great French
cuisine and grills, sometimes including whole roast pigs for special occasions. Entertainment. Expensive. Make reservations.
Closed fall and spring.

Grischuna Grill   St. Moritz   tel: 34 433
The Hotel Monopol offers romantic dining in authentic atmosphere. Expensive. Make reservations.

Sargans [54]

Schloss Sargans   Sargans   tel: (085) 21 488
Fun thirteenth-century inn with lovely view. Closed November
to March. Moderate. Northwest of Bad Ragaz.

Schaffhausen [60]

Fischerzunft (Hôtel du Rhin)   on the Rhine   tel: (053) 53 281
Delightful, riverside stop in charming town. Quite elegant set-

ting and outstanding cuisine. Quenelles, trout, salmon, l'ombre (local fish), and game in season. Expensive.

Sierre [19]

Relais du Manoir   Avenue du Marché (west end of town)   tel: (027) 51 896
Fine inn dating back to 1500s. Lots of atmosphere. Regional cooking with both raclette and fine wines. Smoked meats. Garden. Moderate. Northeast of Sion.

Stäfa [55]

Restaurant Im Kehlhof   Stäfa   tel: (01) 926-1155
Wonderful local choice. Trout, scampi, frogs' legs, and game in season. Moderate. Closed February and Wednesday and Thursday. Just west of Rapperswil.

Verbier [23]

Hôtel-Rôtisserie-Bar Rosalp   Verbier   tel: (026) 72 323
Rustic mountain retreat. Local specialties. Moderate. Closed May through July, September through November.

Vevey [6]

Restaurant du Raisin   Place du Marché   tel: (021) 51 10 28
Good local restaurant with both game and shellfish in season. Fine duck and lamb dishes. Quite expensive. Closed Sunday evening and Monday. Closed in September.

Weggis [47]

Hôtel Albana   Weggis   tel: (041) 93 21 41
Comfortable seventy-room hotel near the lake with nice view. Good regional restaurant. Tennis and sailing. Expensive. Closed late October through March.

Yverdon [14]

Hôtel-Restaurant de la Prairie   *Avenue des Bains 9*   *tel: (024) 21 19 19*
Good local French restaurant. Nice sole and trout. Moderate.
Closed Monday. Southwest of Neuchâtel at the tip of the lake.

Zäziwil [25]

Weisse Rössli   *Zäziwil*   *tel: (031) 91 15 32*
Old inn with twelve modest rooms (none with bath) and a delightful regional restaurant featuring Emmental specialties. Moderate. East of Bern.

Zermatt [22]

Tenne   *Zermatt*   *tel: (028) 77 823*
Very popular hotel with good restaurant. Specialties: grilled
prawns, charcoal-broiled steak, lamb. Moderate. Closed October
through November, May.

Zug [42] (Zoug)

Hôtel-Restaurant Rosenberg   *above town*   *tel: (042) 21 71 71*
Simple spot with lovely view. Nice fish, scampi, veal, and game
in season. Moderate. Closed February and on Wednesday and
Saturday for lunches.

Zürich [40]

Alexander am See   *182 Seestrasse*   *tel: 720-9701*
Six miles from the city at Thalwil. Excellent cuisine. Entertainment. Expensive.

Baur au Lac Grill   *1 Talstrasse*   *tel: 211-7396*
Smart grill room with superb gourmet cooking. Very expensive.
Reserve.

Eden au Lac Grill   *45 Utoquai*   *tel: 47 94 04*
A deluxe restaurant serving the finest in French cuisine. Excellent service and atmosphere. Many consider this hotel restaurant
to be the best in town. Very expensive.

Kronenhalle   *4 Rämistrasse*   *tel: 32 02 56*
Lots of atmosphere. A favorite with painters in the past. Good, hearty cooking. Expensive.

Veltliner Keller   *8 Schlüsselgasse*   *tel: 221-3228*
Dating back to 1551, with a fascinating décor. Once an excellent restaurant—now has an up-and-down reputation. Moderate.

Zum Roten Gatter   *Schifflände 6*   *tel: 34 24 13*
For those who adore chicken.

Restaurant Oepfelchammer   *Rindermarkt 12*   *tel: 32 23 36*
Young in spirit, ancient in atmosphere. Not at all luxurious. Hard to find. Ultrasimple and fun. An offbeat spot where only German is spoken. Very reasonable.

Dezaley   *Römergasse*   *tel: 32 61 29*
Tops for fondue and delicious regional white wines. Expensive, but worth it.

Oscar Huber   *Marktgasse 20*   *tel: 32 52 87*
One of the many guild halls. This one has French cooking with an accent on local specialties.

Casa Ferlin   *Stampfenbachstrasse 38*   *tel: (01) 28 35 09*
Formal Italian restaurant serving excellent lasagne, fettucine, and cannelloni, as well as fine chateaubriand. Expensive. Closed Saturday at lunch and all day Sunday. Closed mid-July to mid-August.

YUGOSLAVIA

YUGOSLAVIA

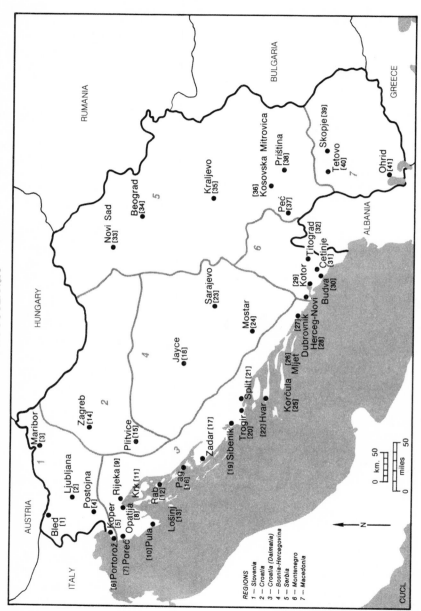

AUSTRIA

ITALY

HUNGARY

RUMANIA

BULGARIA

GREECE

ALBANIA

Maribor [3]

Bled [1]

Ljubljana [2]

Postojna [4]

Rijeka [9]

Koper [5]

Opatija [8]

Portorož [6]

Poreč [7]

Pula [10]

Krk [11]

Rab [12]

Pag [16]

Lošinj [13]

Zagreb [14]

Plitvice [15]

Zadar [17]

Šibenik [19]

Trogir [20]

Split [21]

Hvar [22]

Pag [16]

Jayce [18]

Korčula [25]

Mljet [26]

Dubrovnik [27]

Herceg-Novi [28]

Budva [30]

Kotor [29]

Cetinje [31]

Titograd [32]

Sarajevo [23]

Mostar [24]

Novi Sad [33]

Beograd [34]

Kraljevo [35]

Peć [37]

Kosovska Mitrovica [36]

Priština [38]

Skopje [39]

Tetovo [40]

Ohrid [41]

REGIONS
1 — Slovenia
2 — Croatia
3 — Croatia (Dalmatia)
4 — Bosnia-Hercegovina
5 — Serbia
6 — Montenegro
7 — Macedonia

0 km. 50

0 miles 50

N

CUCL

WHAT TO SEE

Yugoslavia, a unique blend of East and West, has been a popular holiday resort since the Roman conquest. Its lush and rugged coast, with seven hundred offshore islands, is now one of the "in" spots for summer vacations. Many ports remain undiscovered as do the sights and towns of the interior.

The northwest corner of Yugoslavia seems a part of Austria with chalets, scenic mountain resorts, such as *Bled* [1], wandering bands of gypsies, and fine winter skiing in *Kranjska Gora*. Added to this are the fashionable resorts of *Portoroz* [6] and *Koper* [5] on the Adriatic as well as tiny gems like the port of *Piran* [6]. Don't miss the colosseum in *Pula* [10]. Inland you'll find giant caves at *Postojna* [4], the delightful stud farms at *Lipice*, and the lively market in *Llubljana* [2], known as well for its churches. Seasonal attractions include the fall grape harvest around *Ljutomer* [3] and the blossoming orchards around *Maribor* [3] in May.

The two major attractions of inland Croatia are *Plitvicka Jezera* [15] and *Zagreb* [14]. The former is a series of sixteen lakes, spectacular at any time of year. The Old Town of Zagreb is a touristic must with its colorfully tiled church of St. Marks.

The Dalmatian Coast is what many people associate with Yugoslavia. The remote offshore islands (*Losinj* [13], *Mljet* [26], *Rab* [12], *Brac* [22], *Hvar* [22], *Korcula* [25]), rugged coast and sheltered coves for nudists and nature lovers, tiny fishing villages with multicolored boats and red-tiled roofs, and the great medieval city of *Dubrovnik* [29] are the things that attract thousands of visitors to this region each year. You can stay in the fashionable resort of *Porec* [7] or in a miniscule artists haven, *Rovinj* [7], or the fjordside *Herceg-Novi* [28]. Don't miss a visit to the palace in *Split* [21] or an excursion to the medieval towns of *Trogir* [20] and *Zadar* [7]. A seasonal attraction is the fine bird hunting in *Hutovo Blato*.

The long Turkish domination of Yugoslavia is most evident in *Bosnia-Hercegovina*, a region rarely visited by Americans. Winters are rugged here, so you should visit the region from May to late September. Take in the mosques of *Sarajevo* [23], *Banja Luka* [18], and *Mostar* [24], famed too for its lively bazaars. *Remember not to enter a mosque with your shoes on*. Artists will enjoy *Pocitelj* while ardent archaeologists take in *Radimlja* to see the mysterious *stéc-*

chi, unusual tombstones. Trout fishing in April and May is quite good from *Foca* [23] or *Gorazde* [23].

In the northeast you'll find *Belgrade* [34] (Beograd) noted for its National Museum and the bohemian district of Skadarlija. You may wish to make an excursion to the Iron Gates at *Djerdap* or to one of the famed monasteries of *Péc* [37], *Kosovo Polje*, or *Zica*.   *Montenegro*, on the coast near Albania, is one of the most spectacular regions. The inland areas, so remote and untouched, offer a glimpse into another world amid rough, yet inspiring, scenery. Why not base yourself in *Budva* [30] or world-famous *Sveti Stefan* [30]? Make excursions to *Cetinje* [31], the fjord at *Kotor* [29], or the marvelous beach at *Ulcinj* [30].

For a truly uncommon experience, visit *Ohrid* [41] and *Skoplje* [39]. The former offers an assortment of monasteries while the latter is well known for its mosques and fifteenth-century Turkish bathhouse.

WHAT'S THE WEATHER REALLY LIKE?

The weather in Yugoslavia is best in July and August, the peak period, when it's almost impossible to find a room. However, you can swim comfortably from late April to the end of September. Late fall and early spring tend to be cool, colorful, and windy. Winters are quite cold, even along the coast, and many of the hotels are closed. Skiers, hunters, and dedicated sightseers will be attracted to the country at this time and will be able to take advantage of the drastic price reductions. May, September, and early October are the months highly recommended to the off-season traveler.

SOME SUGGESTIONS FOR A MORE ENJOYABLE TRIP

Many homes offer private rooms to visitors. These are often at lower rates than you'd find in hotels. The sign to look for: *sobe* or *privat zimmer*. A stay in one of these often turns out to be a wonderful travel experience. Note that the language barrier is thick in Yugoslavia. Brush up on your German if you had some in school. But try first to communicate in English, since bitterness from the war lingers. If you plan to travel to this country in July and August, be warned that reservations are *essential*. The lines of cars curving along the jagged coast can be a headache as well. If you enter Yugoslavia by car, have the guards note any dents or scratches in your passport. You don't want any hassles about so-called, unreported accidents during your stay in Eastern Europe. In some areas of the country it's forbidden to take photos. You'll see a sign with a line through a camera. Don't take pictures in these areas. As in parts of Greece, you may want to bring extra toilet paper, a rarity in some rural villages. A flashlight is also an excellent idea for occasional blackouts. Be sure to fill up your gas tank whenever you can, especially if you plan to get off the beaten path. Bargaining is expected when shopping, particularly in street markets. Although it goes against the grain in our culture, it's *expected* in many foreign countries. So bargain everywhere and note the price reductions.

WHERE TO STAY

Beograd [34] (Belgrade)

Excelsior   5 Kneza Milosa   tel: 33 13 81
Small hotel with modest rooms. Nice. Moderate.

Majestic   28 Obilićev Venac   tel: 62 10 22
Revamped traditional hotel in city center. Comfortable and quiet. Moderate to expensive.

Bled [1]

Grad Podvin   (Radovljica)   tel: 75 543
A baroque castle with a distinctive Austrian flavor about it. Six miles from Bled in the direction of Ljubljana. Charming forest setting. Gardens. Fine restaurant. Tennis. Pool. Moderate.

Grand Hotel Toplice   5 Cesta Svobode   tel: 77 222
On the lake in a lovely serene setting is this superb and large traditional hotel. Fine furnishings in both public and private

rooms. Extremely comfortable. Out-of-this-world bar. Pool. Access to boating, sailing, and tennis. One of the finest hotels in the country. Moderate to expensive.

Bohinj [1]

Bellevue   Stara Fuzina   tel: 76 331
Small chalet with fine view and lots of rustic charm. Comfortable and relaxing. Inexpensive.

Bohinj-Vogel [1]

Ski Hotel   (Mt. Vogel)   tel: 76 167
Small and modest hotel with a superb view from its mountain perch reached only by cable car. Neat and quite comfortable. Closed in late fall and late spring. Inexpensive.

Bovec [1]

Alp & Kanin Hotels   Bovec   tel: 84 040
Large and lovely modern hotels set in a gorgeous mountain region with lovely views. Extremely comfortable and pleasant. Geared to fishing and hikes. Moderate. North of Trieste; to southwest of Bled.

Budva [30]

Avala   Budva   tel: 82 022
Small hotel near the shore with a sandy "secret" beach. Comfortable. Ask for the corner room. Open April to October. Moderate.

Cetinje [31]

Park   Cetinje   tel: 22 079
Comfortable, if modest, hotel. Inexpensive.

Decani [37]

Visoki Decani   Decani   tel: 72 025
New and fresh inn surrounded by woods. Fine restaurant. Moderate. South of Peć.

Dubrovnik [27]

Argentina   20 Frana Suplia   tel: 23 855
A long walk from the city. A large hotel with a beehive of rooms overlooking the bay. Comfortable but compact. Limited grounds. Private rock beach. Pool. Tennis. Expensive.

Bellevue   Pera Cingrije   tel: 25 075
Small hotel with comfortable rooms at moderate prices.

Dubrovnik Palace   Masarikov Put 20   tel: 28 555
Two miles northwest of town. Large new hotel with the usual clifftop location. Fishing, boating, and pool. Casino. Moderate.

Excelsior   3 Frana Suplia   tel: 23 566
A long walk from the city. A giant honeycomb as well, with lots of life in a commercial sense. Superb view from comfortable rooms. Good restaurant. Private rock beach. Pool. Moderate to expensive.

Grand Hotel Imperial   2 Mise Simoni   tel: 23 688
Nice location with pleasant grounds. Traditional hotel, yet modernized. Pleasant, with some atmosphere. Moderate to expensive.

Libertas   Larceviceva 1   tel: 27 444
Large modern hotel in the luxury class with comfortable rooms looking out from the clifftop setting. Beach and pool. Expensive.

Villa Dubrovnik   8 Vlaha Bukovca   tel: 23 465
Above the ocean, with charming atmosphere. Lovely view, terraces, and garden. Expensive, but highly recommended. A small gem.

Hvar [22]

Adriatica   Hvar   tel: 74 024
Nice small hotel for quiet stay. Good location. Expensive.

Palace Hotel   Hvar   tel: 74 013
Nice location for this small traditional hotel with comfortable
rooms. Pool. Expensive.

Jajce [18]

Turist   Jajce   tel: 21 068
A large hotel on the lake with comfortable, if modest, rooms.
Moderate.

Koper [5]

Zusterna   Koper   tel: 21 640
Only a short drive from the picturesque port. Large but modest
hotel. Pool. Open all year. Inexpensive.

Kotor [29]

Fjord   Kotor   tel: 84 249
Large modern hotel on the bay of Kotor near the center of town.
Pleasant rooms. Pool. Inexpensive.

Kraljevica [9]

Uvala Scott Hotel   Kraljevica   tel: 80 12 26
Three miles from town. A tourist complex on the water with a
fine beach. Large and quite comfortable. Moderate.

Kranjska Gora [1]

Larix   Kranjska Gora   tel: 84 575
Large modern hotel with modest rooms. Moderate. South of
Villach (Austria); near Bled.

Prisank   Kranjska Gora   tel: 84 472
Centrally located. Small and comfortable hotel. Inexpensive.

Krk-Malinska [11]

Palace Haludovo   Krk   tel: 88 55 66
Huge mile-long complex with varying facilities, including luxury
resort apartments. Geared to water sports. Moderate.

Lipica [5]

Hotel Maestoso   Lipica   tel: 73 009
Large hotel with comfortable rooms geared to tourists interested in visiting or riding at the stud farms. Very pleasant. Quite inexpensive. East of Trieste to northeast of Koper.

Mali Losinj-Losinj [13]

Bellevue   Mali Losinj   tel: 86 058
Huge modern resort with modest rooms. Still, quite comfortable. Geared to water sports. Pool. Tennis. Widely varying rates, depending upon room.

Maribor [3]

Slavija   3 Vita Kraigherja   tel: 23 661
Large modern hotel with spacious and comfortable rooms. Good location. Moderate.

Mlini [27]

Plat   Mlini   tel: 86 044
Eight miles from Dubrovnik. Huge secluded hotel with modern rooms—quite modest. Moderate.

Mljet-Govedari [26]

Melita   Mljet   tel: 1
A twelfth-century Benedictine monastery that has been converted into a modest, but very quiet and pleasant, hotel in forest surroundings.

Mostar [24]

Bristol   Mostar   tel: 21 921
Small hotel with charming atmosphere and fine location. Rooms simple, unadorned, but pleasant. Inexpensive.

Novi Sad [33]

Varadin   Novi Sad   tel: 46 393
Small hotel converted from an eighteenth-century fortress. Attractively furnished. Fun. Right on the banks of the Danube. Best restaurant in town. Best gypsy music in the country. Expensive.

Ohrid [41]

Grand Hotel Palace   1-8 Partizanska   tel: 22 030/057
Large lakeside hotel with modern and comfortable rooms. Inexpensive.

Ohrid-Gorica [41]

Inex Hotel Gorica   Gorica   tel: 22 021
Large and comfortable hotel. Moderate.

Opatija [8]

Ambassador   Opatija   tel: 71 671
Large resort hotel on the sea. Comfortable, but touristy. Private beach. Moderate.

Atlantic   Opatija   tel: 71 944
Tiny hotel with comfortable rooms. More intimate. Moderate.

Otocec Ob Krki [2]

Grad Otocec   Otocec Ob Krki   tel: 21 835
A former fourteenth-century castle converted into a delightful, authentic hotel with rustic furnishings. Noted for arranging fishing excursions—hotel is directly on the River Krka near Novo Mesto. Forty miles from Zagreb and forty-five miles from Ljubljana.

Peć [37]

Metonija   Peć   tel: 62 424
Basic resort complex with some bungalows. Comfortable and inexpensive.

Piran [6]

Piran Hotel   Piran   tel: 73 651
Small and modest hotel with some rooms facing the Adriatic.
Clean, with an English inn atmosphere. A bit of a walk from
where you'll have to park your car. Moderate.

Plitvicka Jezera [15]

Jezero   Plitvicka Jezera   tel: 76 355
Huge modern hotel in idyllic setting from which to visit the
lakes. Pool. Expensive. Open all year.

Plitvice   Plitvicka Jezera   tel: 76 340
Small hotel with comfortable rooms. Located with lovely view of
lakes. Very quiet. Moderate. Open April to October.

Porec-Zelena [7]

Parentium   Zelena   tel: 86 522
Four miles from Porec on the beach with comfortable rooms.
Pool. Tennis.

Portoroz [6]

Grand Hotel Palace   Portoroz   tel: 73 542
A huge hotel with a fine central location. Comfortable. Gardens,
pool, and beach. Tennis as well. Moderately expensive.

Pula [10]

Brioni   Pula   tel: 23 888
Large resort one and a half miles south of the city. Set in woods.
Comfortable. Pool, boating, and tennis. Expensive.

Riviera   Pula   tel: 22 299
A converted palace with a wonderful old-world atmosphere.
Great location on the beach. Comfortable. Fine cuisine. Moder-
ate.

Splendid   Pula   tel: 22 370
Huge hotel outside of town with lovely location. Comfortable
and pleasant. Pool. Tennis. Moderate.

Verudela   Pula   tel: 22 370
Huge modern resort complex with some villas in a peaceful setting. Comfortable and inexpensive.

Rab [12]

Imperial   Rab   tel: 87 028
Near the center of town. Large modern hotel. Comfortable. Tennis. Inexpensive.

International   Rab   tel: 87 023
Large hotel with comfortable rooms. Pool. Inexpensive.

Rabac [8]

Laterna   Rabac   tel: 83 213
Modest modern hotel on cliffs overlooking the sea. Open mid-May until the end of September. South of Opatija.

Rijeka [9]

Bonavia   Rijeka   tel: 22 351
Large hotel in the city center with comfortable rooms and some apartments. Quite inexpensive.

Jadran   Rijeka   tel: 41 600
Small hotel in pleasant setting near the sea. Quite casual. Comfortable. Pool. Inexpensive.

Rovinj-Crveni-Otok [7]

Crveni Otok   Crveni   tel: 81 133
A former monastery that has been converted into a quiet, pleasant retreat with modest and nice rooms. Inexpensive. Open April to October only. South of Porec.

Istra   Crveni   tel: 18 144
Modern hotel with quite comfortable rooms. Near the beach. Pool. Tennis.

Sarajevo [23]

Bristol   Josipa Sigmunda 8   tel: 61 48 11
A mile from the center of the city on Highway 10. Large modern hotel. Comfortable, functional. Moderate.

Europa   5 Vase Palagica   tel: 23 481
Large hotel in the center of the city with comfortable rooms. Nice restaurant. Moderate.

Skoplje [39]

Grand Hotel Skoplje   12 Mose Pijade   tel: 34 234/243
Large modern hotel with comfortable rooms in center of town. Good restaurant. Inexpensive.

Split [21]

Lav   Split   tel: 48 288
Three miles to the south of town on a cove. Oriented to water sports. Huge new hotel with comfortable rooms. Moderate.

Marjan   5 Obala   tel: 42 866
Large modern hotel with good location overlooking the harbor. Comfortable rooms and superior suites. Quite fine restaurant. Pool. Expensive.

Stari Dojran [41]

Dojran   Stari Dojran   tel: 4
Ultrasimple but pleasant inn. Near Greek border, far east of Ohrid.

Sveti Stefan [30]

Milocer   Sveti Stefan   tel: 82 233
Formerly a royal residence, now a lovely hotel with some villas. Wonderful garden flavor. Tennis. Open mid-April to mid-October. Expensive.

Sveti Stefan   Sveti Stefan   tel: 82 233
Formerly a fifteenth-century fishing settlement, this large hotel
—consisting of only eight cottages covering an entire island—is
attractive and unusual. Be sure to reserve an outside room well
in advance. Open May to mid-October. Not to be missed. Expensive.

Svetozarevo [34]

Srbija   Svetozarevo   tel: 22 005
Near the monasteries in the small town with quiet countryside
surrounding. Finest restaurant in town. Moderate. Southeast of
Beograd.

Tetovo-Popova Sapka [40]

Popova Sapka   Tetovo-Popova Sapka   tel: 20 489
Comfortable hotel near the ski slopes. Inexpensive.

Titograd [32]

Crna Gora   Titograd   tel: 22 231/321
Very large and comfortable hotel in the middle of town with a
traditional ambience. Inexpensive to moderate.

Pordgorica   Titograd   tel: 42 050
Large hotel on the banks of the river with modern rooms. Comfortable and inexpensive.

Titovo Uzice [35]

Palas Hotel   Titovo Uzice   tel: 21 752
Large, comfortable hotel in the center of town. Moderate. West
of Kraljevo.

Trakoscan [14]

Trakosćan   Trakosćan   tel: 75 124
Modest rooms in an old castle in the forest, forty miles north of
Zagreb.

Ulcinj [30]

Albatros   Ulcinj   tel: 84 144
Large and comfortable. Moderate.

Vodno [39]

Hotel Vodno   Vodno   tel: 35 105
Ten miles west of Skoplje. Very simple inn with superb location.

Zadar [17]

Zagreb   Borisa Kidrica 11   tel: 42 66
An old-style hotel in town on the ocean with comfortable rooms.
Inexpensive.

Zadar-Borik [17]

Borik Complex   Borik   tel: 24 757
A series of hotels oriented to water sports about two and a half
miles from the city. Modern rooms. Pool. Beach. Very secluded.
Moderate.

Pinija   Petrcane   tel: 73 002
Two and a half miles northwest of the city. Seaside hotel with
modern facilities. Moderate.

Zagreb [14]

Esplanade Intercontinental   1 Mihanoviceva   tel: 51 22 22
A large, traditional hotel newly modernized. Now quite comfortable. Casino. Good restaurant. Moderately expensive.

Palace   10 Strossmayerov Trg.   tel: 44 92 21
Small hotel close to the railroad station with comfortable rooms.
Good restaurant. Moderately expensive.

WHERE TO EAT

Beograd [34] (Belgrade)

Dusanov Grad   *Terazije 4*   tel: 32 43 71
Modern restaurant serving local specialties. Moderate.

Dva Jelena   *Skadarska 32*   tel: 33 48 85
Nice regional restaurant with national specialties and music.
Moderate.

Ima Dana   *Skadarska 38*   tel: 33 44 22
Another regional restaurant with local dishes and fine music.
Moderate.

Kalemegdanska Terasa   *Kalemegdan Fortress*   tel: 62 38 39
In the old Turkish fortress you can sample local dishes. Music.
Oriented to warm weather. Moderate.

Skardarlija   *17 Cetinjska*   tel: 334-983
Serbian cuisine in an authentic restaurant, with music. Moderate.

Tri Sesira   *Skadarska 29*   tel: 34 75 01
Local dishes with an emphasis on meat. Music. Moderate.

Bled [1]

Restaurant Bled   *Bled*   tel: 77 413
Old, well-known restaurant with both regional and international
cuisine. Moderate.

Blegas   *Bled*   tel: 77 577
Another nice garden restaurant, with seafood as its main attraction. Moderate.

Grajska   *Bled*   tel: 77 476
Wonderful atmosphere in old castle. Fashionable. Fine dining.
International cuisine. Moderate.

Mlino   *Bled*   tel: 77 531
Lovely, popular garden restaurant—ideal in fine weather. Regional specialties. Moderate.

Podvin Castle   Podvin   tel: 75 543
In the cellar of a castle, a rustic restaurant with regional dishes.
Quite good. Moderate.

Dubrovnik [27]

Astarea   Medu Vratima od Ploca   tel: 25 774
Intimate restaurant with original Dubrovnik cooking. Nice fish
and meat dishes. Moderate.

Dubravka   Od Pila 1   tel: 26 293
Fine fish dishes. Moderate.

Gradska Kafana   Pred Dvorom   tel: 26 402
A café-restaurant combination serving mainly national dishes.
Modest.

Jadran   P. Milicevica 1   tel: 23 547
Thirteenth-century nunnery of St. Clara converted into a
charming restaurant with a spacious courtyard. Just inside the
town gate. Great atmosphere and delicious local specialties.
Quite expensive.

Klub Starina-Astarea   (Fortress)   tel: 24 848
Once a Dominican monastery near the gate on the harbor. Pri-
vately owned with large dining room serving dinners only. Both
fish and meat dishes are excellent. Quite expensive.

Mimosa   Put. M. Tita 27   tel: 26 559
Another modest regional restaurant serving local specialties.
Moderate.

Nada   Zidioska 8   tel: 28 752
Both the game and local stews are especially popular in this regional restaurant. Moderate.

Ocean   Put Marsala Tita 12   tel: 28 075
The best choice here is the seafood. Moderate.

Orsan/Dubrovacka Rijeka   Dubrovnik   tel: 25 467
Charming décor with original Dalmatian cuisine. Moderate.

Prijeko   Prijeko 6   tel: 24 074
Nice restaurant serving both local and international dishes.
Moderate.

Riblji   Siroka 1   tel: 27 589
Both the fish and game are excellent in the off season. Moderate.

Visnjica   M. Pracata 2   tel: 26 486
National specialties with an emphasis on Slovenian recipes.
Moderate.

Grocka [34]

Vinogradi   Grocka   tel: 86 42 14
Ten miles from Beograd overlooking the Danube with superb
fish dishes. Moderate.

Konavlje [27]

Konavoski Dvori   Konavlje   tel: 27 068
Ten miles from Dubrovnik. Charming country restaurant next to
a stream. Pleasant atmosphere. Regional dishes with an emphasis on fresh trout. Moderate.

Ljubljana [2]

Dr. "O"   Draga   tel: 57 893
Small restaurant serving international dishes. Moderate.

Operna Klet   Zupanciceva 4   tel: 20 411
The emphasis here is on seafood. Moderate.

Pri Lovcu   Breg 14-16   tel: 20 423
One of the best restaurants for wild game in the off-season.
Moderate.

Pri Vitezu   Ljubljana Breg 18-20   tel: 24 685
Small restaurant with authentic atmosphere. Fun. Inexpensive.

Sestica   Titova 16   tel: 21 260
A fine restaurant with a pleasant décor serving good local dishes. Moderate.

Zlatorog   Zupanciceva 9   tel: 20 989
A special off-season restaurant with an emphasis on game dishes. Moderate.

Opatija [8]

Villa Ariston   V. Marsala Tita 243   tel: 71 379
Small restaurant in a villa with a view of the sea. Intimate, with lovely antiques. Dining by candlelight. Expensive.

Split [21]

Arkada   Strozanac   tel: 37 81
Near Split is a restaurant with one of the country's more popular night clubs. Quite expensive.

Sarajevo   Ilegalaca 6   tel: 32 74
Local restaurant serving regional dishes. Moderate.

Zagreb [14]

Debeli Martin   Gracanska 48   tel: 36 836
Intimate restaurant with local Croatian dishes. Moderate.

Drina   Preradodiceva 11   tel: 44 78 59
Bosnian specialties. Moderate.

Gradski Podrum   10 Trg. Republike   tel: 36 291
Large cellar restaurant with pleasant atmosphere and music. Local specialties. Moderate.

Lovacki Rog   Ilica 14   tel: 44 54 44
Noted for its wild game in the off-season. Moderate.

Medulić   Medulićeva 3   tel: 442-430
A restaurant specializing in Serbian dishes. Moderate.

Savskom Mlinu   Remetinecka 14   tel: 52 11 18
National specialties with an emphasis on fine meat dishes. Moderate.

Villa Rebar   Gracani   tel: 42 33 01
Lovely restaurant with superb antiques. Excellent continental cuisine. Quite expensive.

Zagorcu   Frankopanska 13   tel: 44 03 81
Zagorje specialties and seafood—tops. Moderate.

Zlatna Skoljka   Marticeva 51   tel: 41 07 12
The main dish here is fish. Moderate.